T0331186

Storytelling for Spatial Computing and Mixed Reality

This is a clear, accessible manual of storytelling techniques and learning activities for spatial computing, augmented reality and mixed reality. It covers the key skills that the next generation of digital storytellers will need, providing readers with practical tools for creating digital stories and adventures out in the real world.

Drawing on more than a decade of experience, veteran immersive storyteller Rob Morgan provides strategies and techniques for augmenting players and places with digital narrative. Readers will try out key ideas through a range of practical exercises, building up their own portfolio of augmented/spatial narrative projects.

Storytelling for Spatial Computing and Mixed Reality provides insight into everything from narrative pacing to conditional and emergent storytelling for augmented/spatial technology. Each chapter addresses key questions about the affordances – and ethics – of augmenting players' realities, helping students and practitioners explore this new storytelling frontier.

This book will be invaluable to experience designers and students of game design, experience design and interactive narrative. It provides theories, best practices and case studies also relevant to creative professionals in games, XR, immersive theatre, theme parks and brand experience.

Rob Morgan is a writer, experience designer, digital dramaturg and founder and creative director of London-based AR design studio Playlines. Rob writes and narrative-designs award-winning VR, AR and spatial computing experiences, and has helped create story worlds and immersive experiences for some of the world's largest licences, attractions and cultural institutions. He is a Visiting Fellow at King's College London and lectures widely on immersive design, storytelling and AR ethics.

A crucial exploration of how augmented reality can redefine storytelling through the blending the digital with the physical. The book is an essential guide for understanding AR and for navigating and shaping the future of immersive experiences.

Leighton Evans, *Associate Professor in Media Theory, Swansea University*

A vision for storytelling in the coming age of spatial computing. Offering a mix of practical guidance and speculative theory, Morgan equips readers for the narrative possibilities ahead. A primer and a gateway to next-gen storytelling in virtual worlds of all kinds. For professionals and hobbyists alike, it's an essential resource for anyone looking to expand their narrative toolkit.

Jay Springett (@thejaymo), *Researcher & Worldrunner*

Storytelling for Spatial Computing and Mixed Reality
The Art of Augmenting Imagination

Rob Morgan

CRC Press
Taylor & Francis Group
Boca Raton London New York

CRC Press is an imprint of the
Taylor & Francis Group, an **informa** business

Designed cover image: Frode Sorensen

First edition published 2025
by CRC Press
2385 NW Executive Center Drive, Suite 320, Boca Raton FL 33431

and by CRC Press
4 Park Square, Milton Park, Abingdon, Oxon, OX14 4RN

CRC Press is an imprint of Taylor & Francis Group, LLC

ISBN: 978-1-032-45928-8 (hbk)
ISBN: 978-1-032-45927-1 (pbk)
ISBN: 978-1-003-37929-4 (ebk)
ISBN: 978-1-032-85344-4 (eBook+)

DOI: 10.1201/9781003379294

Typeset in Times
by KnowledgeWorks Global Ltd.

Contents

Preface: *Play Along*   ix
Acknowledgements   xiii

Introduction   1
Who is this book for?   1
What is this book for?   1
Structure of this book   4
What kinds of technology is this book about?   9
Other key terminology   16
Is this stuff really a big deal?   20
Three rules   28
Over to you: Challenges   30

SECTION 1   Learning From VR   **39**

1.0 LEARNING FROM VR: GETTING STARTED   **41**

1.1 SEEING IN VR   **43**
Seeing ≠ believing   43
Seeing with agency   44
Diegetic and foveated seeing   45
Rebellious seeing   46
From SEEING in VR to IMAGINING and STAGING in augmented/spatial   48

1.2 BEING IN VR   **51**
Out-of-body experience   51
Protagonist-agnostic VR identities   52
Characterised VR identities   53
Identity-discovery   54
From BEING in VR to IDENTITY-BUILDING and BEING-THERE in
augmented/spatial   56

1.3 BEING SEEN IN VR   **59**
Feeling seen   59
The swayze effect   61
Being (un)seen   62
From BEING SEEN in VR to BEING SELF-CONSCIOUS and
OCCUPYING SPACE in augmented/spatial   63

1.4 **JUXTAPOSITIONS: MOVING FROM VIRTUAL REALITIES TO AUGMENTED/SPATIAL REALITIES**   **66**
Parallel realities   66
Unified sensory models   67
The dragon's cave   68
Hybrid realities   69

SECTION 2   Augmenting Players   **71**

2.0 **AUGMENTING PLAYERS: GETTING STARTED**   **73**

2.1 **IMAGINING**   **75**
Active creation of belief   75
Beginning augmentation   76

2.2 **IDENTITY-BUILDING**   **93**
Not quite yourself   93
Protagonist-agnostic vs. Roleplay identities   94
Discovering IDENTITY: Augmented anagnorisis   100
Asserting IDENTITY: *Mise-en-self*   106
Blending IDENTITIES & building complicity   109
Ongoing identities   113

2.3 **SELF-CONSCIOUSNESS**   **116**
This is where you come in   116
Diegetic self-consciousness   118
Augmented self-consciousness   121
Player-as-performer   124
A word of caution: Augmenting/appropriating others   126
Unreliable protagonists   127
Discovering others   129

2.4 **FROM AUGMENTING PLAYERS TO AUGMENTING PLACES**   **133**

SECTION 3   Augmenting Places   **135**

3.0 **AUGMENTING PLACES: GETTING STARTED**   **137**
Place vs space   138
Locative categories   139

3.1 **STAGING**   **151**
All the world's a stage   151

3.1.1 GENERAL AUGMENTED STAGING — 153
General principles of hybrid spationarratives — 153
General augmented staging: Layout — 155
General augmented staging: Spatial pacing — 161
General augmented staging: Boundaries — 171

3.1.2 LOCATION-SPECIFIC AUGMENTED STAGING — 180
Location-specific staging: Surfacing layers of history — 181
Location-specific staging: Layout — 185
Location-specific staging: Spatial pacing — 192
Location-specific staging: Boundaries — 199

3.2 BEING THERE — 205
Found you — 205
Being there through navigation — 206
Egocentric and allocentric mapping — 207
Spatial agency: Forks — 209
Spatial agency: Hubs — 213

3.3 OCCUPYING SPACE — 218
Finding yourself — 218
Spatial subjectivity: Vantage points — 220
Spatial subjectivity: Player-as-performer — 222
Maps of ourselves — 226
Common ground — 228

SECTION 4 Divergent Realities — 231
Journey through space — 231
Better than life: Customised realities and AI — 233
But is it art?: AR graffiti and non-zero-sum cultures — 235
Ar bodies, AR selves: Rights in an augmented era — 237
How do we know when it ends? — 240

Appendix A: Inclusion, Accessibility and Safety — 245
Appendix B: Sliders for Defining Augmented/Spatial Experiences — 253
Appendix C: Example Concept Development Framework — 264
Glossary — 283
Index — 287

Preface: Play Along

I grew up in the Lake District in England's rural North. One Summer, when I was maybe 10 or 11, my Mum sent me and my brother to some kind of weeklong activity camp in the nearby forest of Whinlatter. She was probably sick of us sitting inside playing videogames with the curtains closed (which we'd do even more when dial-up internet arrived a couple of years later).

I don't remember much about the camp. Accompanied by teenage supervisors, small groups of kids would roam the forest and stumble as-if-by-chance onto activities: rope nets strung between trees or streams that needed fording with piles of planks and plastic barrels conveniently close by. There was even a loose storyline to the week. Aliens were coming. I don't remember whether this was a good thing or bad thing, but it justified all the hazard tape and neon paint splashed around the forest. I remember a general sense of being on an urgent mission as we navigated by alien symbols spray-painted on trees, trying to avoid the watchful eye of a shadowy government agency. Chances are, the teenagers running the camp had just been watching too much *X-Files*.

At the end of the week, the story reached a climax in a circular clearing at the top of a hill. For the first time I saw just how many other kids were taking part – maybe fifty. The aliens were nearly here, or maybe the government had nearly caught up with us. Either way this was the final mission. We stood in a circle around a large roped-off area of grass. At the centre, perched on a tree stump, was some kind of alien idol or communication device which we had to retrieve. We couldn't step on the grass inside the rope circle, of course. It was toxic sludge or something. By now we were all primed to re-imagine the forest as being full of glowing sci-fi hazards – or, at least, primed to suspend our snotty prepubescent disbelief long enough to play along.

By completing earlier activities we'd earned a number of plastic milk crates which we threw out into the grass circle/toxic sludge, creating stepping stones to reach the centre. I don't remember why, but it ended up being me who finally had to hop across the crates as the whole circle shouted encouragement and unhelpful advice at me. By this point, even the cool kids were pretty into it.

Suddenly, heart-stoppingly, the sound of a helicopter rapidly approaching, somewhere unseen behind the tall pines that surrounded us. This wasn't actually particularly unusual: the airborne Mountain Rescue frequently ran exercises all over the fells. But the serendipity was too good. One opportunistic teen supervisor with an instinct for story telling shouted out *Quick! They're coming!*

And, right on cue, I fell off the last crate. The circle of kids hooted and heckled and I had to walk back across the grass/sludge and out of the ring. Someone else took their turn, as the helicopter hovered invisibly and impossibly close, and that kid reached the centre and got to save the day. Then we all traipsed back down the hill for juice and biscuits at the Visitor Centre.

The helicopter wasn't part of the script. The whole camp was run on something below a shoestring budget, more like what my indomitable friend and production partner Muki Kulhan would later call a "barefoot budget". The helicopter arriving at that moment was pure coincidence – but my panicked reaction wasn't. The surge of emotion that toppled me off the last crate was a product of a week's cumulative storytelling, intensified by the social pressure of feeling extremely *seen* at such a pivotal moment, and then massively magnified by the lightning-quick narrative instincts of the supervisor who appropriated and incorporated the helicopter into the scene.

Suddenly, in that hybrid of a fictional story and physical game and social test, it became incredibly important that I succeed. And that moment has stayed with me ever since. Not merely the embarrassment at failing (which did fade, eventually), but the feeling of being part of such a dramatic narrative *beat*. The imagination game we'd all been playing was solidly grounded in physical action and social context - then, suddenly, it was also dramatised and amplified by an almost-magical coincidence of of fictional and physical events.

I'd always been happy playing make-believe, or *let's pretend* as we called it in the North. (Or, as I usually called it, *I'll pretend*, while the other lads played football.) So I was already pretty primed to *SEE* the forest as a place of possibility, and to re-imagine it through a narrative filter.

But more than ever before, that convergence of fictional and physical events gave me a powerful sense of *BEING* there, *BEING* part of a story that wasn't just in my head or on a screen but which was happening *where* I was.

And the indelible sense of *BEING SEEN* by the other kids meant that all the real and fictional elements, the story and the stakes and the situation, all got tangled together to build a powerful sense that this story was happening *to me*.

The fact that I failed to save the day didn't diminish the fact that I felt like a *protagonist*.

In many ways, I've been trying to give audiences that feeling ever since.

This book is a manual of techniques for creating compelling narrative moments, in the real world, using digital technology. It focuses on techniques to combine immersive technologies with real, physical places and people to create that sense of protagonism.

Fundamentally, we're going to be dealing with **digital narratives that take place in the player's immediate reality**. These are interactive experiences which, to one extent or another, incorporate the player as a character, rather than just an audience. Digital experiences which, to one extent or another, use the physical world around the player as their stage (and often also as their setting). Narrative experiences in which, more than in almost any other medium, the *player* and the *protagonist* are the same person.

Increasingly today these experiences are created via wearable headsets which can superimpose 2D interfaces onto our vision, or even draw 3D graphics into the world. These are variously called technologies of **augmented reality**, **mixed reality**, or **spatial computing**.

In the Introduction we'll define the key technology and terminology in more detail. But personally, I don't tend to lose a lot of sleep over definitions. The title of this book refers to *augmented*, *mixed* and *spatial* realities. I've been a narrative specialist in immersive technology for well over a decade, so I've seen the terminology shift across these buzzwords as well as *XR, metaverses* and now *spatial computing*.

For simplicity, in this book we'll refer to **augmented/spatial technology**. If the terminology has shifted again by the time you read this, or if you simply have a preferred term, feel free to mentally substitute it. After all, this book is about providing new tools for storytellers to add to, adjust and even edit reality. (We'll also examine the potential dangers and responsibilities that come with these tools.)

Personally I still prefer the term *augmenting reality*, partly out of habit and partly because I think that's the most apt description of what the current technology is actually doing. But even "augmenting" isn't a fixed concept: there's no settled definition of what an augment*ed* reality is or should be, because augment*ing* is always an ongoing, uneven and subjective process. And storytellers don't actually need new technology in order to augment audiences' experiences. Storytellers have been able to create immersion using nothing more than black marks on a white page for thousands of years.

Often terms like *augmented* and *XR* don't stay as solid technical definitions but become hype words: subjective and subject to market forces. But to be fair, immersive technologies are changing, accelerating and diversifying so fast that even the buzzwords can't keep up.

As a result, rather than focusing on specific hardware platforms or software environments which might soon be out-of-date, this book focuses on fundamental storytelling techniques, many of them thousands of years old, and explores how to adapt these storytelling techniques to new reality-augmenting technologies. You'll be given plenty of chance to try out and adapt these techniques yourself in the book's 25 CHALLENGES.

After all, even as technology accelerates, storytellers are changing and re-defining things even faster. Right now artists worldwide are hacking and repurposing immersive technologies: creating new kinds of live or social events; expressing themselves through art; testing out new ideas and ways of being; and building and demanding empathy. Just as storytellers have always done.

Increasingly though, this is happening not just on screens or in virtual spaces, but out on the street. Augmented/spatial technology is creating an explosion of partly-digitised, partly-fictionalised versions of reality, which might be invisible or incomprehensible to anyone else nearby.

And in reality, out on the street, the stakes are high. We as storytellers are gaining access to incredibly powerful new tools to re-contextualise, re-curate and re-make the world. Storytellers have always had this power, of course, but technology is giving us new ways to entwine and embed stories into people's real lives and to influence the way people perceive the world in real time.

New digital reality-interfaces might soon make the world more usable, more content-rich, and more adventurous – for those who can afford the technology. For some people, these interfaces for everyday experience might soon become inseparable from their relationships, their economies and their perceptions – while those new realities remain inaccessible to everyone else.

I've never personally been a big believer in the stereotypical sci-fi dystopia of all-encompassing Virtual Reality, where users "get lost in the simulation" and forget what's real. If that were really a significant threat to the species then storytelling would have been outlawed long ago, like how Plato wanted to banish poets from his republic. The first modern European novel, *Don Quixote*, written more than four centuries ago, is about a guy who reads too many romantic chivalric fables and starts to see a version of the world defined by romance and chivalry. No headset required. And, as we'll see, Quixote didn't get immersed in this fantasy because it was a *convincing* vision of the world, but because it gave him a compelling way to BE in the world.

We're still a long way from any technology that can consistently fool us into truly believing we're somewhere else. But for me, *virtual* realities aren't the biggest concern. Reality-augmenting technologies don't transport players somewhere else; instead, they allow players to hunt Pokémon and feel like heroic protagonists in re-skinned fantasy versions of their own homes and neighbourhoods. But these same AR technologies could also allow different people to live in very different, divergent versions of the world. Even more literally than they do already.

This isn't science fiction anymore. These technologies are already here. There are real dystopian dangers to this stuff. As our reality-customisation tools get more powerful, we storytellers have a responsibility *to reality*. Responsibility to our players' various realities. Because empathy – building it, recognising it, demanding it – is at the heart of all storytelling.

I believe that storytelling will be vital to help us navigate the next wave of technological change, as the beauty and the chaos of videogames and social networks begin to move up off the screen and out onto the street.

Some of the techniques in this book will continue to be relevant even as the technologies change; others will undoubtedly need to evolve or perish. In many ways, our capacity to digitally augment reality is still at its very earliest stage. Yet already, as Forbes says, "the concept of reality is undergoing a paradigm shift".[1] As such, this book is not intended to be definitive or exhaustive. (And anyway, anyone who tells you they've got an ironclad formula for storytelling is trying to sell you something.)

This book aims to provide a grounding in fundamental techniques for building emotional immersion in hybrid digital/physical experiences. Hopefully, the ideas in this book are useful even if you don't agree with them all. My goal is to outfit you with approaches and exercises to help you develop YOUR OWN storytelling in the digital dimension of the real world. This is a manual of possibilities, not parameters. Reality, the hardest and most exciting medium of all, provides plenty of creative constraints already.

So take these techniques out into the real world, find and hybridise your own technologies and techniques, work with your players to tell new kinds of digital stories, and most importantly, find creative ways to **PROVE ME WRONG**.

Nothing would make me happier.

www.augmentingimagination.com

NOTE

1. 'How Immersive Tech Is Redefining the Limits of Human Connection', *Forbes*, 9 Jan 2024, https://www.forbes.com/sites/forbesliveteam/2024/01/23/how-immersive-tech-is-redefining-the-limits-of-human-connection/?sh=3d6b99e41a99

Acknowledgements

This book would have been impossible without my family's love, support and endless flexibility. To Mum for listening, Dad for pride of workmanship and David for comparing notes.

To everyone who's been part of Playlines: Dustin Freeman, Muki Kulhan, Frode Sorensen, Jerry Carpenter, Anya Tye, Denise Koch, Gemma Sanderson and Dan Blaker.

To the students of the first Spatial Narrative Lab, from whom I learned at least as much as I taught: Dan Dawes, Alysha Nelson, Shreya Sharma, Rachel Tookey and Xuechen Xu and to Helen Jewell and Marianna Bielinska at the Old Market Theatre, Brighton.

Much of this book was written while a Visiting Fellow at King's College London. Many thanks to Alison Duthie and Leanne Hammacott.

I am incredibly fortunate in my friends. Unlimited thanks to those who've supported me over the last few years: Leigh Alexander, Amber Boothe, Patti Garcia, Tamasine Herriott, Ben Paul Lafferty, Jak Marshall, Anita Morgan, Sheena Patel, Ian Renouf, Quintin Smith, Nikos Tsouknidas, Jake Tucker and many others.

Huge thanks to the many brilliant friends and colleagues who've advised, commiserated and listened to me think aloud: Luis Felipe Abbud, Kate Bodner, Darrel Butlin, Gordon Calleja, Ben Carlin, Leighton Evans, Tyrone Hannick, Stephanie Janes, Annette Mees, Nathan Sibthorpe, Gabe Smedresman, Joy Stacey, Jay Springett, the XRchiving team and many others.

Special thanks to Chris Hogg.

Introduction

WHO IS THIS BOOK FOR?

It's for writers who want to bring the capabilities of digital interactive narrative out into real homes and streets.

It's for students, artists, and creative types who want to build meaningful careers in the immersive industries.

It's for storytellers who are interested in how augmented/spatial technologies are creating new relationships between *authors*, *audiences*, *content* and *context*.

If these ideas are new to you, but you're excited by them, then this book is for *you*.

WHAT IS THIS BOOK FOR?

There are incredibly compelling new stories to be told, and powerful new kinds of community to be built, as the transformative power of digital narrative really gets a foothold in reality. This book aims to explore (but not define) this new storytelling frontier.

Back in 1999, Ben Russell's *headmap manifesto* set out to "articulate the social implications of location aware devices" like the early, clunky, GPS-enabled satellite phones of the day. *headmap* foresaw "a world in which computer games move outside and get subversive", where "people within a mile of each other, who have never met, stop what they are doing and organise spontaneously to help with some task or other", and where "paths compete to offer themselves to you".[1]

Today, location-aware devices are already everywhere. Increasingly, the devices which we carry and wear are able to detect our local context and then digitally augment that context. This digital re-contextualisation could happen via location-sensitive text, context-aware audio, 2D heads-up-displays, or 3D spatial graphics superimposed into real places. These technologies can deliver contextual information, making places more useful and informative. They can find or gather people with shared interests, making the world more connected. They can anchor digital gameplay and narrative to real things and real places, making the world more adventurous.

Already, many people see the world *through* technology: an augmented version of the world that's very different to the world seen by other people. They might see posts, messages or contextual markup left by others in the digital dimension of real places. They might see quests, magic items or monsters to fight. They will soon be able to

DOI: 10.1201/9781003379294-1

re-skin and re-texture physical surfaces and even bodies, situating themselves within a fantastically re-imagined version of their local reality.

This graphical remaking and overmapping of the world may not be wholly visually *convincing* yet. But, as we'll see, immersive storytelling does not need to be *convincing* to be impactful. It only needs to be *compelling*.

Very soon, if you're standing at a bus stop, the person next to you at that same bus stop might be partially engaged in very different, digitised, divergent version of reality. These different versions of reality might be playful or information-rich. They might be saturated with advertising. They might present a filtered, curated, customised version of the world to suit the user's preferences – or their prejudices.

In 1999, *headmap* foresaw

> computers becoming invisible, mobile, networked and location aware, the real world augmented rather than simulated. [...] technologies facilitating the tagging and annotating of spaces, places, people, animals and things, the emergence of new forms of spontaneous externalised real social interaction, constructs drawn from dreams and myth shap[ing] the outside more tangibly than ever before.
>
> The internet has already started leaking into the real world. headmap argues that when it gets truly loose the world will be new again.[2]

headmap wasn't predicting the virtualised and pre-commercialised New World of a VR "metaverse" (i.e. a network of virtual realms accessed within the confines of a headset). Instead, it foresaw new augmented experiences of existing physical places. Digital experiences with all the tangible impact and emotional stakes of the real world.

Ultimately, physical reality is where the most compelling stuff happens: in the world around us, and within our emotional and sensational bodies. I've been an interactive and immersive writer for well over a decade; I've helped create everything from print game-books to digitised immersive theatre to a VR Awards Game of the Year. But I've always had a desire to make digital stories happen out in the real world, in *players' personal experience* of the real world. Time and again that desire has led me to augmented/spatial technology. This technology allows creators to hybridise digital storytelling with physical play and physical places. And it's now exploding into the global marketplace.

Augmented/spatial technology has all the power of digital storytelling: responding dynamically to the player's actions, invisibly tracking decisions and physical actions, then manifesting real consequences. It can run sophisticated games of skill or chance, and maintain shared world-states that are experienced simultaneously by millions of players.

And all this happens out in the real world with augmented players who are really, physically *there*, in digitally-enhanced versions of ordinary places, experiencing digitally-dramatised versions of their ordinary experience of being-themselves.

These technologies represent a brand new frontier for storytellers, as wide as the real world itself. Artists and audiences will be exploring their new possibilities for many years to come. As the AR designer Heather Dunaway Smith says,

> we are witnessing the birth of a new medium. Which is not something that happens every day. When a new medium arrives, it tends to copy the mediums that existed

before it. So for example, when cinema arrived, it essentially copied theatre. All of the shots were super drawn back and shot wide, like they existed on a stage with a proscenium. And it wasn't until years later – and lots of work – that people realised that there really was no proscenium in film. And on top of that, there were unique things that film could do to tell a story... We're at a similar crux with Augmented Reality now.[3]

One stereotype about new technological media is that when they first arrive they cause audiences to lose track of what's real, like the popular story about early cinema, where audiences fled in fear from Lumière's 1895 film *Arrival of the Train*. Supposedly these first-time cinema audiences were convinced that the train on the screen might physically hit them. Film historian Martin Loiperdinger calls this "cinema's founding myth": there's actually no contemporary evidence of this kind of panic.[4] In fact, audiences wanted to get on board. By 1897, filmmakers in America had created a popular sensation by positioning cameras at the front of trains, filming journeys as if in first-person.[5] These "Phantom Ride" films became enormously popular, and led to the first immersive "virtual travel experiences",[6] where "Phantom Ride" films were shown in mocked-up train carriages which were rocked and vibrated by pistons. Early cinema audiences didn't mistake the train on the screen for real: in fact, they soon wanted more solidity and sense of physical reality to enhance their experience.

Today, storytellers have a chance to position ourselves at the very forefront of a new media technology, with our audiences along for the ride. Whether or not these technologies *look* real or convincing, what is certain is that audiences will be drawn to experiences which *feel* real and compelling. This means we need to start to understand the unique things that these new technologies can do to tell a story, instead of just copying the mediums that came before. We need techniques for designing digital narratives which are anchored in physical sensations and physical places, and which can be meaningfully shared with other people. Some of these techniques will be brand-new, but many will be adaptations of tricks storytellers have been using for eons.

The goal of this book is to communicate how mind-bogglingly exciting augmented/spatial technologies are and to develop techniques to explore their new storytelling capabilities. We'll first examine the technology of augmented/spatial media to understand how they create sensory immersion, then focus on how good narrative design supplies the other half of the immersion equation: *emotional immersion*.

My goal is also to convey some of the **responsibility to reality** which storytellers bear when augmenting reality. People didn't actually flee in fear from early films, unable to discern what was real from what was mere sensation. But sensational and emotive experiences can change people's behaviour in more subtle ways. Augmented/spatial technologies have the potential to be very persistent and pervasive, and they could potentially recontextualise our realities in ways we may not recognise, until we find ourselves living in **divergent realities**. This is particularly significant in our increasingly divided world, where the concept of truth itself is increasingly destabilised, and as we face an existential threat in the form of climate collapse.

I believe the role of storytelling will only become more vital in the new realities in which we find ourselves. The train has already left the station. Let's find out where it goes.

STRUCTURE OF THIS BOOK

Throughout this book we'll use three core **pillars of emotional immersion**. These are three fundamental components of creating compelling immersive narratives:

SEEING
BEING
BEING SEEN

Section 1 will define each of these pillars using examples from Virtual Reality. Then Sections 2 and 3, the bulk of the book, will use these three pillars to examine different aspects of Augmented Reality / spatial storytelling.

Section 1: LEARNING FROM VR

Section 1 is divided into three short chapters, in which we'll examine each of the three pillars in their most basic form as they apply to VR:

1.1: SEEING in VR
1.2: BEING in VR
1.3: BEING SEEN in VR

All three pillars need to be working in concert for a VR narrative to be emotionally immersive. In a VR experience the player might SEE a lush 3D landscape rendered around them. But SEEING alone isn't enough to create a sense of BEING in the place (or the story). The majority of VR experiences do this by embodying the player in a virtual avatar body which moves as they move, often while the story informs them *who* they're virtually BEING. But just BEING there, through the illusion of embodiment and identity, doesn't give players a meaningful *role* in the story. Players also need to feel the possibility of BEING SEEN: either by virtual characters, or in a broader sense by having meaningful impact on the virtual world.

Augmenting Players Vs. Augmenting Places

The three pillars will "evolve" as we apply them to augmented/spatial media. But they'll evolve in two slightly different directions, depending on whether we're focusing on AUGMENTING PLAYERS or AUGMENTING PLACES.

The two main sections of the book deal with these two separate but interrelated aspects of augmented/spatial narrative:

Section 2: AUGMENTING PLAYERS
Section 3: AUGMENTING PLACES

But why divide up "players" and "places"?

When Jerry Siegel and Joe Schuster created Superman in the 1930s, they were heavily influenced by the science fiction heroes of the day, in particular Buck Rogers, and Edgar Rice Burroughs' John Carter of Mars. These heroes were transported into strange worlds where their skills, humanity (and White Western perspectives) were an advantage. Buck Rogers was a fighter pilot who got time-capsuled 500 years into the future: his skills and values proved highly transferrable and he became a hero. John Carter, a Confederate soldier and ideal of Southern courtesy, was mysteriously transported to Mars where he was faster and stronger than Martian natives due to Mars's lower gravity, so he became a hero and a warlord.

These human heroes were fish-out-of-water, but when transplanted into alien waters they usually turned out to be pretty big fish. (The popularity of *isekai* or "in another world" anime and manga today proves the enduring appeal of this formula.)

But Superman was something new: Siegel and Schuster "reversed the usual formula of the superhero who goes to another planet". They "put the superhero in ordinary, familiar surroundings, instead of the other way around, as was done in most science fiction": Superman is an alien who comes to Earth, where our planet's yellow sun gives him superpowers.

It's hard now to appreciate how new this was: according to Schuster, "that was the first time I can recall that it had ever been done".[7]

Not an idealised Earth-man, transplanted into another realm which then swoons over him. Instead, an alien, orphaned on contemporary Earth (where, in most Superman stories, he shows us Earthlings how we can actually be *better*).

However you feel about capes and two-fisted pulp heroes, as an augmented/spatial reality storyteller you may find yourself faced with a similar creative decision:

Do you work on *augmenting the world* around your player, instancing a more adventurous, more empowering or more emotive world around them?
Or,
Do you work on *augmenting the player themselves*, incarnating a version of themselves who is extraordinary within the ordinary world?

Unlike VR, augmented/spatial media don't fully transform the world. They can't entirely transport players to another place, no matter how sophisticated the technology. As the technologist Galit Ariel says, unlike VR which "aspires to transport you into a completely parallel digital world, augmented reality adds a digital layer directly onto or within our existing physical environment".[8]

So we can't just fish players out of their current context and transplant them somewhere new to make them a "hero" (whatever that is). Our players are already in-water. They're in-context and fully immersed in their ongoing experience of BEING themselves and BEING THERE in a real place.

This book is about augmenting stories *into* the player's local reality: stories which feel like they're happening TO the player, and taking place WHERE the player is. *So should we focus on augmenting the player, or the places around them?*

The answer, as you might already suspect, is *both*.

Even while immersed in an augmented/spatial experience, the player is firmly anchored in their real body AND in a real place. So ultimately an augmented/spatial story must be a hybrid of the physical and the digital.

Augmented/spatial technology can't replace or overwrite players' ongoing physical experience. As the word suggests, *augmenting* means *adding to* or *enhancing* this ongoing experience, not subtracting from or overwriting it. Players must experience BEING a hybrid augmented version of themselves, and BEING IN a hybrid augmented version of their immediate reality.

In order to give the player an augmented experience which feels solid, real and emotive, we shouldn't try to overwrite them with a new, authored identity. Or try to fish them out of the real world and transpose them somewhere virtually new. Instead we need to augment their existing identity, and augment their existing relationship with the world around them. We need to combine techniques of AUGMENTING PLAYERS and AUGMENTING PLACES.

These two areas are strongly interrelated, but to keep things organised we'll deal with them separately in Section 2: AUGMENTING PLAYERS and Section 3: AUGMENTING PLACES.

Section 2: AUGMENTING PLAYERS

In Section 2 we'll see how those three pillars of VR emotional immersion begin to evolve when we apply them to augmented/spatial narrative. See Figure 0a for a summary.

2.1: IMAGINING
In chapter 2.1 the pillar SEEING will evolve into IMAGINING. This chapter focuses on fundamental techniques to help storytellers and players co-IMAGINE augmented/spatial scenarios in the real world. No matter what technology we're using, the player's IMAGINATION is our most important resource to get the player SEEING an augmented and recontextualised world.

2.2: IDENTITY-BUILDING
In 2.2 the pillar BEING will evolve into IDENTITY-BUILDING. The player is already BEING someone in their everyday experience, and augmented/

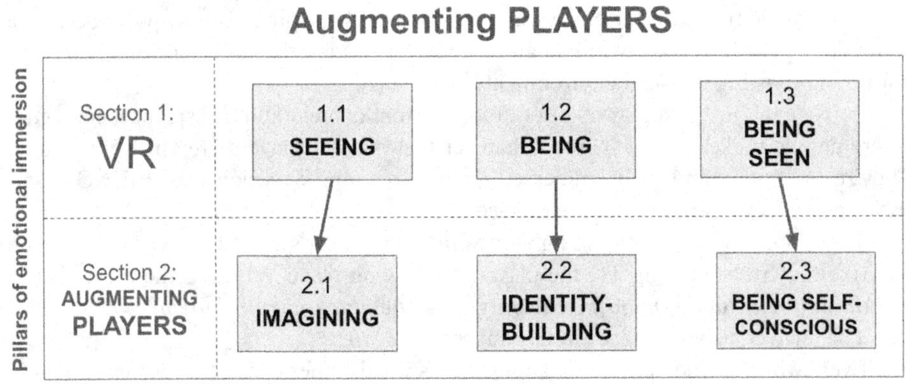

Augmenting PLAYERS

FIGURE I.0a Evolution of pillars of emotional immersion in Section 2: AUGMENTING PLAYERS

spatial technology can only add to that experience, not overwrite it. This chapter focuses on techniques to help the player situate themselves inside an augmented/spatial scenario. In particular this means helping them imaginatively incarnate an augmented player-character IDENTITY.

2.3: BEING SELF-CONSCIOUS

In 2.3 the pillar BEING SEEN will evolve into BEING SELF-CONSCIOUS. This chapter focuses on techniques to acknowledge and leave space for players' SELF-CONSCIOUSNESS. SELF-CONSCIOUSNESS is not the enemy of immersion, especially in augmented/spatial reality. Even "awkward" SELF-CONSCIOUSNESS, which we tend to think of as disruptive to sensory immersion, can be a powerful driver of emotional immersion.

Section 3: AUGMENTING PLACES

In Section 3 those same three pillars will evolve differently. See Figure 0b for a summary. How do we help players instance a new, story-rich, adventurous version of a place, and then situate themselves within it?

3.1: STAGING

In Chapter 3.1 the pillar SEEING will evolve into STAGING. Technology allows us to anchor graphics to physical surfaces, but making a place into the setting of a digital story means helping players to imaginatively STAGE the story. This chapter focuses on STAGING the layout, **spatial pacing** and boundaries of hybrid digital-physical storyscapes.

3.2: BEING THERE

In 3.2 the pillar BEING will evolve into BEING THERE. This chapter focuses on techniques to put the player on-STAGE in the storyscape. Players are always already *somewhere* before augmentation begins, so we need techniques to

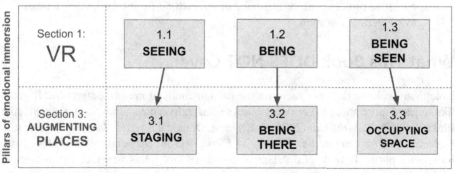

FIGURE I.0b Evolution of pillars of emotional immersion in Section 3: AUGMENTING PLACES

show them which of their pre-existing experiences and sensations are taking place inside the story. In particular, this chapter focuses on designing for players' **spatial agency**, e.g. designing branching paths.

3.3: OCCUPYING SPACE

And in 3.3 the pillar BEING SEEN will evolve into OCCUPYING SPACE. This chapter focuses on techniques for showing players that their presence in the storyscape is impactful and meaningful. You cannot BE someone or BE somewhere without taking up space. We all leave our mark on the world, and have a discernible impact on others. That's part of how we know that we are real – and this is also true in augmented places. This chapter focuses on players' **spatial subjectivity**, e.g. using their vantage point as a storytelling tool.

Section 4: DIVERGENT REALITIES

Concluding the book is Section 4, where we'll look at how the wider implications of AR/spatial technologies might influence the role of the storyteller in the future.

APPENDICES

Appendix A: Inclusion, Accessibility & Safety provides notes and approaches towards making your experiences fair, equitable and safe. Since augmented/spatial experiences always take place partly in the real world, these considerations are very much part of the canvas which storytellers must work with.

Appendix B: Sliders for defining augmented/spatial experiences contains a series of "sliders" or axes which can be used to define an experience, e.g. defining it somewhere on a slider between **location-specific** and **location-agnostic**. Since augmented/spatial experiences are always hybrids, this slider-based approach aims to be more helpful and flexible than strict definitions, helping you explore a wider range of hybrid possibilities.

Finally, **Appendix C: Example Concept Development Framework** provides an example step-by-step process for developing your first augmented/spatial narrative project, with brief advice on everything from concept development to budgeting to testing.

What This Book DOES NOT Cover

Note that this book does not focus on the fundamentals of narrative structure. If you'd like to learn more about the building blocks of narrative, consider writing manuals like Blake Snyder's *Save the Cat* (2005) or Brian McDonald's *Invisible Ink* (2010), or Ursula K. LeGuin's *The Carrier Bag Theory of Fiction* (1986). Appendix C includes Owen Kingston's particularly helpful Adaptive Narrative Plot Beats structure for immersive theatre. But keep in mind that there is no such thing as a foolproof formula for storytelling. The best way to learn about stories is to go out and start telling them.

This book also doesn't cover **scenography**, i.e. the architecture, visual design, set-dressing, lighting etc. of controlled immersive spaces like immersive theatre environments, escape rooms or theme parks. **Scenography** is a complex and beautiful business and is far too broad to be covered here. For a starting point on **scenography** for controlled immersive spaces, I recommend Jason Warren's *Creating Worlds: How to Make Immersive Theatre* (2017).

WHAT KINDS OF TECHNOLOGY IS THIS BOOK ABOUT?

This book isn't going to deal with any one hardware or software platform in detail, because that's the surest way to give it a short shelf-life. Immersive technology is accelerating, and the sheer variety of ways people use the technology is expanding. Our focus is on the fundamental affordances of augmented/spatial media – their capabilities and qualities – and how these affect storytelling. But it's important to establish in general what technologies we're talking about and some key principles of how they work.

Virtual Reality vs. Augmented Reality

Virtual reality is *opaque* (or non-see-through). A virtual reality headset blocks out the world around the player, completely enclosing them and overwriting their sensations of the real world with a virtual world.

In other words, VR "presents a vivid virtual environment while shutting out physical reality".[9]

By contrast, augmented reality appears to be *transparent* or see-through. (Same with mixed reality and spatial computing – more on those shortly.)

As Meta's AR hardware chief Caitlin Malinowski says, "VR takes you somewhere else—a place to focus, or game, or travel. AR is where you are at right now". These are very different use cases: Kalinowski argues that

> we're going to spend a lot more time in AR than we spend in VR. VR will be really important for learning, for deep, immersive experiences, while AR will be used for most of the things that you currently use your phone for.[10]

Augmented reality "allows users to see their physical surroundings and interact with people around them while wearing the headset, tackling a major drawback of VR: the feeling of isolation. It also provides a new way to engage users, making use of their worlds".[11] For John Hanke, CEO of Niantic (creators of *Pokémon GO*), AR is about "selectively adding things which enrich the world a little bit, like a Pokémon that you're chasing. But it's not meant to put you in the Pokémon universe so that you are no longer in reality. That would be VR, and that's a different story—maybe good for escapism, but not as important in terms of the future of technology".[12]

Modern headsets are increasingly capable of both VR and AR. That is, users can "dial" all the way back into a fully virtual reality which overwrites their real environment and situates them in a virtual one. And they can also "dial" all the way forward until they're looking THROUGH the technology at the real world, with graphical elements augmented in.

- **VR is a technology you LOOK AT, while it creates the illusion that you are somewhere else.**
- **Augmented reality/spatial computing are technologies you LOOK THROUGH, while the technology integrates digital elements into your perception of the real world.**

A key quality of augmented/spatial storytelling is that digital narratives appear to be taking place *where* the player is, in their immediate context. Context is highly subjective, which is part of why there aren't many definitive rules for augmenting players' realities. In fact, there are only three hard-and-fast rules we'll use throughout this book: the first rule is that in augmented/spatial media, *context is everything*.

To augment players' context, we first need to detect it, and that starts with location.

Location-based Technology

Storytellers have always been able to make stories which feel local or which hit audiences "where they live". Any good campfire storyteller knows the most effective ghost story is one which happened *in this very campground, on a night just like this*. But in order to make this kind of localised storytelling work in digital formats, we often need to detect and refer specifically to the player's environment. For example, by using location-based or *locative* devices which can detect players' position on a map, usually via GPS. Some location-based technology doesn't use GPS but can locate the user within a specific area, for example by triangulating local Wi-Fi signals or detecting signals from bluetooth location beacons.

Pokémon GO (2016) uses mobile phones' native GPS to populate the player's local environment with in-game features and objectives superimposed onto a map. Location-Based Games (LBGs) like *Pokémon GO* entwine play with everyday life,[13] adding dimensions of narrative and gameplay to players' ordinary walk to the shops.

Environment-tracking Technologies and SLAM

GPS can help situate a digital narrative in a player's general context, but it doesn't give storytellers much information about what the player might be seeing or hearing. Immersive experiences often use environment-tracking technology to feel more specifically contextual.

This typically takes the form of a smartphone camera or a headset with external sensors which scan the player's immediate surroundings while keeping track of the device's position relative to the surroundings. This is broadly known as **SLAM** (**Simultaneous Localisation and Mapping**) technology.

Cameras and depth sensors (such as LiDAR, *Light Detection and Ranging* sensors) detect the physical surfaces of the world and their relative distance from the device. The system then constructs a digital model of its surroundings as a **mesh**, a 3D digital model of a physical space similar to the virtual environments in videogames. (A **mesh** is sometimes also called a map or visual map). Using **SLAM** the **mesh** is overlaid or mapped onto the physical surfaces, so the **mesh** corresponds to the real physical space. This means the system can place virtual objects and characters into the physical space and keep those virtual elements anchored to physical surfaces.

As the player moves, the ongoing **SLAM** process continually tracks the physical surfaces around them and dynamically adjusts the **mesh** so that virtual elements anchored to the physical surfaces stay aligned to those surfaces. Virtual objects anchored to the **mesh** can react to physical motion, creating the illusion that the virtual objects physically touch or react to real objects. If you reach out and touch an augmented object, you might be able feel a real physical surface underneath, giving the augmentation the illusion of solidity.

SLAM allows augmentations to appear to be "world-stable",[14] but it's not perfect yet; a lot of research goes into overcoming AR "drift",[15] where virtual objects move unrealistically in relation to physical surfaces.

Augmenting Graphics into Space

An augmented reality is more than simply a heads-up display. Early smart glasses might superimpose a digital clock or notification HUD (heads-up display) in the corner of your vision, but if this information isn't contextually integrated into your wider experience then it's not an augmented reality. Whereas an interface which detects, refers to and highlights objects or destinations nearby (such as a digital pop-up showing the latest deals when you walk past a shop) is augmenting reality because it's responding to its immediate environment.

Most AR technologies superimpose digital graphics into the player's field-of-view. Mobile AR does this via mobile phones. When a *Pokémon GO* player uses the game's "AR Mode" they hold up their mobile device, and the device's camera sends a live video feed of the surroundings to the device's screen (just like when using the camera normally). The game then draws digital graphics onto the video feed so that the graphical element appears to be present in the world seen through the camera, integrated into a single perceptual experience.

Pokémon GO's AR Mode interprets the camera feed and infers the general shape of the world using a basic form of **SLAM**, creates a basic **mesh** of the physical surface of the floor, and draws a Pokémon onto the video feed so that it appears to be standing on the floor. This improves the illusion that the Pokémon is really there, in physical reality, co-present with the player.

This type of AR called **video passthrough**. The camera feed "passes through" the camera to the screen, and is graphically augmented along the way.

The same **video passthrough** process is happening in augmented/spatial reality headsets like Apple Vision Pro. Cameras on the outside of the headset film the world and send a video feed to screens inside the headset, which are positioned and calibrated so that the displayed video feed appears to be the player's normal vision. Combined with **SLAM**, graphics can then be drawn onto the passed-through video, appearing to be anchored to physical surfaces.

Players' experience of augmented/spatial reality is always first-person. This first-person perspective is in contrast to cinema, where the framing is usually via a camera perspective that's different to the characters' perspectives. This means that an augmented player is always present in the scene, and a protagonist in the story, even if they're watching action unfold between other characters. This is a core quality of AR/spatial storytelling we'll be exploring in detail, and it results in the second hard-and-fast rule we'll use throughout this book: *when augmenting reality, the most important reality you are augmenting is the player themselves*.

Even though we'll spend Section 3 examining how to augment PLACES, nonetheless an augmented/spatial reality narrative always starts by augmenting the PLAYER.

Reskinning

Using a combination of location-based technology, **SLAM**, and global-scale **mesh** data-sets, AR/spatial technologies are increasingly able to overlay the physical surfaces of the world with digital textures and graphics. It will soon be possible for a headset or even a pair of low-profile glasses to be able to fully "reskin" a body, a room or entire street with digital graphics in realtime. For example, reskinning a room like the inside of a submarine, or altering a street into a Victorian fantasy with physical streetlights overlaid with digital gaslamps and so on. You might be able to walk down a street, "theming" it however you choose, able to reach out and touch the augmentations with the illusion of physicality.

We can already do this in realtime to a certain extent; AI is likely to supercharge this capability. Reskinning areas of the world by hand is costly and difficult to scale; but an AI-powered headset might soon be able to infer the physical shape of any street and dynamically reskin it with generated graphics. This has both exciting and potentially dystopian implications, which we'll examine in Section 4: DIVERGENT REALITIES.

XR, mixed reality, and spatial computing

As well as augmented reality, there are other terms at play. Sometimes these are used to define specific types of augmented reality, sometimes as a replacement for that term, and sometimes to encompass even broader technologies. Generally speaking these different terms don't consistently define specific technologies[16]; they reflect different expressions of the same technology, and/or manufacturers and marketers trying to develop a common language to communicate clearly to consumers.[17] Let's try to reduce some of the confusion:

XR

XR is generally used as a catch-all term for VR, AR and spatial computing, and it's sometimes (but not always) taken to mean "eXtended Reality".

Mixed reality

AR which anchors graphics to physical surfaces, or where digital and physical elements can interact,[18] is often specifically defined as "mixed reality".[19] In this definition, physical objects are incorporated into a single hybrid physical-digital perceptual model. For example, a player interacts with a physical prop like a stick, which via a headset is scanned and reskinned as a magic sword. The real-life object provides the sensation of physical substance and texture, while the digital elements overlay magical visuals[20] and incorporate the object into the narrative world.

Some technologists view "mixed reality" as a useful progression or market distinguisher from augmented reality. Others argue "mixed reality" emerged only after the term augmented reality was "diluted" by being applied too broadly.[21] "Mixed reality" is also sometimes used to describe headsets which are capable of both VR and **video passthrough** AR.

In short, the distinction between augmented and mixed reality is still pretty subjective; as the engineer and entrepreneur Louis B Rosenberg says, the distinction "has nothing to do with the hardware and everything to do with the perceptual experience".[22] "Augmented" and "mixed reality" aren't exactly interchangeable; generally speaking they're different implementations of the same technology.

Spatial computing

Spatial computing is a term that's been around for over twenty years, originally defined as "human interaction with a machine in which the machine retains and manipulates referents to real objects and spaces".[23] That is, digital media which we perceive to be taking place in our world, instead of inside the world of a computer. (However, others see "spatial computing" as an even broader term, encompassing autonomous vehicles and robotics.[24])

Apple and Sony have both recently adopted "spatial computing" for their head-mounted displays. Apple requires developers to refer to "spatial computing"[25] not AR or mixed reality in Vision Pro apps, perhaps aiming to create a "cleanly engineered breakaway"[26] from previous buzzwords. Apple might have the casting vote, so spatial computing might become the catch-all term for immersive digital technology.

One of the signs that an artistic medium is maturing is that eventually the terminology settles down, and it's important to agree on general definitions so that investors and audiences alike understand what kind of experience they're being offered. But technology companies are caught between wanting to communicate clearly to consumers, and wanting to differentiate their products with hot new buzzwords.[27] So these terms are likely to continue to change.

In short, if you're confused about the terminology around these technologies, don't worry: it is confusing! These terms are used in different ways by different people for different reasons, and they sometimes reflect hype rather than strict technical definitions.

For simplicity, and to avoid constraining our thinking, in this book we'll use the general term *augmented/spatial media.*

A NOTE ON METAVERSES

One buzzword has been conspicuously absent so far. The term "metaverse", meaning interconnected VR realms, rose and fell in fashion pretty rapidly between 2021 and 2023.[28] But much of the technology underpinning the original VR-based concept also underpins AR/spatial media.

For many, "metaverse" has evolved to encompass concepts much broader than the VR-specific vision initially driven by the newly-named Meta in late 2021. "Metaverse" is increasingly applied to digitisation of the physical world via augmented/spatial technology. In 2024, the CTO of industrial AR developer Magic Leap Daniel Diez said "it's pretty commonly accepted or agreed upon that the true capabilities of the metaverse will come to life when it's a fabric built of digital experiences ingrained or embedded into the physical world".[29] John Hanke has called this the "real-world metaverse".[30]

To avoid confusion we won't refer to technology in terms of *metaverses* in this book, but we're probably not done with that word yet.

Passthrough vs. See-through

Digital devices you look THROUGH have a number of major technical challenges. In augmented reality on mobile phones, your augmented view of the world is confined to a small handheld viewport, the screen of the device itself. Small phone screens present composition challenges, and ultimately more of the world is excluded from the augmented version of reality than is included.

Headsets have a far larger field of view. But currently, many consumer augmented/spatial reality headsets on the market aren't actually transparent: they're still screens you look AT, not THROUGH. **Video passthrough** means the headset is effectively filming the real world, then passing that live feed to screens in the headset and then to your eyes. But like any live feed, this has a delay. Apple Vision Pro has a delay or latency of about 11 milliseconds, a quarter of other contemporary headsets,[31] but it's still detectable by eye. These latency issues cause dissonance or contradiction with our normal vision: we appear to be seeing the world normally, but our brains can detect micro-second lags between moving our head and our "vision" onscreen updating.

And because your eye is always looking at screens just millimetres away, instead of focusing on objects at a range of distances, **passthrough** headsets have to use optical illusions in order to replicate our authentic experience of seeing. (More on this in Chapter 1.1 when we look at SEEING in VR).

Passthrough technologies are improving all the time, but ultimately passing a signal along wires from camera to screen is never going to create a truly authentic experience of vision. As Oculus chief scientist Michael Abrash wrote way back in

2012, "unfortunately, compared to reality, **video passthrough** has low resolution, low dynamic intensity, and a low field of view, all of which result in a less satisfactory and often more tiring experience".[32] **Passthrough** is inherently a compromise: as Nilay Patel said when reviewing the Apple Vision Pro, "you're constantly being reminded that you're looking at video on screens, and reality is a lot more interesting than that".[33]

What's the alternative? Truly "**see-through**" glasses like XREAL Air, or Meta's Orion prototype, superimpose digital graphics onto transparent screens between our eyes and the real world. In **see-through** AR the player is viewing the real world live and in-person, and augmented graphics can be placed in relation to the real scene, rather than digitally painted onto footage. **See-through** is sometimes also called "optical AR", "hard AR" or simply "true AR". As Abrash says, **see-through**

> has the huge virtue of not compromising real-world vision, which is, after all, what you'll use most of the time even once AR is successful. Crossing a street would be an iffy proposition using passthrough AR, but would be no problem with see-through AR, so it's reasonable to imagine people could wear see-through AR glasses all day.[34]

However, true **see-through** visors are difficult and expensive to make, and current visor technology can only produce graphics that are, well, **see-through** and "ghostly".

One of the biggest problems in **see-through** displays is the "black pixel problem". Displaying black is important to make digital objects seem real. Even before Vision Pro was launched, Apple's designers were emphasising how important it was for digital objects to cast shadows: "this grounds them and makes them appear more integrated into the space".[35] Shadows require dark pixels. But in conventional display technology, a black pixel isn't actually "displaying" black: it's *switched off*. In a **see-through** display all the pixels are slightly **see-through**, especially black ones. So as Abrash says, while a **see-through** display "can be bright enough to be the dominant color the viewer sees, it can't completely replace the real world; the real-world photons always come through".[36] It can't overwrite reality.

By contrast, **passthrough** "has the advantage of simplifying the display hardware, which doesn't have to be transparent to photons from the real world, and of making it easy to intermix virtual and real images, since both are digitized".[37] But hardware manufacturers are racing to produce better and better **see-through** displays, since they're much less bulky to wear in public and ultimately yield a better experience.

Regardless, remember that immersive technology always relies on storytelling to stimulate the player's IMAGINATION, because it's their IMAGINATION which fills in the gap between the virtual and the real to create hybrid experiences. Rony Abovitz, founder of **see-through** AR visor company Magic Leap, once said

> we made black with light. And that's not possible. But it was two artists on the team who thought about the problem. And all of our physicists and engineers were like, "well, you can't make black, it's not possible." But they forgot that the whole world you experience is actually in here [tapping his head]. And this can make anything.[38]

Whether or not Magic Leap was able to draw black with light isn't the point: the point is that as with all immersive technology, it's the emotive effects that artists and storytellers create with the technology, by stimulating and collaborating with the player's IMAGINATION, which make it immersive.

As one analysis of the UK Immersive Industry put it in 2019, technologists and artists working in the "immersive" space are often "uncomfortable with the increasingly accepted shorthand of VR/AR/MR/XR as 'immersive technologies'. Immersion is about experience and impact, not about a tech delivery platform: 'immersive tech' is not a given – immersion is *designed for*. The 'tech' part is an appropriate tool which serves the vision not defines it".[39]

Whatever technology you're using to augment your player's reality, remember that the technology is in service of the IMAGINATION – yours, and more importantly, your players'.

- *Virtual Reality* is opaque and overwrites the real world via screens which players LOOK AT inside a headset.
- *Augmented Reality* is transparent and adds digital graphics onto reality via technology the player LOOKS THROUGH.
- *Location-based technology* allows a digital device to understand the player's local context.
- *SLAM and environment-tracking* detects and tracks real surfaces in relation to the device.
- A *mesh* is a 3D digital representation of a physical shape or environment, sometimes also called a map or "visual map".
- *XR* broadly encompasses VR, and AR/spatial.
- *Mixed reality* refers specifically to augmenting physical objects and places. (Sometimes it means VR and AR-capable devices.)
- *Spatial computing* appears to take place in the real world, not in a computer.
- *Video passthrough AR* is used by mobile AR and AR/spatial headsets: a live video feed of the outside world is displayed and augmented via screens.
- *See-through AR* visors or glasses allow vision of the real world to be augmented directly.

OTHER KEY TERMINOLOGY

Player

The interacting audience member.

In augmented/spatial media the audience is implicated in the story and embodied as a character – even if that character is "themselves". But what do we call them? It's a more complex question than you might think.

Immersive theatre moves the audience out of their seats in the auditorium and up onto the stage. It uses a range of terms for audiences, from "visitors" to "audience-participants" "playing-audience" and even "guest performers".[40]

Videogames are similar in that the audience is not just witnessing but enacting part of the story. Rather than completing a story and handing it off to the audience, game writers effectively collaborate with each audience member, who enacts a version of the story which is unique to them.

Videogames have a single stable term: *player*, and this is the term I'm going to use throughout this book. (For the sake of keeping things consistent I'll use "player" even when discussing non-game media like immersive theatre.)

Think of "player" not just in the videogame sense but in the Shakespearean sense, where "players" were the actors who performed plays. (And of course, as Shakespeare knew, in a sense we are ALL merely players.) Your player is not simply the person to whom you're *telling* the story, but also a co-teller, collaborator and performer.

Player-character

The partially-fictionalised version of the player whom the player plays in the story.

We're all the protagonist in our own story all the time. AR/spatial media allows us to give players a heightened sense of protagonism by making them a character in a fictionalised world. This player-character's IDENTITY could be almost (but never quite entirely) the same as the player's IDENTITY, or it may be a **roleplayed** IDENTITY which belongs to the world of the fiction. We'll examine these concepts in detail in 2.1: IDENTITY-BUILDING.

Layer

A coherent set of digital elements presented in relation to physical features. For example, graphics overlaid onto physical surfaces or audio corresponding to physical location.

Some layers are overlaid on reality via maps: e.g. the map view of *Pokémon GO*. Some layers reskin the surfaces of an object or room to totally change its appearance via **passthrough** or **see-through** augmentation.

Some layers might only be visible to some people. You might be able to flip between layers like changing lenses in a pair of glasses. For example, the CityXR system under development by Japanese startup Psychic VR plans to allow players to see the "Social Layer", "Game Layer" or "Art Layer" of a place, all co-existing in the same space.[41]

Zero-sum

Any situation in which two elements cannot co-exist without loss. E.g. two physical objects cannot share the same space.

Chess is **zero-sum**: each square can only contain one playing piece, and there can only be one winner. Physical marks on a physical wall are also **zero-sum**: a wall surface only has two dimensions on which marks can be made, and if two marks exist on the same bit of wall then one must be overwriting the other (or they combine into a new colour, and both are lost in favour of something new).

Whereas digital layers are **non-zero-sum**. More than one layer can exist in the same place without competing for space. A single place can have many **non-zero-sum** digital layers laid over it.

Non-zero-sum digital layering means that there might be numerous different versions or *instances* of a place: some visible, some invisible. And each layer might contain one or more *experiences*.

Experience

Noun. A digital story, application, game or other entertainment product within one or more augmented layers.

It's difficult to pin down a single term for the type of narrative/entertainment products we'll be discussing. They're not necessarily *games*, they may contain many different *stories*, and calling them *plays* comes with its own ambiguity. Although it's a slippery and somewhat overused term, I'm going to describe what we'll be making as *experiences*: discrete interactive products, with narrative elements existing within one (or more) augmented layers.

But don't lose sight of the fact that every moment we're alive we're *experiencing* many different things at different conceptual levels. Augmented/spatial narrative doesn't overwrite players' ongoing, pre-existing experience of the world, or offer them an "escape" from it. We're going to be adding to, curating or re-contextualising players' ongoing experience. Because that's what makes augmented experiences – hybrid digital/physical/imaginative narratives – feel grounded in reality.

Diegetic

An element which is part of a story and exists inside the world of the story.

Whether a physical or digital element is **diegetic** or **non-diegetic** – whether or not it belongs in the world of the story – is a crucial question in augmented/spatial narratives.

Here's an example of the difference: in film studies, **diegetic** music is music whose source you can see in the frame. The music in the cantina in *Star Wars*, for example, is **diegetic** because we can see the band playing their instruments. Music which exists purely in the soundtrack, like the Imperial March in the Emperor's throne room, is **non-diegetic**: the characters can't hear it; it doesn't exist in the world of the story.

Augmented/spatial media doesn't replace the real world with a virtual one the way VR does. So in an augmented/spatial narrative *everything* the player experiences is **diegetic** until they're told otherwise. And, crucially, this includes their experience of BEING themselves. Game researcher Hugh Davies calls this "ludic dramaturgy": "players are able to interpret every action and event as potentially part of the game, making them sensitive to every nuance of reality and giving mundane tasks and events compelling new meanings".[42]

Exploiting this sensitivity to "giv[e] mundane events compelling new meanings" is one of the key tools of the augmented storyteller. An augmented/spatial narrative heightens and dramatises players' decisions and experiences by *diegetic-izing* them, integrating them into a narrative context.

Immersion

A player's state of experiencing and imagining a coherent narrative, scenario or sensory framework. Stimulated by digital media and consensually maintained by the player.

Immersion is a complex concept. It doesn't help that it's become a marketing buzzword used to sell many different kinds of experiences. It's also sometimes used as a subjective measure of how enjoyable and/or realistic an experience is, particularly videogames. But a key design principle throughout this book is that *realistic is not the same thing as immersive* – and it's certainly not the same thing as *engaging*.

Immersion is hard to build, and it's easily broken – particularly if you depend on a simulation being "realistic". Reality sets an almost impossibly high standard. Our senses are incredibly good at spotting falseness, and trying to consistently "fool" them with technology is very challenging and expensive. More importantly for us as storytellers, immersion can be broken just as easily by plain old *boredom* as by graphical glitches. Or by asking players to immerse themselves in events or characters that aren't relatable or don't make emotional sense.

But luckily, as we'll see, immersion is not a trick, nor a spell we cast over the player. It's an agreement. Players *want* to get immersed. This is why we can describe a good book as immersive, even though the technology of a book isn't "simulating" an environment. As the great VR scholar Janet Murray said in *Hamlet on the Holodeck* (1997),

> when we enter a fictional world, we do not merely "suspend" a critical faculty; we also exercise a creative faculty. We do not suspend belief so much as we actively create belief.[43]

The researcher Gordon Calleja notes that "immersion" and "presence" get used almost interchangeably: both are used to describe technologies with the potential to give players "a sense of inhabiting the simulated spaces they offer",[44] that is, not just SEEING fictional places but BEING in them. Activating players' IMAGINATION is a vital part of this. For Calleja, immersive technologies create that sense of BEING "through the use of the player's IMAGINATIVE faculty".[45]

When we're immersed, our brains are never completely un-aware of the real world and our bodily sensations. In fact, some of the most interesting immersive stories deliberately play upon how we can experience a story while simultaneously maintaining various levels of meta-immersion. Calleja actually prefers the term "incorporation" to immersion, to describe how digital situations can be "assimilated into the user's consciousness". That's how we can be part of a fictional story while also still aware of the world around us – the story is "coextensive with our everyday reality".[46]

An augmented/spatial narrative is a partly-digitised version of the real world. So the story will very much be "co-extensive" with elements of the player's everyday reality, including their sensations, feelings, and even their SELF-CONSCIOUSNESS. Our challenge as storytellers is to stimulate players' imagination to "actively create belief" and recontextualise their everyday reality, instead of trying to overwrite it.

Luckily, everyone is already a protagonist (and narrator) of their own story. We just need to play along.

IS THIS STUFF REALLY A BIG DEAL?

This is an important question to ask. New storytelling techniques and technologies come along all the time, and although none of them ever really go away, they don't all have Earth-shaking impact. Augmented/spatial technologies give us some fascinating new tools, but are they going to be more impactful than any of the other buzzwordy technologies we've seen rise and fall?

I believe they're a very big deal. I believe that soon, for many of us, augmented/spatial technologies will have a fundamental impact on how we walk down the street, and how we think about the world. I think this impact will be at least as major as the rise of the smartphone.

Some of the world's most powerful companies – Apple, Baidu, Google, Meta, Microsoft, Samsung, Sony – have invested billions building hardware and ecosystems for a time when many consumers live in a partly-digitised world, with augmentations entwined in day-to-day life. The AR market is estimated to be worth $210BN by 2030.[47]

Our ability to augment the world is rapidly outstripping our ability to understand the cultural, economic and political impacts of doing so. Technology is accelerating, and trying to predict the future is a fool's game. But there are vital ethical questions around augmented/spatial media, which the architecture writer Joshua McWhirter neatly summarised back in 2018:

> What does it mean to filter public space through a highly personalized form of digital sensing? How does the collapse of virtual onto physical space reorder established ways of understanding landscapes? What are the potential pitfalls and possibilities of a technology that promises re-enchantment of space, yet relies on privately-owned data infrastructures and a military-operated ensemble of near-orbit satellites?[48]

Should we storytellers simply concern ourselves with "enchantment", and leave the "pitfalls" to others? Not in my book. After all, as we'll see, much of the power of these technologies comes from the stories we tell about them. More importantly, in a very real sense, these technologies can't exist without storytellers creating compelling experiences which incentivise players to use them.

Let's briefly examine three broad, interrelated areas in which augmented/spatial technology could have a global impact: **world-mapping**, **privacy** and **reality customisation**.

World-Mapping

What are the next big successful apps that we're going to see? Our big bet is on things that make the world come alive, make the world more useful, make the world become connected... Connecting all the physical stuff in the world with the digital things that help you know more about it or help you interact with it.

To do that the big linchpin is not the visual part of AR, in the sense of just overlaying a hologram into the scene. It's knowing where you are in the world and where your gaze is directed.

John Hanke,[49] Niantic CEO

Almost from the beginning, computers have been used to make local places more useful, meaningful or playful. The first public digital bulletin board, the precursor to every social network and imageboard on the internet, was a location-specific network called Community Memory, a series of computer terminals in wooden or cardboard boxes placed around Berkeley, California in 1973. The vast majority of content was hyper-local: bagel store recommendations, carpool requests and bands seeking drummers.[50]

Today, GPS apps show curated overlays of hyper-local information, helping make the places around you more navigable and meaningful. Early commercial augmented/spatial experiences tended to focus on players' own homes. But with increasingly portable headsets, many developers are overlaying graphics on outdoor places for games, fitness and advertising applications. This overlaying is partly done in realtime, with the user's device sensors detecting their physical location through **SLAM**. But for contextual information the system must also refer to online datasets about the location.

These datasets, which Hanke describes as "visual maps", comprise pre-scanned **meshes** of the physical shape of the world. These spatial datasets "let the camera [on an AR device] know exactly what it's looking at in the world. And then you can make the Pokemon hide behind the park bench... Or provide information about a public artwork",[51] because these 3D spatial datasets also have contextual metadata about landmarks or businesses.

Spatial-contextual datasets are the infrastructure that underpins global-scale augmentation, and spatial-contextual data has rapidly become one of the most valuable commodities in the global data economy. Companies are investing billions to build these datasets in order to create augmented/spatial applications, but players who use these applications are often contributing their own data too.

As a result, according to the NYU Stern Center for Business and Human Rights, "major technology companies continue to pour billions of dollars into immersive technologies, signalling their intention to retain their dominance in the transition from the 2D to the 3D web".[52] Companies like Apple and Google see augmenting the world not just as a way to sell devices, but also as the next logical frontier in their service/content/data business models. With augmented/spatial reality, these business models will move off the screen and out onto the street.

As the location-based media researcher Leighton Evans says,

The overlaying of information over physical space can lead to a strengthening of our relationship to that space... We are spatial beings. The idea that we feel comfortable somewhere, the idea that we have a contextual history with a particular environment is very important to us. We are more likely to spend time somewhere like that. We are more likely, from a commercial point of view, to spend money in a place like that.[53]

And ultimately, this all comes down to money. Look at your local area via the mapping app on a smartphone. The geolocated content on the map on your device will be slightly different to the content seen by another user, even if they're standing in the same place. These different digital versions of the same place might highlight different routes, amenities or local businesses. Sometimes this is helpful, like if you have particular access needs or food preferences. But this shifting, subjective digital geography doesn't happen simply because places *mean* different things to different people. The map is trying to *sell* different things to different people. The companies that make mapping apps don't give them away: they provide the apps for free in exchange for your user data, to be used or sold to partners, mainly in order to contextually sell products to you.

Augmented/spatial advertising is currently still somewhat gimmicky (it's still in what sci-fi writer Karl Schroeder calls "the flying-whale stage of visual grab-assery"[54]). But as augmented advertising becomes more widespread, those 3D "visual maps" will likely be combined with contextual datasets of users' preferences, movements, friends and shopping habits. AR adverts will be able to provide contextual suggestions, recommendations, and offers. As Evans says, if you walk past a shop while wearing AR glasses,

you're going to get pop-ups. You're going to get an overlay of information that says "call in here for 20% off a soy oat milk" or whatever… and ten minutes later you've got another offer and another offer, and all of a sudden you are being commercially exploited by the partners of this application.[55]

Artist Keichii Matsuda's 2016 short film *HYPER-REALITY*[56] shows one vision of an augmented world: it's saturated with contextual augmented advertising on almost every physical surface, and users' attention is minutely monetised. Today, some companies are already selling the advertising rights to the still-mostly-hypothetical digital dimension of physical places.

These commercial drivers are a big part of the reason AR/spatial technology is being developed, and hence the reason storytellers like us will have the opportunity to populate the world with digital narratives.

In advertising terms, augmenting the world with highly personalised and contextual content is potentially far more impactful and lucrative than advertising on 2D browsers. This requires those vast spatial-contextual datasets.

Those datasets aren't built simply via satellite or drone, but also by harvesting data from users. For Hanke, building a global "visual map" is a big part of Niantic's contribution to the development of augmented/spatial technologies. Niantic's approach is to design games which incentivise players to contribute data about the world through their device cameras. In Niantic's first game *Ingress* (2014) high level players were incentivised to contribute photos and metadata about local landmarks. Many of those same landmarks, with their user-contributed photos, then showed up in Niantic's later games. Hanke describes the dataset which powers Niantic's products as a "UGC [user-generated content], collaboratively built map".[57] Today, Niantic's Lightship platform uses those same spatial-contextual datasets to allow developers to create their own location-based AR games and applications. Products built on the platform can in turn harvest more user data for the ecosystem.

In effect, all current AR/spatial technologies are entangled with the service/content/data business models of some of the world's largest companies. The same technology that lets us *write* new kinds of stories into the world might also be *reading* our players as they play. There may soon be financial incentives to design experiences that induce augmented players to behave in certain ways, e.g. to maximise data capture. Platform-holders may seek to create demand for products which refine their datasets of products, places, businesses, and demographics. For good and ill, this is the landscape in which AR/spatial storytellers operate.

Privacy

We carry on daily life assuming that no-one has access to our innermost thoughts, medical conditions, sexual preferences, and emotional vulnerabilities. The possession of such information would amount to an inordinate amount of power to extort, manipulate, and coerce.

XR technologies are designed to collect and process precisely such intimate information.

In fact, XR technologies cannot function adequately without collecting and processing large quantities and various types of personal data – specifically, bodily data that can also be used to infer behavioural and psychological information about individuals.

Mariana Olaizola Rosenblat, NYU/Stern Center for Business and Human Rights[58]

VR, AR and spatial technologies constantly scan users and the surrounding world, acquiring "bodily data". Bodily data is extremely valuable in identifying us and quantifying even "intimate" things about us – and platform-holding companies want to keep[59] it[60].

One 2023 study showed that individual users of the VR game Beat Saber (2019) could be identified from body language alone with more than 94% accuracy using only 100 seconds of motion data. 50% of all users could be identified with only *two* seconds of data.[61] Lead researcher Vivek Nair said:

Moving around in a virtual world while streaming basic motion data would be like browsing the internet while sharing your fingerprints with every website you visit... the streaming of motion data is a fundamental part of how the metaverse currently works.[62]

Even the basic motion data required to control a virtual avatar, use gestures, or be reskinned in AR, is as unique as a fingerprint. And it can be read at a distance by CCTV or other people's wearables. As Rosenblat says, XR wearables have

the potential to capture the gait patterns, facial expressions, and eye movements of bystanders, who have not given their consent. Furthermore, headsets are equipped to constantly scan physical objects for spatial cues. When used en masse, such perpetual scanning of the world and its inhabitants could enable constant surveillance of public and semi-public places.[63]

Moreover, as a 2022 report to the UN High Commissioner for Human Rights says, this data

> is not just the user's real identity, which is mostly already known by the platforms... Instead, it is a new quality of information that is comprised of the user's real identity combined with their reactions to particular stimuli – indicating what someone uniquely may think and like and want.[64]

There's no question that the technology required to augment the world will be prohibitively expensive for many years. AR/spatial technology may end up widening the existing gap between technology "haves" and "have-nots" by allowing "haves" to effectively live in more user-friendly versions of the world.

If consumer AR technology does become affordable, even for technology "haves", it'll likely be because platform-holding corporations provide the hardware at a discount because they're able to scrape lucrative data from users, via the very technology that makes immersion possible.

It's not just about "reading" players: these technologies can exert enormous influence on players too. In early 2024 researchers found they could inject "inception attacks" into Meta Quest headsets, diverting VR players into alternative virtual realities without their knowledge.[65] Back in 2018 researchers were already able to

> find[] vulnerabilities in VR systems [and] control the movements of immersed users and lead them to predetermined locations without their knowledge—a type of attack they called the "human joystick." They were also able to... trick users into hitting real-world physical objects and walls.[66]

Even *Pokémon GO* has been used to manipulate players into unwitting political acts. At the height of the first *Pokémon GO* craze, players in Munich were unknowingly co-opted into a counter-protest action to disrupt a right-wing demonstration. By placing lure modules at the location of the counter-protest, rare Pokémon – and players – were drawn to the event. According to one report, "the plan worked out perfectly: playing against xenophobia".[67]

For Louis Rosenberg, the platform-holders of immersive technologies could soon pair real-time surveillance with real-time influence: companies

> could track billions of people and impart influence on select individuals by altering the world around them in targeted and adaptive ways.[68]

In general, modern users are aware that their data is being commoditised. But even if you're happy to be part of the content-data ecosystem, being tracked in this way can affect your behaviour. According to the UN report,

> there is a risk of self-censorship, in the most fundamental way, if users find themselves trying to limit what they feel, think, or express for fear that information will be monetized or researched.[69]

If you've ever swiped past a video in order to *train your algorithm* (i.e. so that the video platform doesn't show you more of the same), you've self-censored in this way. Now imagine recreating that dynamic in the real world.

Under a capitalist system, this might mean averting your gaze from real objects so that your algorithm doesn't decide you want to buy them.

Under a totalitarian system, you might need to self-censor your gaze by not-looking at banned or marginalised elements of the real world. Your wearable system might be tracking your gaze (or even censoring these elements out of your vision altogether).

AR/spatial technology might give us "super-vision" in the form of information-rich interfaces for everyday reality. But the price we pay might be corporate or even state *supervision*. And we all behave differently when we're being supervised.

Reality Customisation

In effect, a player of *Pokémon GO* is moving through a slightly altered version of the world. The game doesn't constantly superimpose graphics into the player's field of view, but it recontextualises the world through a pervasive extra dimension of play. We know it's just a game, and we might be playing it in parallel with ordinary errands. Still, in order to engage with the game we have to treat its fictional premise with some level of reality, and let its fictional objectives influence how we move through space. In other words, as researchers Larissa Hjorth and Ingrid Richardson say,

> location-based hybrid reality games such as Pokémon GO [...] require us to adopt an "as-if" structure of experience, moving through the environment "as if" it were game terrain or an urban playground. That is, Pokémon GO is not just a casual mobile game, for while we might play it in the midst of other daily activities, it also explicitly intervenes with and modifies those activities and relations—sometimes in positive ways, sometimes negative.[70]

There are implications for player safety when augmenting layers of content and gameplay onto reality. Especially if those layers influence how players behave. Appendix A looks in more detail at storytellers' responsibilities when augmenting the world.

But there's nothing inherently wrong with viewing the world through an "as-if" structure, whether that's viewing it through "rose-tinted spectacles", seeing the world as a romantic quest like Don Quixote, or perceiving things from a given political or moral standpoint. We all experience and perceive the world differently based on our physiology, upbringing, attitudes and biases. In many ways, storytelling is the analogue technology humans developed so that we could compare notes and find common ground despite our very different, highly subjective experiences of reality.

But the world is increasingly saturated with complex information. For most of us, our perspective is influenced by the media we consume, whether that's journalists, politicians, influencers or ideologues. We in turn curate and filter our media intake to focus on things we find engaging – or we allow an online platform to algorithmically curate media for us. This curation of cultural and political information has a huge impact on our worldview.

Many of us already receive all our news, culture and political commentary through a self-selected filter – often consciously or unconsciously tuned to affirm our existing opinions and validate our values. Scholars have been warning of the dangers of ideologically-personalised news and "customized truth" since the earliest days of the[71] internet.[72] Today we can all self-curate a selection of news and commentary to corroborate almost any ideological perspective. It's easy and enticing to stay within "filter bubbles", or within communities which speak the same cultural language we do. But if these bubbles filter out all differing perspectives, they can become **echo chambers**.

Echo chambers don't have to be self-curated; one of the services provided by social networks (in exchange for your data) is the almost-invisible, algorithmic personalisation of your feed to suit your tastes and drive your engagement.

If you're exclusively fed content filtered by ideology, excluding a diversity of perspective, your attitudes to the world can quickly harden and radicalise. When you're in an **echo chamber** – a customised, filtered version of reality – it's easy to begin to see the perspectives and actions of other people in other **echo chambers** as alien and deplorable. Over the last few years we've seen the radicalising effects of **echo chambers** and their very real effects on culture and politics, particularly in the rise of extremist far-right conspiracy theories. And this all happened in 2D **echo chambers** on screens and browsers. Now, with technology increasingly able to augment and personalise various versions of reality, it's possible to imagine people living in bespoke, 3D **customised realities**.

In a **customised reality**, hardware and software services would curate reality via headsets or glasses to suit our needs and desires. This might mean simple and convenient interfaces for the daily shop, but it might also the ability to reskin or even overwrite certain elements of reality.

Of course, we all see the world differently already, right? This is true even without technology. Buy a philosopher a drink and they'll tell you that we all perceive different, subjective versions of reality. The world is, in the words of the poet Louis MacNeice, "incorrigibly plural".

However, empowering players to customise their individual reality in augmented/spatial reality could have a particularly strong effect in shaping their attitudes or behaviour. AR/spatial technology might empower some people to live within custom, reskinned realities curated by ideology. These **divergent realities** could pervasively influence those players' perceptions.

There are major risks, real potential dystopias, inherent in AR/spatial technology. For me, these dangers don't come from people getting lost in virtual worlds and believing that the fantastical is real. The danger comes when technology empowers humans' existing tendency to be highly selective about ordinary reality: to be selective about what we treat as *valid*. And *who* we treat as valid.

What would it mean if individual, customizable reality browsers, mediated by wearable technology, allow us to see different, personalised versions of the same street? Today, when we step away from browsers and **filter bubbles** and go out into the world, we inevitably encounter the plurality of other peoples' perspectives. We might not agree, but we encounter the world's diversity of perspective. What happens if, instead, we're able to selectively opt-out of seeing different objects, ideas, or people?

If you stand at a bus stop wearing AR/spatial glasses, and look at an augmented advert on the bus stop wall, that advert doesn't have a physical presence in the world which everyone can see and touch. It could be an image personalised to you. It might advertise something else entirely to others or be invisible to them.

What happens if it's a political advert? Or graffiti? Or reality-markup specific to a closed community? You are effectively seeing a completely different version of local reality compared to the other people at the bus stop. And their **custom realities** might be completely invisible and inaccessible to you. At that point you are effectively living in different realities – much more literally than ever before.

Some players might choose to live inside a game layer which visualises the world "as-if" it's a space of colour-coded contested territory, and visualises people from other game factions "as-if" they're demons or orcs.

Some might choose to view a world overlaid with hidden or encrypted layers of ideological messages. These "dark layers" could be exploitative, or embed illegal content into real places, or manifest crypto-political perspectives into reality. They could be "dark layers", the "Dark Web" of the real world.

In a future "marketplace of realities" we might be able to pick and choose what version of reality we want to live in. This will deepen the real and perceptual divisions between ourselves and other people living in other realities nearby. Our realities might not overlap with our neighbours' at all. That phrase "marketplace of realities" has been used to describe the vast potential of augmented reality,[73] but it's also been used by researchers into conspiracy theories and internet radicalisation, to describe the online environment in which it's all too easy to fall down an alternate reality "rabbit hole".[74]

This doesn't necessarily mean that the answer is censorship or centralised control of augmented reality technology. John Hanke again:

> I think people should be able to theme the world however they choose to theme the world. If I want to see the world that's a little bit more like it's Nintendo everywhere and it's bright and happy and has Marios popping up from behind park benches, I think that should be my choice. I don't think someone should assert some right to control what's happening on my body and in my eyes or ears.[75]

If a corporation or government had full control over both the hardware and software of an AR/spatial ecosystem, it's possible they could impose a particular reimagination or reskin of the world onto all users. This would be a supercharged form of the kind of authoritarian "reality control" we see in dystopias like *1984*.

By contrast, the danger of "**customised realities**" isn't that any particular re-versioning of the world is imposed onto everyone. Instead, it's that people will be able to live in bespoke versions of reality – just as they always have, but now supercharged with full 3D graphical treatments, perhaps personalised by contextual datasets or AI. These **divergent realities** might be comfortable, compelling and all-encompassing, yet invisible and impenetrable to others.

Divergent realities might be so siloed that they make it even harder for us to understand how and why other people see the world differently to ourselves. Augmented/spatial technology might end up making it harder, not easier, for humans to communicate about our different experiences.

And of course, while some of us live in an increasingly digitised world, for the vast majority of people these technologies, and whatever realities they unlock, will remain financially out of reach.

Augmented/spatial storytellers are engaged with these issues, whether or not they want to be.

If *context is everything*, then recontextualising people's reality has the power to *change* everything, one person's perceptions at a time.

And if these technologies are *augmenting the player themselves*, then they could have profound effects on players' behaviour, their identity, and how they treat others and the environment.

That's why the third hard-and-fast rule for augmenting reality is:

when augmenting a player's reality, we have a responsibility TO their reality.

Players have a responsibility to their reality too. They can always switch technology off. And no matter how much an interface or entertainment product might re-version the world, people bear a responsibility for their own safety and behaviour in the physical world.

But judging by recent history, it's easy to imagine a world where many people prefer to live within a particular *edit* of reality. Maybe because it's fun or useful, or emotionally compelling, or they're involved in its digital economy, or simply because it's where all their friends hang out.

And even if you choose to opt-out of this technology altogether, you might have no control at all over how other people use it to re-skin *YOU*.

That's why this stuff is a big deal. And that's why developing realistic, responsible approaches to augmented/spatial storytelling is vital now, as these technologies are just beginning to proliferate.

THREE RULES

I've mentioned three hard-and-fast rules we'll use throughout this book. These are drawn from my decade-plus as an immersive storyteller across a wide variety of immersive formats. They're intended to foster good quality storytelling and to make storytellers conscious of the sheer power of the new tools available to them.

But if there's no foolproof formula for storytelling, why have rules at all? Moreso than other media, augmented and spatial narratives are partly composed by (and partly composed *of*) real players and places. This means that, even more than other media, any discussion of storytelling techniques for AR/spatial is a discussion of people's real and varied experiences of the world. Effective AR/spatial storytelling can't be done merely with a mechanical collection of tools. It must engage with perspectives, principles and even politics: all the unpredictable elements which make physical reality the most difficult and exciting artistic medium.

Accordingly, these three rules are not necessarily here to help you create fictions: they're here to keep you grounded in reality.

Rule 1

Context is everything

All augmented/spatial realities, no matter how sophisticated, use the real world as a substrate or basic structure. You might be using technologies which can fully reskin the physical surfaces of a player's whole neighbourhood, making it appear to be a steampunk fantasy or a post-apocalyptic wasteland. Or you might simply be playing location-triggered factoids to your player as they go about their day, like a museum audio tour. Regardless, the player's perspective and physical sensations – their context – is what anchors augmented/spatial elements and makes them meaningful.

Augmented narratives become compelling when they acknowledge and incorporate the player's context, and situate themselves *within* the player's context.

Unlike virtual reality, augmented/spatial technology does not "transport" the player elsewhere or transpose them into a virtual world. We must meet players where they are and use their world as a foundation, no matter how much digital superstructure we then build upon it. The player's context is our canvas.

Rule 2

The most important reality you are augmenting is the player themselves

The player is the most important part of the context which forms our canvas. The player's identity, and their ongoing sensory and cognitive experience of being themselves, must be a **diegetic** part of the narrative.

Augmented players are not unaware of everyday reality. They don't have to believe your fiction is "true" – even temporarily – to get immersed. Immersion doesn't mean the player has "forgotten" who or where they are. Immersion doesn't mean you've successfully distracted them from the fact that they're wearing plastic goggles and looking at pixels. Augmented players are not just *suspending* their disbelief; they are actively *creating belief*.

Immersion is not a trick – it's an agreement. A negotiation. A conversation. Players don't get immersed because an augmented world is *convincing*. They get immersed IF it's *compelling*. This means they need to be involved. Augmentation starts with them; we must augment the player before we start augmenting the world.

Rule 3

When augmenting reality, you have a responsibility TO reality

Once you start augmenting and editing reality, the stakes get very high very quickly. Humans already tend to choose to live in selective realities. AR/spatial technologies may accelerate the ongoing divergence of different peoples' realities.

Some people's realities are harder than others'. Rich and powerful people have always had an outsized ability to influence the realities of others – and to be selective about which realities they themselves have to deal with. To adapt a quote from William Gibson, reality is already here – it's just not very evenly distributed.

Ultimately, the promise of AR/spatial storytelling is the ability to leave each other notes in the digital margins of reality. As storytellers we have a particular responsibility to make sure that these technologies do not end up further empowering those who are already powerful, and pushing those who are already marginalised further into the margins of their own reality.

As augmented/spatial storytellers, these issues are also part of our canvas. We have to address them head-on in our work and our practice, or we will be part of the problem.

OVER TO YOU: CHALLENGES

Throughout this book are CHALLENGES designed to get you prototyping augmented/spatial storytelling principles and applying them in your own work. Shortly we'll conclude this introductory section with the first of these CHALLENGES.

Augmented/spatial narratives always take place *somewhere*, so the CHALLENGES will often ask you to design an augmented experience for your own home or to choose a real-world location. You can find locations via GPS mapping software like Google Maps, or by finding floorplans for locations online (later Case Studies refer to London's Tobacco Dock venue; floorplans and a Virtual Tour can be found at https://www.tobaccodocklondon.com/3d-tour/). But often a CHALLENGE will ask you to visit a location in-person, so you can respond to its unique features.

In order to keep things accessible, in the CHALLENGES you'll often prototype augmented/spatial storytelling techniques using only text, audio or basic locative technology.

Audio Prototyping

When students ask me how to get started in augmented/spatial storytelling, I tell them to first find a place they love, then write and record a short audio narrative designed to be heard in that place. There's no faster or cheaper way to prototype contextual narrative layers. My own early augmented reality theatre designs combined audio, locative technology and live performance. I was following in the footsteps of artists like Chris Harding, Teri Rueb, RIXC collective, Mark Shepard, Hive Networks, Blast Theory and especially Janet Cardiff and George Bures Miller.

Location-specific audio narratives are the AR equivalent of student short films. They can be easily made using just a smartphone, and easily shared as part of a portfolio. They allow you to experiment with using narrative to augment *how* and *why* a player navigates the world. They teach you many of the fundamental storytelling techniques you'll need when working with more technology.

Accordingly, some of the CHALLENGES will ask you to record location-based audio tracks. Simply use any audio recording application, e.g. on a smartphone, then play it back while in the location. (Later on you'll also be asked to use platforms like caught.nu to geolocate recorded audio so that it triggers seamlessly as players reach a location.)

Why Audio?

Next time you're on a trip to the shops, imagine a dramatic, gravelly "trailer voice" contextually narrating your every action as if it's a momentous decision. What would it say? How would it change the way you feel, and what you do, as you shop?

Audio has the great advantage of being *heads-up*. Listening via headphones allows players to be *co-present* in a narrative while highly present in a real location. Their experience is a hybrid of the audio layer and the immediate context. Hence, location-based audio can inject evocative narrative elements into ordinary experience, and recontextualise players' relationships with the places and people around them.

Audio can also be both *public* and *private*. One of the exciting (and potentially dystopian) aspects of AR/spatial technology is that people sharing a public space might be perceiving that space in entirely different ways in the privacy of their headsets. This idea isn't new. It all started with the Sony Walkman, not only the first truly *portable* consumer audio player, but in many ways the first *private* audio player. As the media theorist Jay Springett says, when the Walkman launched "the cultural phenomenon... of isolating yourself in your own auditory world in public was when looked at objectively, weird and new... Fast forward, and now almost everyone is plugged into their individual auditory universes while navigating the cityscape".[76]

Janet Cardiff describes how audio can "accentuate the visual and accentuate the reality. You know how it is when you're walking along, listening to music on a headset. It's like the real world becomes a film with a soundtrack".[77] As one designer who worked on early Walkmen said, they added "a kind of spectacle to daily life and made humdrum activities feel cinematic".[78] For musicologist Shuhei Hosokawa, the Walkman augments and "theatricalizes" players' experience of the world.[79]

The pioneering digital theatre maker Chris Hardman describes the moment in 1980 when, having forgotten to bring a book on a plane, he tried the "new fangled bizarre device called a Walkman":

> Just as the airplane lifted into the sky "The Ride of the Valkyries" began to play. Suddenly I realized that there was this amazing theatrical event happening and it was called synchronicity! The visual and the audio were working in sync and furthermore instead of watching from afar, I was literally inside the event.[80]

Hardman's use of audio to "theatricalise" experience led to several "site-specific location walk-through"[81] theatre productions using audio. But Hardman saw further, writing in 1983 about his vision for "Walkmanology" as immersive interactive theatre:

> In this theatre of the future, you, as the audience, will clip on a radio transceiver no larger than a saltine cracker... By digital encoding/decoding, your unit will be able to pick up its own discrete channel and yet all the units will be perfectly synchronised...

Your pre-taped intervoice asks you to step through a red door and start walking down a hall. Soon you're approached by a humanoid; it could be a hologram, an actor, or a fellow audient. You hear him talk to you over your tape. The hall is now full of beings and the sound grows deafening. Your inservice asks you to step through a side door and you are alone...

Suddenly a man bursts in with a drawn knife. You are given a choice: join or fight. Your decision determines your play: the mother computer triggers either the fight or the join tape and the play continues. Perhaps next you'll be asked to engage in Hesse-like games of chance or feats of skill. Each decision or result will determine the next step in your adventure.[82]

This pitch, now over forty years old, sounds pretty "augmented reality" to me. Every effect Harding describes is now technically possible – with a big enough budget – and is becoming more possible every day.

When it comes to storytelling there's nothing really new under the sun. What matters is how you utilise the affordances of your chosen media. That's why this book's CHALLENGES will often ask you to augment and "theatricalise" players' realities using audio, the most accessible and flexible technology currently available.

On that basis, let's do an initial CHALLENGE: augmenting a place with audio narrative to create a hybrid spatio narrative.

This CHALLENGE might seem a little daunting, but it's designed to be a quick-and-dirty first try at digital storytelling for real places. You don't need to tell a complex story or use technical tools besides a smartphone. You'll continue developing this story concept in later CHALLENGES. Many of the CHALLENGES build upon earlier ones, so you'll have chance to iterate upon your ideas.

CHALLENGE #1: SHADOW PLACE

Goal: Augment a place via audio narrative to create a hybrid spatio-narrative experience.

SUMMARY

You're going to create a **5-7 minute** audio spationarrative which dramatises a player's presence in a location. Provide **navigation** narration/dialogue to guide them along a short **path** through the location.

Use narrative to recontextualise the location, and "theatricalize" the player.

First, **select a place**. Choose somewhere you can physically access – somewhere you know well, or can visit for inspiration.

Now **develop a narrative concept** which reveals a hidden "shadow" side to that location.

It's up to you what this "shadow side" is like. It could be a "ghost tour" through a historic location with a tour guide who turns out to be a ghost. You could reveal fragments of conversation from a train station's parallel dimension. Or show players their local park is actually a field of magical, invisible flowers, and they need to walk a pattern to restore the flowers' enchantment.

Make sure the player is a character in your narrative. What is their role? Are they themselves, or **roleplaying** a character? Why are they able to perceive the "shadow" side? What does the story need from them?

Now **visit** the location and **plot** your narrative onto the location by choosing a **path**.

Select a **start point** and **end point**, and note any landmarks along the way. You will need to provide **navigation** through narration or dialogue to tell players where to go and when. What landmarks or other physical features can you describe to provide **navigation** from the start point to the end point?

Now, **write** and **record** your audio dramatisation to narratively augment the place (and the player!)

Finally, **test** by playing the audio as you move through the space. If possible, ask some friends to do the same. Do they accurately follow the navigation? Does their attention wander? Will they relate to the location differently next time they visit? **Assess** your narrative and consider how you'd improve it next time.

TASKS

- **Select a place**.
- **Develop a narrative concept** about the place's "shadow side".
- **Visit the site**.
- **Plot** a narrative **path** with a **start point** and **end point**.
- **Write** your script, incorporating **navigation**.
- **Record** as audio.
- **Test**.
- **Assess** and **iterate**.

NOTES

Remember that a location-based digital narrative is only as **accessible** as the physical place, so consider physical access for people with different mobilities, as well as social and safety factors affecting different people's access. (We'll look at accessibility in more detail in Appendix A.)

NOTES

1. Ben Russell, *The headmap manifesto*, 1999, p. 5, http://www.technoccult.net/wp-content/uploads/library/headmap-manifesto.pdf.
2. *Ibid.*
3. Heather Dunaway Smith, "AR Design Principles: Creating Immersive Experiences", Adobe MAX 2021 https://youtu.be/JO1Qw-JTVqc
4. Martin Loiperdinger, "Lumière's 'Arrival of the Train': Cinema's Founding Myth", *The Moving Image 4:1*, 2004.

5. *The Haverstraw Tunnel*, American Mutoscope and Biograph Co., 1897, https://archive.org/details/haverstraw_tunnel

6. Christian Hayes, "Phantom Carriages: Reconstructing Hale's Tours and the Virtual Travel Experience", *Early Popular Visual Culture*, 7:2, 2009.

7. *NEMO: The Classic Comics Library* #2, Fantagraphics, 1983.

8. Galit Ariel, "How AR Can Make Us Feel More Connected to the World", TEDWomen, 2018.

9. James J. Cummings, Jeremy N. Bailenson, "How Immersive Is Enough? A Meta-Analysis of the Effect of Immersive Technology on User Presence", *Media Psychology* 19:2, 2016

10. Caitlin Kalonowski, quoted in Tech at Meta blog, 1 Feb 2023. https://tech.facebook.com/ideas/2023/2/meta-ar-future-wearable-tech-caitlin-kalinowski/

11. Tom Emrich, "2024, the Year Spatial Computing Takes Off", *The Drum*, 22 Jan 2024. https://www.thedrum.com/opinion/2024/01/22/mixed-reality-wearable-tech-and-ai-2024-the-year-spatial-computing-takes.

12. John Hanke/Cristina Criddle, "A Real-world Metaverse Will Be More Magical Than VR", *Financial Times*, 3 Oct 2022, https://www.ft.com/content/40d81fa4-67e6-40ea-b077-ba09484ba151.

13. Adriana de Souza e Silva, Ragan Glover-Rijkse, Anne Njathi, Daniela de Cunto Bueno, "Playful Mobilities in the Global South: A Study of Pokémon GO Play in Rio de Janeiro and Nairobi", *New Media & Society* 25:5, 2021.

14. Philipp A. Rauschnabel, Reto Felix, Chris Hinsch, Hamza Shahab, Florian Alt, "What Is XR? Towards a Framework for Augmented and Virtual Reality", *Computers in Human Behaviour* 133, 2022

15. Carter Slocum, Xukan Ran, Jiasi Chen, "RealityCheck: A Tool to Evaluate Spatial Inconsistency in Augmented Reality", *IEEE International Symposium on Multimedia*, 2021

16. Louis Rosenberg: "Mixed Reality or Spatial Computing", 16 Feb 2024 https://medium.com/predict/mixed-reality-or-spatial-computing-346e62148026

17. Stephanie Llamas, "We Don't Know What We Are Talking About" in *Charlie Fink's Metaverse*, Charlie Fink (ed.), Cool Blue Media, 2018

18. Laia Tremosa, "What is the Difference between AR vs. MR vs. VR vs. XR?", Interaction Design Foundation, 2023. https://www.interaction-design.org/literature/article/beyond-ar-vs-vr-what-is-the-difference-between-ar-vs-mr-vs-vr-vs-xr

19. "Extended Reality Technologies", US Government Accountability Office, January 2022 https://www.gao.gov/assets/gao-22-105541.pdf.

20. Cesar Lucho Lingan, Meng Li, Arnold Vermeeren, "The Immersion Cycle: Understanding Immersive Experiences through a Cyclical Model", *Proceedings of the Design Society* 1, 2021

21. Rosenberg, 2024.

22. *Ibid.*

23. Simon Greenwold, "Spatial Computing", MIT Masters Thesis, 2003. https://acg.media.mit.edu/people/simong/thesis/SpatialComputing.pdf

24. Emrich, 2024.

25. Apple, "Submit Your Apps to the App Store for Apple Vision Pro", https://developer.apple.com/visionos/submit/

26. Ewan Spence, "'Apple Vision Pro Apps Hide A Crafty Mac Decision'", *Forbes*, 13 Jan 2024, https://www.forbes.com/sites/ewanspence/2024/01/13/apple-vision-pro-app-store-sdk-macos-apple-silicon/

27. Rauchsnabel *et al.*, 2022.

28. Dean Takahashi, "The Metaverse Is Back. But Let'S Not Call It the Metaverse", *VentureBeat*, 9 February 2024 https://venturebeat.com/games/the-metaverse-is-back-but-lets-not-call-it-the-metaverse-the-deanbeat/

29. Daniel Diez, interviewed by Dean Takahashi, "With $590M in More Funding, Magic Leap Looks to the Future", *VentureBeat*, 16 January 2024, https://venturebeat.com/games/with-590m-in-more-funding-magic-leap-loosk-to-the-future-interview/

30. Hanke/Criddle, 2022.

31. Tomislav Bezmalinovic, "Optifidelity Measured the Passthrough Latency of Quest 3 & Vision Pro", *Mixed News,* 16 Feb 2024 https://mixed-news.com/en/quest-3-vision-pro-passthrough-latency-measurement/

32. Michael Abrash, "Why You Won't See Hard AR Anytime Soon", *Valve,* 20 July 2012, https://web.archive.org/web/20120722110736/http://blogs.valvesoftware.com/abrash/why-you-wont-see-hard-ar-anytime-soon/

33. Nilay Patel, "Apple Vision Pro Review: Magic, Until It's Not", *The Verge,* 30 Jan 2024 https://www.theverge.com/24054862/apple-vision-pro-review-vr-ar-headset-features-price

34. Abrash, 2012.

35. "Principles of spatial design", Apple, https://developer.apple.com/videos/play/wwdc2023/10072 WWDC 2023

36. Abrash, 2012.

37. Abrash, 2012.

38. Rony Abovitz, "2015 EmTech Digital – Magic Leap" https://www.youtube.com/watch?app=desktop&v=bmHSIEx69TQ&feature=youtu.be&t=35m18s&ab_channel=RuthalasMenovich 35:22

39. Jon Dovey, *Framing Immersion,* Watershed, Bristol, 2019. https://www.swctn.org.uk/wp-content/uploads/2019/07/SWCTN_Immersion_Showcase_Publication_D.pdfEmphasis added.

40. Josephine Machon, *Immersive Theatres*, Palgrave Macmillan, London, 2013, p. 74.

41. "CityXR: A Vision For Augmented Cities In The Shadow Of Hyper-Reality", Harry Baker, UploadVR 2 November 2023, https://www.uploadvr.com/cityxr-augmented-cities/

42. Hugh Davies, "Place as Media in Pervasive Games", IE '07: Proceedings of the 4th Australasian conference on Interactive Entertainment, 2007, p. 2.

43. Janet H. Murray, *Hamlet on the Holodeck: The Future of Narrative in Cyberspace (Updated ed.)*, MIT Press, Massachusetts, 1997, p. 110.

44. Gordon Calleja, "Immersion in Virtual Worlds" (2014) in *The Oxford Handbook of Virtuality*, Mark Grimshaw (ed.), OUP, Oxford, 2015, p. 222.

45. *Ibid.*

46. *ibid.*

47. Meticulous Research, Jul 2024, https://www.prnewswire.com/news-releases/augmented-reality-market-to-be-worth-210-1-billion-by-2031--exclusive-report-by-meticulous-research-302202506.html

48. Joshua McWhirter, "City Skins: Scenes from an Augmented Urban Reality", Failed Architecture, 20 Sep 2018 https://failedarchitecture.com/city-skins-scenes-from-an-augmented-urban-reality

49. John Hanke, interview with Nilay Patel, "The Metaverse is already here and it's full of Pokemon", Decoder Podcast, 14 Dec 2021 https://www.theverge.com/22832490/niantic-ceo-john-hanke-metaverse-pokemon-go-ar-vr-podcast-decoder-interview

50. "Guide to the Community Memory Records", Online Archive of California, https://oac.cdlib.org/findaid/ark:/13030/c8cv4p5k/admin/

51. Hanke/Patel, 2021.

52. Rosenblat, 2023.

53. Leighton Evans, Personal correspondence, July 2023. See also Evans and Michael Saker, *Intergenerational Locative Play: Augmenting Family*, Emerald Publishing, UK, 2021.

54. Karl Schroeder, "'The Suicide of Our Troubles'", Slate.com 2020.

55. *Ibid.*

56. Keichii Matsuda, *HYPER-REALITY*, 2016 https://www.youtube.com/watch?v=YJg02ivY zSs&ab_channel=KeiichiMatsuda

57. Hanke/Patel, 2021.

58. Mariana Olaizola Rosenblat, "Reality Check: How to Protect Human Rights in the 3D Immersive Web", NYU Stern Center for Business and Human Rights, Sept 2023 https://bhr.stern.nyu.edu/tech-immersiveweb-report

59. Joseph Jerome, "Pretty Soon, Your VR Headset Will Know Exactly What Your Bedroom Looks Like", *Wired*, 3 Oct 2023, https://www.wired.com/story/virtual-reality-meta-wearables-privacy/

60. Kyle Orland, "Meta will start collecting "anonymized" data about Quest headset usage", Ars Technica, 27 February 2024, https://arstechnica.com/gaming/2024/02/meta-will-start-collecting-anonymized-data-about-quest-headset-usage/

61. Vivek Nair, Wenbo Guo, Justus Mattern, Rui Wang, James F. O'Brien, Louis Rosenberg, Dawn Song, "Unique Identification of 50,000+ Virtual Reality Users from Head & Hand Motion Data", USENIX Security 23, 2023

62. Vivek Nair, quoted in Louis Rosenberg, "New Research Suggests That Privacy in the Metaverse Might Be Impossible", *VentureBeat*, 20 Feb 2023, https://venturebeat.com/virtual/new-research-suggests-that-privacy-in-the-metaverse-might-be-impossible/

63. Rosenblat, 2023.

64. Brittan Heller, "Privacy and the Metaverse", 4 Jun 2022, Submission to OHCHR, https://www.ohchr.org/sites/default/files/documents/issues/digitalage/reportprivindigage2022/submissions/2022-09-06/CFI-RTP-Brittan-Heller.pdf

65. Melissa Heikkilä, "VR Headsets Can Be Hacked with an Inception-Style Attack", *MIT Technology Review*, 11 Mar 2024 https://www.technologyreview.com/2024/03/11/1089686/hack-vr-headsets-inception/

66. Rosenblat 2024, citing Peter Casey, Ibrahim Baggili, Ananya Yarramreddy, "Immersive Virtual Reality Attacks and the Human Joystick", *IEEE Transactions on Dependable and Secure Computing* 18:2, 2021

67. Christian Orth, "With Pokémon against Pegida", puls, 19 Jul 2016, Google Translate, 19 Sep 2023

68. Louis Rosenberg, "The Metaverse: from Marketing to Mind Control", Future of Marketing Institute, 30 Oct 2022, https://futureofmarketinginstitute.com/the-metaverse-from-marketing-to-mind-control/

69. Heller, 2022, p. 33.

70. Larissa Hjorth, Ingrid Richardson, "Pokémon GO: Mobile Media Play, Place-making, and the Digital Wayfarer", *Mobile Media & Communication* 5:1, 2017.

71. Cass Sunstein, *Republic.com* (Revised Edition), Princeton University Press, 2001.

72. Nicholas Negroponte, *Being Digital*, Hodder and Stoughton, 1996.

73. Nilay Patel, Hanke/Patel, 2021.

74. Alyssa Rosenberg, "I Understand the Temptation to Dismiss QAnon. Here's Why We Can't", *Washington Post*, 7 Aug 2019, https://www.washingtonpost.com/opinions/2019/08/07/qanon-isnt-just-conspiracy-theory-its-highly-effective-game/

75. Hanke/Patel, 2021.

76. Jay Springett, "Thoughts on the Apple Vision Pro", 6 Jun 2023 https://www.thejaymo.net/2023/06/06/thoughts-on-apple-vision-pro/

77. Janet Cardiff, "Pleasure Principals: The Art of Janet Cardiff and George Bures Miller", interview by Meeka Walsh, Robert Enright, *Border Crossings*, May 2001, https://bordercrossingsmag.com/article/pleasure-principals-the-art-of-janet-cardiff-and-george-bures-miller

78. Stephen Holt cited by Phil Patton, "Walkman", https://web.archive.org/web/20070814024224/http://www.philpatton.com/walkman.html

79. Shuhei Hosokawa,"The Walkman Effect", Popular Music 4, 1984, CUP, Cambridge, p. 176.

80. "Audient", Antenna Theater, https://www.antenna-theater.org/audient.html. The artist David Hockney created a similar synchronicity with his "Wagner drives", drives through the Santa Monica hills choreographed to Wagner's music. A "Wagner Drive" was a centrepiece of Hockney's 2023 immersive exhibition *Bigger & Closer (not smaller & further away)*.

81. Chris Hardman, "Walkmanology", *The Drama Review* 27:4, 1983, 45.

82. *Ibid.*, p. 43.

SECTION 1

Learning From VR

Learning From VR

1.0

Getting Started

This book is about storytelling for players who are looking at the physical world THROUGH augmented/spatial technology. Virtual Reality, by contrast, creates virtual worlds which players look AT within a headset. So what could augmented storytellers have to learn from VR? Though they're very different, these technologies share many storytelling qualities, and in my decade or so of creating VR narratives, I've learned a lot that's applicable to my augmented/spatial storytelling too.

In this section, we'll use VR to introduce many of the key concepts we'll use throughout the book. But this section doesn't provide a comprehensive study of VR narrative design: that's already been well covered by other authors. For more detail on VR storytelling, I recommend Melissa Bosworth and Lakshmi Sarah's *Crafting Stories for Virtual Reality* (2018) as a starting point.

This Section 1 establishes the three fundamental pillars of emotional immersion we'll use throughout the book: SEEING, BEING and BEING SEEN. We'll explore these pillars using examples and techniques from VR. Then later in Section 2: AUGMENTING PLAYERS and Section 3: AUGMENTING PLACES we'll build upon these pillars, and see how each of them change when digital narratives move out of VR headsets and into the augmented world (Figure 1.0).

The first pillar of emotional immersion we'll examine is SEEING. SEEING is such a fundamental part of VR technology that it's easy to mistake VR for a purely visual experience. But only when all three pillars – SEEING, BEING and BEING SEEN – are working together can you create an emotionally immersive simulation.

Virtual Reality aims to simulate our sensory and tactile experience of BEING in physical reality – generally called *embodiment* or *presence*. But good VR storytelling requires more than just BEING there: the player's understanding of WHO they're BEING in the simulation is also vital to emotional immersion. If a simulation asks the player to BE someone whom they don't understand, don't relate to, or just don't care about, it's as disruptive to immersion as any graphical glitch.

Worse, if the player gets the sense that their presence doesn't matter or has no meaningful impact on the story – if they aren't BEING SEEN – then that player will likely never even get immersed in the first place.

DOI: 10.1201/9781003379294-3

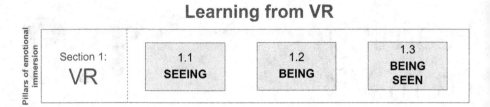

FIGURE 1.0   Pillars of emotional immersion in VR

SEEING in VR

1.1

How do we SEE in VR?

How does this affect VR storytelling?

How is this useful for AUGMENTING PLAYERS?

How is this useful for AUGMENTING PLACES?

SEEING ≠ BELIEVING

It's worth dispelling a common assumption about how audiences relate to what they SEE in VR. It's easy to think that VR is immersive because it is visually convincing, but the truth is that **"realistic" is not the same as "immersive"**. It's certainly not the same thing as *compelling*. Whether working in VR or augmented/spatial, our job as immersive storytellers isn't to create *convincing* situations; it's to create compelling situations in which players actively participate in the process of getting immersed.

As the engineer, interface researcher and storyteller Kevin Brooks said back in 2003,

> when sights and sounds in a VRE [Virtual Reality Environment] are particularly well designed and coordinated, the mind follows the senses. Belief, or at least the suspension of some disbelief, follows what is sensed… It is belief that puts the real into virtual reality.[1]

When the poet Coleridge coined the phrase *willing suspension of disbelief* in 1817, he was trying to explain why his poetry included unrealistic and even supernatural elements like fairies, ghosts and magic. These had fallen out of fashion during the Scientific Enlightenment, but Coleridge, like any good storyteller, knew that the vast majority of audiences wouldn't get any less immersed in a story just because it wasn't *realistic*. Coleridge knew his audience wouldn't object to these "shadows of imagination" as long as the situations he created were relatable and engaging: then the reader would supply "that willing suspension of disbelief for the moment, which constitutes poetic faith".[2]

And as Brooks says, "this is nothing new. Storytellers have been providing this sort of believable immersive experience with stories since the beginning of humanity. The human animal is a narrative animal".[3] Ghosts and goblins have always been part of how we humans talk about the world and relate our experiences to one another, since long before we learned to write (let alone put on a headset).

DOI: 10.1201/9781003379294-4

Remember, immersion isn't a trick: it's an agreement we make with the player. In VR the technology does not do the immersing for you, no matter how realistic it looks. For proof, we just have to look at popular VR experiences like *Beat Saber* (2018), *Gorilla Tag* (2021) or especially *VRChat* (2014); these experiences are fantastically non-naturalistic but still immerse millions of players. It's easier for players to suspend disbelief and get immersed if a simulation is visually consistent, and if the way the player SEES the simulation feels similar to their ordinary experience of SEEING the world. But it certainly doesn't have to be photorealistic.

As Crescent Jicol, lead researcher on a major study into VR immersion[4] said in 2023: "a lot of money goes into making VR headsets and screens better and rendering virtual worlds more realistically, but more effort needs to be centred on improving the user's emotional experience."[5] Jicol et al's study was the first to examine how technical factors (specifically, visual realism and field of view) interact with human factors to build immersion – and as Jicol says, "the main takeaway is that emotion and agency are crucial to inducing presence, but visual realism is not". As we'll see, the same is true of augmented/spatial realities.

SEEING WITH AGENCY

One key similarity between VR and augmented/spatial technology is that the storyteller can't control what the player SEES – nor should they try to. Traditional flatscreen media like cinema present a pre-meditated framing of the action, determined by the director and cinematographer. But in VR the "camera" is the player's gaze, and it's freely controlled by them the same way they're freely in control of SEEING the real world. As the VR filmmaker and theorist Jessica Brillhart puts it, "attempting to craft a pre-meditated frame is futile when VR involves worlds of potential frames".[6] In film terms, the player IS the director, free to frame their own perspective.

When I worked on the early prototypes of the PlayStationVR in 2014, it was challenging and counterintuitive to discover we could never take camera control away from the player. At the time, when videogames had a chunk of story to deliver, they'd typically switch into a cutscene or "cinematic" in which the player had no control. But in VR we quickly found that cutting away to an external camera felt weird and disorienting for the player, and seizing control of the player's camera-gaze and *making* them look at something caused a dissonance between what their body was feeling and what their eyes were SEEING. In testing, these conflicting signals caused instantaneous, sometimes catastrophic nausea. Today's VR hardware is much better at reducing motion sickness, but the basic principle remains the same: the player must control the "camera" the same way they control their own head and eyes. Trying to move the camera FOR them causes immersion-breaking dissonance. When you try to *make* the player SEE, you're telling them that they are a passenger in their own perspective, and their brain rebels.

I've worked with a lot of storytellers coming into VR from other media industries, especially film. Film and VR might seem superficially similar, but when I'm reading a spec VR script, one dead giveaway that the writer is still thinking in film terms is that sooner or later the direction tells us.

And then we see…

In VR there is no *we*. There is just the player, alone in the headset. More importantly, in VR the storyteller cannot define what the player SEES because the VR player has the agency to look in any direction.

DIEGETIC AND FOVEATED SEEING

But VR players aren't just SEEING. VR players are usually embodied as a virtual avatar, usually the story's protagonist. So while they have agency over where to look moment by moment, they're also BEING a character when they look. We'll examine BEING in more detail shortly, but VR storytellers need to remember that how a player SEES also says a lot about the character they're BEING. Choosing where to look defines the player's perspective on the action, but that choice also becomes part of the action – it is **diegetic**. What the player chooses to SEE is also a choice made by the story's protagonist. So choosing where to look is done in-character – and in turn it *characterises* what kind of protagonist they are.

And these choices matter. As Brillhart says, VR involves "worlds of potential frames". But we can't look everywhere at once. Choosing to look in one direction means we may miss other things happening behind us. But this is part of life: every choice *for* something involves choosing *against* unnumbered possible alternatives. Having the agency to frame our perspective on reality, and exclude everything outside that frame, feels authentic to everyday sensory experience.

Recent VR headsets greatly improved their simulation of ordinary SEEING with a technique called **foveated rendering**, which mimics how our gaze focuses on one small area and excludes everything else. When you focus your gaze on *these words*, the other words elsewhere on the page are out of focus. This is called foveal vision. Your vision is actually pretty blurry other than a small area at the centre of your gaze called the fovea. But in VR, until recently, everything was rendered fully in-focus.

Modern **foveated rendering** mimics our everyday experience of vision by dynamically lowering the resolution and de-focusing everything in the field of view, *except* what the player is directly gazing at. As Marques Brownlee describes, the headset is "only actually rendering in high resolution exactly what you're looking at when you're looking at it. The rest is soft and fuzzy. That works really well because that's exactly how our eyes work".[7] (Or, as VR YouTuber habie147 says, "everything in your peripheral vision looks like mashed potatoes. But since it's in your peripheral vision, you don't see it."[8]) This creates a better illusion of normal vision and avoids a dissonance between what we're SEEING and what our brain and body is *feeling*.

Foveated rendering simulates the naturally selective nature of our foveal vision. Having agency over what we include and exclude in our visual frame is part of our normal experience of SEEING – and that agency is crucial to VR SEEING too. Even if every single player of a VR experience moves through the same scenario, triggering the same events, each player's visual "edit" of the scenario will be unique based on where they chose to look. The VR creator might control the scene and the scenario, but not how the player's eye edits it, OR what their gaze-behaviour implies about the protagonist-character they're embodying. A big part of VR storytelling is learning to live with this loss of control over both camera and character. VR creators must surrender control over how the story is SEEN, and how the story's protagonist behaves.

Later, when we start augmenting players' realities, it will be vital to acknowledge the player's freedom to choose and **foveate** their own framing or "edit" of the story. And it'll also be vital to show players that those moment-to-moment choices are **diegetic** and are characterising their protagonist identity.

REBELLIOUS SEEING

Giving VR players the agency to frame and **foveate** their SEEING is fundamental to emotional immersion. But this represents a storytelling challenge: what if they miss a crucial detail? In fact, players often unconsciously rebel when a simulation seems to want them to look somewhere specific. But many VR experiences fail to acknowledge or reward this agency over SEEING. Brillhart gives an example:

> Next time you're in a virtual reality experience, I encourage you to try and identify where the creator may want you to look—and then I want you to turn and look in the opposite direction. What do you see when you do that? Chances are, probably not much.[9]

Many VR creators, especially those still thinking in film terms, want to direct the player's eye to where the story is happening. This might involve lighting, sound cues, set design – but often also means creating emptiness everywhere *else*. So the player has no need to **foveate** or risk missing out – there's only one place worth looking.

But this isn't what real SEEING feels like – there's rarely just one perspective on a situation or one interesting thing to look at. Worse, if the simulation is empty except where the storyteller wants the player to look, the player who makes a choice to look somewhere *else* will discover that their choice isn't meaningful. They should look where they're told. Remember, when the player is embodied in the scene, everything they do is **diegetic** – including their choice to "rebel". If the creator creates a mostly-empty world to try to control the player's eye, this shows the player their actions aren't **diegetic** unless they do what the storyteller wants. Their agency doesn't belong in the world of the story.

These "rebellious" players aren't necessarily trying to break the simulation, but they are subconsciously testing its limits. These are some of the most engaged players, because they are trying to treat the simulation the same way they'd treat the real world – acting as though there are multiple perspectives and things to look at. But if a VR creator creates a mostly-empty world to try to direct the player's eye, they miss an opportunity to create multiple different **vantage points** on the story, and reward players' agency over SEEING.

Rewarding players' agency over SEEING means creating story elements which some players might never see. VR players may miss a crucial element of the story if they're looking in the "wrong" place, but the solution to this is to construct stories which make sense when framed from multiple different perspectives – and potentially have different meanings and interpretations.

(There are actually plenty of examples of this working well in flatscreen videogames: the groundbreaking shooter *Half-Life* (1998) had no cinematics and never arrested camera control, so it was easy to simply miss whole chunks of the plot by looking elsewhere. As a kid I mainly consumed videogames by watching my older brother play, but *Half-Life* was the first game I still wanted to play for myself even after watching him finish it. Because *Half-Life* empowered players' agency over SEEING, I knew I'd experience a completely different version of the story to my brother.)

VR players are embodied in the narrative by default, so ignoring their agency leaves a huge hole at the heart of the story. Acknowledging small "rebellions" goes a long way. VR players who SEE in unexpected ways are usually doing so in order to subconsciously calibrate their experience of BEING in a virtual environment: how much agency do they have? How **diegetic** is their agency? How much does their presence matter?

One way to acknowledge and reward agency over SEEING is through what Brillhart calls "greeting the rebel". In her VR film *Resonance* (2015) the initial framing of the scenario focuses on a young woman practicing violin. If players choose to look elsewhere, they might see her parents watching from the doorway. This extra detail acknowledges the player's agency and provides insight which completely changes the context of the scene – and remember, ***context is everything***. Effectively the scene exists in different versions, where the player did and didn't turn and see the parents.[10] The player who "rebels" against the default framing of the scenario gains a new perspective – so their agency is shown to be empowered and meaningful.

It's worth stepping outside the VR headset for a moment and thinking about how these ideas could help build emotional immersion in augmented/spatial narratives.

CHALLENGE #2: EMPOWERED SEEING

Goal: Adapt the idea of "Greeting the Rebel" from VR storytelling to augmented/spatial narrative.

SUMMARY

Use the location-based narrative concept you developed in CHALLENGE #1, **"Shadow Place"**. You're now going to imagine ways to reward players who behave unexpectedly or who test the boundaries of the story in its opening moments.

In the **"Shadow Place"** CHALLENGE you **plotted** a **path** onto your chosen place. In theory, the story progresses as the player moves along the **path**. But you're not simply *telling* this story – the player is enacting it. So it's up to them whether they follow the **path**.

At the starting location, identify **three rebellions**: things the player could do at the beginning of the story OTHER than follow the **path**. For example: they could hold still without doing anything; they could start to exit the location; or they could examine a nearby object that isn't directly relevant to the story.

Assume you can reliably detect when a player performs a **rebellion** and then trigger a story element. For each of the **three rebellions**, **write** story elements in the form of narration or dialogue to **acknowledge** the player's choice. Players might discover a hidden detail which recontextualises the events they're seeing. Or a character might respond to the player's **rebellion** or make a judgement about them.

Finally, **record** your new dialogue as audio and **test** with friends by watching their actions and playing the appropriate audio. Do they perform the rebellions you expected? What other rebellions come to light?

TASK

- **Identify the starting location** and the **path**.
- List **three rebellions**.
- For each rebellion, write **dialogue** or **narration** to **greet the rebel**.
- **Test.**

NOTES

Remember a "**rebellion**" doesn't have to be deliberate: often they happen because the player is confused by navigation or their attention wanders.

From SEEING in VR to IMAGINING and STAGING in Augmented/Spatial

As augmented/spatial storytellers we can place magical and exciting graphics into the player's visual field, and even recontextualise their relationship to the things around them. But augmented players' agency is even more manifest than in VR, because they're out in the real world. We must surrender even more control to players, collaborating with their imagination as a "co-director". The player is also "co-editor", so some of our story might be left unseen on the cutting-room floor.

On the other hand, in VR everything the player SEES is a virtual object which needs to be made by someone. VR players never run out of the ability to look, but creators might eventually run out of virtual objects for them to *look at* (at least, without the help of AI). In this sense, augmented/spatial storytelling has a big advantage: reality itself seamlessly surrounds the player with visuals at all times without any inherent cost to creators. How much you can graphically "reskin" reality, versus simply recontextualising it using narrative, is determined by your technology platform and budget. But fundamentally, reality is cheap and plentiful. In videogame terms, reality has excellent graphics, and rarely glitches out (though it also has notorious balance issues and uneven difficulty, which affects some people more than others – more on this in Appendix A).

But just like a VR player, an augmented player can't choose to SEE everything, and they can't BE in two places at once. AR/spatial narratives, like all narratives, are inherently selective. Even moreso because of the player's agency. By framing and **foveating** reality the player will determine their "edit" of the story. But as we'll see, just like in everyday un-augmented experience, the player's imagination plays a crucial role in filling in the gaps between what they SEE and don't SEE.

So in Section 2: AUGMENTING PLAYERS, the pillar SEEING will evolve into IMAGINING. The player can't SEE everything, but if an augmented story creates space for their agency in SEEING, their IMAGINATION will come flooding in fill in any gaps. Creating areas of ambiguity leaves space for the player's IMAGINATION to anchor the digital and real worlds together. This allows augmented narratives to be more than the sum of their parts: to feel wider, richer and more coherent.

Like VR storytellers, augmented/spatial storytellers can't control where the protagonist looks. But we also don't have much control over an augmented story's setting, because it's a version of the physical world, with all its distractions and unpredictability. As the XR researcher Timoni West puts it,

> Storytelling folks who are annoyed by VR because they 'can't control the camera' are in for a wild ride when they move to AR and realise they can't control the set either.[11]

So when we come to Section 3: AUGMENTING PLACES, the pillar SEEING will evolve into STAGING, because players will need to not just SEE the world in a new way, but imaginatively STAGE digital events in their unpredictable local reality.

SEEING IN VR: SUMMARY

HOW DO WE SEE IN VR?

- *Ideally, as much a possible like we SEE in reality. This means respecting the player's agency to frame their gaze.*
- *The player is embodied in a virtual avatar, so everything the player does through that avatar, including where they look, is **diegetic** and characterises them.*
- *VR uses effects like **foveated rendering** to simulate our visual senses. Our eyes don't try to focus on everything at once; we're highly selective in SEEING.*

HOW DOES THIS AFFECT VR STORYTELLING?

- *Never take camera control from the player.*
- *Allow players to **foveate** like they do in real life: construct scenes and stories robust enough that players can look where they choose.*
- *As far as possible, treat their choice of where to look as **diegetic** and characterising their in-story identity.*
- *Show them their agency is meaningful when they are first calibrating to a VR experience: try Greeting the Rebel.*

HOW IS THIS USEFUL FOR AUGMENTING PLAYERS?

- *When AUGMENTING PLAYERS, we have even less control over SEEING.*
- *Yet the player's agency over SEEING must be incorporated as **diegetic** to their player-character.*

HOW IS THIS USEFUL FOR AUGMENTING PLACES?

- *When AUGMENTING PLACES, imagination and subjectivity will be key in stimulating players to help STAGE augmented events in unpredictable reality.*

NOTES

1. Kevin Brooks, "There Is Nothing Virtual about Immersion: Narrative Immersion for VR and Other Interfaces", Motorola Labs/Human Interface Labs, 2003, p. 3.
2. Samuel Taylor Coleridge, *Biographia Literaria*, 1817, Edinburgh University Press, 2014, Ch. XIV.
3. Brooks 2003, p. 3.
4. Crescent Jicol, Christopher Clarke, Emilia Tor, Rebecca M Dakin, Tom Charlie Lancaster, Sze Tung Chang, Karin Petrini, Eamonn O'Neill, Michael J Proulx, Christof Lutteroth, 'Realism and Field of View Affect Presence in VR but Not the Way You Think', *CHI Conference on Human Factors in Computing Systems,* 2023.
5. Crescent Jicol, "VR Users Need an Emotional Connection to Virtual Worlds, Not Better Graphics", Bath University, 11 Dec 2023: https://www.bath.ac.uk/announcements/vr-users-need-an-emotional-connection-to-virtual-worlds-not-better-graphics-study-finds/.
6. Jessica Brillhart, *In the Blink of a Mind – Engagement*, Jul 6 2016: https://medium.com/the-language-of-vr/in-the-blink-of-a-mind-engagement-part-1-eda16ee3c0d8.
7. Marques Brownlee, "Apple Vision Pro Review", 4 Feb 2024: https://youtu.be/86Gy035z_KA?si=AiNgtxxP6jXtamcC 4:05.
8. "No Man's Sky in VR 7 Years Later", habie147, 16 Sept 2023, 6:01: https://youtu.be/5A8eFXe9_D0?si=7hqYillivGFNXr4h.
9. Jessica Brillhart, *How to Greet a Rebel: Unlocking the Storyteller in VR,* Dec 7 2015: https://medium.com/the-language-of-vr/how-to-greet-a-rebel-unlocking-the-storyteller-in-vr-d40b2cc05f55.
10. Brillhart 2015.
11. Timoni West, Twitter post 7:57 pm, 28 Apr 2018: https://twitter.com/timoni/status/990304008853110785 retrieved 17 Sept 2023.

BEING in VR

1.2

How does VR create a sense of BEING in a story?

How does VR storytelling convey to a player WHO they are BEING?

How is this useful for AUGMENTING PLAYERS?

How is this useful for AUGMENTING PLACES?

OUT-OF-BODY EXPERIENCE

A key aspiration of VR technology is to mimic the sensory experience of BEING in a physical place by simulating sensations of presence. So most VR narratives embody the player as a virtual avatar – and this body is usually also a character whom they're playing or BEING in the story.

Early in my career I was lucky enough to sit in a lot of user tests watching first-time users of VR headsets. One of the things first-time players consistently did when entering a VR sim was look *down*, and move their limbs to discover what kind of virtual body they were embodied in. Whether or not the player was doing it consciously, they started calibrating how their virtual body would spatially relate to the virtual world. And they also started to gather clues about their in-sim identity, so they could understand how to emotionally relate to the simulated scenario.

In augmented/spatial storytelling, the player can sense physical reality all around them, so their sensations of presence are authentic. But *who* they're BEING in the narrative is still a crucial question.

So it's useful to first understand how VR storytellers make players feel a sense of BEING inside a simulation, and how they make players feel like they're BEING *someone* – sometimes themselves, sometimes someone else altogether.

VISUOTACTILE CONGRUENCE

If a VR player is embodied as a VR avatar, their bodily agency is always manifest because their virtual body is animated by their actual movements.

Achieving a sense of authentic BEING in VR requires **visuotactile congruence –** what the player's SEEING has to match or be *congruent* with what they're feeling. Even if we can't SEE what our body is doing (for example, if we're

DOI: 10.1201/9781003379294-5

wearing a headset) we can still feel it – this is called *proprioception*. So the movements of a VR avatar must be *congruent* with the player's actual body motions to achieve full embodiment.

Research shows that when VR players are placed into a virtual version of their real environment, but embodied in a virtual body which appears larger than their own, the player will subconsciously begin moving as if they inhabit a larger physical body – provided that **visuotactile congruence** is maintained.[1] This shows that players can BE many different people in VR, provided that the body they're BEING reflects their bodily[2] agency.[3]

So virtual motion must match the player's physical motion. But virtual identities don't have to match real identities. Some VR experiences, like the story-driven *Assassin's Creed: Nexus* (2023) impose fully-formed protagonist identities onto the player. This can establish emotive relationships with people and places for the player to **roleplay**. But other experiences like the arcade game *Beat Saber* treat the player more as-themselves, keeping the player's own identity close to the action. We can call these **protagonist-agnostic** experiences, since the protagonist could be anyone.

PROTAGONIST-AGNOSTIC VR IDENTITIES

Even story-driven VR games often impose relatively little characterisation on the player. Back in 2014, I wrote the earliest playable narrative demo for the PlaystationVR. The player-character, an unnamed scuba diver, was trapped inside a malfunctioning underwater cage and attacked by a shark. The player-character never spoke, so the only dialogue came from the operator of the cage winch speaking via radio. In early versions, this operator character responded to the shark attack, their voice becoming frightened and urgent as the shark bashed and bent the cage bars. I assumed that because the player was in a proxy body and couldn't speak, that another character's voice was needed to express the emotions of fear and urgency. But user testing showed that this experience was unsatisfying. I had assumed that I needed to characterise and vocalise the player-character's reaction for them. Instead, I started cutting dialogue. In the final demo, the operator character was completely unaware the player was in danger. This was more realistic, but also made the experience much more emotive. Via radio, the operator would be blithely asking you to sit tight as the shark gnashed away inches from your face.

A golden rule of screenwriting is "show, don't tell". The shark cage taught me that in immersive media you need to not just *tell*, not just *show*, but to let the player *BE* in the story. In the shark cage demo, there was no need to narrate or ventriloquise the anonymous diver's emotions to the player. In the absence of a strong player-character identity, the player's own emotions became paramount. And this was easier if you left the player alone to be themselves!

Because the diver wasn't characterised and had no voice, the action could have been happening to anyone. It was protagonist-agnostic, in the sense that the protagonist could have been anyone. So the action felt like it was happening TO the player.

The operator's cheery dialogue was in stark contrast to the terror of the situation, which invoked isolation and fear: the player-character was alone with the shark, and the only person who could help had no idea they were in danger. There was no character between the player and the threat. In the absence of characterisation the emotions of the player and player-character were free to merge.

CHARACTERISED VR IDENTITIES

The anonymous, voiceless scuba diver was appropriate in a short horror demo with a disempowerment plot. But not every story can have a silent protagonist, and even horror stories are generally more satisfying with emotionally contextualised heroes. So VR storytellers often ask players to **role-play** a character who already has some characterisation within the story.

In the early VR adventure *The Assembly* (2016) we experimented with different ways to characterise the game's two protagonists. The player played two named, characterised player-characters in alternating chapters, one male and one female, and initially the two protagonists had different heights and gaits, affecting the camera's movement and position as they walked. Early user tests showed that players found these transitions disorienting and disruptive to immersion. Players stumbled when they suddenly switched into a differently-proportioned virtual body. Eventually all physical differences between the two virtual bodies were removed – only their footsteps sounded different. User testing showed that this alone was enough for players to noticeably change their body language while embodying the different characters.

It wasn't the shift of identities which disrupted immersion – this is an imaginative leap which our minds seem to be able to make quite easily. In fact some studies have shown that players tend to act more outgoing or confident when embodying a virtual avatar which they perceive as more attractive.[4] But in *The Assembly* the shift of embodiment was much more disruptive because players had begun identifying with one way of physically relating to the world, and then suddenly woke up in a different body with different arms and legs. This shows that VR creators can ask players to **role-play** a surprising amount, provided we maintain **visuotactile congruence**.

What about representing the player's own body in VR? Some studies have suggested VR avatars which closely resemble the player can increase **visuotactile congruence** and presence.[5] This is relevant since in augmented/spatial narratives the player is often simply embodied as themselves. But creating a compelling sense of BEING doesn't have to mean realistically BEING-in your physical body, or even a realistic human body – identifying with an identity is more important.

Meta's *Horizon Worlds* (2019) focuses on abstract but representational human avatars, whereas the indie social platform *VRChat* (2014) allows players to visualise themselves however they choose. The visual effect of *VRChat* is eclectic at best, chaotic at worst, but it has consistently attracted higher engagement than the multi-billion-dollar Meta platform. Many *VRChat* players seem to find the ability to manifest themselves in alternative physical identities allows for greater emotional identification with themselves and others; some players have used *VRChat* to explore body dysmorphia and experiment with different identity-presentations.[6]

IDENTITY-DISCOVERY

So physical embodiment, and even **visuotactile congruency,** is only part of the story when building emotional immersion in VR. Identity is also crucial. In those early user tests, when I saw those first-time VR users look down at their bodies, they were trying to identify and calibrate not just what body they were in but WHO they were BEING.

The moment where a player discovers their in-sim identity is key to building emotional immersion – it's the equivalent of the establishing moment when we first meet a character in fiction. But in VR this is a complex moment, since the player is discovering the body and identity that they're *already* embodying.

In early flatscreen first-person shooters like *Wolfenstein 3D* (1992) and *Doom* (1993), the protagonist's face was always visible as part of the game's UI (User Interface)– you couldn't miss the fact that you were playing a hefty white guy. Whereas in the revolutionary first-person puzzler *Portal* (2007) the main character Chell was not in the UI or on the box; it was only possible to see your avatar by arranging the game's iconic portals in a particular configuration. This gave the moment of discovering your in-game identity the satisfaction of solving a puzzle. Some players might have been surprised to discover they were playing a mixed-race woman, but the game only made it possible to "see yourself" after a few levels, once the narrative had created solid, emotive reasons for the player to care about Chell's predicament.

In the first-person RPG *Deus Ex: Human Revolution* (2011), otherwise-fairly-standard protagonist Adam Jensen undergoes a Frankensteinian transformation with cybernetics replacing much of his body. This body-transformation was heavily depicted in promo art, but the impact on Jensen's psyche is more ambiguous. There's a mirror in Jensen's apartment – but it's shattered. Nearby there's a note reminding Jensen to contact his concierge about getting ANOTHER new mirror. On Jensen's laptop an email from the concierge tells us that the new mirror hasn't arrived yet. But, if you choose to break into the concierge's office, you discover the mirror HAS arrived, but they're holding it because they're so annoyed at Jensen for constantly breaking his mirror. We discover Jensen's disgust at his physical appearance – a core but unspoken aspect of the identity we're playing – and we discover it indirectly, via exploration and implication.[7]

In VR, moments of identity-discovery like this can be used to create powerful and surprising moments. In the Emmy-nominated VR documentary film *Travelling While Black* (2019) the player's 360° perspective is positioned in a diner booth for much of the film, a witness to first-hand interviews about Black people's experiences of racism. The wall next to the booth is mirrored, but for most of the experience the player's reflection – or where it would be – is obscured by a diner sign. This was probably done to hide the 360° camera's physical presence in the scene, but it also anonymises the player and focuses our attention on the interviewees.

Until one speaker, activist Courtland Cox narrates a bus journey to Mississippi during the Jim Crow era. As Cox describes his fear of racist violence, the mirrored diner wall next to the player transitions to the window of a bus, travelling past rolling fields, with the reflection of a young Black man in Jim Crow-era costume staring out[8] as though he is the player's own reflection. Suddenly the player goes from anonymous or identity-agnostic to being embodied in a Black identity. Director Roger Ross Williams notes: "in VR… you are forced to a place of deep empathy, or you are forced to confront the pain of what you have been living. There's something about not being able to escape it …".[9] Depending on the player's real identity this "mirror moment" might be an empathy-building experience of being embodied as a Black person, or might express the player's own experience of Black identity. Either way the mirror moment conveys the inescapable influence of racist violence on Black lives and identities, not just through *showing* or *telling*, but BEING.

In VR, these moments of identity-discovery allow the player's own authentic emotions to be part of their embodiment and characterisation of the player-character. Depending on the story you're telling, the player's moment of self-identification could have the satisfaction of solving a puzzle like in *Portal*, or convey a horrible, creeping realisation about yourself like in *Deus Ex*, or the sudden empathic experience of BEING in a body that's the focus of prejudice and violence as in *Travelling While Black*. This blend of the player's real, grounded emotions with the protagonist's identity and predicament gives immersive narratives enormous emotive power. It's not just what you're SEEING, but who you're BEING, that counts.

When we look at AUGMENTING PLAYERS in Section 2, we'll take these "self discovery" ideas further to develop techniques for moments of "augmented *mise-en-self*".

For now let's try adapting this type of moment of IDENTITY-discovery to your own augmented/spatial storytelling:

CHALLENGE #3: SELF-DISCOVERY

Goal: Explore ways of introducing an augmented player to the in-fiction IDENTITY they embody.

SUMMARY

You're going to further develop the narrative concept you created in CHALLENGE #1, "Shadow Place".

If you haven't already, **assign the player a role or identity** to embody. Remember that the player experiences the story by moving through the **place**, so a motivation to follow the **path** should be part of their character. If your "Shadow Place" involved hidden ghosts, they could be a ghost investigator; if it's a magical flower garden, they could be the gardener.

Outline the first moment that the player realises/discovers something about their identity. Don't *tell* or *show* the player who they are; construct a moment of discovery which involves them BEING or expressing their character. If the player-identity is a spy or has a secret, make them feel that other characters are suspicious of them; if they are a "second-class citizen" in your fiction, make clear that they are unwelcome in certain areas.

Finally, **write** a new opening to the narrative which incorporates the self-discovery moment.

TASKS

- **Adapt** your "Shadow Place" narrative (or **identify** a new **place** and conceptualise a new narrative)
- **Assign** the player's in-story IDENTITY
- In three bullet points, **outline** the self-discovery moment.
- **Write** a new opening to your narrative incorporating self-discovery.

From BEING in VR to IDENTITY-BUILDING and BEING-THERE in Augmented/Spatial

As we've seen, VR players are more than capable of **roleplaying** someone un-like themselves, both in terms of physicality and identity. But creating a sense of BEING in VR always means leaving some space for the player's self. All **role-playing** requires the player to create a composite of their real self and the in-fiction character. This is even more true in augmented/spatial narrative.

In Section 2: AUGMENTING PLAYERS, the pillar BEING will evolve into IDENTITY-BUILDING. Augmented players are always already BEING somewhere, present in the real world, and they start off BEING themselves. We need to help them to build an augmented IDENTITY which belongs in the world of the story too. Section 2 will also distinguish augmented/spatial experiences which ask players to **roleplay** a character, and experiences which are **protagonist-agnostic**, i.e. in which the player "plays themselves". We'll explore the different ways that these approaches, and the spectrum in-between, create different emotive effects on augmented players.

Then, in Section 3: AUGMENTING PLACES, BEING will evolve into BEING THERE. Unlike VR, augmented/spatial creators can't confine players to a virtual environment. Augmented players don't only have agency over SEEING; BEING in the physical world means they have full **spatial agency** over where they go. We'll explore ways to build players' sense of presence in augmented places, by designing moments for players to express **spatial agency** within the story.

But first, there's one more pillar we'll need. What players SEE in VR, especially about themselves, feeds directly into their sense of who they're BEING. But, just like in real life, VR players may not feel that how they're SEEING and BEING has a meaningful impact – until they feel that they're BEING SEEN.

BEING IN VR: SUMMARY

HOW DOES VR CREATE A SENSE OF *BEING* IN A STORY?

- *Building and maintaining **visuotactile congruence** is key to embodiment.*
- *But a virtual avatar body doesn't need to correspond to the player's body for embodiment to take place. Players can adopt the physicality of the virtual body fairly readily, and this can have emotional effects in turn.*
- *Identifying with in-story IDENTITIES is as important as **visuotactile congruence**; players can **roleplay**, or embody versions of themselves, or somewhere in between.*

HOW DOES VR STORYTELLING CONVEY TO A PLAYER WHO THEY ARE *BEING*?

- *Player-character identities can be anonymous or **protagonist-agnostic** in order to allow the player's own identity to feel close to visceral VR action.*
- *Narrative-driven experiences often require characterised protagonists. Even when **roleplaying** characterised protagonists, players bring in their own emotions.*
- *Moments of identity-discovery or "**mise-en-self**" can be compelling: the player discovers their identity through BEING.*

HOW IS THIS USEFUL FOR AUGMENTING PLAYERS?

- *2.2: IDENTITY-BUILDING will show how to design "**mise-en-self**" moments to help players BE someone in a hybrid digital-physical narrative.*
- *We'll examine the differences between **protagonist-agnostic** IDENTITIES (player "plays themselves") and **roleplay** IDENTITIES.*

HOW IS THIS USEFUL FOR AUGMENTING PLACES?

- *In AUGMENTED PLACES, players are really BEING THERE in physical space. **Visuotactile congruence** is crucial to build presence in hybrid digital-physical places.*
- *Players have **spatial agency** in the real world; 3.2 will examine how to design for **spatial agency** to diegeticize it into the story.*

NOTES

1. Marius Rubo, Matthias Gamer, "Visuo-Tactile Congruency Influences the Body Schema During Full Body Ownership Illusion", *Consciousness and Cognition* 73, 2019.
2. Mel Slater, Bernhard Spanlang, Maria V. Sanchez-Vives, Olaf Blanke, "First Person Experience of Body Transfer in Virtual Reality", *PLoS ONE* 5(5), 2010.
3. Konstantina Kilteni, Jean-Marie Normand, Maria V. Sanchez-Vives, Mel Slater, "Extending Body Space in Immersive Virtual Reality: A Very Long Arm Illusion", *PLoS ONE* 7(7), 2012.
4. Nick Yee, Jeremy Bailenson, "The Proteus Effect: The Effect of Transformed Self-Representation on Behavior", *Human Communication Research* 33(3), 2007.
5. Thomas Waltemate, Dominik Gall, Daniel Roth, Mario Botsch, Marc Erich Latoschik, "The Impact of Avatar Personalization and Immersion on Virtual Body Ownership, Presence, and Emotional Response", *IEEE Transactions on Visualization and Computer Graphics*, 2018.
6. "Making Sense of VRChat, the 'Metaverse' People Actually Like": People Make Games, May 2022. https://www.youtube.com/watch?v=4PHT-zBxKQQ&t=963s&pp=ygUKdnJja GF0IHBtZw%3D%3D.
7. Years ago a senior artist who'd worked on *DE:HR* confided to me that the mirror was broken because rendering a real reflective mirror was too processor-heavy. As so often in game writing, the writers retroactively justified a technical limitation.
8. *Travelling While Black*, 2019, Dir. Roger Ross Williams, https://youtu.be/7UUFn7iyymo?si= ckG_WtW6L8urWY3e 7:30.
9. Roger Ross Williams, "Oculus VR for Good: Travelling While Black", 12 Dec 2019. https://www.youtube.com/watch?v=aOBwXOgIIb8&ab_channel=MetaQuest.

BEING SEEN in VR

1.3

Why is BEING SEEN important in VR?

How can VR narratives make players feel SEEN?

How is this useful for AUGMENTING PLAYERS?

How is this useful for AUGMENTING PLACES?

FEELING SEEN

In VR, as in life, just BEING there isn't quite enough. If a VR player detects that there's no physical consequences to their actions, the virtual world feels rubbery, unresponsive and boring. Even more so if the player realises that they can do whatever they want without any *social* consequences. Emotion and agency are essential for VR presence. But for the player-character's presence to matter within a story, and for players to feel authentic emotions that are **diegetic** in the story, they have to BE SEEN.

VR creators have to ask themselves the *It's A Wonderful Life* question: how would things unfold differently, and how would the NPCs (non-player characters) in the scenario feel and act, if the player didn't exist? If everything would be the same, it's a dead giveaway that the creator hasn't left room in the story for the player-character's agency. The player might BE there as an invisible spectator, but if this has no impact on the scenario then they quite literally have no skin in the game.

Since the earliest days of VR, creators have recognised that BEING SEEN gives virtual reality a special power to empathetically place players into *social* realities. In 1999 Kevin Brooks (who we've already met), Carol Strohecker and Larry Friedlander helped build *Tired of Giving In*, a virtual depiction of the 1955 arrest of Rosa Parks and events leading to the Montgomery Bus Boycott during the American Civil Rights era.[1] *Tired of Giving In* was only ever implemented on flatscreens, but set out the team's ambitions for the early virtual environments they were building at Mitsubishi Electric Research Laboratories. As Brooks said,

> If an adolescent of today had a way of experiencing a reality where a choice that they would normally take for granted was death defying... like the decision to walk down a certain sidewalk or talk to a particular person in Montgomery of 1955, then they would

DOI: 10.1201/9781003379294-6

have a better understanding of that time and place. An implemented TOGI [Tired of Giving In] virtual environment would allow a participant to experience first hand that the skin that immersed them also defined them, and much of their experience.[2]

Earlier in *Travelling While Black* we saw a moment of identity-discovery as a Black identity, but this was a moment of SEEING yourself in VR. For Brooks, the capacity of VR to impose onto players the experience of BEING SEEN with hostility, because of their virtual identity, would "communicate culture by communicating firsthand experience. This is a noble role for VEs [Virtual Environments] to play in the future".

But even today, effective BEING SEEN in VR is difficult to achieve. During the first Covid-19 lockdown, the Wired journalist Tristan Cross tried to recreate his local pub Skehan's in VR. Cross succeeded in recreating the pub's architecture and fixtures from off-the-shelf virtual assets. But people are much harder than objects. Cross wrote,

"I did it, I made Skehan's!", I keep thinking to myself... But something doesn't feel right... I've made an empty room that looks like Skehan's. It's not the same.[3]

Pubs are extremely social environments. In the isolation of the lockdown, Cross wasn't missing the pub building: he was missing its social environment. Cross introduced NPCs to the virtual Skehan's, but they didn't react to the player's presence. He interviewed me for the article and talked about his eerie, antisocial virtual pub full of unresponsive NPCs:

"I've seen this happen in a lot of user tests," says Morgan. [That's me.] "The first thing first-time users do in VR is go right up to an NPC and get right up in their grill. They violate social norms in order to quickly calibrate the level of social realism in their environment. If your NPC doesn't react, like "woah, back off", the NPC is immediately revealed to be fake.

Users don't do this because they're hell-bent on spotting the strings or ruining the trick, but because they want to know whether they are in an environment of social consequence. Is there a real person watching me? Is there the potential to be embarrassed? These questions are absolutely crucial to how we subliminally approach situations, and how seriously we take situations".[4]

This idea of "getting up in an NPC's grill" might seem like a joke, but it reflects players' desire to calibrate to the emotional dynamics of whatever immersive scene they find themselves in. If a VR simulation is a free-form sandbox designed for players to indulge mischievous instincts, then having no social consequence, no sense of BEING SEEN, can be good. Without social consequence, the player relaxes – but they also relax out of emotionally engaging with any characters present in the simulation. A virtual person who has no social needs of their own, no personal space, no ability to say *woah, back off,* is safe to treat as a true "NPC", a non-person. More narrative-driven VR requires socially realistic characters, whom the player feels SEEN by.

Luckily, a little BEING SEEN goes a long way. It's not possible to produce enough dialogue and animation for virtual characters to specifically react to everything the player could possibly do. But if an NPC gives generic-but-appropriate reactions to common, general social violations, e.g. backing away when a player gets up in their grill, then players will tend to assume they're in a consequential environment and behave accordingly. It's like the principle of **panopticon**: if you give the player the sense that at any time they *could* be BEING SEEN, they will internalise this sense of consequence and treat the simulation as consequential going forward. Finding resource-efficient ways to induce this type of BEING SEEN is the stuff of good VR storytelling.

THE SWAYZE EFFECT

Without social consequence the player is just a ghost: as Cross said,

> I'm there, in Skehan's with my nearest and dearest, but they can't see or hear me. It's like I've died and been sent to haunt them on a night out. The simulation is nearly there. It has the pub and the people, but you, the player, are absent.[5]

In VR design this phenomenon is named after a famous ghost (or rather, an actor who played one): the **Swayze Effect**. The term was coined by environment artist and immersive storyteller Matt Burdette when he worked at the Oculus Story Studio. In 2015 Burdette described working on the early Oculus demos "Lost" and "Henry": in "Lost", "the more [the team] added to enrich the feeling of presence, the more the narrative felt disconnected", until the team introduced a moment where main NPC character Hand "directly acknowledge[d] the viewer... Suddenly, [the team] noticed viewers seemed more connected with the character... Many even leaned forward as though they were looking at another person".[6] Even though the character in this case was a gigantic robotic hand which behaved more like a dog than a person, the key thing was that the player's presence had been acknowledged.

Without this BEING SEEN, the player got "the sensation of having no tangible relationship with [their] surroundings despite feeling present in the world... the feeling of yelling "I'm here! I'm here!" when no one or nothing else around seems to acknowledge it". Burdette named this effect after Patrick Swayze, whose character Sam in the 1990 movie *Ghost* is invisible and experiences exactly this *I'm here! Why can't you SEE ME!?* sensation.

Burdette describes a variation of the **Swayze Effect** in another early Oculus demo, "Henry", a Pixar-style short about a lonely hedgehog celebrating his birthday by himself. The player had no role in the scenario, nor any particular identity: they were just an invisible, flying camera. As Burdette says "lots of people [were] just happy to be there". A relatively new feature, "look at" behaviour, allowed Henry's eyes to snap to the player-camera, so Henry would periodically make eye contact with the player, implicitly acknowledging their presence. This countered the uncomfortable invisibility of the **Swayze Effect**, but it contradicted the narrative scenario in which Henry was alone. This created "a dissonance between presence and story: why is Henry so lonely if I'm sitting right here with him?"[7]

The fact that Henry SAW the player implicated the player in the scene. But because it didn't change the narrative, it actually made the player feel *complicit* in Henry's loneliness. BEING SEEN made the player feel they were BEING there, but the story told them they weren't *there for* Henry on his birthday.

BEING (UN)SEEN

BEING SEEN can be a disempowering experience – after all, we can't control how we are seen by others. But nonetheless it lends crucial emotional authenticity to VR and gives storytellers new tools to stimulate empathy. BEING (UN)SEEN can also create powerful effects. The weird, voyeuristic **Swayze Effect** of "Henry" would hit very differently if the player was supposed to be, say, *spying* on Henry's birthday. Or, like in the Shark Cage demo, it can be powerful to make players feel UN-SEEN while also making them *want* to BE SEEN because they're in danger.

The VR pioneer Nonny de la Peña's *Use of Force* (2013) is an early VR experience which hinges on dynamics of BEING (UN)SEEN. *Use of Force* dramatises citizen journalist footage of the 2010 killing of Anastasio Hernandez Rojas by US border patrol agents.[8] Rojas was caught crossing the US-Mexico border trying to return to family in the US; he was detained by border patrol agents who beat and tasered him while restrained. The incident, which was ruled a homicide, was captured on cameraphone by multiple witnesses.[9]

De la Peña built on work by Mel Slater and Maria Vives Sanchez to develop "immersive journalism" for VR: she said "I never want my viewers to be sitting passively in some chairs out in the audience again".[10] But active participation doesn't mean players can change the outcome in *Use of Force*. Players use a handheld peripheral to control a cameraphone inside the simulation, but their only means of interaction is to film. Embodied as one of several witness to the beating of Rojas, the player is physically separated from the incident and unable to intervene. The player SEES but is not SEEN in any way which changes the outcome. Yet BEING (UN)SEEN places the player in the role of witness/citizen journalist, which charges the scenario with an emotive sense of complicity and disempowerment in the face of institutional violence.

The question for us as storytellers is: how can we achieve similar impactful, empathy-building narrative effects using augmented/spatial reality technologies? Most importantly, how do we responsibly use these technologies to, as Brooks puts it, "communicate culture by communicating first hand experience"? Let's try implementing BEING SEEN in an augmented narrative:

CHALLENGE #4: CREATIVELY BEING SEEN

Goal: Explore ways of making augmented players feel SEEN.

SUMMARY

Continue developing the concept from **CHALLENGE #1: Shadow Place**.

Your narrative should already contain an **identity** for the player, and a **motivation** for them to move through the location.

Introduce (or adapt) two **characters**. An ASSISTANT character should share the player's **motivation** and want them to fulfil it. An OPPOSING character should oppose the **motivation** and try to hinder or stop them fulfilling it.

Remember that these characters can't physically make the player do anything; they exist only in the audio layer. So in this story, they're going to ASSIST/ OPPOSE purely through making the player feel SEEN (or NOT SEEN). **Outline** how they will do so.

The ASSISTING character could tell the player that they look like the sort of hero the story needs; the OPPOSING character might whisper that people nearby are watching and laughing. The ASSISTANT might tell the player that invisible ghosts everywhere will recognise them for their good deeds; the OPPONENT might tell them their kind isn't welcome here. The voices might speak to the player in one key moment, or whisper throughout the story.

Write dialogue/narration introducing these two characters and showing how they use BEING SEEN.

Record audio for these characters and **test** it. What effects do moments of BEING SEEN have on your test players?

TASKS

- **Develop** two new characters; an ASSISTING character and an OPPOSING character.
- For each character, **outline** in bullet points how they will ASSIST/ OPPOSE by exploiting the player's sense of BEING SEEN.
- **Write** new dialogue/narration adding these moments to the story.
- **Record** audio.
- **Test.**

From BEING SEEN in VR to BEING SELF-CONSCIOUS and OCCUPYING SPACE in Augmented/Spatial

The techniques that VR storytellers have developed to achieve a sense of BEING SEEN will be very helpful to us in understanding augmented/spatial storytelling, where the player is out in the real world and might even be surrounded by real people. An augmented player might be SEEING the world through augmented layers, which might alter their behaviour in front of others. Players might also be aware that others around them may not be SEEING things the same way.

Even more significantly, as the technology to augment reality proliferates, we might start to lose control over how we're SEEN by others via their AR glasses or reality-browsers. We've already seen how AI-driven "nudify" apps can extrapolate a pornographic image from an ordinary image of a person. Stable diffusion-driven technology can already detect and re-texture human bodies in realtime. Combine these technologies together, and it's now easy to imagine a future where our own bodies might be BEING SEEN and being re-skinned, in ways we can't control or even perceive, by people simply passing us on the street.

This is why it's vital that we develop techniques to augment the world with narrative which builds empathy, instead of empowering users to isolate themselves in bespoke **customised realities**. VR shows us the empathic value of BEING SEEN. Now we need to figure out how to begin creating these kinds of effects in augmented/spatial realities.

In Section 2: AUGMENTING PLAYERS the VR pillar BEING SEEN will evolve into BEING SELF-CONSCIOUS. Augmented players are **diegetically** present in the story, more or less as a version of themselves; as a result, we'll develop techniques to acknowledge and incorporate their sense of how they SEE themselves. This means changing how we think about the player's SELF-CONSCIOUSNESS: it's not inherently disruptive to immersion, and it can be a **diegetic** emotion that's part of their player-character's experience.

Then in Section 3: AUGMENTING PLACES, BEING SEEN will evolve into OCCUPYING SPACE. This is because "OCCUPYING' space means more than simply BEING there; it means that your presence is **zero-sum**, and therefore has an impact on the place and on other people co-present there with you. This will manifest in techniques to design for **spatial subjectivity**, showing players that their choice of **vantage point** is **zero-sum** and can influence their perspective. We'll also look at ways to turn players into performers for other players and passers-by. Finally, we'll briefly examine the importance of allowing players to leave a mark on space.

BEING SEEN IN VR: SUMMARY

WHY IS BEING SEEN IMPORTANT IN VR?

- *We're social creatures. A sense of social consequence is key to giving emotional significance to virtual presence.*
- *BEING SEEN reinforces a player-character's in-story IDENTITY and embodiment.*
- *BEING SEEN can also place players into the experiences of IDENTITIES other than their own. This isn't some magic solution for discrimination, but it can be effective in building empathy.*

HOW CAN VR NARRATIVES MAKE PLAYERS FEEL SEEN?

- *Use the principle of **panopticon**. A small selection of high-probability high-impact NPC reactions is an efficient way to create a sense of BEING SEEN without having to program a vast array of potential reactions.*
- *Avoid the **Swayze Effect** by making players' presence visible and meaningful. Players might be happy to just invisibly "be there" for a while, but this limits engagement and emotional immersion.*
- *But BEING (UN)SEEN can have powerful effects too: voyeurism, tension, complicity or disempowerment.*

HOW IS THIS USEFUL FOR AUGMENTING PLAYERS?

- *Augmented players also SEE themselves, so acknowledging and **diegetically** incorporating SELF-CONSCIOUSNESS is key.*
- *Acknowledging player presence and avoiding the **Swayze Effect** is vital in AR. Stimulating positive SELF-CONSCIOUSNESS can be a driver, not a disruptor, of immersion.*

HOW IS THIS USEFUL FOR AUGMENTING PLACES?

- *BEING (UN)SEEN is a crucial dynamic to make players feel they're meaningfully OCCUPYING SPACE in augmented places.*
- *Techniques of **spatial subjectivity** will show them they OCCUPY **zero-sum** space in the physical-digital storyscape. Perspective and **vantage point** will be all-important to their experience.*
- *Allowing players to leave a mark is an important way of showing them they OCCUPY diegetic SPACE.*

NOTES

1. Carol Strohecker, Kevin M. Brooks, Larry Friedlander, "Tired of Giving in: An Experiment in Narrative Unfolding", Mitsubishi Electric Research Laboratories, 1999.
2. Brooks, 2003, p. 3.
3. Tristan Cross, "I've Made My local Pub in VR", *Wired*, 8 May 2020, https://www.wired.co.uk/article/i-made-my-local-pub-in-vr.
4. *Ibid.*
5. *Ibid.*
6. Matt Burdette, "The Swayze Effect", Oculus Story Studio, 18 Nov 2015, https://www.oculus.com/story-studio/blog/the-swayze-effect/.
7. *Ibid.*
8. Nonny de la Peña, "Use of Force", MIT Open Documentary Lab, https://docubase.mit.edu/project/use-of-force/.
9. William J. Aceves, "Op-Ed: U.S. Border Killings Evade Justice", *Los Angeles Times*, 30 Nov 2022, https://www.latimes.com/opinion/story/2022-11-30/u-s-border-killings-anastasio-hernandez-rojas-death-hearing.
10. Nonny de la Peña, "Use of Force Incorporates Virtual Reality to Achieve a Unique Impact", interview with Karen Kemmerle, Tribeca, 16 Apr 2014, https://tribecafilm.com/news/use-of-force-nonny-de-la-pena-interview-storyscapes.

Juxtapositions: *Moving from Virtual Realities to Augmented/ Spatial Realities*

1.4

PARALLEL REALITIES

In the Summer of 2016 *Pokémon GO* launched, and millions of players began SEEING and BEING in public places recontextualised as augmented hunting grounds. Many were also BEING SEEN by a critical mass of fellow-players.

Pokémon GO remains to date the most successful augmented reality game ever. Yet the game had an "AR mode" which, within a few days of launch, most serious players had switched off. "AR mode" superimposes Pokémon into the real world with video **passthrough**. It took a heavy toll on device batteries and was nonessential to gameplay.

But even with "AR mode" switched off, the game was still augmenting players' reality.

The majority of *Pokémon GO* gameplay takes place on a map of the player's immediate locality, onto which in-fiction objectives like hunting spots and PokéStops are marked. Some players participate in the game as part of normal errands around their neighbourhood, while others travel far afield specifically because of the layer of collectibility and competition which the game superimposes on the world. Even with "AR mode" off, this digital/fictional recontextualisation of reality is powerful enough to alter players' behaviour, whether they're deviating slightly from their ordinary route to the shops or flying abroad to hunt a rare shiny pokémon.

Researcher Christian Licoppe studied how mobile locative games like *Pokémon GO* influence players' experience even without actually augmenting graphics into their field of view. Licoppe refers to players' experience of multiple simultaneous realities, some physical and some digital, being "folded" together: "Users may experience their environment both as mobile bodies and through the screen and locative media interface, both referring to the same "here-and-now".[1]

DOI: 10.1201/9781003379294-7

But creating and maintaining multiple realities risks creating juxtapositions, which can result in an experience that's less than the sum of its parts. As Licoppe says, "users are particularly aware of the possibility of mismatches between these two different ways of experiencing the same spatio-temporal reality".[2]

UNIFIED SENSORY MODELS

Back in 2023 Brendan Sinclair, Managing Editor of gamesindustry.biz, coined the term "**ludocorporeal dissonance**" to describe these kinds of juxtapositions. *Ludocorporeal* is an unholy mashup of *ludic*, meaning play, and *corporeal*, meaning physically real. So **ludocorporeal dissonance** means contradiction between how a game plays and how the world feels. It's a development of a common term in videogame theory, "*ludonarrative* dissonance", a contradiction between how a game plays and how the story makes you feel. (For example, there's ludonarrative dissonance when a game story features deadly jeopardy, but the player knows they'll respawn if they die.)

As we've seen, **visuotactile incongruities** between what a player SEES in a VR headset and what they physically *feel* create dissonance which can disrupt immersion. For Sinclair, augmented/spatial technology takes that same problem out into the real world. He says AR/spatial will always risk **ludocorporeal dissonance** because there will always be a clear and visible juxtaposition between the real world and the kind of visuals that commercial digital experiences will augment into the world. In his article "Games will need a radical rethink to work in AR", Sinclair says:

> So many video games work because they present a heightened fantasy of coolness for people to inhabit for a while, but AR by its nature seeks to juxtapose that fantasy with a mundane reality many users would like to escape…
>
> Video games are often power fantasies, and they place a premium on things that are, for lack of a better word, cool… But when you take those cool things out of the stories and environments that exist to reinforce their coolness, and you instead put them in our contemporary everyday world, they are going to stick out like a sore thumb.[3]

Let's set aside for a minute the assumption that compelling interactive narratives must include traditionally "*cool*" things. I believe that augmented/spatial media, for all their technical challenges, may actually represent LESS fundamental juxtaposition with reality than VR.

When I started work in videogames around 2012, the widespread assumption in the games industry was that games would continue to follow the same trajectory as the previous decade: ever-better graphics,, driven by more powerful hardware, larger screens and higher visual fidelity. At PlayStation at the time we were preparing to launch next-generation games for 3DTVs. (Remember 3DTVs? If you don't, don't worry: they never took off.)

But meanwhile, the smartphone revolution was already well underway. And that's what actually changed the games industry in the 2010s: not a continuation of the hardware-graphics arms race, but small games for small devices. Games which fit in your pocket and fit around your everyday life. There are still lucrative segments of the industry trading on more and better graphics year-on-year. But it wasn't bigger screens and more visual fidelity that expanded the gaming market to billions of *new* users; it was compelling pocket-sized experiences that added new dimensions to everyday life.

Remember, immersive experiences do not need to be "convincing"; only compelling. Louis Rosenberg argues that although augmented/spatial reality is a greater technical challenge than VR, nonetheless AR/spatial will be a more relevant and useful technology to more people because of the way it can fit into their real lives:

> The fact is, visual fidelity is not the factor that will govern broad adoption. Instead, adoption will be driven by which technology offers the most natural experience to our perceptual system. And the most natural way to present digital content to the human perceptual system is by integrating it directly into our physical surroundings.
>
> Of course, a minimum level of fidelity is required, but what's far more important is perceptual consistency. By this, I mean that all sensory signals (i.e. sight, sound, touch, and motion) feed a single mental model of the world within your brain. With augmented reality, this can be achieved with relatively low visual fidelity, as long as virtual elements are spatially and temporally registered to your surroundings.[4]

But in VR, creating "a unified sensory model of the world" is much harder, because any inconsistency between what's SEEN and what's *felt* causes dissonance – "this inconsistency forces your brain to build and maintain two separate models of your world – one for your real surroundings and one for the virtual world that is presented in your headset".[5]

Like smartphones, AR has the power to provide contextual information when the player is out and about – and to add new story and game contexts to everyday life. Remember, when augmenting reality, the first rule is that *context is everything*. Incorporating digital elements into a truly "unified sensory model" will probably require true **see-through** AR not **passthrough**. But if augmented elements can be successfully integrated, anchored or "registered" to the physical world, the effect may ultimately be more "immersive" than VR – and more relevant, compelling and useful to more people.

THE DRAGON'S CAVE

This is where storytelling comes in: that's how we get players to play along, willingly "creating belief" to integrate digital elements into their emotional and sensory experience.

Like all media technologies, AR/spatial technologies have their drawbacks. As storytellers our job is to understand how players relate to these media, understand their strengths, and turn their drawbacks into opportunities.

When comparing the storytelling affordances of VR and AR, I use the example of the dragon's cave. Let's say you want to tell a story featuring a dragon. This premise presents a significant juxtaposition with reality: tragically, dragons aren't real. Different storytelling media may present even harsher juxtapositions: a theatrical dragon prop might not look convincing, or a videogame dragon might be boxy and polygonal. But with good storytelling, players easily suspend their disbelief long enough to fly with dragons.

In VR, you can transport the player into a dragon's cave, presenting their sensory model with the appearance of being in a cave with a dragon.

But augmented/spatial reality isn't great for telling the player "you are in a dragon's cave". Most of what an augmented player experiences is still the real world. AR can't completely overwrite and replace reality with a fully virtual environment. Even if you have a headset that can reskin the player's room like a dragon's cave, that reskin is still anchored to the physical substrate of reality, so it's vulnerable to physical-digital juxtaposition. If you're trying to "transport" your player somewhere completely fictional, you're better using VR.

Virtually "transporting" the player doesn't play to AR/spatial technology's main strength: being grounded in the solid real world, which allows it to evoke to solid real-world emotions.

Remember the second rule of augmenting reality: *the most important reality you are augmenting is the player themselves*. AR isn't well suited to trying to convince the player, "you are in a dragon's cave". What augmented/spatial technology is REALLY good at is whispering in the player's ear,

What if you were secretly a dragon?

This little mote of narrative recontextualises the way that players see and relate to the world around them. It imaginatively augments the PLAYER, and this in turn creates an augmented relationship to the PLACES around them.

This recontextualisation doesn't require a full reskin of the world. It doesn't even require the player to perform or **roleplay** in a specific way, because suddenly they are **diegetically** present in a story that's already ongoing and happening *to* them. Everything they were already doing is now in-character as a secret dragon-person – even while they're just going about their day.

HYBRID REALITIES

As researcher Jeff Ritchie says, it takes mental work to navigate digital narratives set in real places. Players must "successfully navigate two spaces (digital and physical)... requiring audiences to continually discern what does or doesn't belong within the storyworld".[6] So although AR can be integrated into the player's perceptual model, they're always conscious they're navigating multiple kinds of reality. And there will always be dissonances between fictional and physical realities, between the game layer and the real world.

Sinclair describes these as *ludocorporeal dissonances*, adapting the concept of ludo*narrative* dissonance to the *luidic* + *corporeal* experience of AR. But this leaves *narrative* out of the equation. And I believe it's narrative that can bridge this dissonance, by stimulating players' imagination to "actively create belief".

In augmented/spatial media, we need to collaborate with the player's imagination to co-create *with* them a hybrid experience incorporating digital and physical elements. Done right, this doesn't trigger **ludocorporeal dissonance**, because humans have an enormous capacity to hybridise and move through different realities. (In fact, modern media increasingly seems to demand that we navigate multiple layers of reality.)

Stories always contrast with reality. Yet stories still recontextualise how the player sees themselves and sees the people and places around them. And though we create a "unified world-model", that model is made up of many different contexts, layers of reality and versions of ourselves. As Springett says, "we take world-views on and off like glasses all the time in our personal lives. In the supermarket, in the bank, at a train station, in the pub".[7]

Augmented players don't have to be "convinced" to be immersed – they understand they're navigating multiple realities. Nevertheless, remember the third hard-and-fast rule: **when augmenting reality you have a responsibility TO reality**. Since AR takes place in the player's own context, their unique perspective(s) and the way they move through the world are both core to their experience. This includes any physical or social barriers the world presents to them. These aspects of their experience can't be digitally overwritten.

In short, compared to VR, an augmented/spatial narrative is even more of a collaboration with the player's imagination. As augmented/spatial storytellers our primary job is to **augment context**, creating compelling re-contextualisations in which players can take part. This begins with **augmenting the player**: stimulating them to re-imagine partially-fictionalised versions of themselves and the world. And we must do this **responsibly**.

NOTES

1. Christian Licoppe, "From Mogi to Pokémon GO: Continuities and Change in Location-Aware Collection Games", *Mobile Media & Communication* 5:1, 2016.
2. *Ibid.*
3. Brandan Sinclair, "Games Will Need a Radical Rethink to Work in AR", 23 June 2023, gamesindustry.biz, https://www.gamesindustry.biz/games-will-need-a-radical-rethink-to-work-in-ar-this-week-in-business.
4. Louis Rosenberg, "Why AR, Not VR, Will Be the Heart of the Metaverse", *VentureBeat*, 28 Dec 2021 https://venturebeat.com/2021/12/28/future-augmented-reality-will-inherit-the-earth/.
5. *Ibid.*
6. Jeff Ritchie, "The Affordances and Constraints of Mobile Locative Narrative", in *The Mobile Story: Narrative Practices with Locative Technologies*, Jason Farman (ed.), Routledge, New York, 2014.
7. Jay Springett, personal correspondence, 20 Jul 2023.

SECTION 2

Augmenting Players

Augmenting Players

2.0

Getting Started

Is the audience member present in the piece?
Not just as a mute listener or impotent observer,
but as a physical body with embodied experience.

Is the interaction you offer meaningful, are you
creating more than a toy to play with?

When and where is the audience, if they still have
a sensation of the room they are in, the body they
inhabit, can you really ignore that?

Have you acknowledged that the audience has
already crossed the fourth wall?

– Duncan Speakman, *No Vantage Point*[1] (2019)

Duncan Speakman is an immersive artist whose work focuses on site-specific audio. He's spent years augmenting people's experience of the world with new narratives and sensory contexts, all without using headsets. As we're moving out of VR and into augmented realities, Speakman's provocations give us a useful checklist for building emotional immersion, by focusing on the player:

Is the player present? Is the interaction meaningful?

In VR, creating a sense of "inhabiting" a virtual body is crucial. We need to do the same in AR, but the player is *already* embodied as-themselves, so our story must acknowledge them, create space for them, and create meaningful interactions for them.

Can you really ignore their sensations?

Augmented players are already present in a physical place and in their own body. Their senses constantly update them on *where and when* they are. These real sensations exist before we start augmenting their reality, and continue throughout. We can't afford to ignore the player's sensations of the world or of themselves – and we shouldn't try to completely overwrite them.

DOI: 10.1201/9781003379294-9

Have you acknowledged the audience has already crossed the fourth wall?

Your player is already immersed in one version of the world. Successful augmented realities allow players to find themselves inside new, augmented versions of the world – without ever knowingly crossing a fourth wall.

In an augmented/spatial narrative the player is both the substance and the audience of your story, and they are story's co-teller, and probably its protagonist too. The are a big part of your canvas, and they supply a lot of your paint. Remember the second hard-and-fast rule for augmenting reality: *the most important reality you are augmenting is the player themselves.*

Accordingly, this Section 2 focuses on AUGMENTING PLAYERS (Figure 2.0).

Telling compelling stories using augmented/spatial technology is about collaborating with ongoing processes already at play within the player – IMAGINING, IDENTITY-BUILDING, and dramatising their relationships with the world and other people through SELF-CONSCIOUSNESS.

Augmenting PLAYERS

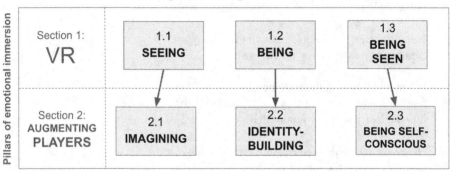

FIGURE 2.0   Evolution of pillars of emotional immersion when AUGMENTING PLAYERS

In Chapter 2.1, we'll examine ways to augment players' IMAGINATION so they can go beyond SEEING and begin experiencing hybrid digital-physical narratives with meaningful interactions.

In Chapter 2.2, we'll explore techniques for co-creating augmented IDENTITY, so players know not just when and where they are, but who they're BEING and how they fit **diegetically** into the narratively-augmented world.

Finally in Chapter 2.3, we'll look at ways that augmented/spatial media can interact with players' existing SELF-CONSCIOUSNESS and use it to drive immersion, so that players feel SEEN as their augmented in-story self.

NOTE

1. Duncan Speakman, *No Vantage Point* V1.0, South West Creative Technology Network 2019, p10. CC 4.0.

IMAGINING

2.1

How do we activate the player's IMAGINATION to help augmented/spatial technology to STAGE the story?

How do we collaborate with the player's IMAGINATION so the story feels anchored in their own reality?

ACTIVE CREATION OF BELIEF

The pleasurable surrender of the mind to an imaginative world is often described, in Coleridge's phrase, as "the willing suspension of disbelief." But this is too passive a formulation even for traditional media. When we enter a fictional world, we do not merely "suspend" a critical faculty; we also exercise a creative faculty. We do not suspend belief so much as we actively create belief. Because of our desire to experience immersion, we focus our attention on the enveloping world and we use our intelligence to reinforce rather than to question the reality of the experience.

Janet H. Murray, *Hamlet on the Holodeck*[1] (1997)

In her incredibly prophetic study of VR narrative, Janet Murray argues that, given the right prompts, an immersed player's brain doesn't focus on unrealistic elements. Instead it focuses on imaginatively filling-in the gaps. When we're immersed in a story, we don't outsource all the imagining to the creator: we engage with what they have imagined and then we reframe and retell it to ourselves. Through this re-imagination, the story gains emotional traction within our own minds.

As Kevin Brooks puts it, "by experiencing a good story well told, we create our own immersive environments, with details unrivalled by electronic media". These environments comprise elements created by the storyteller, hybridised with our own imagined sensations: "we are able to see the anxiety in faces… we can smell the food in kitchens, we can feel the hairs on the back of our neck react to scary situations".

And this is happening just when we're being *told* a story, even without a headset. Hence, for Brooks, technology "should complement the immersion already present in the human system. In a sense, narrative experiences (reading, listening, watching) are merely catalysts for a mental activity that we also call narrative".[2]

So even when we're immersed, we're not completely surrendering to an imaginative world created by someone else. Immersion comes from our active co-imagining and making-believe.

This comes so naturally to us that we don't even notice, because this ongoing narrative-making mental activity is also part of our baseline experience of life. Just

DOI: 10.1201/9781003379294-10

as our vision is highly **foveated**, focusing only on a small area at a time, our brains only perceive the world one piece at a time while our imaginative capacity fills in the gaps, building a coherent world-model. That's why we're able to fully and emotionally engage in a story, even if that story is told only through black marks on a white page. We "actively create belief", without at any point needing to believe the story is "real".

Even in VR, which might seem superficially to enclose us in a complete, authored vision of a new reality, we're still **foveating** and focusing on small areas at a time while our brain imaginatively constructs a full model of the scene. Our imagination fills in small gaps in **visuotactile congruence**, too, and allows us to feel embodied in a virtual body and identity.

In augmented/spatial media, immersion relies even more on the player's **IMAGINATION**.

As Calleja observes, "immersion" is fundamentally a metaphor rather than a specific mental state. This goes back to Murray:

> "we seed the same feeling from a psychologically immersive experience that we do from a plunge in the ocean or swimming pool: the sensation of being surrounded by a completely other reality".[3]

This idea of total submergence in another reality is considered the gold standard of immersion in other media. But an augmented player isn't "submerged" in a fictional reality to the exclusion of physical reality. To the augmented player, physical reality is manifest all around them. Their physical and bodily sensations are ongoing. They have not been "transported" anywhere.

An augmented/spatial experience is a hybrid of digital elements plus the physical world – to which the player is still firmly anchored. They can still sense physical reality *through* the technology. And an augmented/spatial experience is also a hybrid of the storyteller's and the player's IMAGINATIONS.

If you want to get technical, according to immersive researchers Lucho Lingan, Li and Vermeeren "the engagement and involvement factors [of immersion] are linked to imagination and imaginative immersion".[4] These researchers propose a "Immersive Cycle", and put the "User's Imagination" at the very centre. They argue that when an immersive experience "possesses a cohesive narrative or story, the user's imagination can be guided, making sense of what users are experiencing... The ITE's [Immersive Technological Experience's] narrative or story will help the user in reaching the "being there" effect".[5]

In short, it's the player's IMAGINATION that unifies augmented/spatial resources into coherent, emotive hybrid experiences. The player's augmented IMAGINATION is a far more powerful immersive storytelling resource than even the most powerful software or hardware. (And it's a lot more cost-effective.)

BEGINNING AUGMENTATION

So how should an augmented story begin? We need to stimulate the player's imagination. This means providing "catalysts for [the] mental activity that we also call narrative".

Remember, *the most important reality you're augmenting is the player them-selves.* An augmented story always begins *inside* and *around* the player. It's part of an ongoing continuity of experience. If your narrative tries to draw a sharp bound-ary between where reality ends and the story begins, it isn't playing to the storytelling strengths of augmented/spatial technology. If the story begins *Once upon a time, in a land far away*, this doesn't allow the player to use their immediate reality as a catalyst for imagination.

In theory, when we enter a game's "magic circle" we suspend our real identities and the norms of the outside world. As immersive theatre practitioner and theorist Jessica Creane says, "the conventional wisdom of the magic circle (Huizinga 1949) suggests that we press pause on our real lives when we enter a game space".[6] But reality can't be paused. The augmented player can see reality still manifestly carrying on around them. There isn't a "magic circle" in augmented narratives – it's more like a porous bubble. Digital storytelling elements can catalyse the player's mental process of narrative-making, but the world around them will also carry on and provide other catalysts too.

Unlike film, which creates and shows us a new reality within the frame, augmented/spatial stories always seem to take place in a version of the player's immediate reality. Therefore the "establishing shot" of an augmented reality will always be a modification to or partial transition from normal ongoing reality. Hence, instead of trying to establish a brand-new story reality, it's better to begin by giving the player a narrative prompt to imaginatively modify or reskin what's already there. Instead of *once upon a time*, it's better to establish that the story is happening *where* the player is, and happening *to* them.

So in a sense, **all augmented/spatial narratives begin *in medias res*** (in the mid-dle of the story). Augmented/spatial stories mix digital elements with the real world and the player's real self – both of which are already in-progress. As a result, in augmented/spatial storytelling it's vital to establish continuity with the player's ongoing experience and immediate context. Many **room-scale** and **table-scale** AR experiences (see 3.0.5 and 3.0.6) start with a status quo of ordinary reality followed by a "breaking" of reality: a portal opens, something breaks through from the outside, or something is revealed to be enchanted.

Remember, in augmented/spatial media *context is everything*. Merely placing digital story elements *alongside* the player's context doesn't put them *in-context*. In *No Vantage Point* Speakman describes a locative audio experience in which a Dutch city was aug-mented with a location-driven audio layer of voices from a historical Spanish setting:

Soon I am walking the busy streets... But [via digital audio] I can also hear other voices, people walking the Compostela pilgrimage. I try to concentrate on their words but instead I am constantly distracted by my surroundings... I want to sympathise, to empathise, to feel that their story somehow connects with mine, but they don't know I'm here.[7]

Speakman highlights the dissonance between the physical city around him and the decontextualised audio narrative:

The city wants to consume me,
to show me its splendour,

the voices want me to hear their story,
neither gives the other space, the edge between them is a brutal, not a flickering
*   blur that allows me to easily transition. I find myself between two layers of*
*   immersion that do not care for each other.*
I am stranded
de-mersed[8]

Speakman contrasts this with a more successful AR experience: a sound installation by Francisco Lopez. The installation's abstract "resonant metallic tones" initially "consume" Speakman, but ultimately the experience doesn't submerge him but attenuates him to the real world around him:

My immersion was an existing condition, the sound had not created it, only
*   highlighted it, the fuzzy edges of the transition let multiple things interweave*
Intermmersive
They let things co-exist
Commersive[9]

Players' immersion is a pre-existing condition. They're already immersed in ongoing physical and mental worlds before we even begin any augmentation. So when an AR narrative starts it shouldn't try to compete with, or overwrite, the player's existing reality; it should add to and commingle with it. This means creating *intermmersive* or *commersive* moments which activate the player's imagination, so they start to re-imagine and build upon the ongoing reality in which they're already immersed.

In the establishing moments of an augmented/spatial narrative, you're not asking the player to pause their identity, overcome cognitive dissonance or flit between two contradictory realities. You're relying on their pre-existing ability to sustain multiple immersions and navigate across different versions of reality. Given the right catalysts, the player's imagination will criss-cross and hopscotch playfully back and forth across these realities, gaining emotional momentum from narrative and sensory inputs across the digital and physical layers.

We can summarise this in three key criteria:
Augmented/spatial narratives must:

1. *Be compatible with what the player can sense around them,*
2. *Include space for the player and inspire their imagination and participation,*
3. *Be in-progress and maintain continuity with the player's ongoing experience.*

In the remainder of this chapter, we'll look at three core storytelling techniques that show how augmented storytellers can fulfil those three criteria:

Plausibility
Desirability
Faits accomplis (which means a done deal, something which is already occurring, or an offer you can't refuse.)

Plausibility

A digital narrative scenario needs to be **plausible** in the player's immediate context, in order to be commersive and activate the player's IMAGINATION. Luckily, "**plausible**" is not the same as "realistic'!

Like with VR, consistency and congruence is far more important than "realism" in building **plausibility**. As immersive researchers Von der Au *et al* say, "humans seek consistency and congruence in their sense-making activities, and it is no surprise that these matter in a digital world where "reality" is exceptionally fluid".[10] Players are perfectly capable of emotionally engaging with even quite cartoonish augmented elements – so long as they are consistent and congruent; that is, they appear to be solidly anchored to the real world and to obey its general rules.

(In fact von Der Au *et al*'s study suggests there may be a kind of Uncanny Valley in AR: "matching context with augmented content might backfire, as realism may present a higher bar to clear".[11] As augmented objects become more realistic they might actually diminish in effectiveness, because they're subject to higher standards of **plausibility**.)

Picture yourself being about six or seven, playing an imagination game while running around outside. You have an imaginary ray gun, and you're trying to fire it at a fellow-player. You point with your fingers (or with a suitable stick) and say "pew pew! I shot you!" "Nuh-uh!" says the other player, "you missed!" If this were a video game, there would be millions of calculations being run every second to track the trajectory of every bullet to make sure everyone knows who shot whom. But in an imagination game, you're both collaborating on a shared instance of reality, so your word is as good as your fellow-player's.

So to be sure, you take more careful aim, announce "I'm taking careful aim!", then you "pew pew!" again. But no, this time they tell you, "my forcefield was up!"

Again, compared to digital experiences, IMAGINATION is collaborative and malleable. Did your fellow-player make up the forcefield on the spot in order to avoid being hit? Or was it always part of their imaginary loadout? There's no way to prove it wasn't. All warfare is based on deception, after all, and today's six-year-olds have to grow up so fast.

Let's say your opponent now *pew-pews* at you. You could claim they missed, or pull your own forcefield out of your imaginary loadout. But if you want to avoid being hit AND avoid an argument over imaginary rules, your best bet is to duck behind a real, physical tree. There's no arguing with a tree: if the other player can't see you, they can't very well say they definitely hit you. In your collaborative imagination you might reskin the tree as a Martian cyber-oak or whatever, but this imagining is staged upon the physical tree, which provides a solid substrate underpinning the game. The tree lends **plausibility** to otherwise-subjective imaginings.

For an augmented story to have congruence and consistency with reality, the player's IMAGINATION requires a few secure anchor points in physical reality. When we create these anchor points in AR, we can call them "**merged reality moments**", because they're points in the story where the real world lends its solidity to the narrative. (And, in turn, the narrative lends its emotive extra dimension to reality.) Agreeing that the tree is a Martian cyber-oak which blocks lasers is a **merged reality moment** because the fiction is now firmly anchored in the real.

The key quality of a **merged reality moment** is that it establishes **plausibility** by aligning or anchoring a digital event to a physical surface or phenomenon. This could be a floor, a wall, a sound, the time of day or the weather. Experiment with building **merged reality moments** in your own storytelling in the next CHALLENGE:

CHALLENGE #5: BUILDING PLAUSIBILITY: MERGED REALITY MOMENTS

Goal: Explore ways to anchor events in a digital layer to events in the physical world.

SUMMARY

Continue using the **place** and concept you developed in **CHALLENGE #1: Shadow Place**. (Or develop a new idea; make sure to **visit** the new **place**.)

Identify three physical phenomena which commonly take place in the **place**. This could be a clock striking, the sound of sirens or a shift change at a shop.

Assume that you could reliably detect these events happening and respond to them in-story.

Now, **conceptualise three story events** which take place in the digital layer; each should be **aligned or anchored** to one of the **physical phenomena**.

Each **story event** should **acknowledge, adapt,** or **contextualise** a physical phenomenon into your story. A clock striking could be **acknowledged** as a reminder that the player-character's time is running out; sirens could be **adapted** as the sound of nearby dragons; a shift change could be **contextualised** as the moment when a treasure is unguarded.

Write new dialogue or narration as a continuation of your CHALLENGE #1 concept. **Write three merged reality moments**, each triggered by one of the **phenomena**. When one of the three **physical phenomena** occurs, it should **merge realities** by triggering one of the **story events**.

TASKS

- (If you're using a new idea/place, **visit** the **place** and outline the **concept**.)
- **Identify three physical phenomena** in the location.
- **Conceptualise three story events** anchored to **physical phenomena.**
- **Describe** how each **story event acknowledges, adapts,** or **contextualises** its **physical phenomenon**.
- **Write** new dialogue or narration for these **three merged reality moments.**

BONUS CHALLENGE: AT HOME

Now try to make a version of this CHALLENGE which might work in any player's own home. Try to conceptualise general phenomena which might occur in homes worldwide, and create **merged reality moments** for them.

Phenomena like "doorbell rings" may not occur or be relevant to some people's homes. The most reliable phenomena are ones which the player themselves enacts. These usually have an emotive context. If the player enters the kitchen, the player might naturally think about food – you could **acknowledge** this event by having a character ask when the player last ate. If the player sits at a computer, the player could be at risk of getting distracted – **adapt** this event by telling the player that all screens have been taken over by hypno-droids. If the player gets into bed, the player may think of sleep – **contextualise** this by telling them they're already asleep, and this is all a dream.

Remember, **plausibility** is subjective. We all see the world differently. Our job as storytellers is not to fill the player's perceptions edge-to-edge. As the live game designer Tassos Stevens says, storytellers can deploy the "minimum fiction necessary" to "play with the real world and, in so doing, recast it as otherworldly in the imagination and experience of the beholder". [12] Plausible storytelling means building-in empty, ambiguous or subjective areas where the player's imagination can act. A lot of augmented/spatial reality storytelling is about getting the player telling *themselves* a story. Once the player's imagination has been activated, they will fill in these gaps and ambiguities – and these imagined elements will be far more emotive and **plausible** story elements than even the most specifically anchored element created by the storyteller.

Immersive Artist Joon Moon's "Augmented Shadow" work is an example of highly subjective AR/spatial storytelling, with large swathes of ambiguous imaginative space. In Moon's installations, characters often peek into our world from their own hidden realm.[13] In Moon's "Inside" (2023[14]), the audience moves around a darkened physical space with a hand-held spotlight. As they point the spotlight at various areas, augmented shadows are superimposed onto the spotlight, so the player can see the shadows of "invisible" characters and infer their presence.

The spotlight empowers the player but also restricts their perspective to wherever they focus the "gaze" of their spotlight, leaving darkness in which their IMAGINATION can act.

Giving your players clues about how to **foveate** their experience – e.g. by creating areas of focus and un-focus – is resource-efficient storytelling because you can concentrate your assets on focused **merged reality moments**. Players will naturally gravitate to areas of focused story, and this is a good way to manage players' progress through a plot (more on this when we look at **spatial pacing** and **boundaries** in 3.1.1). But if you've activated the player's imagination with a compelling scenario, then you can outsource much of the peripheral world-building to their subjective IMAGINATION, which will get better with the world around them anyway. In this way, you can build fantastical augmented scenarios which still have all the **plausibility** AND subjectivity of reality.

Desireability

Plausibility isn't everything. *Don Quixote* is about an ageing, small-time landowner who reads too much heroic poetry and begins to imagine the world as a heroic adventure full of monsters to slay and great deeds to perform. He sees himself as a knight errant, imagines his clapped-out old horse Rocinante as a fine noble steed, and charges windmills which he perceives as hostile giants.

This is a relatively un-**plausible** way to imagine the world. Fundamentally, Quixote imagines the world in this way because it is more **desirable** than his forgettable real life. Augmented/spatial narratives must create space for the player and their imaginings; one reliable way to do this is to make sure the narrative invites the player to re-IMAGINE the world – and themselves – in a **desirable** way. This doesn't necessarily mean giving the player whatever they want – more on that later – but generally speaking **desirability** should go hand-in-hand with **plausibility**.

Don Quixote's way of seeing the world isn't entirely un-**plausible**, since it is based on the coherent and congruent system of romantic chivalry. But it is fantastical. People regularly mock him for his implausible actions. But his re-IMAGINING only needs to be coherent to him. In fact, Don Quixote does not overwrite other peoples' perspectives. He is very aware that other people do not see the world in the same way he does; his fantasy has a built-in justification for this. When his "squire" Sancho Panza wonders whether Quixote's stories of derring-do are "just wind and lies", Quixote explains away any juxtaposition between his vision and reality:

> There is a crew of enchanters always amongst us who change and alter all our deeds, and transform them according to their pleasure and their desire either to favour us or injure us.[15]

One of these "enchanters" follows Don Quixote around, you see, transforming everything. Thus:

> everything to do with knights errant appears to be chimaera, folly and nonsense, and to go all contrariwise… what seems to you to be a barber's basin appears to me to be a Mambrino's helmet, and to another as something else.[16]

The mythical Mambrino's helmet was supposed to grant invulnerability to its wearer. In chapter XXI, Quixote perceives a mounted knight wearing a glittering gold helmet. (In fact, as Sancho observes, it's a barber riding a mule, wearing his bronze basin on his head to keep the rain off.) Quixote scares off the "knight" and triumphantly dons the "helmet". But he's aware that to others it seems a mere basin. The fantasy of "Mambrino's Helmet" needs to be anchored to a physical object to be **plausible**. But more importantly, for Quixote, seeing the basin as a mythical helmet is **desirable**; and the fact that others *do not* see it is also a **desirable** part of his fantasy – it means he's in on a great secret.

Quixote can't actually transform the world around him, or force others to see the world his way. But in a sense, it's *essential* to Quixote's fantasy that others see him a ridiculous basin-wearing clown. The enchanter who supposedly remakes the world around Quixote is his ally, and Quixote's clownishness is a *disguise*. "It shows a rare foresight in the sage who is on my side to make what is really and truly Mambrino's helmet seem to everyone a basin", he says, "for, as it is of such great value, the whole world would persecute me in order to get it from me".[17]

The real appeal of Quixote's fantasy is the idea that his own undignified everyday reality is a disguise he wears to hide true heroism. In that sense, he's a superhero. (Wish-fulfilment stories of superpowered-everypeople represent the same fantasy, from Superman to *Everything Everywhere All At Once* (2022).) In short, **desireability** makes up for any lack in **plausibility**.

The next thing Don Quixote does after claiming Mambrino's helmet is to free a group of prisoners destined to be galley slaves (a fate which the author may himself have suffered earlier in life). There's no illusion involved in *why* Don Quixote does this: he just doesn't think free men should be enslaved.[18] The only illusion is his superheroic role of knight errant: i.e., someone who rights wrongs without fear of the consequences.

Quixote's fantasy is a world which *needs* him, where he can make a difference. Seeming laughable is a small price to pay for doing his duty as he sees it. His "duty" might be self-appointed, even absurd, but what matters is that Quixote treats it as if it's important.

When the video game theorist Steven Conway compared football video games with actual football, he argued that the common element across the digital/physical divide was "commitment to a set of primordial as-if statements: behave as-if the soccer ball is valuable, indeed the most valuable entity in this world at the moment of play".[19] This "as-if" isn't **plausible**, but it creates the **desirable** condition of competitiveness, which players need in order to treat the game *as-if* it is real and important.

So a **desirable** reality-version should give the player-character an important role and perhaps hint at their special knowledge or status. We can break down these **desirability-**building elements into four ingredients: Purpose, Stakes, Secrecy and Exclusivity.

Purpose

Quixote's sense of duty was critical to his imagined self-image. As John Fowles puts it, "duty largely consists of pretending that the trivial is critical".[20] "Pretending the trivial is critical" is a pretty good definition of play: play is often driven by players adopting **objectives** which they treat with the seriousness of primordial duty.

Purpose is often but not exclusively expressed through gameplay **mechanics** and **objectives** (more on these in Appendix C). Basically, an augmented story should *need* something from the player, giving them a task or role. This creates a framework for their interactions as well as creating a **desirable** sense of purpose.

EMPOWERMENT AND ENTITLEMENT SIMULATORS

Bear in mind it's possible to go too far when creating a world that needs a hero. Action videogames in particular tend to depict worlds which seem to be waiting for a hero to come along and save them. This "damsel world" fantasy is empowering for the player but often relies on the in-fiction characters being completely disempowered. This approach results in many videogames being, as the theorist Matt Boch describes, "entitlement simulators".[21] As feminist and queer theorists such as Mattie Brice have pointed out, this emphasis on player empowerment makes it difficult to tell digital stories about marginalisation or oppression.[22] More sophisticated game stories often use mechanics of disempowerment. These might allow designers to convey experiences of economic oppression or racialised or LGBTQ+ experiences.

Empowerment simulators might be **desirable** for some players, but in AR/spatial media their **plausibility** is limited, since in the real world everyone is theoretically an empowered protagonist of their own story – yet at the same time your players may well experience marginalisation, discrimination or disempowerment. These realities can't be augmented away.

Augmenting purpose onto players usually does mean giving them a bit of **desirable** "Main Character Syndrome": a sense that their actions are important and consequential. But as storytellers we have a responsibility not to encourage augmented players to simply treat other people around them as "NPCs",[23] or inadvertently replicate the ways that the **zero-sum** physical world disempowers people'.

Stakes

A compelling purpose requires un-**desirable** consequences if the purpose isn't fulfilled. An augmented scenario should have stakes. These stakes should be emotive but also **plausible**, i.e. anchored to reality and coherent in the logic of the story.

A quick way to test whether your story has real stakes is to ask the *It's A Wonderful Life* question: "what would happen if the player-character didn't exist? How would the story be different?" If there would be no difference if the player-character never showed up, the player's actions have no stakes.

Player-characters don't have to be saving the world all the time. Stakes don't have to be big, just compelling. Be wary of raising the stakes with major jeopardy, as this can create insurmountable juxtaposition between reality and fiction. In most cases it's difficult to threaten an augmented player with death, because how will you augment a death scene? Unless it's done cleverly, it's the opposite of a **merged reality moment**; a stark juxtaposition between story and experience.

Secrecy

Secrets are a highly **desirable** type of "glamour" to augment onto the player. Secrets activate IMAGINATION because they represent special ways of seeing and being-in the world. Even better, if you give players a secret to keep, then they're instantly in-character as someone-with-a-secret.

Provided the secret is story-significant, everything a secret-keeper does is dramatised in terms of the secret. *Am I keeping the secret? Will I share it? Are my actions inadvertently revealing the secret?*

Secrecy can make stakes more compelling while minimising the risk of juxtaposition. Say you set an experience in a busy train station. If you tell the player, "you are a bomb disposal expert. There is a bomb in the station. Find and defuse it", you've augmented a context onto both player and place. (This is just an illustrative example: for obvious reasons be very cautious dramatising this type of scenario in public places.)

This scenario asks the player to IMAGINE a high level of jeopardy, which sets a standard of **plausibility** that augmentation cannot meet. The player knows the station is unlikely to blow up. But if you tell the player "there is a bomb in the station. Find the bomb *without letting anyone know about the bomb*", you have augmented the player with a secret. Although the fiction is still ultimately in juxtaposition with reality, in the sense that a bomb won't actually go off, the player's focus is directed much more to the emotive and embodied experience of not-giving-away-the-secret. **Diegetically** speaking, everything the player now does is an enactment, either concealing or accidentally revealing the secret.

Secrets can be highly dramatic while not requiring any actual changes to the world. With the heightened drama of secrecy, even acting completely normal is dramatised while the player embodies the emotive secret-keeping scenario. It's also a type of **panopticon**: the player continues to experience this dramatic sense of being (un)seen even when the story isn't talking to them directly, so it's an efficient use of storytelling resources.

Exclusivity

There's something fundamentally **desirable** about having special insight and seeing the world differently to others. Don Quixote's perception of himself as "knight errant" makes him part of an exclusive club; the special protection of his "enchanter" even moreso. Like secrets, exclusivity is inherently enacted. But unlike secrets, exclusivity only really counts for something when it's SEEN by others.

In the mid-2010's my studio Playlines made several site-specific AR theatre installations using layers of location-triggered interactive audio laid across busy festivals or conferences.[24] These were "barefoot budget" AR narratives built using the tools available to us: mobile audio, location beacons, and physical performers.

Players wore headphones and moved around the busy conference venue. Moving into different areas or rooms triggered different audio, and players' choices of where to go were tracked, allowing players to choose from multiple **forking** paths with different consequences in the audio layer.

Often we'd designate a "VIP area", closed off with a red rope, with a live performer acting as "bouncer". Entry required speaking a password to the bouncer, and the only way to get the password was via certain story paths in the audio layer. Whispering the password to the bouncer and then being let into the VIP room created a **merged reality moment**, manifesting the digital story in physical reality.

Better still, the player's exclusive access to the VIP area was being seen by non-player bystanders at the conference. The red rope would always attract attention from non-players, who'd want to know how to get into the VIP. This moment granted players a very tangible sense of exclusivity grounded in a real social dynamic. (And by inspiring Fear of Missing Out, it conveniently served as a great advert to non-players.)

CHALLENGE #6: MAMBRINO'S HELMET

Goal: Explore ways to narratively augment *purpose, stakes, secrecy* and *exclusivity* onto players.

SUMMARY

Conceptualise a simple narrative that takes place in **the player's own home**. The player-character has a special **identity** which is hidden to the world around them but which gives them special insight, status or duties. They might be able to sense the thoughts of objects, be an alien sleeper agent, or be a disgraced billionaire fallen on hard times.

Identify a common object which most people might have in their home. This is your basin/Mambrino's helmet.

In-story, this object is going to represent the player-character's special **identity**. It might be the object which leads them to discover their superpower, represent a message from alien HQ, or be a symbol of their former life.

Maybe their housekey is a magically transfigured sword; maybe their mattress hides the stash of money which troubles their conscience; maybe their toilet is haunted.

Write a short dialogue or narration associated with the object. It could be the voice of the object's spirit, an omniscient narrator, or the player-character's own inner thoughts. Convey a sense of *purpose, stakes, secrecy* and/or *exclusivity*.

Define the conditions under which this content will be heard. Does the object simply start speaking one day? Does the player's inner monologue draw attention to it? Does it respond only when the player touches it? (Assume you can reliably detect these **conditions** to trigger content).

Record audio and **test** it on a friend by playing the audio as they move around the home or classroom and interact with the object. Can you alter their relationship to the place and the object using only narrative?

TASKS

- **Conceptualise** a simple narrative in the player's own home or classroom.
- Create a player **identity** with special status.
- **Identify** a common object to represent the player's status.
- **Write** a short dialogue in which the object conveys or symbolises the *purpose, stakes, secrecy* and/or *exclusivity* of the player's status.
- **Define trigger conditions.**
- **Record** audio.
- **Test**.

Faits Accomplis

Our third criteria for stimulating augmented IMAGINATION was that augmented scenarios should be *in-progress and maintain continuity with the player's ongoing experience*. Often this means that it's best to start an augmented narrative with the story *already* happening to the player. A *fait accompli* is a done deal, and by making the call-to-adventure a done deal we we can get the player actively playing the role of hero before they even realise they've started **role-playing**.

In *The Hero With a Thousand Faces* (1949) the writer and mythologist Joseph Campbell codified the "hero's journey", a basic structure for storytelling which has influenced generations of storytellers. George Lucas called Campbell "my Yoda" and built much of *Star Wars* in his "hero's journey" structure.[25]

(Bear in mind that in many ways storytelling has moved on from Campbell's principles. Some aspects of Campbell's approach are best left behind: for starters there's little room for female agency. When asked by students, "but what about the heroine's journey?" Campbell is reputed to have said "women don't need to make the journey. Women are where the journey is trying to get to".[26] Furthermore, Campbell's structure was based on spectator media like oral myth and literature. As we'll see, it can be unhelpful when writing for interactive media where the player is the protagonist.)

Campbell's structure is organised into story phases or "beats". The first beat establishes an "Ordinary World" which is disrupted by a "Call to Adventure". In Campbell's rubric this is usually followed by the "Refusal of the Call" beat, where the hero tries to go on with life as normal. In *Star Wars* this is when Obi-Wan Kenobi offers to show Luke Skywalker the ways of the Force: despite being desperate to leave his backwater home planet, Luke "refuses" and chooses to return home. It's only when Luke finds his parental figures murdered by the Empire that he agrees to take on the adventure.

The "Refusal" functions well in cinema partly because it makes the hero relatable: their everyday concerns overwhelm the temptation to fly off on an adventure. But in interactive formats this becomes complicated: you don't really want to give audiences the opportunity to Refuse the Call, because they might just opt to end the story ten minutes in.

(Some games like *The Stanley Parable* and *Far Cry 4* allow players to Refuse or just go home, but this is usually played for laughs and rarely lasts long. Refusing the Call might be relatable and give the player more true agency, but also robs the player of the adventure they've paid for.)

In augmented and spatial narratives, offering a "Refusal" is even trickier because the player is securely anchored in the real world, with all its distractions. It can be difficult enough to keep your player imaginatively engaged without also giving them perfectly relatable reasons to Refuse and resume their unaugmented ordinary life.

In a sense the principles of **plausibility** and **desirability** are ways of setting up effective Calls to Adventure to your players: compelling invitations to co-IMAGINE a change to their Ordinary World and to play along with the Call to Adventure. But in AR/spatial the player-protagonist's experience is in continuity with their ongoing experience of the ordinary world. If they "Refuse" and walk away, they'll seamlessly resume their ordinary reality, cutting off the story before it's really begun.

So how do we get player-protagonists invested in re-IMAGINING the world when they can always Refuse, and when Refusing is such a common and relatable thing for protagonists to do?

One approach is to simply skip the Refusal altogether. Instead, ensure the story starts with a *fait accompli*: it's a done deal. The adventure's already happening to them. The player is already aboard the story train, and it has left the station.

Alfred Hitchcock's film *North by Northwest* (1959) sidesteps the Refusal by simply kidnapping the protagonist into the role of hero. Roger Thornhill (impeccably played by Cary Grant) is a Manhattan advertising executive who gets mistaken for government spy George Kaplan and is kidnapped by villains.

When the villains interrogate him, the baffled and cranky Thornhill denies all knowledge of Kaplan, just like a spy would. He survives a murder attempt, then ends up in the frame for another murder. This kicks off a locomotive cross-country adventure where Thornhill escapes pursuit by acting like *he thinks* a secret agent would.

George Kaplan, it turns out, was himself a fiction: a red herring created by the government as a distraction from their real operation. Thornhill accidentally embodied the character and attracted the attention of the villains. Later Thornhill willingly steps into the role of Kaplan in order to fool the villains, and finally he transcends the role altogether, escaping the government handlers who have co-opted his identity, and saving the day for real.

North by Northwest is constructed around *faits accomplis*: Thornhill is continually kidnapped, cornered and pushed into situations with no opportunity to Refuse. Stubbornly improvising his way out of situations, Thornhill becomes more relatable and more glamorous than any of the film's legit spies, until finally, at the climax he willingly embodies the role of a true hero, and risks his life when it really counts to rescue love interest Eva Marie Saint. He "fakes it till he makes it".

This is good inspiration for augmented *faits accomplis*. "Kidnapping" the player lets them know they're already implicated in the adventure. They're already a protagonist *in medias res*. As the AR designer Heather Dunaway Smith says,

> If I make a digital flood [in AR], then as the waters rise that will feel like a personal, borderline dangerous experience for that person, even though they're clearly going to be fine.... The whole point is that when you have objects or experiences or events that happen next to your body, they take on personal meaning. They just do. And it's one of the most powerful and exciting aspects of AR storytelling.[27]

It's not the **plausibility** of the digital flood which makes it emotive – as we've seen, real jeopardy is hard to augment. It's the player's involvement which is emotive – and they are already involved, the flood is happening. Like with the VR shark cage, an ongoing scenario has been created and the player's body is already up to their neck in it; their visceral gut reactions are both authentic and in-fiction.

When players discover an augmented story has already begun, they find themselves already inside the fourth wall, already embodied. Everything they're already doing is now in-character, **diegetic**, the act of a protagonist. Thornhill has to "fake it till he makes it"; with *faits accomplis* you can skip augmented players straight to "already making it" as the hero of the story.

CHALLENGE #7: CONSTRUCTING *"NORTH BY NORTHWEST* MOMENTS"

Goal: Explore ways to bring augmented players into events already in motion through *faits accomplis*.

SUMMARY

Identify an everyday activity the player could be doing while alone. They could be sitting in a bar, shopping in a supermarket, or washing the dishes. You're now going to **interrupt the player** via narrative.

Conceptualise a scenario which places a duty or demand upon the player and has in-story **consequences** if they **refuse**. This could be anything from "follow a secret agent out of the bar" to "build a crockery assault course for fairies". Present it as a *fait accompli*: it's happening, whether the player likes it or not.

Identify a medium to convey the narrative. You could send in-character text messages to the player's phone, play dialogue via a smart speaker, or augment fairies onto their dish rack via a headset.

Think about why the *fait accompli* is happening to the player. Is it a case of mistaken identity? Are they a destined Chosen One? Are they just in the right place at the right time?

Write short narration or dialogue for the moment the player is interrupted. Remember you are bringing them into an in-progress story. Introduce the demand and the consequences as *faits accomplis*.

Finally, **identify** how and why the player could **refuse**. Could they ignore the dialogue? Stop washing the dishes and walk away? Assume you could reliably detect **refusal**; **outline** how your narrative would respond to this **refusal**.

TASKS

- **Identify** an everyday, solitary activity which you will **interrupt**.
- **Conceptualise** a scenario with a demand on the player and **consequences** if they **refuse**.
- **Identify** a medium/technology to interrupt the player and communicate the scenario.
- **Write** a short narration of the moment the player is interrupted. Introduce the demand and consequences.
- **Identify** 3x ways the player could **refuse**.
- For each **refusal**, outline how your narrative responds.

(Note that using *faits accomplis* is just one approach to getting players on-board an *in medias res* narrative; immersive theatre impresario Owen Kingston argues for "Debate" as an equivalent story beat to Refusal in interactive theatre, allowing players to willingly opt-in. More on Kingston's "Adaptive Narrative" beat structure in Appendix C.)

FAIT ACCOMPLI PHRASES

There are certain phrases which will instantly throw our IMAGINATIONS into overdrive and change our relationship to everything around us. "Get in the car, you're being kidnapped" works like this, but so do phrases like

You're being watched.
I know what you did.
Try to act normal.

Try to act normal is particularly powerful yet completely non-specific. It could mean you're in danger, or simply that other people are disappointed in you. These phrases play on BEING SEEN, our sensitivity to social situations. Sidle up to someone at a party and whisper "look, just try to act *normal*", and you've ruined that person's night.

As a rule, augmented/spatial narrative is ill-suited to delivering large chunks of exposition. Starting an augmented narrative with an emotive, gut-reaction *fait accompli* phrase like "try to act normal' allows us to hotwire the player, bypassing any need to TELL them who they are in-fiction. They cut straight to already BEING a player-character – someone who's instinctively trying to act normal, playing along with the fiction. They activate gut reaction emotions, and those emotions are both authentic and **diegetic**.

This is helpful because maintaining a boundary between "in-character" and "out-of-character" is a big part of why **roleplaying** is daunting for many potential players. With *faits accomplis*, however the player authentically reacts **is diegeticized** into their player-character.

In this chapter we've begun developing techniques to stimulate players to IMAGINE an augmented scenario. But we can already see how much of the player's IMAGINING focuses on the augmented version of themselves who is participating in the scenario.

The player's experience of BEING themselves is part of their ongoing mental process of narrative-making. And it's a key part of their experience that's available for us to augment. So let's move on to the second pillar of Augmenting Players: IDENTITY-BUILDING.

IMAGINING: SUMMARY

How do we activate the player's IMAGINATION to help the augmented/spatial technology to STAGE the story?

- *Collaborate, don't overwrite. You can rely on the player's IMAGINATION to co-create and fill in gaps and ambiguities. Subjectivity makes experiences more authentic.*
- *Understand that immersion is a pre-existing condition. Augmented scenarios should be "commersive" with players" immediate context, allowing them to imaginatively hybridise the digital and physical.*
- *In effect all augmented/spatial narratives begin **in medias res**. Stimulate the player to IMAGINE a modified version of their situation.*

Augmented/spatial narratives must:

- *Be compatible with what the player can sense around them,*

- *Include space for the player and inspire their imagination and participation,*
- *Be in-progress and maintain continuity with the player's ongoing experience.*

How do we collaborate with the player's IMAGINATION so the story feels anchored in their own reality?

- *Build **plausibility**, but remember it's not the same as realism. Use **merged reality moments** to anchor your story layer.*
- *Make sure your story layer is a **desirable** way to SEE and BE in the world: purpose, stakes, secrecy and exclusivity all work well.*
- *Use **Faits accomplis** to put your players on the story train: look for **North by Northwest** moments.*

NOTES

1. Murray, 1997, p. 110.
2. Brooks, 2003, p. 4–5.
3. Murray, 1997, p. 110.
4. Lucho Lingan *et al.*, 2021.
5. *Ibid.*
6. Jessica Creane, "Let the Magic Circle Bleed", *Gamevironments* 15, 2021.
7. Speakman, 2019.
8. *Ibid.*
9. *Ibid.*
10. Simon von der Au, Philipp A. Rauchsnabel, Reto Felix, Chris Hinsch, "Context in augmented reality marketing: Does the place of use matter", *Psychology & Marketing* 40(11), 2023.
11. *Ibid.*
12. Machon, 2013, p. 25.
13. Joon Moon, *Augmented Shadow: Chasing Stars in Shadow,* 2022. https://joonmoon.net/Chasing-Stars-in-Shadow.
14. Joon Moon, *Augmented Shadow: Inside,* 2020. https://www.joonmoon.net/Inside
15. Miguel de Cervantes, *Don Quixote* I.XXI, trans. J.M. Cohen, Penguin Classics, London 1950, p. 204.
16. *Ibid.*
17. *Ibid.*
18. *Ibid.*, ch. XXII.
19. Steven Conway, "FIFA: Magic Circle", *How to Play Video Games* eds. Matthew Thomas Payne, Nina B. Huntemann (eds.) NYU Press, New York 2019.
20. John Fowles, *The Magus,* 1965, Vintage Classics 2004.
21. GDC Microtalks, 2015.
22. Mattie Brice, "Death of the Player", 2013. http://www.mattiebrice.com/death-of-the-player/.

23. NPC (slang): "someone who is perceived as lacking independent thought or blindly follow-ing trends." Later.com Social Media Management, https://later.com/social-media-glossary/npc/

24. *Coming Out*, Playlines & Roundhouse Radio with support from NESTA, 2016; *CONSEQUENCES,* Harry Shotta & Playlines, 2018.

25. Lucas Seastrom, "Mythic Discovery Within the Inner Reaches of Outer Space: Joseph Campbell Meets George Lucas", starwars.com, 22 Oct 2015.
https://www.starwars.com/news/mythic-discovery-within-the-inner-reaches-of-outer-space-joseph-campbell-meets-george-lucas-part-i.

26. Thanks to Christopher Morrison for this well-attested but unproven quote.

27. Heather Dunaway Smith, "AR Design Principles: How to Create Immersive Experiences", Adobe MAX lectures, 28 Oct 2022, https://www.adobe.com/max/2021/sessions/ar-design-principles-how-to-create-immersive-exper-s478.html.

IDENTITY-BUILDING **2.2**

How do we co-create the augmented player's in-fiction IDENTITY?

What makes a good player-character IDENTITY?

How do we get players to self-identify as their in-fiction IDENTITY?

NOT QUITE YOURSELF

As we saw in 1.2, in VR narratives the player's experience is defined not just by what they're SEEING but by who they're BEING. When creating any immersive media, some of the first questions the storyteller needs to ask are *WHO is the audience in this story? What is their role? How does the story communicate this to them?*

WHERE is the audience? is usually a simpler question. In VR creating a sense of BEING in a simulated location is crucial to immersion. But in augmented/spatial media the audience is already situated *somewhere* before the story begins: their local reality. Everything the player sees and senses around them is **diegetic** until they're told otherwise. Not just their location, but also the body they're in and their experience of BEING themselves. As Duncan Speakman said, "if [the player] still has a sensation of… the body they inhabit, can you really ignore that?"

And the player's experience of BEING somewhere, virtual or otherwise, is inextricably tied up with their ongoing experience of BEING *someone*. We're now going to examine techniques for helping players to play as different "someones" in different augmented narratives. Augmenting IDENTITY is probably the most complex concept we're going to examine in this book. To keep things simple, we'll break it down into its components. First, what is an "augmented IDENTITY"?

IDENTITY is the context through which we experience reality and one of the interfaces through which we interact with reality. In VR, an avatar's virtual hands embody the player in the simulation, AND are the player's primary interface with virtual objects. In the same way, in AR/spatial narratives the player's augmented IDENTITY is a key character in the story, and also the player's interface with the story. This is true whether the player is playing a slightly-augmented version of themselves, or **roleplaying** a fully-characterised persona.

So *WHO ARE* augmented players? Immersive theatre practitioners call their audiences everything from "visitors" and "audience-participants" to "playing-audience" and "guest performers".[1] In performance art, the audience's IDENTITY "alternates between that of a passive consumer, and that of a witness, an associate, a client, a guest, a co-producer and a protagonist".[2]

Audience-participant. Spectator-producer. Consumer-protagonist. An augmented player is a character within the story, the narrator of the story (i.e. the perspective or aperture through which the story gets told), AND the audience of the story. But how much are they "themselves"?

To date, AR experiences generally haven't projected strong player-character IDENTITIES onto players, instead offering simple character silhouettes like the "Agent" and "Pokemon Trainer" personae in Niantic LBGs *Ingress* and *Pokémon GO*. These don't ask players to **roleplay** too heavily: *Ingress*'s Agent personae draw on broad, tropey espionage/thriller archetypes, and part of *Pokémon GO*'s success is because it piggybacked on a well-established childhood fantasy. As John Hanke says, being a Pokémon trainer "is a fantasy that, in many cases, people are already in love with".[3]

These fantasies are broad and flexible enough that they can sit on top of a player's own IDENTITY; players imagine *themselves* as Pokémon Trainers. (In fact research shows that being able to represent your own IDENTITY via LBG avatars is a priority for players, particularly for people whose IDENTITIES are underrepresented.[4])

Effective augmented IDENTITIES always contain elements of the player's own IDENTITY, because their IDENTITY is part of their ongoing embodied experience. It's where their emotions are grounded. Many AR/spatial experiences simply treat the player as themselves, or as a slightly-alternate-reality version of themselves to whom the story is happening. We'll call this approach where the player-character is a slightly fictionalised version of themselves **protagonist-agnostic** (or just **protagnostic**). **Protagonist-anostic** means that the player could be anyone, and therefore so could the player-character.

This is distinct from **roleplaying** approaches, where the player embodies a characterised player-character defined within the world of the story.

- *Protagonist-agnostic:* Player plays themselves (with minor augmentations).
- *Roleplay:* Player plays a fictional persona characterised by the story.

PROTAGONIST-AGNOSTIC VS. ROLEPLAY IDENTITIES

In **protagonist-agnostic** experiences the player finds themselves as-themselves in an augmented scenario. *Pokémon GO* is primarily **protagnostic**, because your experience of playing it is primarily the experience of BEING yourself walking through your neighbourhood. The game augments in-fiction **objectives** on to that experience, as well as the broad IDENTITY of Trainer. Any additional IDENTITY augmented onto the player is superficial (though players could choose to **roleplay** more if they want).

In **roleplaying** augmented IDENTITIES, the **roleplayer** adopts and embodies a persona different to their own, usually one which has already been more-or-less characterised by the story world. Combined with AI, AR technology is increasingly able to visually reskin players' bodies to give them a visual IDENTITY, so we're likely to see augmented players stepping into **roleplay** IDENTITIES more often.

MOST augmented IDENTITIES exist on a spectrum between **protagnostic** and **role-playing,** incorporating elements of the player's self plus fictional characterisation. Which is fitting, as IDENTITIES often shift and change in reality as well as fiction. In the real world, performing and shifting IDENTITIES is one of the most interesting parts of being human.

Protagonist-Agnostic Identities: Possible Selves

In a **protagnostic** narrative, players play "themselves". But they may nonetheless internalise minor IDENTITY augmentations to **diegeticize** themselves into the fiction (or to bring the fiction into their reality). The AR game *Five Nights at Freddy's: Special Delivery* (2019) *fait accompli*'s the player into a horror story: the story purports to be happening to *you*, but a version of you who signed up for a deadly delivery service. Why exactly "you" signed up to this service isn't clear, but it's a plausible-enough "possible self".

Other games provide minor but aspirational IDENTITY augmentations, because an aspirational "possible self" is easy to internalise. Many people want To Be The Very Best, Like No-one Ever Was. The pervasive social game *SFZero* (c.2006) gave players social tasks including meeting new people and exploring their city. The game specified that your player-character "looks exactly the same as you, [has] all the same skills and attributes as you, and even the same memories and feelings", except this possible self "is able to do things that you may be unable or unwilling to do yourself[5]… things like fear, lethargy and the police don't prevent your character from achieving their goals".

Psychologists Hazel Markus and Paula Nurius (1986) argue that imagined "possible selves" are critical to our psychological processes of self-assessment and goal-formation.

> Possible selves represent individuals' ideas of what they might become, what they would like to become, and what they are afraid of becoming, and thus provide a conceptual link between cognition and motivation. Possible selves are the cognitive components of hopes, fears, goals, and threats.[6]

Markus and Nurius give an example (which feels a little close to home): "the assistant professor who fears he or she will not become an associate professor carries with him or her much more than just a shadowy, undifferentiated fear." They are likely to conceptualise "a well-elaborated possible self", a future version of their IDENTITY they can imagine "as having failed, as looking for another job, as bitter, as a writer who can't get a novel published."[7]

Markus and Nurius argue that conceptualising these personal "possible selves" is crucial to how we form goals, like the goal of becoming an associate professor. That IDENTITY certainly feels personal to Markus and Nurius, right? As they say, "there is a piece of self in that goal space".[8] Our brains personalise our goals by IMAGINING possible *as-if* versions of our IDENTITY. We dramatise a story, not just IMAGINING possible futures but IMAGINING them *as-if* they're happening *to us*.

"Possible selves" seem to be rooted in goal-setting. So creating **objectives** and motivations is key to helping players to incarnate a compelling augmented version of their own IDENTITY inside an augmented narrative.

If your experience has gameplay **mechanics**, then these will likely shape the player's **objectives** (more on **mechanics** and **objectives** in Appendix C). But motivations are more complex. To incarnate an augmented IDENTITY, to know WHO they're BEING, players need a strong sense of WHY they're participating in the narrative.

Even gameplay-heavy experiences like Escape Rooms need to supply players with in-story motivations if they want to build a narrative. These narrative motivations can be basic and reactive: *you are trapped. Escape* is the most basic ur-narrative of all Escape Rooms. But sophisticated Escape Room narratives might require players to internalise active motivations, like taking part in a heist. Charles Melcher discussed this idea with Victor van Doorn, co-founder of groundbreaking Escape Room designers Sherlocked, in 2023:

MELCHER: *In traditional storytelling, there always has to be a motivation for the character that's consistent with their arc… [In Escape Rooms] the actions of the guests, of the players, those actions have to have the same consistency of motivation, right? They have to be woven into the fabric of the story; you're doing some random puzzle but your physical actions and challenges are moving the narrative forward or fit in with an integrity into the narrative.*

VAN DOORN: *Well said. [Player motivations] have to make sense because if they don't, on some level you will be taken out of the story and then the immersion is broken.*[9]

Making player motivations compelling means stimulating players to conceptualise "possible selves", such as IMAGINING a "possible self" who has escaped or completed a heist. Even when players are "playing themselves", like in an Escape Room, this is crucial to emotional immersion.

Conceptualising these "selves" helps players internalise **diegetic** motivations. Storytellers need to ask, how is this successful "possible self" different from the player's current self? Are they wealthy, famous, or simply out-of-danger? The storyteller then needs to give the player enough information that they can imagine the "possible self" who has completed the story successfully – and a "possible self" who failed. This means taking the *purpose* and *stakes* of the story and encouraging players to humanise and internalise them in terms of their in-story IDENTITY. By working backwards from their in-fiction "possible selves", players are better able to incarnate and embody a version of themselves who plays along with the narrative. This is their **diegetic** IDENTITY: themselves, but augmented with motivation.

CHALLENGE #8: PROTAGONIST-AGNOSTIC IDENTITY: MESSAGE FROM A "POSSIBLE SELF"

Goal: Augment the player's everyday **IDENTITY** with a message from a future "possible self".

Conceptualise a secret characteristic, aspect or trait which can be augmented onto the player's **IDENTITY**. They could have superpowers, be a mythical Chosen One or secretly be a ghost.

Your player isn't currently aware of their secret characteristic. They will receive a message from the future revealing the secret and describing the player's future self. **Select** the **medium** of the message: it could be a voicemail, a note hidden in a book or an AR encounter with a time traveller.

Establish an **objective** for the player to fulfil. The player's future self might need their help. Or their future self might have become dangerous or evil, and need stopping. How does the message motivate the player to fulfil the objective? How does the "possible self" impact the player? Will they want to fulfil or avoid this possible version of themself?

Develop the **IDENTITY** of the player's future self. **Outline** in bullet points how the secret characteristic has changed them and their life. Be as **protagonist-agnostic** as possible: the secret characteristic should be compatible with whoever your player happens to be.

Write the message from the future. Communicate how the secret characteristic has changed the player. Are they a jaded superhero or regretful supervillain? Are they a ghost? How do you make this message **protagnostic**?

TASKS

- **Conceptualise** a secret characteristic, aspect or trait.
- **Select** your **medium.**
- **Develop** the **IDENTITY** of the player's future self with the characteristic. Keep it **protagnostic**.
- **Write** a message communicating an **objective** to the player.

BONUS CHALLENGE

Test the message with various friends. How **protagnostic** is it? Do they find it **plausible** as a "possible self"? Ask them to write their own messages from the future using the same secret characteristic.

Roleplay Identities: Performance of Self

As AR technologies proliferate, especially combined with AI, we're likely to see massive increases in our capacity to visually reskin players' bodies and superimpose fantastical visual IDENTITIES onto them. Furthermore, not all stories can feature agnostic, everyperson protagonists; some stories need to characterise the player with a backstory or role which they ask the player to **roleplay.**

But **roleplaying** is a daunting prospect for many players. It invokes anxieties of performance and BEING SEEN. It feels too much like making-believe, which we're all supposed to have grown out of, right? But in psychological and sociological terms, even when we're "BEING ourselves" we're usually also **roleplaying** an IDENTITY to others.

In the groundbreaking sociological text *The Presentation of the Self in Everyday Life* (1956) Erving Goffman pioneered the idea that "we are constantly projecting a definition of [a] situation and thereby making an implicit or explicit claim to be a person of a particular kind".[10] Research shows that children from the age of two rehearse this social identity-performance by adopting and blending multiple personae in play.[11]

Think about the kinds of roles and personae we commonly see in fiction. They're often roles which have an inherent drama or which are given a special sense of purpose or significance in society. As Goffman points out,

> The roles of prizefighters, surgeons, violinists, and policemen… allow for so much dramatic self-expression that exemplary practitioners—whether real or fictional—become famous and are given a special place in the commercially organized phantasies of the nation.[12]

To most adult players these roles – athlete, doctor, artist, cop – would be a challenging proposition to **roleplay** out in the real world. As job descriptions, they all imply knowledge or competency to which the player may not have access. Players may not feel confident **roleplaying** as a doctor (or impersonating a cop) because this implies qualifications, authority and social signifiers. Similarly, there might be implied skills (or the risk of embarrassment) in making-believe you're an athlete or an artist. Superficially, these roles seem to set a high bar for **roleplay**.

Yet these types of roles are exactly those we see most often dramatised in books, TV, films, games and other "commercially organised phantasies".

Roleplay is not the same as impersonation. To understand how to get augmented players **roleplaying** we need to understand why roles like these are so often dramatised.

Each of these roles implies heightened *purpose* and *stakes*, but also increased conflict, commitment and confrontation compared to most "job descriptions". It's the dramatic, emotive yet relatable predicaments which these roles imply which make them so apt for dramatisation – and much easier to **roleplay** than they first seem. Compellingly **roleplaying** a doctor doesn't require a player to impersonate the competencies of a doctor – it requires them to internalise the potential *conflicts* of a doctor.

Five C's of Compelling Roleplay Characterisation

What makes a compelling **roleplay** IDENTITY? What kinds of information do players need to understand WHO they are BEING?

In 2009 John Harper, creator of the tabletop roleplaying game *Blades in the Dark*, outlined "Four C's of Character" for **roleplaying**: *Connections, Capabilities, Commitments* and *Conflict.*[13]

LARP creator Chloe Mashiter subsequently adapted the Four C's for LARP **roleplaying** and added a fifth C, *Comfort.*

LARP or Live Action Roleplaying is an embodied form of **roleplay**: as Mashiter says, "you're doing what your character is doing… You're not sat around a table describing what you're doing, you are BEING that character – that's the live aspect".[14] The IDENTITY play of **roleplaying** is particularly heightened in LARP because the player is embodied as themselves, so Mashiter's adaptation is highly relevant for digitally augmenting IDENTITY.

- *Connections* – How is the character related to the world? Who do they know? What things are they associated with? What are their most important relationships?
- *Capabilities* – What can the character do in the world? What resources or influence can they access? What do other characters think they might be capable of?

- *Commitments* – What are the character's principles? What are their loyalties? What people or things exert an influence or power over them? Is the player **roleplaying** these commitments, or are they carried over from the player's ordinary self?
- *Conflict* – How do the above three stand in tension? How might they clash? Do they want something they aren't capable of? Are their loyalties divided?
- *Comfort* – What stands between what the storyteller wants players to do, and what players might be naturally comfortable with? What non-**diegetic** social norms, access needs, preconceptions (and more) might you have to account for to empower players to play?

Harper/Mashiter's **Five C's of Characterisation** are a great way to generate characters who are more than just a job description. They have complex wants and needs, shoulds and shouldn'ts, principles and compromises.

Take the iconic roles identified by Goffman. By incorporating *Conflicting Connections, Capabilities* and *Commitments*, a **roleplayer** gets all the benefit of these roles' iconic familiarity, and can concentrate on their character's conflicts without worrying about their competencies. This greatly improves the *Comfort* of the **roleplay**.

Roleplaying a cop might be daunting, but adding a *Conflict* between their *Connections* and *Capabilities* might mean **roleplaying** a *disgraced* cop. This is an emotive and relatable predicament, not a job description. The player can focus on embodying an in-progress IDENTITY instead of the potentially un-*comfortable* situation of impersonating the police.

Players may struggle to IMAGINE themselves BEING a heavyweight boxer, but by adding a *Conflict* between *Capabilities* and *Commitments* we might have a boxer *who has lost their nerve*. Now the player's **roleplay** is not focused on impersonation, but on emoting and empathising.

As Goffman says, the roles above are all in a sense public performances. Harper/Mashiter's **Five C's** add drama and relatability by introducing elements of BEING SEEN – tension between characters' inner and outer lives. This core tension between self and SEEN-self is fundamentally relatable, whatever the job description, and this helps players to imagine and perform a "performed self" who is very far from their own "possible selves".

Effectively a **roleplayer** is drawing on their own emotions and IDENTITY when playing a "performed self". It's more heavily characterised than a protagonist-agnostic "possible self", but still fundamentally draws on the player's self to help them perform as a player-character.

Three techniques for building augmented IDENTITY

"Possible selves" and "performed selves" give us a framework for understanding how players can co-create and relate to augmented IDENTITIES, both as **protagonist-agnostic** and **roleplay** characters.

For the remainder of this chapter, we'll apply these ideas to augmented/spatial reality. We'll examine how media including ancient drama, immersive theatre, videogames and theme parks establish characters, and adapt these into techniques for establishing augmented player-character IDENTITY. Finally we'll examine the phenomena of **conceptual blending**: how players construct hybrid IDENTITIES through both real and imagined components, and how this helps build player-character **complicity**.

Discovering IDENTITY: Augmented *Anagnorisis*
Asserting IDENTITY: Augmented *Mise-en*-self
Blending IDENTITIES & building complicity

Discovering IDENTITY: Augmented *Anagnorisis*

In AR stories, you can't simply tell the player who they are, or why they should care about what's happening. Their continuity of experience with unaugmented reality, and the 'pieces of self' they bring into the experience, mean it's too big a jump to simply impose a character upon them and ask them to play along. But allowing players to *discover* their in-fiction IDENTITY allows us to spirit the player across the border between ordinary self and augmented self, without them consciously beginning the daunting process of **roleplay**. Even if you're asking the player to **roleplay** an augmented IDENTITY, if the player discovers they're *already* embodying that IDENTITY, they haven't had to step through the fourth wall, or worse, step from the darkness of the wings out onto a spotlit stage. They're already on-stage, performing a version of themself, which is something they do every day.

This IDENTITY-discovery is the AR/spatial equivalent of the VR mirror moments we looked at in 1.2, like the IDENTITY-discovery experience in *Travelling While Black*. Literary criticism already has a technical term for this dramatic discovery-of-IDENTITY: *anagnorisis*.

In ancient Greek *anagnorisis* specifically means recognition of a person or their nature. In the *Poetics* (c.335 BCE), the founding text of media criticism, Aristotle used it to describe moments in drama when a character discovers their own IDENTITY.

In Euripedes' *Medea* (c.431 BCE), the audience sees Medea decide to kill her children. Medea knows they are her children, and after much exposition she does indeed kill them. The audience was likely familiar with the myth of Medea so they already knew the ending, and the play didn't construct an *anagnorisis* or IDENTITY-discovery.

Aristotle criticises *Medea* for lacking emotional impact, and contrasts it with Sophocles' more emotive *Oedipus Rex* (c.429 BCE). We-the-audience know that Oedipus is going to unknowingly kill his father and marry his mother, so there's dramatic irony because we know something Oedipus doesn't. Better still, the play constructs a moment of *anagnorisis*: the climax of the play is not the murder, nor the marriage, but the moment we see Oedipus realise who he is and what he's done. (Similar *anagnorisis* moments occur throughout literature, from *King Lear* to (spoilers) *Game of Thrones*.)

ANAGNORISIS AND DRAMATIC IRONY

Dramatic irony is when the audience knows something the characters don't. In passive media like film or theatre this creates a pleasing dramatic tension: the audience knows there's a monster behind the door, but the characters don't, so it's emotive when the characters unwittingly approach the door.

But dramatic irony is difficult to pull off in interactive media when the player has agency. If the player knows there is a monster behind the door, and the story-teller wants their player-character to walk through the door anyway, you're asking the player to **roleplay** ignorance. This forces the player up against a hard boundary between their meta-knowledge (*"there is a monster behind the door"*) and their **diegetic** knowledge (*"my player-character does not know what's behind the door"*).

It can be fun to play with fiction and meta-fiction: reality TV stars, VTubers and Pro Wrestlers do it all the time. But in interactive media where the audience has agency, dramatic irony requires them to enforce a fourth wall within them-selves. The player must imaginatively divide what they know from what their character knows. If the player can't do this successfully, it feels like having their agency curtailed – *"why does my character HAVE to walk through the door?"*.

But *anagnorisis*/discovery-of-IDENTITY can function without dramatic irony. The famous "Shyamalan" twist endings of *The Sixth Sense* (1999) and *Unbreakable* (2000) are both realisations of self-IDENTITY that come as a sur-prise to both audience and protagonist. *Bioshock* (2007) adapts an *anagnorisis*-twist into videogames; a key moment of IDENTITY-realisation is a shock to both player and player-character.

Constructing moments of *anagnorisis* is a powerful technique for conveying IDENTITY to a player. Like the IDENTITY-discoveries in *Portal* and *Driving While Black*, the moment of discovery can come with the satisfaction of a puzzle solved, or be an empathy-building experience like BEING in a racialised IDENTITY. This moment is embodied through the experience of BEING the IDENTITY, not getting *told* or shown who you're supposed to be. It's like the establishing moment which tells you who a movie character is – but here the player discovers they're already successfully BEING the IDENTITY.

Let's try constructing a moment of augmented *anagnorisis*.

CHALLENGE #9: *ANAGNORISIS:* MISPLACED IDENTITY

Goal: Explore augmented *anagnorisis* techniques by "discovering" an **IDENTITY**.

SUMMARY

Identify a room in your own home. Think about what the objects in the room might say about you (or others who share the space).

Conceptualise a scenario in which a fictional character visits your home. Based on the objects in your home, this character will mistakenly imagine a completely fictional, **false IDENTITY** for you. They might mistake you for a spy, a superhero or an alien.

Think about what kind of character, under what circumstances, could imagine this **false IDENTITY**. Use the **Five C's** to **outline** that character. Maybe they're a paranoid spy who sees patterns in innocuous objects; a journalist who's convinced you are a superhero; or an alien anthropologist who doesn't understand humans.

The **false IDENTITY** should be anchored to objects. **Outline** how one or more objects suggested the **false IDENTITY** to the fictional character.

Think about how small changes could recontextualise the room and help suggest the **false IDENTITY**. How could you completely change the apparent IDENTITY of the room's occupant with the smallest number of changes? Could you do it by writing on a whiteboard, hiding a note, or playing a soundtrack?

TASKS

- **Identify** a room in your home.
- **Conceptualise** a scenario in which a character visits your home and imagines a **false IDENTITY**.
- **Outline** the character using the **Five C's:** *Connections, Capabilities, Commitments, Conflict* and *Comfort*.
- **Outline** how one or more objects in the room led to the character imagining the **false IDENTITY**.

BONUS CHALLENGE

Now, the twist: the character is correct! Your own IDENTITY is actually an illusion, and the **false IDENTITY** is your true self. I'm sorry you had to find out this way.

How did this happen? How does this affect you? What is your future now that you have discovered your true IDENTITY?

Outline your true self's character using the **Five C's**. Anchor the realisation-of-IDENTITY to an object in the room and **write** a short dialogue or narration depicting the *anagnorisis.*

Anagnorisis and character development

In 2.1, we looked at *fait accompli* **phrases** as a tool for sparking IMAGINATION. Often they work by discovering to the player an augmented IDENTITY they're already embodying. This is what's happening when you sneak up to a player and whisper in their ear, "you are secretly a dragon". If they imaginatively engage with BEING a secret dragon, you have recontextualised their relationship to themselves and the world around them.

"You're a secret dragon" might seem like a major augmentation to IDENTITY, but it's primarily **protagnostic** because suddenly everything the player is already doing is in-character as a secret dragon.

Nonetheless this type of *fait accompli* IDENTITY-discovery can be the beginning of a character arc where players develop more characterisation of their augmented IDENTITY and even begin to **roleplay**. Once the player is onboard a *fait accompli*, you can then begin to help the player IMAGINE and embody what their new in-fiction IDENTITY is like. Over the course of a storyline you can develop an initially highly **protagnostic** character, whom the player is comfortable playing, into a character who has been changed by the storyline. At the end of a storyline the player may find themselves playing an IDENTITY which has developed characterisation and is differentiated from the player's IDENTITY – as different as mundane grump Roger Thornhill at the start of *North by Northwest* is from heroic survivor Roger Thornhill at the end. Starting with *anagnorisis*/IDENTITY-discovery means players can build upon their own IDENTITY while you take them through a heroic arc. Their arc will be all the more compelling because they were themselves to begin with – and can become a "possible self" by the end.

Exclusivity and *secrecy* can also be powerful forces in *anagnorisis*. If the player discovers they're a secret dragon, they're also automatically embodying a glamorous secret. This is a kind of inverse dramatic irony: the player experiences the thrill of being privy to information or context that others can't access.

That *I-know-something-you-don't* feeling is compelling even if your secret knowledge is part of a fiction. In his visionary 2008 short story "To Hie From Far Cilenia", Karl Schroeder depicted a hidden global underworld of augmented reality layers: *"Millions of kids around the world put virtual overlays and geographical positioning information over the real planet, and made up complicated games"*.[15] There are players who consider themselves to have no citizenship other than the transnational perceptual layer they're part of; characters who have many bodies and who play freely across genders, identities and national borders. Players of one game layer, *Rivet Couture,* enter a gaslight Victorian reskin of reality, with "ghostly" overlays of Victorian floral wallpaper and brass gas fixtures.

[Players] walked alone in the ordinary streets of Berlin or Minneapolis, yet at the same moment they walked side by side through the misty cobblestoned streets of a Victorian Atlantis. Many of them spent their spare time filling in the details of the places, designing the clothes and working out the history.[16]

These perceptual "overmappings" are complete, coherent realities with their own social dynamics and functioning economies, invisible to the vast majority of people. Players can construct parallel IDENTITIES for themselves – and discover they're BEING SEEN in those identities by a select few others. The narrator likens the effect to wearing lingerie under business clothes, giving "much the same sense of owning a secret uniqueness".[17]

CHALLENGE #10: *ANAGNORISIS*: DISCOVERING SECRET IDENTITY

Goal: Explore ways to have players discover secret **IDENTITIES**.

SUMMARY

Using the **Five C's, develop** a **roleplay IDENTITY** for the player-character. The player will start as themselves, then discover their new **roleplay IDENTITY**.

Conceptualise a secret characteristic, aspect or trait as part of the **role-play IDENTITY**. Your player-character could have superpowers, be a mythical Chosen One or secretly be a ghost. The player-character is NOT aware of this characteristic.

Outline an *anagnorisis* scenario where a secondary character visits the player in their **own home** and deliberately or accidentally reveals the player-character's secret characteristic. The secret should change the way they relate to the world around them.

Write a short narration or dialogue showing the moment of *anagnorisis*.

TASKS

- Using the **Five C's**, develop a **roleplay** IDENTITY with a secret characteristic.
- **Develop** a secondary character who reveals the secret.
- **Outline** a scene showing this *anagnorisis* moment in **the player's home**.
- **Write** dialogue or narration for the scenario.

BONUS TASK

Now, flash forwards: the same character visits the player's home some time after the *anagnorisis*. It might be days, months or years. Consider how the player's recontextualised perspective might have changed over time. Is the player's hidden characteristic normalised, or still strange? **Write** flashforward narration/dialogue for the scene.

Identity-discovery in immersive theatre

"Immersive theatre" is a broad category comprising many different kinds of experience. Generally speaking immersive theatre breaks down the spatial divides between performer and audience. The audience are, to one extent or another, present in the scene. This creates new and sometimes ambiguous roles and IDENTITIES for players. As immersive theatre practitioner Jason Warren says, "unclear rules of engagement" in immersive theatre can make players "unsure about what is 'allowed' in an immersive production and to what extent they are expected to push the apparent boundaries they are given".[18]

> "Much of the embarrassment a new immersive audience member experiences actually comes from a fear that they will somehow behave in a way that is 'wrong'",[19] disrupting either the play's action or story. Audiences accustomed to more conventional theatre sometimes redraw fourth-wall boundaries themselves, disincluding themselves from the play's action due to "ingrained stay-out-of-the-play's-way behaviour".[20]

Some immersive theatre asks players to **roleplay**, but many of the most successful – including the enormously influential Punchdrunk Theatre – are deliberately structured as **protagonist-agnostic**. Punchdrunk's "masque" productions require audiences to wear anonymising masks, and the play's characters treat them as – mostly – invisible. As theatre creator and researcher Nathan Sibthorpe says,

> in other immersive productions, when a performer-character looks at me I am easily distracted by complex and unexplained interpersonal dynamics – what is this space between my reality and their fiction, between what I bring with me into the space and what their illusion depends on? They have rehearsed their character but I'm trying to guess what version of myself I'm allowed to be here. My unrehearsed, unresearched, untrained presence in their carefully-constructed world feels like an imposition.[21]

In Punchdrunk, wearing a mask removes this anxiety over IDENTITY, and **dieget-icizes** the player:

> I can lose myself in the mask… Our role is that of a ghost – which is mythic in its connection to the story (after all, Punchdrunk's worlds are Greek, Shakespearean, Epic) but also readily understandable in its rules. We can watch, but we cannot influence.[22]

Punchdrunk Artistic Director Felix Barrett describes his inspiration for using masks: while directing a prototypal immersive play as a student

> "four days before [the play] opened, I remember thinking this is good, it's atmospheric. But the audience get in the way. And I had the epiphany: oh my gosh: if we just put the audience in masks suddenly they disappear".[23]

Punchdrunk's masque shows are designed to deliver immersive experiences at scale, to a general audience. Part of the purpose of the masks is to anonymise players to allow them a **protagonist-agnostic** experience while still being **diegetically** present (or semi-present) in the story, albeit as a ghost. For Barrett,

> the Punchdrunk approach is that we want to be a REALLY instinctual experience: you need to be yourself inside the environment… We would never want someone to have to suspend disbelief or to have that layer or buffer of pretending to be another, because I feel that it would be a psychological block…
>
> The mask is one device that allows the audience to be contextualised within the work… Rather than having to pretend you're going through it, or pretend you're a character, it's yourself experiencing it.[24]

That sense of players "losing [them]self in the mask" is due to the absence of any in-story IDENTITY. Players can be physically present in the immersive scene, but are liberated from worrying about performing; this allows players to BE themselves without their IDENTITIES being **diegetically** present in the story.

Nonetheless, even in anonymous masque productions, immersive creators have to ask themselves WHO the audience is. Players may discover their in-story IDENTITY has more significance than they thought. Punchdrunk's masked ghost-audiences are invisible to the performers, EXCEPT at key story moments, such as in *Sleep No More* (2011-) where

Macbeth, haunted by guilt, suddenly is able to see "ghosts" – the masked audience – all around him. The players' IDENTITY is "discovered" by the character and by themselves.

This *anagnorisis* is pivotal: the audience have not simply been hidden voyeurs. They are augmented with an IDENTITY: they are spectres of guilt. But while the masks remove the pressure to **roleplay,** they also provide little opportunity for players to assert their identity or have agency in the story.

Asserting IDENTITY: *Mise-en-self*

Constructing moments of IDENTITY-discovery can be useful in showing players they're already in-character and already in-story. But if you stimulate players to assert their in-story IDENTITY *themselves*, their experience of augmented IDENTITY can be even more emotive.

In cinema, *mise-en-scène* is all the visual elements – sets, lighting, actors – everything which establishes the look of the scene, except the framing itself. When augmenting IDENTITY, the equivalent establishing moment is the *mise-en-self*.

Mise-en-self techniques create space for players to establish, assert and characterise their in-story IDENTITIES. This helps players embody both **protagonist-agnostic** and **roleplay** IDENTITIES.

In the 1980s, theme park performer, writer and consultant Ron Schneider helped originate the character of the Dreamfinder at Disney's Epcot. The Dreamfinder was a magician of imagination, who wore a purple top hat and puppeted a purple dragon called Figment. Schneider writes about developing the beloved character in his remarkable book *From Dreamer to Dreamfinder* (2012). Part of the Dreamfinder's job was to roam the park and engage child guests to talk about the power of their imagination. But Schneider was frustrated by operational reality:

> all anyone wants is to have their picture taken and to get my autograph… how can I get these people to engage with me creatively?

Kids have no problem engaging with magic or blurring imagination into reality, but when confronted by a strange adult, especially one wearing a purple top hat, they tend to want to feel safe from embarrassment. Despite Schneider's efforts to engage, the autograph book gave kids a clear structure for a low-risk social exchange with a magical character, with minimal engagement. They didn't engage in the Dreamfinder's fiction. Until, one day, Schneider "spontaneously react[ed] to a small child as if [he'd] never seen one before". Dreamfinder challenges the child to explain himself, and the child

> grows very serious, and explains to me what he is (a boy named Michael) and where he comes from (Orlando). I act fascinated… and he is suddenly thinking about himself and his life in a new and objective way.[25]

What's a child? Why are you shorter than these other people? Why is a child different to a grown-up? This feigned ignorance became the basic premise of Schneider's Dreamfinder interactions. It emphasises the Dreamfinder's theme – *everyone has the childlike power of imagination*. Plus, Dreamfinder's otherworldly ignorance takes all the risk of embarrassment out of the encounter by placing the child in the role of comedy straight-person.

But most important, asking *what's a child?* challenges the child to self-identify, "turning the spotlight on the child as a unique and wonderful being".[26] This creates a moment of **protagonist-agnostic *mise-en*-self**. The player establishes and asserts their IDENTITY, and does so within the fiction.

The child isn't fictionalising their IDENTITY, but the moment they respond to the question they have already accepted a fictional premise – that the Dreamfinder is so strange and magical that he doesn't know what a child is. Responding to the challenge to self-identify, in asserting their IDENTITY the player "finds themselves" already inside the bubble of the fiction, firmly embodied in their own IDENTITY but situated **diegetically** at the centre of an encounter with a magical being. The autograph book, with its anonymising effect and clear rules of engagement, can be dropped like a mask, while the player's IDENTITY is foregrounded and played with in the fiction.

How does this type of ***mise-en*-self** apply in augmented/spatial narrative? At the start of my career I was a lead game writer at the sadly now-closed PlayStation London Studio, working on the groundbreaking Wizarding World AR game *Wonderbook: Book of Spells* (2012). The game used the Wonderbook peripheral, a physical cardboard book with every page covered in QR code-like markers. The user activated their PlayStation Eye Camera and sat in front of their TV, which showed a live feed of themselves and their room. As the user interacted with the Wonderbook, graphics were augmented onto the book's pages in the live feed. So the player, holding a physical book, saw their ordinary selves in their ordinary room, but holding a graphically-augmented magical spellbook. Gameplay sequences animated a magical origami dragon which flew up from the book, or burned the book with harmless digital fire. The digital experience, and its rendering of magical things, was firmly anchored in reality because of the solidity of the book in the player's hands – an ongoing **merged reality moment**.

When I watched kids test early builds of the game, it struck me that from the player's perspective the story wasn't happening to a character or an avatar. They could see themselves BEING the main character, with the story happening *to* themselves in their real surroundings in realtime. And the narrative addressed them directly, referring to them simply as "you".

So WHO were these players as they were playing?

At the start of the game, we'd found that when asked to "open the book" players often didn't figure out they needed to physically turn the pages; they looked for a button to press on a controller. At the time players found it counterintuitive that manipulating a physical object would affect the digital object on the screen. I'd written an "idle prompt" for this circumstance, i.e. an instructional line which would prompt the player if they didn't open the book. I wrote the line with a strong call-to-action based on a quote from the Wizarding World books:

"Come on, open the book! **Are you a wizard or not?**"

I wondered if this might come off as too aggressive. But, in testing, watching first-time players try the game, I saw this call-to-action work even more strongly than I'd intended. "YES!" kids would shout, grabbing the book and opening it. "Yes, I AM a wizard!"

The players could SEE themselves, as-themselves, in their own living room. But when challenged, players immediately self-identified as a hybrid of their own IDENTITY and a magical, in-fiction IDENTITY.

Like *Pokémon GO* this IDENTITY built on the core fantasy of the IP: that anyone could turn out to be a wizard. The player was already through the fourth wall; in fact the fourth wall was completely transparent and they could SEE themselves on the other side, in-story, holding their spellbook. They didn't have to suspend disbelief, or suspend their own IDENTITY, in order to take on an IDENTITY that belonged in the story. "Wizard" was an augmentation to their existing IDENTITY which could be worn as easily as the wizard hats which many players chose to wear while playing.

Protagonist-agnostic augmented IDENTITIES consist mostly of the player's own IDENTITY, so challenging players to "explain themselves" doesn't disrupt immersion. And questions like *what's a child?* and *are you a wizard or not?* challenge players to actively create moments of assertive self-identification within the fiction.

These **mise-en-*self*** moments allow players to augment **diegetic** elements onto their IDENTITY while maintaining their continuity of experience. What's more, the sense of asserting IDENTITY means the player's **diegetic** presence in the scene is always as an active, assertive participant. They can be confident of one solid, anchoring thing in the fiction – themselves – and the rest of the "rules of engagement" can follow.

CHALLENGE #11: *MISE-EN-*SELF: IDENTITY ASSERTION

Goal: Challenge players to assert their player-character **IDENTITY**.

SUMMARY

Adapt the "secret identity" scenario you created in the previous **CHALLENGE #10**. Now the player-character is well aware of their hidden characteristic.

Using the **Five C's, develop** a secondary character who visits the player in their own home.

Outline a *mise-en*-self scenario in which the secondary character questions or challenges the player-character in a way which motivates the player-character to assert their secret **IDENTITY**. The secondary character could be sceptical about whether magic exists, or simply accuse the player of being a boring nobody.

Remember, don't just *tell* the player who they are: construct a moment which invites them to **assert** their augmented **IDENTITY**.

TASKS

- **Adapt** your CHALLENGE #10 scenario: the player-character is now aware of their hidden characteristic.
- Using the **Five C's Develop** a secondary character.
- **Outline** a scenario which constructs a moment of augmented assertion, challenging the player to self-identify.

Blending IDENTITIES &
Building Complicity

Whether players are playing themselves or **roleplaying**, augmented IDENTITIES aren't all-consuming method-acting performances. Augmented players don't leave behind their own IDENTITIES by entering a "magic circle". Augmented IDENTITIES are complex hybrids, and just like the personae we play in the real world, they're composed partly of fiction and partly of fact. Ensuring a compelling experience of augmented IDENTITY means maintaining that fifth 'C' – *Comfort* – and that means allowing players to control their diegetic involvement and engagement with the character.

In fact, players are in control of their level of **diegesis** whether you like it or not, since they might at any point remove a headset, receive a notification or focus on an extra-diegetic detail in the real environment. Because augmented players always have one foot in the distracting real world, it's best to design augmented narratives which acknowledge that the player is operating on multiple layers, rather than trying to submerge them in a singular seamless fiction. Immersion doesn't have to be all-or-nothing. Immersive Experience Network researchers identify different immersive theatre audience archetypes, who desire different levels of diegetic engagement at different times (sometimes called "paddlers", "swimmers" and "waders"[27]). Similarly, LARP designer Chloe Mashiter argues against trying to achieve "continual immersion" in LARP, likening immersion to being in a swimming pool – continual immersion would get boring and tiring after a while, and "getting in and out of the pool doesn't make being in the pool less enjoyable."[28]

In game design, *lenticular design* means a game is designed to be fun and rewarding for different players at different levels of skill and engagement. In AR, like immersive theatre and LARP, we need to take a *lenticular* approach to immersion, creating experiences which are rewarding for players who swim and submerge deep in immersion, AND players who paddle in and out. While VR aspires to create continuous all-consuming immersion, in AR this approach means that the slightest unpredictable element in the real world – or ordinary emotion within the player - must be **nondiegetic** and immersion breaking. Augmented realities and spatial computing, by definition, appear to be happening in the distracting real world around the player, and happening *TO* their distractable selves. If the player becomes "distracted", we have a choice: we can take this as a break in immersion, treat it as extra-diegetic, and demand the player suppress that part of themselves to fit into the fiction. Or, we can treat the distractable side of themselves as **diegetic** and authentic, and create fictions flexible enough to incorporate unpredictable elements. These fictions can gain authentic real-world serendipity and solidity.

IDENTITY-BUILDING can help us create that fictional/meta-fictional flexibility, and show players that their authentic selves belong in the fiction: we can show them they are *already* performing in-character (*anagnorisis*) or create opportunities for them to assert/perform their character in a self-aware way (*mise-en-self*). Techniques like these allow players, in the words of immersive theatre creator Katie Lyons, to "play with the distance"[29] between themselves, the fiction, and a fictional self.

In 2002 cognitive scientists Fauconnier and Turner developed the idea of "Conceptual Blending" to describe how humans subconsciously blend ideas to conceptualise possible outcomes – in other words, to IMAGINE. Fauconnier and Turner argue we evolved this "**blending**" to improve our survival: "the great evolutionary change that produced cognitively modern human beings" was the capacity to "run off-line cognitive simulations so that evolution did not have to undertake the tedious process of natural selection every time a choice was to be made".[30]

By conceptually **blending** what *is* with what *could be*, humans evolved the ability to plan and hypothesise, as well as to empathise: to IMAGINE other humans' perspectives.

As we've seen, when players have agency it's challenging to authentically **roleplay** dramatic irony. If you, the storyteller, tell your player out-of-character that the seemingly-kindly court wizard is actually the scheming villain, the player might struggle to authentically **roleplay** a character who still trusts the seemingly-kindly wizard.

But of course, trained actors do this all the time. Fauconnier and Turner argue that actors engage in a **blend** in which their "motor patterns and power of speech come directly into play, but not their free will or foreknowledge of the outcome",[31] As theatre scholar Bruce McConachie says,

> before stepping onstage as Hamlet, the actor knows that his character will die at the end of the play, but, performing "in the **blend**" as actor/Hamlet, he suspends that knowledge in his moment-to-moment interactions.[32]

As a result, the actor is in control of their level of **diegesis**. They can live the character, while also drawing on their own IDENTITY for authentic emotion in the performance, while at some level also knowing how it ends.

But allowing the player complete control over their **diegetic** blend might allow them to distance themselves from the emotions at play in the narrative. The player might be able to "**un-blend**" themselves. In her essay *Let the Magic Circle Bleed* Jessica Creane observes that **roleplaying** a new IDENTITY can allow players to "compartmentalise" their in-story actions. "Buy-in to the story ultimately allows us to justify abiding by (or not abiding by) an entirely different social contract than the one we are accustomed to in our out-of-game lives".[33] In other words, an engaged **roleplayer** might do things in-character they never would in real life.

But interactive narratives create their most powerful emotional effects when, via the **blend**, players feel a measure of complicity in their player-character's actions. If the player **roleplays** a villain, but the player can compartmentalise all complicity in their villainous player-character's actions, this risks "thereby absolving the player of contextualizing what their in-game decisions can teach them about their present out-of-game lives".[34]

(Of course, some players want game worlds free from consequence: fantasies of, for example, acquiring criminal wealth and mowing down pedestrians. Impunity simulators like *Grand Theft Auto* serve a purpose in escapism. But these fantasies can't – or shouldn't – be uncritically ported straight into augmented/spatial reality as game layers laid across real streets, where people can physically get hurt.)

Without complicity or emotional consequence, an interactive scenario isn't compelling. VR players are enclosed in a simulation, so they have to calibrate to the level of social consequence – e.g. by getting up in NPCs' grills. But augmented players are pre-immersed in the real world, where cause-and-effect is already very real. If an augmented narrative layer fails to make the player feel complicit in their player-character's actions, it doesn't just make the narrative feel limp; it also fails **plausibility** because it's not authentic to how the real world works.

Sometimes players voluntarily introduce **blending** to *create* complicity. In Chris Harding's early "Walkmanology" interactive theatre, players' actions were tightly scripted. They enacted roles and actions described in the audio layer. This meant players were able to adopt these roles easily: "you can't forget your lines, they're all on the tape; you're not responsible for your performance, you're just doing a job", But this didn't eliminate the player's agency or complicity in their actions: Harding wondered "will people stop playing if they are asked to do morally repugnant acts?"

In Harding's *Artery* (1982) the player was given a specific IDENTITY, "a desperate young man named Jay", and an objective: "steal the girlfriend's necklace". Even if the agency to refuse was only implied, players were still making a choice to comply. And some players "refused to lift the ice and maintained their own moral character".[35] Players who refused to take the necklace weren't "**un-blending**" their IDENTITY from the character of Jay; they were **blending** their own moral character into BEING Jay.

Sometimes *withdrawing* characterisation of a **roleplayed** character at key moments can create greater complicity. In the early VR adventure *The Assembly* (2016), there's a sequence which mimics the famous Milgram Experiment. The player is instructed to repeatedly press a "torture button" which they're told causes pain to an innocent victim. The player, embodied in a VR avatar, was **roleplaying** a characterised, named player-character who spoke throughout the game. I had initially scripted a whole monologue for the player-character to articulate how the "torture button" situation made them feel. But after testing, I ended up removing almost all this dialogue. I didn't want to allow the player to feel "absolved" of their actions while pressing the torture button, by hiding behind a character or being "absolved" by **roleplay**. So the character fell silent, **blending** more of the player's IDENTITY into the scene at the moment of greatest complicity.

In augmented/spatial narrative, complicity has to be situated "in the **blend**" for it to be effective. This means digital events should be securely anchored to physical phenomena, to create the strongest possible sense that the consequences of complicity could affect the player's own body and IDENTITY. Remember, as Dunaway Smith says, "when you have [digital] objects or experiences or events that happen next to your body, they take on personal meaning".[36]

Let's do a complicity-focused CHALLENGE:

CHALLENGE #12: THE TELLTALE AR

Goal: Explore conceptual **blending** to build complicity.

SUMMARY

Develop a new player-character IDENTITY for the player to **roleplay**. It is defined by some guilt, taint or curse which haunts them and changes how the player sees the world.

They could be haunted by memories of a person they wronged, or carry the risk that anyone who gets close to them will die. Outline the IDENTITY's **Five C's.**

Identify a public location, and **identify an everyday sound** (or other phenomenon) which can act as a *leitmotif* or sensory anchor for the guilt/curse. The phenomenon should regularly occur in the location, but the player should also encounter it in other contexts. Birdsong, sirens, train sounds, etc. all work well.

Conceptualise a short scenario for the player to play out in the **public location**. The scenario should draw attention to the *leitmotif* and clearly anchor it to the guilt/curse.

Your goal is to anchor the narrative guilt/curse to the *leitmotif* so strongly that the player cognitively **blends** the real-world phenomenon with in-character emotions.

Even when your narrative is finished, the player should be reminded of the guilt/curse narrative whenever the *leitmotif* recurs in ordinary life.

Outline any characters you need for the scenario and **write** the narration or dialogue, then **test** with an unsuspecting friend.

TASKS

- Using the **Five C's develop** an **IDENTITY** for the player to **roleplay**, defined by a **guilt, taint or curse**.
- Identify a **location** and an everyday phenomenon to act as a *leitmotif.*
- **Conceptualise** a short scenario anchoring the **guilt/curse** to the *leitmotif.*
- **Outline** the scenario.
- **Write** the narration or dialogue
- **Test**.

NOTES

Associating an emotional state with external stimuli is also called *Pavlovian* or *Classical Conditioning*. It's a way of manipulating people, and it should be done with care. Be conscious of how others may experience a "curse" differently to you. Remember that *when you're augmenting peoples' reality you have a responsibility TO their reality*.

BONUS CHALLENGE

Now, play out the same scenario, but in a **protagnostic** context. Treat the player as themselves – but a version augmented with a guilt/curse. How does this affect the scenario you developed? Does your choice of *leitmotif* still work or does it need to change? How far do you think you can get the player to internalise a fictional curse augmented onto their real IDENTITY? How do you feel about this?

ONGOING IDENTITIES

In augmented/spatial narrative, players will not be constantly in contact with your worldbuilding: remember, you can't contain them within a dragon's cave. Players' sense of BEING-in an augmented/spatial narrative needs to be reinforced through reiteration, because the real world is so open and distracting that the narrative can easily be forgotten or disrupted. As game scholar Henry Jenkins says, "within an open-ended and exploratory narrative structure like a game, essential narrative information must be redundantly presented across a range of spaces and artefacts".[37]

But much of the reiteration and "redundant presentation" needed to maintain AR worldbuilding can happen as augmented IDENTITY. *The most important reality you're augmenting is the player themselves.* Once the player feels established within an augmented IDENTITY, they can be both protagonist and narrator, IMAGINATIVELY filling in any gaps in the storyscape with the ongoing experience of self-narrating their **blended** IDENTITY.

Acting as both protagonist AND narrator (as well as audience) isn't a cognitive stretch for players, because that's what it feels like when we're living/narrating the story of our everyday life. As the philosopher Adriana Cavarero says, "Every human being, without even wanting to know it, is aware of being a narratable self – immersed in the spontaneous auto-narration of memory".[38]

The story the player tells themselves is far more powerful and immersive than any story we can impart to them. Our job is to augment just enough fictional elements onto their "narratable self", so that the player "auto-narrates" themselves into a compelling story. Augmenting IDENTITY is our most powerful tool to do this.

As I said, augmenting IDENTITY is probably the most complex concept we'll examine in this book. This chapter just scratched the surface of what's possible. But the concepts in this chapter also touch on the scariest and most potentially dystopian aspects of AR/spatial technology. The ability to digitally reskin other people's appearance or IDENTITY-presentation, potentially without their knowledge, is no longer science fiction. Remember that *when augmenting reality we have a responsibility to the player's reality.* Altering or overwriting people's IDENTITIES, even in play, is something we should never do lightly. More on dystopian possibilities in Section 4, and more on **role-playing** safety in Appendix A.

In the meantime, when co-creating augmented IDENTITIES with the player, remember that IDENTITIES are performative, porous, and multifarious. We all perform and blend between immersions and IDENTITIES throughout our lives, which why "active creation of belief", "performance of self" and immersion in stories all come so naturally to us.

It's also why our IMAGINATION and IDENTITY are so resilient to the potentially-disruptive element of SELF-CONSCIOUSNESS. In immersive design, we tend to think of SELF-CONSCIOUSNESS as immersion-breaking. But as we're about to see, SELF-CONSCIOUSNESS is not the enemy of immersion – in fact it can be immersion's most powerful driver.

IDENTITY-BUILDING: SUMMARY

How do we co-create the player-character's in-fiction IDENTITY with the player?

- *Understand that an in-fiction IDENTITY is the player's interface with the story. They need a chance to learn how to operate it.*
- *Understand that an in-fiction IDENTITY will be just one of several IDENTITIES which the player has "**blended**" that day.*

What makes a good player-character IDENTITY?

- *A solid IDENTITY should have:*
- *Connections – who do they know and what's the dynamic?*
- *Capability – what can they do in the world?*
- *Commitments – what guides their action?*
- *Conflict – how do the other three C's stand in tension?*
- *Comfort – how do you allow players to control their diegetic distance?*

How do we get players to self-identify as their in-story IDENTITY? How do we make that moment powerful?

- *Psychologically anchor IDENTITIES by formulating them as "possible selves" of the player OR a **roleplayed** character.*
- *Create moments of dramatic **anagnorisis** ("realisation of IDENTITY").*
- *Challenge the player to self-identify and assert IDENTITY in-story with **mise-en-self** techniques.*
- *Play with the "blend" to build complicity e.g. by withdrawing characterisation at key moments.*
- *Augment IDENTITITES responsibly.*

NOTES

1. Josephine Machon, *Immersive Theatres*, Palgrave Macmillan, London, 2013, p. 74.
2. Nicholas Borriaud, *Relational Aesthetics*, Les presses du réel, Dijon, 2002 p.168.
3. John Hanke/Cristina Criddle, "A Real-world Metaverse Will Be More Magical Than VR", Financial Times, 3 Oct 2022, https://www.ft.com/content/40d81fa4-67e6-40ea-b077-ba09484ba151
4. Maximillian Clark, Aneesha Singh, Giulia Barabareschi, "Towards Greater Inclusion and Accessibiliy for Physically Disabled Players in Location Based Games". *Proceedings of the ACM on Human-Computer Interaction* 7:7, 2023.
5. *SFZero*, http://sf0.org/about, retrieved 14 Dec 2023.
6. Hazel Markus, Paula Nurius, "Possible Selves", *American Psychologist* 41:9, 1986.
7. *Ibid.*
8. *Ibid.*

9. Victor van Doorn, Charles Melcher, "How to Design an Escape Room", *Future of Storytelling* Podcast 3, 16 Feb 2023.

10. Erving Goffman, *The Presentation of the Self in Everyday Life*, University of Edinburgh, 1956, p. 6.

11. John Gerstmyer, "Toward a Theory of Play as Performance". University of Pennsylvania, 1991.

12. Goffman, 1956, p. 20.

13. John Harper, "The Four Cs of Characters", 29 Dec 2009 http://mightyatom.blogspot.com/2009/12/four-cs-of-characters.html.

14. Chloe Mashiter, "Creating Tools for Play: Writing for LARP", Immersive Experience Network Huddle 1, 20 Feb 2023, https://youtu.be/GaJwr8jPDQ4.

15. Karl Schroeder, "To Hie from Far Cilenia", (2008) in Metatropolis ed. John Scalzi (ed.), Subterranean Press, Michigan, 2009, p. 224.

16. *Ibid.,* p. 220.

17. *Ibid.,* p. 224.

18. Sarah Wiseman, Janet van der Linden, Ad Spiers, Maria Oshodi, "Control and Being Controlled: Exploring the use of Technology in an Immersive Theatre Performance", *Proceedings of the 2017 Conference on Designing Interactive Systems*, 2017.

19. Jason Warren, *Creating Worlds: How to Make Immersive Theatre*; Nick Hern Books, 2017, p. 29.

20. *Ibid.*

21. Nathan Sibthorpe, Personal correspondence, 4 Aug 2023.

22. *Ibid.*

23. *No Proscenium* 11 2022.

24. *ibid.*

25. Ron Schneider, *From Dreamer to Dreamfinder*, Bamboo Forest Publishing, USA, 2012, p. 102.

26. *Ibid.*

27. Immersive Audience Report 2024, Immersive Experience Network, Joanna Bucknall, Andy Barnes, and Nicole Jacobus (eds.), https://immersiveexperience.network/articles/immersive-audiences-report-2024/

28. Chloe Mashiter, 'How "Immersion" Is Ruining Your Immersion", https://chloemashiter makesthings.wordpress.com/2024/07/09/how-immersion-is-ruining-your-immersion/

29. Katie Lyons, Personal correspondence, 31 May 2023.

30. Gilles Fauconnier, Mark Turner, *The Way We Think: Conceptual Blending and the Mind's Hidden Complexities*, Basic Books, New York, 2002, p. 217.

31. *Ibid.*, p. 266–267.

32. Bruce McConachie, "An Evolutionary Perspective on Play, Performance, and Ritual", *TDR* 55:4, 2011.

33. Jessica Creane, "Let the Magic Circle Bleed", *Gamevironments* 15, 2021.

34. *Ibid.*

35. Chris Hardman, "Walkmanology", *The Drama Review* 27:4, 1983, p. 45.

36. Heather Dunaway Smith, 'AR Design Principles: Creating Immersive Experiences', Adobe MAX 2021 https://youtu.be/JO1Qw-JTVqc.

37. Henry Jenkins, "Game Design as Narrative Architecture", in N. Wardrip-Fruin, P. Harrigan (eds.), *First Person: New Media as Story, performance, Game,* MIT Press, Cambridge, MA, 2004.

38. Adriana Cavarero, *Relating Narratives: Storytelling and Selfhood*, trans. Paul Kottman, Routledge, London, 2000, p. 33.

SELF-CONSCIOUSNESS 2.3

What role should the player's SELF-CONSCIOUSNESS play in an augmented/spatial story?

When is an audience member too SELF-CONSCIOUS to get immersed?

How can we use SELF-CONSCIOUSNESS within augmented/spatial narratives?

THIS IS WHERE YOU COME IN

As we saw in 1:3, BEING SEEN is crucial to VR immersion. Similarly, in augmented/spatial narrative it's vital the player not only perceives the story, but also feels perceived as a player-character. This reinforces presence and creates meaningful consequence. Without BEING SEEN (or a dynamic of BEING (UN)SEEN) the player doesn't have a **diegetic** presence in the story.

This might mean BEING SEEN by characters in the digital layer. In *Augmented Shadow* Joon Moon aims to "create[] the fun of observation between overlaid layers of reality". His piece *Inside* is populated with digital characters: "the audience observes them from the real world, but they also observe the audience from their own world".

But augmented players might BE SEEN by other real people too. *Inside* is technically a single-player experience, but while one player is interacting, "at the same time, the other members of the audience observe the stage from outside". So the player inside the story-space is conscious of BEING SEEN not just by fictional characters but by other real people outside. "Thus, the [outside] audience finds themselves an active part of the story"[1] because they add a dynamic of SEEING/BEING SEEN.

Social multiplayer is a big part of Niantic's *Ingress* and *Pokémon GO*, especially in high-level play. At launch *Pokémon GO* was so popular it achieved a critical mass of players SEEING and BEING SEEN by one another, reinforcing the shared fantasy.

Nonetheless, making-believe out in the real world can be a vulnerable experience. That social risk can be exacerbated by the actual technology: a big factor in the failure of early smart glasses Google Glass (2013) was the negative image of headset-wearing "glassholes".[2] Niantic's own CTO called the way *Pokémon GO* players need to hold their smartphone to view AR "unnatural": "it makes them look like a total doofus if they're doing it for an extended period of time".[3] Even Apple Vision Pro was criticised as "too big and dorky to wear in public"[4] at launch.

DOI: 10.1201/9781003379294-12

This "doofus factor" is a result of our fundamental self-awareness or, in more negative terms, SELF-CONSCIOUSNESS. Psychologists often divide self-awareness into "private self-consciousness", "public self-consciousness" and "social anxiety".[5] Psychologists still debate the stimuli and effects of SELF-CONSCIOUSNESS, but broadly speaking, when something reminds us of ourselves (e.g. seeing ourselves in a mirror) we often compare ourself with an ideal standard – an imagined "possible self". Then we either regulate ourselves to try to meet the ideal standard, or avoid the thing that confronts us with ourselves.[6] I.e. we adjust our appearance or behaviour, or we avoid mirrors.

When a VR player gets right up in the grill of an NPC, they're trying to determine whether they're BEING SEEN. Do they need to regulate their behaviour with SELF-CONSCIOUSNESS? Or can they act free of social consequence? If the NPC reacts to the player-character, this is a social consequence, and social consequences also help build the player-character's sense of who they're BEING. Finding out how others SEE you is another type of IDENTITY-discovery.

In fact, BEING SEEN actually causes players to form stronger psychological attachments to **roleplayed** IDENTITIES. Theatre performers Leslie Hill and Helen Paris researched experiences of performing in traditional theatre vs. immersive theatre. For performers, a conventional theatre performance might "go by in a bit of a blur" because they're "in a skills mode, performing something we [the performers] have learned in the same way a musician performs a song". Whereas in immersive theatre "even though we [the performers] have memorised lines and rehearsed a sequence of actions, we are engaged in an experience with the audience members and remember the event in the same cognitive manner that we process episodes in our lives". The performers can see "how [the audience] reacted, what they looked like, what they laughed at and when they looked thoughtful, and so we also remember ourselves and what we were doing in those moments more distinctly".[7]

Similarly, for theatre researcher Nandita Dinesh, BEING SEEN by performers implicates the audience in the performance, and this "seems to cause emotions-based empathy that is more likely to evoke autobiographical memories"[8] for audiences.

This "autobiographical" memory-forming and narrative-making, where performers and players experience and remember story events in the same cognitive manner as real events, is crucial to immersion. So making augmented players feel SEEN is a powerful tool.

But in AR/spatial media, players' SELF-CONSCIOUSNESS is likely to be highly alert because they're embodied in-the-world. What's more, there may be non-players around who are not seeing the augmented layer, creating a risk of the "doofus factor" and the vulnerability of making-believe in public. A digital narrative layer might be invisible to others, but if the player's SELF-CONSCIOUSNESS is activated they might still regulate their own in-story behaviour due to the extra-**diegetic** gaze of others – or "un-blend" altogether. Fear of doofusness is emotive: it disrupts the *Comfort* that's essential for IDENTITY-BUILDING. Augmented players always have one foot in the real world and one in the digital, but this becomes complex if they try to regulate their in-story behaviour so they don't seem strange in the real world. This forces players to enforce barriers between their real self and their player-character self.

Nonetheless, SELF-CONSCIOUSNESS is not inherently disruptive to immersion. It's a perfectly natural thing to feel when wearing a headset and making-believe. It's our job to **diegeticize** players' SELF-CONSCIOUSNESS and show that there is room in the story for this part of their experience.

In immersive design we tend to think of the moment a player becomes SELF-CONSCIOUS as the moment immersion has broken. But SELF-CONSCIOUSNESS is part of their ongoing, authentic experience of everyday reality. Being CONSCIOUS of the gaze of others can be a positive experience because we are social animals. Clay Shirky describes the odd economics of bars and pubs: the product being sold is only a small part of the overall experience, most of which is made up of other people. A bar is in the "curious business of offering value above the products and services [it] sells, value that is created by the customers for one another".[9] This is what was missing from Tristan Cross's virtual version of his local pub Skehan's: BEING SEEN. And, yes, BEING SELF-CONSCIOUS.

DIEGETIC SELF-CONSCIOUSNESS

According to Machon, in Punchdrunk theatre the audience's masks represented Artistic Director Felix Barrett's desire "to remove the other audience-being-audience from the picture", as Barrett felt that SEEING other players "was detrimental to an individual's connections with and interpretation of the work".[10]

Nonetheless, even when a masque show signals that we-the-audience are **dieget-ically** invisible, BEING SEEN is still at play. Suddenly BEING SEEN is critical to moments like Macbeth seeing the audience "haunting" him. And Punchdrunk creates some zones, such as the bar, where players are encouraged to remove their masks.

But some story elements can cause Punchdrunk players to visibly behave in ways which might create dissonance for other players. *Masque of the Red Death* (2007) briefly incorporated a module of gameplay designed by renowned experience designers Coney, called "The Goldbug". A small number of players were challenged to hunt down specific clues during the show, to unlock secret storyline elements. Barrett has described the ideal experience of shows like *Sleep No More* and *Masque of the Red Death* as an "instinctual experience", like "floating around in [a] fever dream". But creating a sub-population of players in "pure mission mode" was disruptive "in terms of rhythm and sensibility". According to Barrett:

> you had 90% of audience floating around in their fever dream of the show, with a proper underwater tempo with them slowly moving through the space, and then suddenly you'd get someone barrel up, and say 'have you seen the Goldbug?'... The collision was so brutal that we had to take away the Goldbug... Two different audience drivers: each was destroying the other ones' experience.[11]

This went beyond the aesthetic: players in the "fever dream" might SEE other players in "pure mission mode", potentially making both player types SELF-CONSCIOUS, and disrupting the overall **diegetic** mood.

But this disruption was due to the specific aesthetic of those masque shows. In other contexts, SEEING other players in "mission mode" could enhance the overall mood of an experience. Players might even act as player-performers, if their presence and behaviour enhances the experience for others. When interviewing Barrett, critic Noah J. Nelson articulated the potential to

> harness that audience energy to solve [Goldbug-style puzzles]. To be, if nothing else, amusing to everybody else. So that when someone comes up with that gold fever, looking for the goldbug, it enhances the experience for the audiences floating through the world… like they belong there somehow.
>
> BARRETT: Absolutely, I totally agree. What's interesting is, it doesn't work with the masque form because the mask removes the rest of the audience, I hope… So you're individuals. Actually I think it would only work in a different kind of construct where the audience are present.[12]

In "a different construct", with audience members un-masked and fully **diegetically** present, the implied social regulation of others' gaze and behaviour could become part of the aesthetic and the experience.

Even a competitive context could contribute to mood: seeing other players "gaming" the scenario could enhance an experience, as long as the SELF-CONSCIOUSNESS this invokes is incorporated into the experience. Immersive theatre shows like *Arcane: Enter the Undercity* (2021) and *Peaky Blinders: The Rise* (2022) incorporate competitive elements in this way.

At a meta-level, Punchdrunk shows have always been a competitive environment. Critics have observed that masque formats can create a "perpetual fear of missing out".[13] Each show is so large, players must choose which storylines to follow, and will see only a fraction of the show's total content. This "self-consciously imposed scarcity model"[14] drives some players to meta-play: sharing information on forums about how to best optimise their routes through the experience. Like the Goldbug players, it's relatively easy to spot "completionist" audience members driven by meta-objectives moving with purpose through masque shows.

But this layer of meta-gameplay, and the dissonant audience behaviour it causes, is only non-**diegetic** because the masks and the "fever dream" aesthetic explicitly *exclude* the audience's presence, their IDENTITY, and their SELF-CONSCIOUSNESS from the diegetic story world. In a different construct, competitive meta-gameplay could be integral to the story.

Barrett himself, always influenced by video games, is now moving towards incorporating more objective-driven play and more competitive BEING SEEN:

> BARRETT: My challenge now is, I really want to come back for [elements like the Goldbug]. Because I really believe in objective and mission… How do you "level up" within this sort of work? [E.g.] there's a doorway that's locked and you can only access it if you're level five audience member – that feels like it's the ultimate in democratising the work.

Put simply, in immersive experiences, the player's SELF-CONSCIOUSNESS is only disruptive to immersion *if you treat it as something that doesn't belong in the world of the story.*

In the real world, SELF-CONSCIOUSNESS doesn't go away even if you do get caught up in a romance story or a hair-raising adventure, believe me. SELF-CONSCIOUSNESS is integral to our everyday "auto-narration of memory", our ongoing experience of self-narration. And after all, SELF-CONSCIOUSNESS is a hallmark of relatable, authentic fictional characters. That's why Roger Thornhill is always complaining in *North by Northwest*; it's why superhero movies add authenticity to their heroes by making them SELF-CONSCIOUS (and showing the challenges of being SEEN by the world).

Even SELF-CONSCIOUS uncertainty about the "rules of engagement" can be used to power immersion, if you allow it into the story. At the start of Janet Cardiff and George Bures Miller's binaural experience *The Paradise Institute* (2001) audiences were asked to switch their phones off, in typical fashion. Then the sound of a phone going off somewhere in the audience was played, prompting "outraged turning and tutting"[15] from audiences – until they realised it was part of the show. Collapsing the fourth wall like this helps reassure players that they don't need to enforce a fourth wall inside themselves, or exclude their SELF-CONSCIOUSNESS, to participate in the story.

Janet Cardiff often uses a SELF-CONSCIOUS "Janet" persona in her work, a character who's aware she is both creator and protagonist. In the video walk *Night Walk for Edinburgh* (2019), players were asked to arrive and wait at a specific, public location in Edinburgh. As the show begins, the voice of "Janet" articulates worries which the player might well share: "I was supposed to be playing a night walk game but the people didn't show up… but maybe they're tricking me and this is all part of it".[16] The player's own SELF-CONSCIOUSNESS is normalised and incorporated into the show. There's no barrier between the player's everyday SELF-CONSCIOUSNESS and SELF-CONSCIOUSNESS in the story.

The Janet-persona is not just a fellow-player but a co-creator: "Janet" goes on to say "I was supposed to be playing a night walk game but it seems like I might be the one designing it".[17] Through shared SELF-CONSCIOUSNESS, the player is alerted to being a co-creator too. This collapses the boundary between author/narrator/player and emphasises the player's authority to co-create their own experience. The barrier between **diegetic** and non-**diegetic** is destabilised, showing the player that even uncertainty and SELF-CONSCIOUSNESS can all be part of the show, and part of their in-story IDENTITY.

The potential emotional impacts of SELF-CONSCIOUSNESS – both good and bad – are heightened in augmented/spatial media where the player is embodied in the real world, may be wearing technology, and may be seeing things others don't see. SELF-CONSCIOUSNESS is a fundamental, gut feeling. It can cause discomfort and dissonance. But if we give it space inside the story, it can help authenticate the player's experience. Then, the player's augmented IMAGININGS and augmented IDENTITY are securely anchored to an embodied gut feeling – **diegetic SELF-CONSCIOUSNESS.** Already in-progress and in continuity with their ordinary experience.

This is what Ron Schneider was doing when he asked *what's a child?*: creating space inside his fiction for the player's SELF-CONSCIOUSNESS. Holding up a fun-house mirror to the player, alerting them to their self, and challenging them to self-identify within the terms of the fiction. Kids who put away their autograph book to respond, even for a second, were made SELF-CONSCIOUS without being embarrassed.

And that SELF-CONSCIOUSNESS meant they self-identified as a version of themselves who was already inside the magical scenario, helping to co-author it.

We cannot augment SELF-CONSCIOUSNESS away, and attempting to overwrite it creates a heightened risk of juxtaposition. Too often immersive creators end up demanding that players regulate out their own SELF-CONSCIOUSNESS, partitioning it off with internal fourth walls, before they can play along. If we try to eliminate SELF-CONSCIOUSNESS, or ask players to exclude it, we're cutting out a vital and authentic part of their ongoing experience, which can help power their immersion. We miss an opportunity to play with the whole of the player, as their whole, authentic selves.

And worse, if we exclusively try to create scenarios in which we think a player will be UN-SELF-CONSCIOUS, we may end up constructing scenarios in which only *some* people feel welcome. Different physical, sensory, cognitive and identity factors can make different people SELF-CONSCIOUS in different contexts.

As we saw in 1.1, historically the videogame industry has often attempted to create "neutral" protagonists, whom players could theoretically embody UN-SELFCONSCIOUSLY. But this just ends up revealing game developers' preconceptions about what a "neutral" person looks like – usually a stocky white guy.

In AR/spatial media, if a storyteller tries to exclude a central component of the player's ongoing experience like SELF-CONSCIOUSNESS, they might just inadvertently reveal their own preconceptions about WHO their audience is. Preconceptions about what types of identities can belong UN-SELF-CONSCIOUSLY in a story. Preconceptions about what kind of person gets to be a hero.

So instead of trying to chase down and eliminate SELF-CONSCIOUSNESS, in augmented/spatial stories we must show players that the new reality *includes* their SELF-CONSCIOUSNESS. We must show them that their native SELF-CONSCIOUSNESS is a part of their augmented IDENTITY, an authentic hallmark of their player-character.

At the start of this chapter one of our key questions was:

When is an audience member too SELF-CONSCIOUS to get immersed?

But, as you may have already guessed, I believe that the answer to this question (at least in principle) is "**never!**"

AUGMENTED SELF-CONSCIOUSNESS

So how do we use and augment SELF-CONSCIOUSNESS to support augmented narratives?

Once we have co-developed the player's augmented IDENTITY – whether **protagonist-agnostic** or **roleplayed** – we also need to allow players to experience what being SELF-CONSCIOUS feels like *as* that augmented IDENTITY.

This means providing pathways to in-character SELF-CONSCIOUSNESS. Once this is established, we can use dynamics of BEING SEEN and (UN)SEEN to activate powerful SELF-CONSCIOUSNESS-driven emotions that take place in-story.

Luckily, a little "BEING SEEN" goes a long way. We've already talked about the principle of **panopticon**: if you establish that someone *could* be watching, players will tend to act as though someone is ALWAYS watching. From then on, socially-aware parts of their brain will heighten their experience with socially-charged emotions.

AUGMENTED SELF-CONSCIOUSNESS CASE STUDY: *COMING OUT*

In 2016 my studio Playlines installed one of our early locative AR theatre pieces within a busy tech festival called #FutureFest at London venue Tobacco Dock (*Coming Out*[18], devised in collaboration with young artists at Roundhouse Radio). Players freely roamed the space wearing headphones while their location was tracked via Bluetooth iBeacons.

Character voices in the audio layer guided players to specific locations. Players heard context-appropriate audio when moving into new areas or rooms: their mobile devices detected that room's associated iBeacons and played the appropriate audio. Using basic **conditionality** also allowed us to create branching paths, with players encountering **forks** in the road where they could choose which storyline to pursue. These **spatial agency** choices were tracked and created consequences which followed them through the story and changed the ending. (More on **conditionality** in 3.1 and designing for **spatial agency** in 3.2)

Some choices led players to a "VIP area" with a red rope and bouncer. Players were given the password to the VIP area through the audio layer. (In 2.1 we saw how this created a desirable element of BEING SEEN through *exclusivity*).

Coming Out was set in Tobacco Dock thirty years in the future, and was presented as a futuristic dating app where users could go on "asynchronous dates" around the venue, guided in the audio layer by the date character of their choice.

In the physical layer, players were surrounded by attendees of a busy tech festival – often friends and colleagues. It would have been pointless to try to augment away players' SELF-CONSCIOUSNESS. So we leaned into it.

One of the characters was not actually romanceable, but rather a free trial of a futuristic personal "wingman" service. The "wingman" was specifically designed to incorporate the social situation and the player's sense of BEING SEEN. She remotely guided you around the venue while (in-fiction) accessing data on people nearby to suggest romantic prospects, and she also gave advice on the player's self-presentation. Early on the "wingman" guided the player to a balcony, a location where they would definitely BE SEEN. The "wingman" character used this as a moment to boost the player's confidence: "put your hands on the railing, shoulders back, don't look at your phone; just look around. There's nothing more confident than someone just looking around".[19] Often we saw players' body language change in this moment, gaining a confidence which they would carry forward through the experience. Their SELF-CONSCIOUSNESS had been acknowledged and positively incorporated into the story.

AUGMENTED SELF-CONSCIOUSNESS CASE STUDY:
GENTRIFICATION: THE GAME (2010)

Gentrification: The Game at New York's *Come Out & Play* festival played with SELF-CONSCIOUSNESS in a big way. *Gentrification* narratively augmented groups of players with faction-based IDENTITIES : players were greedy property developers or concerned locals.

Gentrification used an actually-gentrifying Brooklyn neighbourhood as its game board. Players roamed the streets completing objectives: depending on which faction they were in, they were challenged to "claim" properties by taking digital photos, or to hand out flowers and organise protest marches.

As researcher Dan Dixon writes, players were well aware that *Gentrification* was, in 2010 parlance, "a hipster game". Players playfully embodied various gentrifier archetypes, and their ironic SELF-CONSCIOUSNESS was part of the experience. Players shared the risk of making-believe in public (and worse, potentially being mistaken for *actual hipsters*) but felt a sense of community and critical mass as a player-group. As Dixon says, the presence of fellow-players invoked "social immersion and deep social engagement... It's that drunken "I love you man" sentiment. It's also the sense of oneness that helps convince someone to join in looting when everyone else is doing it".[20]

This sense of permissive critical mass was part of the point. *Gentrification*'s play-performances took place in a real neighbourhood with real, pressing gentrification issues. The game brought a self-selecting population of mostly-young, mostly-privileged experimental game players into this gentrifying neighbourhood. This was a self-fulfilling prophecy: one player who was actually local felt "alienated whilst in her own neighbourhood, the players of *Gentrification* unwittingly colonising the local space".[21]

Gentrification: The Game was a combination of game, flashmob, protest and embodied satire. It not only co-opted its players' presence, it also SELF-CONSCIOUSLY co-opted the in-progress gentrification of the neighbourhood and the stereotypical image of the self-aware "hipster". It transformed players into performer-perpetrators. Players weren't necessarily in control of how they were SEEN, and this was part of the experience. The game destabilised the barriers between **diegetic** and non-**diegetic**. Players might begin to realise that acts of play, acts of protest, even their own mostly-privileged real-world IDENTITIES, could all be part of the gentrification ecosystem.

CHALLENGE #13: ACTIVATING SELF-CONSCIOUSNESS

Goal: Experiment with activating players' SELF-CONSCIOUSNESS to drive emotional immersion.

SUMMARY

Conceptualise a narrative moment which **interrupts the player** while they're in a public place, and augments their sense of BEING SEEN.

First **select your medium**. You could whisper to the player via headphones, flash messages on AR glasses or take over a digital billboard.

Conceptualise a scenario in which the player is BEING SEEN (or UNSEEN) by in-story characters, AND/OR by non-player bystanders. (Consider stimulating the player to enact behaviour which causes others to look.)

You could tell the player they're being hunted by interdimensional cops, or that all the non-players around them are secretly vampires.

Your goal is to change the player's relationship to themselves and those around them. Don't impose a **roleplay** character onto the player; keep it **protagonist-agnostic**.

Write the initial narration or dialogue which will interrupt the player. Try to write a *fait accompli* **phrase** opening line which immediately activates their SELF-CONSCIOUSNESS: *act normal; everyone's watching; I know what you did; don't even blink.*

Create a sense of **panopticon**. Assert to the player that someone could *always* be watching; how can you anchor this impression in their local reality without requiring any physical changes in the environment?

Finally, **test** with unsuspecting friends. Observe the moment the narrative begins; can you see their demeanour change?

TASKS

- **Select media.**
- **Conceptualise a scenario** which **interrupts the player** and augments SELF-CONSCIOUSNESS.
- **Write** a short dialogue or narration to introduce the narrative. Use a *fait accompli* phrase and create **panopticon**.
- **Test.**

PLAYER-AS-PERFORMER

In 1979, Sony held a Tokyo launch event for their brand-new Walkman. It was what we'd now call a flashmob or immersive activation. According to Sony's archives, journalists were given Walkmen, bussed to a park, and asked to put on the headphones and press play. "The tape the journalists were listening to asked them to look at certain demonstrations, including a young man and woman listening to a Walkman while riding on a tandem bicycle... For onlookers [i.e. bystanders not wearing Walkmen], a lack of any public announcement or audible sound was rather puzzling".[22] The bicycling performers' actions meant different things depending on whether or not onlookers were privy to the audio layer.

As we saw with the Goldbug, players can become performers and knowingly or unknowingly influence other players' experiences. The presence of other players is a useful resource to enact parts of an augmented narrative and create **Merged Reality Moments.** And it can be powerful to alert players that they in turn might be performers (or props) in other peoples' stories.

In *Virtual Ambrose*, an augmented reality theatre prototype I helped create in 2019, players moved through the public and backstage areas of the Grand Theatre in Kingston, Ontario, hearing the voices of various historic ghosts and choosing which storyline paths to follow. Some of those paths indirectly intersected. One path we prototyped led players out onto the lit theatre stage in front of a darkened auditorium. They were asked to kneel down on the stage and perform a kind of ritual. Another path took players to a box at the back of the auditorium, where they could see the stage. In their digital layer, the player in the box heard a description of a ritual taking place on the stage. If the players' paths intersected as designed, the narrative heard by the player in the box would be embodied by the player-performer onstage. Just as the audio narrated, someone would enter onto the stage and perform the ritual. The player onstage might never realise they were BEING SEEN – but the player in the box was alerted to the possibility that they, in turn, might be performing to someone else, creating a **panopticon** effect.[23]

CHALLENGE #14: PARALLEL PLAYERS-AS-PERFORMERS

Goal: experiment with intersecting player paths to make players into performers.

You're going to create two parallel audio paths for two players. The two paths should indirectly intersect. At the intersection, one player will enact a performance which is SEEN by another.

This could be a moment of intimate performance in a shared space, or one player may voyeuristically witness another from a distance. Think about how you will deploy SELF-CONSCIOUSNESS and **panopticon** to heighten players' experience.

Identify a **place** and draw two paths through it. **Conceptualise** two parallel narratives which will guide two players along two **paths** through the **place**.

The players could be two characters within the same fictional world, or exist in entirely different realities, but they must be, in some way, part of the same story.

Plot your two narrative paths through the **place**. Ensure that they intersect either at a location or via a suitable **vantage point**.

At the point of intersection, the narrative should ask at least one player to enact something. This enaction will be witnessed by the other player. Incorporate the performance of the acting player into the narrative of the witness player.

Think about ways to synchronise the players. You could start both players at the same time and location, and trigger the performance after a fixed duration. But people move at different speeds. Can you use phenomena in the physical realm to cue the performance, e.g. a clock striking?

Write, record and **test** your experience with two friends. What impact does the player-performance have on each player?

TASKS

- **Identify a place.**
- **Conceptualise a narrative** with two parallel paths.
- **Plot** both paths onto the place and include an **intersection.**
- **Design** a performance moment.
- **Write** both path scripts.
- **Record audio.**
- **Test.**

BONUS CHALLENGE

If you haven't already, **conceptualise** a version of your story where the two players are unaware of one another until the convergence. Make at least one player remain unaware of the presence of the other player throughout. How does this impact each player's experience? How much harder is it to co-ordinate the experience?

A WORD OF CAUTION: AUGMENTING/ APPROPRIATING OTHERS

At one point in *Coming Out* the "wingman" character, searching for a suitable date for the player, starts describing the (fictional) dating profiles of the (real) people nearby. The wingman highlighted a bearded person with glasses and a plaid shirt, whom they said was near to the player. Unlike other shows, we didn't use any actors to fill this role. But, the show took place at a technology conference in the mid 2010's, so chances were very high that there was a bearded person with glasses wearing a plaid shirt somewhere nearby.

Players would often see a person fitting the description, incorporating them into their fiction. If they didn't see anyone, players tended to assume they'd just missed them, AND/OR they would get the joke about the contemporary tech bro stereotype. (Numerous players fitted that description themselves, as did I.) Like *Gentrification: The Game*, players were alerted to the fact that the game was co-opting people nearby into the narrative – and that they themselves might be being co-opted too.

Tom Maller of Immersive Everywhere has called this "endowing" members of the public with a touch of the story: "an experience where you can't tell who's a character and who's public".[24] It can be powerful. However, we need to be cautious with this kind of co-opting or appropriation of other people's identities as props in our stories. Reskinning or imposing narrative onto an unsuspecting bystander could constitute an unwanted appropriation of their body or their identity – a form of what Mary Flanagan calls "entertainment colonisation".[25] In reality, some people have much less control over how they're SEEN than others. Keep in mind your ***responsibility to players' realities,*** and don't allow augmented/spatial narratives to exacerbate humans' existing tendency to view other people as "NPCs".

UNRELIABLE PROTAGONISTS

If you're reading a book or watching a film, you're free to interpret the story however you want, but that interpretation exists outside the text. Whereas augmented players are the protagonist, so their perspective is paramount. It's their story, AND they're part of the text. And players always bring a "piece of self" into whatever character they're embodying, so their perspective will always be subjective in ways we can't necessarily predict or control. An augmented player is simultaneously character, narrator and audience in/of the story. This means their subjective interpretations will influence what happens in the story, AND how the story is told, AND how it is received by its audience.

In most literature, the perspective of the protagonist (and/or the narrator) tends to have a large influence on who and what we sympathise with in the story. In a story narrated from a narrator's point of view, they're our window into the story world so we tend to receive and accept their interpretation of events – up to a point. But sometimes we discover that narrators are unreliable, biased or just plain lying. **Unreliable narrators** are perspective characters whom we gradually realise are misrepresenting things or deceiving themselves or us. They highlight how subjective and self-serving our own perspectives can be.

An **unreliable narrator** has a **diegetic** IDENTITY in the story world, and though they might claim to be an unbiased or omniscient (all-knowing) narrator, their in-story attachments mean they are just as susceptible to bias or self-justification as any other character. Everyone from Chaucer to Jane Austen to Kazuo Ishiguro has used **unreliable narrators** to examine human self-deception and to build empathy in their readers.

In 2.2 we saw how augmented narratives need to create space for the player's IDENTITY. In this chapter we've seen the particular importance of including players' natural SELF-CONSCIOUSNESS as a player-character trait – whether they're playing themselves or **roleplaying**. Augmenting SELF-CONSCIOUSNESS creates continuity and relatability between **blended** player/player-character IDENTITIES. And it allows powerful, authentic emotions to exist "in the **blend**".

Players' perspectives will always be both subjective and SELF-CONSCIOUS. This means we can show players that even though they're the protagonist of the story, nonetheless they may not have all the answers. They may not, in fact, be the "hero".

In a sense, every augmented player is an **unreliable protagonist**. Their subjective perspective isn't the whole picture. They aren't present in the story as an omniscient narrator. Theirs is just one perspective among many. Just like in real life.

Unreliable protagonists are a character just like any other. This means that their interpretation of the story is defined by their perspective (which is subject to their IDENTITY) and their **vantage point** (which is subject to their position in space; we'll look at **vantage points** in more detail in 3.3: OCCUPYING SPACE.)

Using SELF-CONSCIOUSNESS to convey to the player their status as an **unreliable protagonist** will make their experience more compelling and authentic. This means augmented storytellers must acknowledge that the story which the player ends up telling themselves may be a radically different story to the one the storyteller set out to tell. But for the player, that story will be all the more immersive because of its authentic subjectivity.

CHALLENGE #15: UNRELIABLE PROTAGONISTS

Goal: Experiment with making an augmented **IDENTITY** feel more complete by showing the player they're an **unreliable protagonist**.

Conceptualise a short scenario to be augmented onto a table or other flat surface in the player's own home (More on **table-scale** design in 3.0).

Make sure you explain why the story is confined to the single flat surface. It could be a doll's house that's home to magical gnomes; the player could be viewing a diorama of a crime scene or performing an alien autopsy.

Develop an **IDENTITY** for the player to **roleplay**. Use the **Five C's**. The **IDENTITY** should imply a certain **perspective** on events: if they are the kindly maker of a doll's house, they might have a caring and sympathetic perspective towards the gnomes who live there; a crime scene detective might be obsessively looking for a culprit; an alien investigator might be obsessed with proving aliens are hostile.

(Don't worry about *mise-en-self* for now; assume you can *tell* your player an **IDENTITY** to **roleplay**.)

Outline a **perspective** you'd like the player to adopt as part of **roleplaying** the **IDENTITY**. Your goal is to get the player to adopt that perspective on the scenario.

Write a **description** of the player-character for the player to read before the scenario begins.

Write the scenario as an augmented scene which plays out on the table.

Now, **add a twist** to the scenario which shows the player that their initial **perspective** is incorrect or incomplete. A secret room in the gnomes' house could reveal the gnomes' plan to take over the world; viewing the crime scene from a different angle could reveal that the murder was actually an unlikely accident; the alien could awaken and insist it isn't hostile.

Test your scenario on a friend. Afterwards, ask them if they feel differently about **roleplaying** their protagonist perspective as a result of the **twist**. How would they approach the same scenario differently next time?

TASKS

- **Conceptualise** a scenario to augment onto a table surface. It will need a **twist.**
- **Develop** an **IDENTITY** for the player to **roleplay**.
- **Outline** the **IDENTITY**'s specific **perspective** on events.
- **Write** a **character description** and convey the **perspective.**

- **Write** the scenario.
- **Add a twist** to show the player-character their perspective was incomplete or incorrect.
- **Test** and review.

BONUS CHALLENGE

Implement a *mise-en-self*. After the **twist**, add dialogue or narration which **challenges** the player-character on their **perspective** or **identity**. Use voices from within the story to highlight the player-character's limited **perspective**. Characters could accuse them of being single-minded or prejudiced, or speculate about their motives. They might be given an opportunity to reassess their opinion. **Test** the scenario again; how does the player react when **challenged**? Does this reinforce their augmented **IDENTITY** or disrupt it?

DISCOVERING OTHERS

There's evidence that immersive experiences have a particular power to build players' empathy with characters and fellow-audience. Nandita Dinesh conducted a 2017 study comparing the emotional impact of immersive and non-immersive versions of the same theatre piece about the experience of immigrants.

Dinesh found that immersive audiences' interest was "oriented toward the ways in which individual audience members, and their peers, negotiated their respective immersive situations. In contrast the proscenium piece seemed to generate topic interest, where spectators constantly returned to the topic of authenticity and whether to not the story of the [immigrant] protagonist could be trusted".[26]

In other words, conventional, passive proscenium audiences tended to focus on their individual reactions, coloured by their perceived knowledge of the subject matter, and the perceived verifiability of characters' perspectives. Meanwhile, immersed audiences tended to experience encounters with other people's subjective perspectives, and to relate these perspectives to their own.

Outside of **echo chambers**, when we're in the real world, we're forced to encounter the fact that other people SEE things very differently. This is continually reinforced by our SELF-CONSCIOUSNESS, our tendency to seek social referencing and our inability to control how we're SEEN by others. Augmented/spatial narratives have a special power to create these kinds of encounters, because they take place (partially) in the real world.

An augmented narrative purports to be happening *WHERE* the player is, *TO* the player and often also *TO the people around the player*. So we're not being shown a singular perspective the way we are in the dark of a movie theatre. Other augmented players nearby might be experiencing the same story, but nonetheless their **blended** IDENTITY and different spatial **vantage point** gives them a different perspective. And if there are non-players nearby who are not aware of the augmented story layer, this highlights the way that augmented/spatial media can instance multiple, multifarious versions of reality.

It has to be said, some people definitely seem to believe that they have a definitive, objective, un-prejudiced **vantage point** on things. Most of us allow ourselves to believe this to a certain extent. But storytelling is the business of building empathy. This means showing how totally different, but how highly relatable, our disparate experiences of reality really are.

As the theatre scholar Chiel Kattenbelt says, the essence of creativity is when someone "stage[s] themselves in words, images and sounds, in order to make [their] own experiences perceptible to the audience... with the intention to explore to what extent life experiences are shared with other human beings".[27]

Ultimately, this is the value of making room for the player's SELF-CONSCIOUSNESS in an augmented story. Co-creating augmented IDENTITIES allows players to "stage themselves", partially-fictionalising themselves to make their own experiences perceptible to themselves in new ways. Then, SELF-CONSCIOUSNESS "stages players" in front of others, alerting players to BEING SEEN by their audience. Then, in turn, it alerts players to the subjective ways they themselves may be "staging" and perceiving others.

Leaving space for player SELF-CONSCIOUSNESS (or better still, augmenting it into the story) allows players to bring a larger "piece of self" into the story and to feel more authentically present as a player-character. But it also gives storytellers new tools to make players encounter other people – or even versions of themselves. Doing so builds the empathy that allows us to IMAGINE the world beyond our own subjective experience.

Or, as the novelist Joseph Conrad, master of the **unreliable narrator**, puts it:

> It is when we try to grapple with another man's intimate need that we perceive how incomprehensible, wavering, and misty are the beings that share with us the sight of the stars and the warmth of the sun.[28]

This is the stuff of great storytelling: being conscious that other peoples' needs and perceptions are incomprehensible to us, as ours are to them. Yet, understanding that we must share the world with one another. By figuring out ways to activate this SELF-CONSCIOUSNESS, we can allow our players to encounter or "stage themselves" as emotive, flawed, human characters who grapple with their own as well as others' ordinary, human "intimate needs".

BEING SELF-CONSCIOUS: SUMMARY

What role should the player's SELF-CONSCIOUSNESS play in an augmented/ spatial story?

- *It's part of them, so it should have a place in the story.*
- *SELF-CONSCIOUSNESS is a hallmark of authentic characters.*
- *Trying to eliminate or overwrite SELF-CONSCIOUSNESS may reveal your preconceptions about your audience.*

When is an audience member too SELF-CONSCIOUS to get immersed?

- *Trick question. In theory, never. **SELF-CONSCIOUSNESS is only an enemy to immersion if SELF-CONSCIOUSNESS is excluded from your story world.***
- *Asking players to exclude SELF-CONSCIOUSNESS demands that players enforce internal fourth walls and partition emotions they can't control.*

How can we use SELF-CONSCIOUSNESS within augmented/spatial narratives?

- Create moments that **diegeticize SELF-CONSCIOUSNESS.**
- *Use **panopticon** to create lasting SELF-CONSCIOUSNESS with minimal story resources.*
- *Alert players to BEING SEEN by:*
  - *Designing moments when players converge to turn **players into performers**.*
  - *Consider co-opting non-players, but consider how you might be appropriating others' IDENTITIES.*
  - *Cultivate **unreliable protagonists** by showing players their perspectives are incomplete.*

NOTES

1. Joon Moon, Augmented Shadow: Inside, https://www.creativeapplications.net/environment/augmented-shadow-inside-joon-moon/ retrieved 31 Aug 2023.
2. Quinn Myers, *Remember the Internet #3: Google Glass*, Instar Books, 2022.
3. Phil Keslin, TechCrunch Disrupt San Francisco panel, 2017 https://techcrunch.com/2017/09/18/pokemon-go-creators-next-game-will-incorporate-audio-into-the-ar-experience/.
4. Tomislav Bezmalinovic, "Apple Vision Pro: Review Roundup with verdicts", Mixed News, 30 Jan 2024, https://mixed-news.com/en/apple-vision-pro-review-roundup/.
5. Fenigstein, A., Scheier, M. F., Buss, A. H., "Public and Private Self-Consciousness: Assessment and Theory", *Journal of Consulting and Clinical Psychology*, 43:4, 1975.
6. Duval, S., & Wicklund, R. A., *A Theory of Objective Self-Awareness*, Academic Press, 1972.
7. Leslie Hill, Helen Paris, *Performing Proximity: Curious Intimacies*, 2014 Palgrave, London, p.16–17.
8. Nandita Dinesh, *Memos from a Theatre Lab*, 2017 Routledge, London, p. 82.
9. Clay Shirky, *Cognitive Surplus: Creativity and Generosity in a Connected Age*, Penguin, NY, 2010, p.58.
10. Machon, 2013, p.73.
11. Felix Barrett, interview with Noah J. Nelson, *No Proscenium Podcast 366*, 11 Nov 2022, 31:10.
12. *Ibid.*, 34:30.

13. Ian B. Faith, "Of Actors and Non-Player Characters: How Immersive Theatre Performances Decontextualize Game Mechanics", *Journal of Games Criticism* 4:1, Aug 2020.
14. *Ibid.*
15. Fiona Bradley (ed.) *Night Walk for Edinburgh,* 2019, The Fruitmarket Gallery, Edinburgh, p. 35.
16. Janet Cardiff, interviewed in Bradley, 2019, p. 3.
17. Bradley 2019.
18. *Coming Out*, 2016, Playlines and Roundhouse Radio. With support by Nesta. Devised by Roundhouse Radio volunteers and Rob Morgan. Technical development by Dustin Freeman.
19. *Coming Out*, 2016.
20. Dan Dixon, *Playing with Reality: A Technocultural Ethnography of Pervasive Gaming* University of the West of England, Bristol 2016 p. 171–172.
21. Dinesh, 2017, p. 177.
22. Sony History Ch6: "Just Try It", Sony, sony.com/en/SonyInfo/CorporateInfo/History/SonyHistory/2-06.html.
23. *Virtual Ambrose* (Prototype), Playlines / Single Thread Theatre. Rob Morgan, Dustin Freeman, Liam Karry, Amanda Baker, Adam Seybold.
24. Tom Maller, IEN Design Symposium, 9 Oct 2023.
25. Mary Flanagan, "Locating Play and Politics: Real World Games & Activism", *Leonardo Electronic Almanac* 16:2–3, 2007.
26. Dinesh, 2017, p. 87.
27. Chiel Kattenbelt, "Intermediality in Theatre and Performance: Definitions, Perceptions and Medial Relationships", *Culture, Language and Representation* VI, 2009.
28. Joseph Conrad, *Lord Jim* (1900), Wordsworth Classics, London, 1993.

From AUGMENTING PLAYERS to AUGMENTING PLACES

2.4

In this Section 2 we've examined techniques for AUGMENTING PLAYERS. Making digital stories that feel like they're happening *TO* the player, by finding ways to stimulate players to "stage themselves" as **diegetic** characters in the story.

Remember, this book is not intended to be definitive or exhaustive. It's just too early in the technology's development. We're just scratching the surface of how to AUGMENT PLAYERS and get them to incarnate compelling augmented IDENTITIES; there will be many more techniques for you to discover with your players. Go out and creatively PROVE ME WRONG.

But before you do, we need to look at the other half of the augmented equation: AUGMENTING PLACES. Section 3 will explore ways of making digital narratives that feel like they're happening *WHERE* the player is. This means stimulating players to "stage" augmented scenarios in the physical places around them.

DOI: 10.1201/9781003379294-13

SECTION 3

Augmenting Places

Augmenting Places

3.0

Getting Started

In this section, we'll develop techniques to solidly anchor players' augmented experiences in re-imagined versions of the places around them.

Previously in Section 2 we saw how the three pillars of emotional immersion, SEEING, BEING and BEING SEEN, evolved into IMAGINING, IDENTITY-BUILDING and BEING SELF-CONSCIOUS. Now we need to help the player instance a narratively-augmented version of their local reality, and situate themselves within it.

Let's return to Duncan Speakman for four more provocations, this time regarding the role of place in immersive experiences:

> Does the thing you're making care where it is?
> Why this place?
>
> What is unique to this place, and what does it
> share with others?
>
> How does my experience change if I know this
> place well, or if I've never been here?
>
> What aspects of the thing you're making will linger
> on for the audience?
>
> Duncan Speakman, *No Vantage Point*[1]

Why this place? What is unique about it?

All augmented/spatial narratives take place somewhere, and this is almost always a version of *where the player already is*. We need to get them to SEE that place and context differently, and imaginatively STAGE digital narratives there. This means understanding how to align and anchor the digital elements of AR narrative to a place. We also need to understand what makes different locations suitable for different narratives.

DOI: 10.1201/9781003379294-15

How does my experience change if I know this place?

We need to understand how the player's subjective perception of BEING IN a place influences their emotional state. We also need to show that their physical movements in the place have a presence in the digital dimension – and the story.

What aspects of the story will linger there?

What traces will the story, and the player-character, leave behind in the digital-physical story-scape? We need storytelling techniques to show that they, as a player-character, OCCUPIED SPACE and had a meaningful impact.

AR/spatial media is ill-suited to "transporting" the player to a virtual environment like a dragon's cave. This "transporting" is best left to VR. AR/spatial narratives need to be firmly anchored to the player's immediate reality.

Hence, we need techniques to help players' IMAGINATION to STAGE augmented narratives in real places.

We need to show players that their in-story IDENTITY can interface with an augmented place to create a sense of BEING THERE.

And we need to show players that their presence is consequential and carries weight: making them CONSCIOUS of their SELF in the hybrid digital-physical place, by showing them they OCCUPY both physical and digital SPACE.

In this Section 3 the three pillars of emotional immersion, SEEING, BEING and BEING SEEN will evolve in completely new ways:

In Chapter 3.1: STAGING, we'll explore techniques for stimulating players' IMAGINATION so that they're not just SEEING digital graphics, but STAGING digital narratives fully anchored in a place. (This chapter is divided into sub-chapters for **location-agnostic** and **location-specific** design; see below.)

In Chapter 3.2: BEING THERE, we'll adapt presence-building techniques to empower players' **spatial agency,** so that players feel a strong sense of BEING THERE in an augmented place.

And in Chapter 3.3: OCCUPYING SPACE, we'll see how **spatial subjectivity** can help players go beyond BEING SEEN and give them a sense of meaningful and consequential impact on the storyscape.

PLACE VS SPACE

Before we start AUGMENTING PLACES, we have to understand what a *place* is. A *space* is just a set of coordinates without any human meaning attached. Place, according to geographers Carter, Donald and Squires, is "space to which meaning has been ascribed".[2] A place rarely has just one meaning: according to Doreen Massey places resist single identities and are "constructed out of the juxtaposition, the intersection, the articulation, of multiple social relations".[3] A place is "always under construction[4]" because it comprises "a particular constellation of social relations, meeting and weaving together at a particular locus".[5]

For Massey, a place is *a simultaneity of stories-so-far*.[6]

When ambient literature researcher Matt Hayler visited a university in Australia, he felt:

> you can't help but be struck by the different stories that we tell about the landscapes we inhabit [...] 'this is the economics and sciences building, and it's also sacred land, a fact we shouldn't ever forget.' It's also where John and Tiffany met, where Edith and Jerome broke up, where that kid tripped downstairs in the middle of class...
>
> The stories swirl around us, mix with one another to become the place. Experience of place, then, becomes something co-constructed; rather than place being something immanent in a boundaried location it instead becomes the palimpsestuous product of every voice that passes, and has passed, through.[7]

(A *palimpsest* is a writing surface which can be written on, erased and re-written on; Hayler is punning it with *incest* to mean a re-writing that's also a merging and inter-relating.)

In other words, a place can sustain many different interrelated, intermingling meanings, written into it by different people, yet a place always presents a fresh surface ready for someone else to write something new. Just as we have multiple IDENTITIES which co-exist within us, a single space can be multiple places. Augmented/spatial technology is starting to supercharge this "simultaneity of stories-so-far". It may soon be possible to "channel-hop" between different layers, instances or digital dimensions of the same place.

Just as *a player's immersion is pre-existing*, the many meanings of a place are already *in-progress* when the player arrives. This means that in the establishing moments of an augmented/spatial narrative the player is joining an ongoing place-story that's both *in medias res* and *in situ* (i.e. already in place).

Finally, because of the collision and co-existence of meanings, "place" always has a relationship to power and politics. People don't always get to control the meanings of their places, and often only culturally-dominant place-meanings get recorded while those on the margins are lost. Augmented/spatial technologies create the possibility of hidden or encrypted "versions". The "layering" of digital meta-places could easily allow users to choose to live within custom versions of places, excluding or rewriting elements they don't like.

This could result in people physically sharing the same *spaces* but existing in separate sensory and ideological *places* – maybe even **customised realities**. John Hanke argues players "should be able to theme the world however they choose".[8] But remember, *when augmenting places we have a responsibility to reality*. (More on this in Section 4: Divergent Realities.)

LOCATIVE CATEGORIES

An augmented storyscape could be any tabletop surface. It could be the player's own home, or a specific venue or location chosen by the storyteller. But augmented experiences can also be designed work almost anywhere, like *Pokémon GO*.

Brendan Sinclair (who coined the term ludo-corporeal dissonance) identified some of the challenges of augmenting different kinds of places:

> If AR gaming is going to be anything grander than a new way to play games entirely possible in other formats, then the games need to understand and interact with the player's environment. And that only makes sense if the environment where you play – the specific arrangement of furniture and things around you – is meaningful to gameplay.
>
> If the environment significantly impacts the gameplay, that suggests people are going to be having wildly varying experiences depending on the size and relative clutter of the place they happen to be. Will someone be able to play in the middle of an open field? How about on a crowded bus? In a bathroom stall? The more the game relies on the geography of one's immediate surroundings, the harder a design problem it becomes to avoid possible environments that would be sub-optimal or completely unviable.
>
> The more designers control for that potential, to ensure that every environment can still work, the more abstracted the impact of the environment becomes.[9]

In other words, if a storyteller wants to specifically use or refer to the player's environment, with **location-specific** design and storytelling, they're more likely to require players to be in a specific kind of location, or even a single designated location.

But if the designer wants to make the experience work in many possible locations, to make it **location-agnostic,** the relationship between the narrative and the player's location becomes much less specific. This makes it more likely that the narrative will feel vague and un-anchored to the player's immediate reality, and/or that players will encounter juxtapositions or **spationarrative dissonances.**

Throughout this Section 3 (Figure 3.0), we'll draw a key distinction between **location-specific** design and **location-agnostic** design.

The different storytelling affordances of **location-specific** and **location-agnostic** design particularly affect STAGING. Accordingly, Chapter 3.1 is divided between 3.1.1: General Augmented STAGING and 3.1.2: Location-Specific Augmented STAGING.

Broadly speaking, **location-agnostic** experiences have much larger potential audiences, but there are real limits to how contextual they can be. **Location-specific** design

Augmenting PLACES

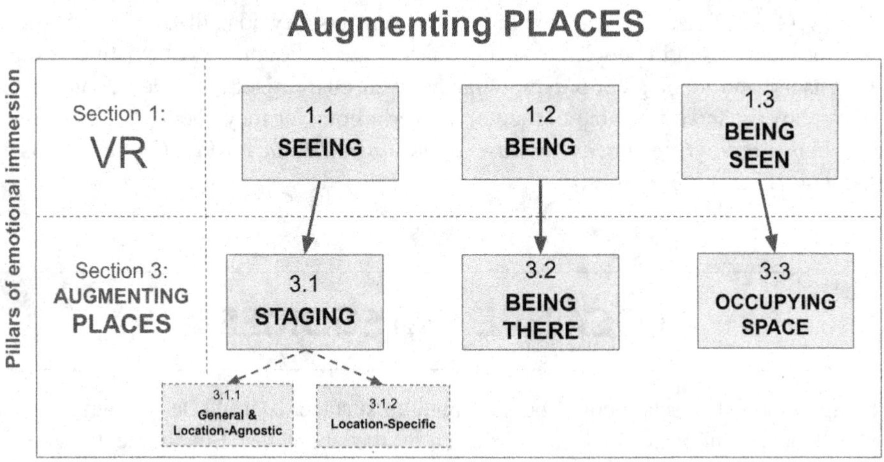

FIGURE 3.0   Evolution of pillars of emotional immersion when AUGMENTING PLACES

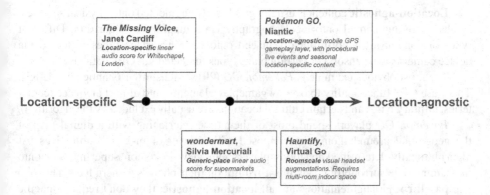

FIGURE 3.0.1 Different experiences on a spectrum between location-specific and location-agnostic

allows storytellers to create context-specific **merged reality moments** that anchor the narrative to the player's surroundings. But specifying a location limits the number of people who can access the experience, which has implications for inclusivity and business models. The first really financially successful locative AR experiences were all **location-agnostic** (with hybrid elements).

Both **location-specific** and **location-agnostic** are capable of creating social or multiplayer experiences. With **location-specific** design this tends to require scheduled "show times" to bring together enough players into a shared instance. **Location-agnostic** might require a critical mass of players worldwide in order to create serendipitous multiplayer encounters in any given location. Hence, even *Pokémon GO*, the archetypal **location-agnostic** AR game, orchestrates partially **location-specific** experiences such as Safari Zones where the spawn rates of rare Pokémon are increased in specific locations to attract players (Figure 3.0.1).

In addition to **location-specific** and **location-agnostic** design, there are four other sub-categories of location-based AR/spatial design: **generic places**, **location-portable**, **roomscale/at-home** and **table-scale**.

These different **locative categories** have very different design affordances. We'll examine the different categories of location-based digital narrative design in more detail in this chapter's subsections:

Location-Agnostic
Location-Specific
Generic Places
Location-Portable
Roomscale/At-home
Table-Scale

Location-Agnostic Experiences

A **location-agnostic** or (**locagnostic**) augmented/spatial experience uses the player's immediate surroundings as the setting, but can be played *anywhere*.

Location-agnostic content is usually graphically augmented onto physical surfaces, or abstractly augmented onto local geography via a map, by an algorithm. Different types of content are algorithmically placed onto certain surface types (detected via device cameras and sensors) or certain place types (detected via GPS databases).

The most obvious example is *Pokémon GO* (2016) and similar Niantic-style LBGs. These use GPS functionality to overlay gameplay elements onto almost anyplace (cemeteries, military bases and certain cultural locations are usually excluded by the algorithm).

Pokémon GO players spend most of their time interfacing with a digital map of the geography around them, superimposed with a layer of in-fiction **objectives**. At algorithmically-determined locations players can view Pokémon superimposed onto their immediate surroundings via **passthrough** on their phone's camera feed. The map and **passthrough** augmentations are all **location-agnostic**: they don't require specific physical features to work.

Other examples of **location-agnostic** augmented/spatial experiences include early LBGs like *Insectopia* (Peitz, Saarenpää, Björk 2007[10]) which turned any bluetooth device into a spawn point for collectible digital insects, and the narrative fitness game *Zombies, Run!* (Sixtostart, 2012) which doesn't use any sensors to detect context, simply asking players to go for a run then augmenting that experience with a context of drama and gameplay.

Advantages of **location-agnostic** design

- **Access.** Global reach, potentially global audiences. Players need the relevant hardware (e.g. a smartphone), and the majority of LBGs work better in cities, but nonetheless **location-agnostic** experiences can potentially access a vastly bigger audience than **location-specific**.
- **Scalability.** The early mobile Java/GPS game *Mogi* (Newt Games, 2003) was a digital scavenger hunt which was only playable in Tokyo.[11] Early LBGs like this were **location-specific** by necessity: each content node had to be geolocated by hand, which is prohibitively expensive at scale. Today GPS datasets and sophisticated algorithms allow content to be populated **location-agnostically** into any neighbourhood, which is much more cost-effective.
- **Flexible business models.** Access to a larger audience enables more scalable pricing structures. Most LBGs are "freemium" (the game is free with optional in-game purchases). At scale this model can be highly profitable: *Pokémon GO* made $5BN in its first five years.[12]

Disadvantages of **location-agnostic**

- **High development and running costs.** Global-scale datasets are expensive to build and access. Niantic was a spinoff from Google and benefited from access to Google's global mapping data. (Niantic LBGs often incentivise players to contribute contextual data, so Niantic has accrued rich "visual map" datasets – but this was only achieved through critical mass.) Algorithmic content distribution systems are also complex to develop and maintain. AI and third-party spatial content tools (including Niantic's own Lightship platform) are making this process easier and cheaper for smaller developers. But nonetheless making LBGs sustainable is challenging; even Niantic have been forced to shut down games like *Wizards Unite* (2019) which failed to achieve critical mass.

- **Dispersed userbase.** Without a designated focal point for play (as in **location-specific**), **locagnostic** players may be sparsely populated around the globe with little chance of encountering each other. LBGs like *Pokémon GO* are able to orchestrate multiplayer moments like Raids, but this requires a critical mass of players locally. Coupled with high costs, this is why global **locagnostic** experiences often count on licensed IPs to attract a minimum viable audience – and they're still a financial gamble.

- **Context-blindness.** Global datasets contain only limited amounts of contextual information, so it's hard to orchestrate anchored **merged reality moments**. It's all too easy for **location-agnostic** narratives to feel like they could be happening ANYWHERE, which makes it hard to feel like they're happening TO the player. Combined with algorithmic rather than scripted content distribution, this can result in experiences which feel generic or repetitive, or lack narrative **pacing**. We're currently seeing a move from algorithmic identification of location-types via GPS to algorithmic recognition of physical features of the player's environment via device cameras. This semantic parsing of the player's environment will continue to improve, driven by AI, allowing for headsets to recognise specific elements of a players' environment and augment them. These experiences will feel more contextual while still being **location-agnostic**. However, this level of scanning and detection of the player's immediate environment has major privacy implications.

- **Potential safety concerns.** **Locagnostic** design isn't necessarily aware of the player's particular circumstances, or any hazards or inequities which might affect them. As a result algorithms can place content in areas which might be inaccessible or unsafe for players because of mobility or social factors,[13] and might even inadvertently encourage unsafe behaviours.[14]

In short, **location-agnostic** experiences are highly accessible and scalable, but they can't be specifically anchored to the player's local reality. The **merged reality moments** they create generally have to be ad-hoc or **emergent** rather than scripted (more on **emergent** locative storytelling in 3.1.1 when we look at **spatial pacing**). Multiplayer moments can be orchestrated, but these require both global and local critical mass. There are also privacy, liability, safety and responsibility issues associated with populating places with recontextualised content. (More on this in Appendix A.)

Location-Specific Experiences

A **location-specific** experience uses a specific location as its setting.

Augmented/spatial experiences implemented within immersive theatre, theme parks, escape rooms, museums, historical sites or commercial activations are all likely to be **location-specific**. (Unless those experiences are designed to tour to multiple venues, when they will incorporate elements of **location-portable** design, see below.)

To a large extent the structure and the feel of a **location-specific** story is influenced by, and grounded in, the structure and the feel of its chosen place. There might be some variation according to the weather or time of year or day, but generally **location-specific** storytellers can design highly contextual spatio-narratives.

The work of Janet Cardiff and George Bures Miller can only be fully experienced at specified places (and often only during specific times). Cardiff's audio walk *The Missing Voice: Case Study B* (1999) is highly **location-specific** to Whitechapel in East London. The experience consists of an audio track which guides the player through the area. The player starts the audio track at the Whitechapel Gallery, and is directed to find a specific book on a specific shelf in the library next door. The player is then directed through a maze of East End streets as the "Janet" character's voice dramatises their journey and recontextualises the neighbourhood with narrative. *The Missing Voice...* might be just a scratchy audio track from decades ago, but because it is so **location-specific** it's able to create a hybrid spationarrative experience which changes how players look at a place.

Other examples of **location-specific** experiences include Geocaching and digital scavenger hunts like *Mogi*; hybrid digital-physical flashmobs like MoMA's Augmented Reality Flash Mob (Veenhof, la Poutre, Domhan 2010[15]) and #arOCCUPYWALL-STREET (various artists,[16] 2011); and site-specific AR layers like Gorillaz' Skinny Ape AR shows in Times Square and Piccadilly Circus (Gorillaz & Nexus Studios, 2022[17]).

Advantages of **location-specific**

- **Highly contextual. Location-specific** narratives can be securely anchored to local context, and the place can be used as a setting to help tell the story. Storytellers can refer to particular features or **landmarks** and ask players to interact with them. Creators can deliberately move players through areas with specific moods or textures in order to emotionally **pace** a narrative (though the player is in control of their movements, so the storyteller can't completely dictate the **pacing**.) Players can also be directed to and choose physical **forks** in the road representing choices in the story. (More on this when we look at **layout** and **spatial pacing** in **location-specific** design in 3.1.2.)
- **Concentrated playerbase.** Though only accessible to a much narrower audience (see below), it's easier to gather a critical mass of fellow-players in specific places and/or at specified times for multiplayer experiences. This also allows creators to market experiences with conventional theatre or exhibition business models with scheduled showtimes.
- **Control over setting.** Depending on the place the storyteller may have a degree of design control over the space to enhance it as a setting. This could include involve everything from physical design and set-dressing to **merged reality moments** orchestrated using live actors.

Disadvantages of **location-specific**:

- **Narrow accessibility**. The audience for a **location-specific** experience is largely limited to people who live nearby. **Location-specific** experiences are almost always confined to large cities, which excludes large numbers of people. Due to ticketed business models they often also exclude many people due to cost. Free or freemium **location-specific** experiences are rarely sustainable without external funding. If profit is one of your goals, then **location-specific** design is only sustainable if it can appeal to a critical mass of local audience. A **location-specific** experience is also only as physically accessible as its location, so anyone unable to access due to mobility or social inequalities will be excluded.

- **Potentially high physical & infrastructure costs**. To provide scarcer but higher-quality experiences, especially if players are required to travel, **location-specific** experiences often have to reward players with more "wow". This might include live actors or set-dressing, and these represent costs. Venue hire or fees may be required to use specific locations. Even in public places, liaison with local authorities may be required if an experience will attract large numbers of users or be potentially disruptive to others. All of these elements potentially increase cost and complexity.

Basically, **location-specific** experiences allow for **location-specific** storytelling with more specific **merged reality moments**. Narratives can be more grounded, more contextual, and generally stronger hybrids of place and narrative. Multiplayer moments can be orchestrated – but only if enough players are prepared to travel and potentially pay higher costs-of-entry. In addition, the storyteller is more directly responsible for the accessibility and safety of the location. (More on accessibility and safety in Appendix A.)

Generic Places

A **generic place** is a type of place with some common qualities, found worldwide.

Think of the last time you were in a supermarket. Now think about a time you visited a supermarket in another state or country. Although the sights, sounds and smells in these different supermarkets would have been very different, there would be many common features too, from an aisle-based layout to features like refrigerator cabinets. Our globalised world is full of generic locations which share basic features: airports, multistorey carparks, multiplex cinemas and the like. The academic Marc Augé called these anonymised spaces "non-places".[18]

Generic places are often liminal spaces where people are in transit or "between things". If no-one lives in a space, or it has only transitory meaning to everyone, then the space is "deterritorialized"; it is not local to anybody and nobody is building or competing to build its meanings. (However note that "non-place" is a highly subjective concept; if you work in an airport every day, it might be full of individualised meaning as a place.)

Examples of digital narratives designed for **generic places** include Silvia Mercuriali's *wondermart* (2009), which can be played in any supermarket. Mercuriali describes her work as *autoteatro*, using "instruction-based theatre"[19] to create a theatre piece which the player is both audience and performer, enacting a performance based on an audio track. *wondermart* is accessible to anyone who lives near a supermarket – billions of people worldwide – yet the story can still ask the player to enact specific things, like filling a shopping basket or drawing a heart on the condensation of a freezer cabinet.

Similarly, ZU-UK's groundbreaking *Radio Ghost* (2023) uses specific showtimes to gather small audience groups, but can be mounted in any busy shopping centre or mall. Like *Gentrification: The Game*, *Radio Ghost* is a form of embodied site-specific satire, highlighting the common, exploitative features of hyper-commercialised spaces.

Designing experiences for **generic places** combines some of the advantages of both **location-agnostic** and **location-specific** design:

- **Access**: A **generic place** location type like a supermarket is fairly accessible to a wide range of audiences worldwide.
- **(Semi-)contextual design**: Experiences can use certain location features to anchor and amplify the story through **merged reality moments**.
- **(Semi-)context-blindness**: Even globalisation has its limits; like **homes** (see below), **generic places** are very different worldwide, and creators may simply reveal their own cultural preconceptions if they assume that all supermarkets or airports will share specific features. Smaller **generic places** can be more reliably generic – toilet stalls, roads, car interiors – but even here local variations abound, and the more generic the place the less specific the spationarrative.

Location-Portable Design

Location-portable experiences are designed to work in multiple specific locations.

Due to the narrow accessibility of **location-specific** digital experiences, some are designed to be later re-mounted in a new location with minimal alteration. Immersive theatre and experiential installations often have to tour to be sustainable, but remounting physical installations can be extremely expensive. Digital location-specific narratives, on the other hand, can often be transposed to new locations relatively easily.

Examples of **location-portable** experiences include the *Green Planet AR Experience* (BBC, Factory42, 2022), which was installed at Regent Street in London, but which could work in any location with a similar layout.

Making a narrative feel site-specific across multiple sites, and making the process of re-mounting relatively straightforward and inexpensive, requires modular design. This is much easier if it's designed in from the start. Playlines' AR theatre work was designed to be **location-portable**. Our augmented reality hip-hop opera *CONSEQUENCES* (2018), written and performed by the incredible MC Harry Shotta, consisted of a mobile app and an array of bluetooth location iBeacons. The experience transformed its venue into an augmented nightclub, with players navigating a layer of interactive narrative (set in London's Drum n' Bass scene) which was laid across the venue.

Although initially designed for a specific nightclub location, we designed-in **location-portability** so that the show could tour. We ended up re-mounting it in historic sites, busy festivals and even office buildings, without rewriting the story. Accordingly, the show was designed with modular components: some remounts added set-dressing and live performers to the venue, while other remounts removed certain storylines due to limitations of **layout**.

The only physical infrastructure required to run the show was a set of beacons, each representing different "rooms" in the nightclub setting. The beacons could be removed (or cloned) and re-mounted to augment the show's "rooms" onto new venues. The show's digital **layout** was also designed to be loose and modular, with unlimited **journey** and **dwell times** in order that it could be overlaid across sites with very different physical **layouts** (more on these in 3.1.2).

Modular **location-portability** is common in art installations. Turner Prize-nominee Ghislaine Leung's **location-portable** installations are so modular that they are different in every venue. Each installation is defined by a "score", which is implemented into different sites by local curators. The "score" for Leung's 2022 "Fountains" reads simply "a fountain installed in the exhibition space to cancel sound". The same artwork has multifarious versions in different locations: Leung calls these "scores" because she is "theoretically the composer, and the institution is the performer".[20]

Again, the **location-portable** approach combines some advantages and disadvantages of **location-specific** and **location-agnostic**:

- **Access**: **Location-portable** experiences allow for **location-specific** designs to reach a larger number of audiences through touring.
- **Challenging design**: The more contextual the spationarrative design, the more the show may require redesign for each venue. Modular branching narrative design is complex, as is crafting the mood of an experience that can work in multiple locations. *CONSEQUENCES* effectively superimposed its "digital nightclub" setting onto whatever location it was mounted in. However, it was a very different experience, with a higher baseline of **spationarrative dissonance**, when played in daylight in an office building compared to when we mounted it in an actual nightclub.

Roomscale/At-home

Roomscale AR/spatial experiences take place in an augmented version of the room around the player.

In Virtual Reality, **roomscale** refers to experiences in which headset-wearing players are able to physically move in an indoor space, with their movements tracked by sensors. The player can gesture and, to a limited extent, walk around the virtual space, within the confines of the physical room, and their movements are replicated by avatar movements in the virtual environment. But the player cannot see the room around them because the VR headset is situating them in a virtual environment. The dimensions of the virtual environment seen in the headset usually do not correspond to the physical dimensions of the room. So the player is blind to their physical surroundings: headset sensors detect walls and furniture in relation to the player's location and alert them with in-headset warnings when they are about to bump into an obstacle. (Meta's Guardian interface is an example of these warnings.)

VR **roomscale** design needs to **diegetically** explain to players seeing a virtual environment why they can't physically walk farther than the length of the actual room they're physically in. Or they need to provide alternative ways of virtually moving which don't correspond to physical body movements (e.g. via a joystick).

In augmented/spatial technology, **roomscale** design uses similar room-scanning technology, but the player is looking *through* the technology at an augmented version of their real room.

An augmented/spatial **roomscale** experience might augment digital characters into the physical room, or augment graphics onto the walls. *Prepare to Dive* (2024) depicts your room as a submarine interior, augmenting portholes and control panels onto your walls, and spawning undersea enemies which clamber through the portholes and into the room; *Starship Home* (2024) does the same with a spaceship.

Other **roomscale** experiences might almost completely reskin the room, such as the AI-based room-texturing DreamSpace[21] project by TikTok developers ByteDance.

The dimensions of the augmented environment still correspond to the physical dimensions of the room. This reduces the risk of players physically bumping into walls, and also solidly anchors the experience to the physical surfaces of reality, providing opportunities for **merged reality moments**.

Consumer **roomscale** experiences are generally designed to be played **at home**, which means that they also have an emotive anchoring in the player's home. We all have an emotional connection with the places we live – and we also tend to know their layout. *Espire 2: Stealth Operatives*'s Mixed Reality mode (2023) spawns enemies inside the player's home; players are encouraged to use their meta-knowledge of the physical layout to sneak up on enemies.[22]

Many experiences exploit the emotive distinction between the inside of the **home** and the outside world. *First Encounters* (2023) and *Drop Dead: The Cabin's* Home Invasion mode (2023) augment windows or apertures onto your walls, showing an augmented world outside, often with players "defending the **home**" from enemies "breaking in" from the outside. The augmented "outside world" glimpsed through the apertures is very different from whatever is actually outside the **home**'s walls. This allows these experiences to create the sense that the player's home has been transplanted *Wizard Of Oz*-style into a new place. It's often part of a *fait accompli* scenario such as defending the home from attacking zombies.

Some experiences detect physical features of the **home** and augment them, bringing the scenario into closer alignment with the player's surroundings. AR horror game *Hauntify* (2022) allows players to close doors for protection while being hunted by ghouls through their own home – but then uses this physical solidity to create a horrifying **merged reality moment** – more in 3.1.1: when we look at **spatial pacing**.

Roomscale/at-home experiences share some advantages and disadvantages with **generic places**. **Homes** may have some common features, but few of these can be counted on as homes are very different worldwide.

- **Access: Roomscale/own-home** experiences are intended to meet players where they already are. They often require relatively large rooms clear of furniture, but many players worldwide can access an appropriate space.
- **Semi-generic design:** Players' **homes** might have similar abstract qualities but great physical variations; highly adaptive modular design is required to incorporate physical features.
- **Strong visuotactile congruence**: The player's sense of the immediate reality of their environment is strong due to digital-physical correspondence. Firmly anchoring narrative or gameplay to features in this immediate reality can increase **plausibility**.
- **Established relationships**: An established sense of home can be **diegeticized** into the AR narrative to create highly **desirable objectives**, such as defending the home from attack.

Table-Scale

Table-scale experiences take place on any flat surface.

Many early augmented reality experiences STAGED their action onto a tabletop or a similar flat surface. These experiences have the advantage of very broad accessibility, since almost all players have access to suitable flat surfaces. Many use small-scale characters like animated scale models or a "puppet theatre" aesthetic.

Table-scale experiences can be "in-the-round", i.e. players are able to view the action from any angle around the tabletop, which can be used to reward player **agency** in their choice of **vantage point**. Players might only discover a hidden clue by viewing the **table-scale** drama from a certain **vantage point**. (More on this when we look at **spatial subjectivity** in 3.3.)

Examples of **table-scale** AR experiences include the National Theatre's *All Kinds of Limbo* (2022[23]), which superimposes a miniature concert onto any flat surface. Other experiences such as *Mirrorscape* (2023) and *Demeo* (2021) replicate tabletop miniature games like *Warhammer* or *Dungeons and Dragons* by superimposing scale-model graphics onto table surfaces, while boardgames such as *The Arkham Asylum Files* (2023) have physical boardgame components enhanced with AR graphics.

Arkham Asylum Files also incorporates **at-home** elements, augmenting some clues and features onto physical walls in the player's surrounding room[24] using surface detection. This overcomes a typical weakness of the "puppet theatre" model – lack of reference to the player's surroundings.

Without adopting techniques from **roomscale** or **generic place** design, **table-scale** experiences are generally unable to refer to anything beyond the horizontal surface they are anchored to. As a result most **table-scale** experiences are stories-in-a-box: dramas taking place upon a miniature stage, but not meaningfully taking the player's context as a setting.

Table-scale has the advantage of flexibility and the broadest possible accessibility, but in storytelling terms it's constrained by its small scale and relative context-blindness:

- **Access**: **table-scale** experiences are truly **location-agnostic**, requiring only the most basic of features, a flat surface, which provides a strong anchor to reality.
- **Confined, context-blind design**: Many creators have produced compelling dramas at this scale. But without reference to the player's immediate environment there is limited potential for **merged reality moments** or contextual narrative.

NOTES

1. Speakman, 2019, p. 25.
2. Erica Carter, James Donald, Judith Squires (eds.), *Space and Place*, Lawrence & Wishart, London, 1993, p. xii.
3. Doreen Massey, *Space, Place and Gender*, University of Minnesota Press, 1994, p. 137.
4. Doreen Massey, *For Space*, Sage, London, 2005, p. 1.

5. Massey, 1994, p. 154.
6. Massey, 2005, p. 1.
7. "The Voices of Place", Matt Hayler, *Ambient Literature* 18 Apr 2018, https://research.ambient lit.com/index.php/2018/04/18/the-voices-of-place/.
8. Hanke/Patel, 2021.
9. Sinclair, 2023.
10. Johan Peitz, Hannamari Saarenpää, Staffan Björk, "Insectopia – Exploring Pervasive Games through Technology already Pervasively Available", *Proceedings of the International Conference on Advances in Computer Entertainment Technology, 2007.*
11. "Mogi = Socially Connected GPS Gaming", Wireless Watch Japan, 2 Jul 2004 https://wirelesswatch.jp/2004/07/02/mogi-socially-connected-gps-gaming/.
12. Craig Chapple, "Pokémon GO Catches $5 Billion in Lifetime Revenue in Five Years", SensorTower, July 2021 https://sensortower.com/blog/pokemon-go-five-billion-revenue.
13. de Souza e Silva *et al.,* 2021.
14. Ono Sachiko, Ono Yosuke, Michihata Nobuaki, Sasabuchi Yusuke, Yasunaga Hideo, "Effect of Pokémon GO on Incidence of Fatal Traffic Injuries: A Population-Based Quasi-Experimental Study Using the National Traffic Collisions Database in Japan," *Injury Prevention* 24:6, 2017.
15. Sander Veenhof, Johannes la Poutre, Tobias Domhan, *Augmented Reality Flash Mob*, MoMA 2021 https://www.moma.org/interactives/exhibitions/2011/talktome/objects/146407/.
16. *#arOCCUPYWALLSTREET* https://aroccupywallstreet.wordpress.com/ retrieved 26 Aug 2023, recorded in Mark Skwarek, "Augmented Reality Activism" in V. Geroimenko (ed.), *Augmented Reality Art*, Springer, Switzerland, 2014, p. 24.
17. *Skinny Ape*, Gorillaz/Nexus, https://nexusstudios.com/work/skinny-ape/.
18. Marc Augé (2006) [1992], *Non-Places: Introduction to an Anthropology of Supermodernity*, John Howe (trans.) Verso, London, 1995.
19. Silvia Mercuriali, *Macondo*, https://www.silviamercuriali.com/macondo retrieved 24 Aug 2023.
20. Nicholas Wroe, "Toys, Twisted Rollercoasters, Rooftop Fountains", *The Guardian* 23 Sept 2023 https://www.theguardian.com/artanddesign/2023/sep/23/turner-prize-2023-barbara-walker-ghislaine-leung-rory-pilgrim-jesse-darling-towner-eastbourne.
21. Bangbang Yang, Wenqi Dong, Lin Ma, Wenbo Hu, Xiao Liu, Zhaopeng Cui, Yuewen Ma, "DreamSpace: Dreaming Your Room Space with Text-Driven Panoramic Texture Propagation", ByteDance / Zhejiang University, 2023, https://ybbbbt.com/publication/dreamspace/ retrieved 16 Feb 2023.
22. Alan Truly, "Hands-on with Espire 2's New Procedural Mixed Reality Missions", *Mixed News* 26 Nov 2023 https://mixed-news.com/en/hands-on-with-espire-2s-new-procedural-mixed-reality-missions/.
23. *All Kinds of Limbo,* National Theatre / Dimension Studios https://www.allkindsoflimbo.com/.
24. Todd Martens, "Using Augmented Reality and Novel-like Storytelling, L.A. Designers Want to Upend the Board Game", *LA Times*, 27 Jul 2023, https://www.latimes.com/entertainment-arts/story/2023-07-27/augmented-reality-storytelling-los-angeles-designers-want-to-upend-board-game.

STAGING

3.1

How do we activate player IMAGINATIONS to help STAGE digital narratives in real places?

How do we design for and co-opt real physical layouts to create augmented spationarratives?

How do we pace augmented spationarratives?

How do we create and communicate the boundaries of augmented spationarratives?

ALL THE WORLD'S A STAGE

In AR/spatial storytelling, the player merges with the protagonist, and the player's location also merges with the story's setting. Every element in your narrative, whether it's audio dialogue or graphical reskinning of physical surfaces, should support the player in imaginatively STAGING the narrative as something that's happening WHERE they are.

Our first pillar of emotional immersion in VR, SEEING, will now evolve into STAGING as we begin augmenting the player's location. In this Chapter 3.1, we'll explore ways to anchor digital elements to physical features and use this to enhance the player's sense of **spatial agency** and complicity in a narrative that's happening around them.

We'll look at techniques to help concretely anchor digital elements to the world; to exploit the existing **layouts** of places to help tell our story; to use spatial design to help **pace** our story while maintaining player agency; and to communicate the **boundaries** of a storyscape.

You might be reading this at a time when AR headsets and neural resonance AI or similar technologies have made large-scale graphical reskins of the real world possible – maybe with **passthrough** video, or even true **see-through** glasses. Players may even be able to choose to SEE different narrative or gameplay layers or versions of the same location. But remember, what makes an experience emotionally immersive is not how *convincing* it is, but how *compelling*. No matter how fully you can digitally overlay the world, you need to ask the same questions as storytellers in other media: *how do I get players to engage with a narrative when they're surrounded by the real world with all its distractions? How do I engage them when they're surrounded by an increasingly competitive ecosystem of content?*

3.1: STAGING is divided into two sub-chapters:

3.1.1: General Augmented STAGING
3.1.2: Location-Specific Augmented STAGING

Both sub-chapters explore **layout, pacing** and **boundaries,** as well as examining hybrid locative categories like **generic places** or **roomscale** where relevant.

3.1.1 includes CHALLENGES to explore the general techniques of augmented STAGING.

3.1.2 begins a sequence of CHALLENGES which will incorporate all the techniques you've learned so far to build up a full prototype spationarrative for a specific location.

General Augmented STAGING

3.1.1

GENERAL PRINCIPLES OF HYBRID SPATIONARRATIVES

We often tend to think of media, especially immersive media, in terms of "escapism" or being "transported" elsewhere. When fuelled by narrative, our IMAGINATION can be so powerful that we can be situated in one physical place while imaginatively STAGING ourselves somewhere else. Researcher Jay Springett talks about playing a tabletop RPG (or TTRPG) set in Terry Pratchett's indelibly vivid Discworld. Though the players were situated "sitting around a student kitchen table, an overflowing ashtray at its centre… coexisting with the memory of nights spent in that smoky room are very real memories of being in the cobbled streets of Ankh-Morpork." So, as Springett says, "I have two memories, in the kitchen AND in the Discworld. What is this called? Two co-located realities on top of one another. A hybrid or hyper memory"?[1]

A Virtual Reality appears to transport the player somewhere else entirely. But augmented/spatial media appear to be taking place in the world around the player. So augmented players experience a similar *co-location of multiple realities* – they are co-located in an IMAGINED and a real location simultaneously. Unlike TTRPG players, augmented players are not IMAGINING themselves to be *somewhere else* like a dragon's cave: augmented players are imaginatively helping to STAGE augmentations into their actual surroundings. Their minds help cohere digital elements into the real, physical environment – so long as those elements are congruent and emotionally engaging enough to prompt "active creation of belief". The augmented player can then experience a hybrid- or hyper-place.

So in augmented/spatial storytelling, we need to think not about "escapism" but about *scapism*: introducing narrative elements to exploit and dramatize and **diegeticize** the actual features of the player's physical location, rather than trying to transpose the player somewhere else.

As we saw in 2.1, players are very capable of re-IMAGINING physical features as hybrid physical/fictional features, like blocking ray gun blasts by hiding behind a tree/ Martian cyber-oak. Springett talks about him and his friends co-opting the features of a playing field during shared imagination games, "LARPing our way around the

DOI: 10.1201/9781003379294-17

school field. The white lines of the football pitch recast as the dark and dank corridors of 'Zombie Dungeon'".[2] Similarly, a study from 2012 found that child Pokémon fans engaged in imaginative play in their neighbourhoods would "intimately, contingently and formatively co-implicate" the world of Pokémon "with/in everyday geographies".[3] In other words, five years before *Pokémon GO* these kids were routinely "integrat[ing] Pokémon play into the structure of their mundane spatial practices and daily space-time routines, effectively remaking their homes, local shops, and neighbourhoods as inter-volved with the Pokémon universe".[4]

With enough imaginative engagement, players can experience their local physical geography "intervolved" with both imagined and augmented elements. And through augmented IDENTITY, players can feel a strong sense of BEING THERE in these hybrid physical/narrative storyscapes (more on this in 3.2).

In short, we need to let go of the idea of helping players "escape" and focus on intervolving both theirselves and the physical features around them – and that includes intervolving unpredictable elements like the weather. Like augmented IDENTITIES, we have to co-create augmented places with our players. But this can be an advantage, because we have relatively little control over an augmented story's setting, especially in location-agnostic experiences like LBGs. As co-creators, players' IMAGINATIONS can fill in any gaps to STAGE a coherent spationarrative.

We might be able to reskin the physical world around the player, but we have to fol-low its basic shape. So what physical aspects of our STAGE – the player's local reality – most impact storytelling? What aspects of a place should you be looking for to use it as an augmented setting?

As AR/spatial storytellers, we aren't able to construct or architect the dimensions or basic features of our settings; we have to work with the places where the player finds themselves, or meet them in their home. However, there's still much to learn from digital storytellers who get to fully design and control virtual settings. In her essay "Challenges of a Broad Geography" the pioneering interactive fiction writer Emily Short lays out three key principles for designing the geography of interactive fiction worlds:

[1:] "Build a **layout** that is easy for the player to understand without extensive mapping".
[2:] "Control access to parts of the geography in a way that sets the desired **pace** for the game, through puzzles and other design techniques;
[3:] "Disguise the **edges** of the map from the player so that [the map] doesn't feel claustrophobic".[5]

Short is talking about text-based interactive fiction (which includes some of the earliest videogames ever made, and is still a thriving medium today through visual novels and narrative RPGs). These games have to build coherent, evocative virtual geographies, often through words alone, so Short's challenges are helpful as a framework when we're thinking about overlaying navigable and compelling story-scapes onto real geography. We'll use these three principles (**layout, pac-ing** and **edges/boundaries**) to establish some techniques for STAGING augmented narratives. In this chapter, we'll examine these in general terms, then in 3.1.2 in **location-specific** terms.

GENERAL AUGMENTED STAGING: LAYOUT

The first and most fundamental physical quality influencing spatial narrative is **layout**: the immediate physical geography and how the story is overlaid onto it. Designing augmented spationarratives requires us to use physical **layout**, not overwrite it: as locative narrative researcher Jeff Ritchie says, while designers are "constrained in their ability to create the architecture or details of the spaces in which they unfold their narratives, storytellers can still take advantage of the opportunity afforded by the language of physical space and the interplay between digitally-mediated and physically-mediated story elements".[6]

So what kinds of physical features comprise spationarrative **layouts**? How do we use them to help the place tell the story? And how do we communicate **layout** so the storyscape is "easy for the player to understand without extensive mapping"?

Augmenting Spatial Elements

Emily Short describes several geographical features or "memorable topologies" helpful for building interactive fiction storyscapes, including street maps, rivers, hubs and landmarks.[7] These features are similar to the five basic elements of "urban legibility" which, according to urban theorist Kevin Lynch, build up people's "mental maps" of a city: **paths, edges, districts, [hubs]** and **landmarks.**[8]

(Lynch actually uses "node" instead of **"hub"**, but in spationarrative design **"node"** is typically used to describe any located piece of content, and this is how it's used in this book. To avoid confusion, we'll use **hub** as the **spatial element** or geographical feature, and use **node** to refer to location-based digital content.)

(Note that **edges** (such as rivers in Short's example) shape the topology *within* a storyscape: we'll consider these kinds of **edges** here under **layout**. But we'll deal separately with the *outer edges* of the storyscape under **boundaries**.)

To illustrate how Lynch's five elements apply in storytelling environments, researcher Sarah Perry helpfully related them to the "marvellously internally legible environment" of Disneyland:

> **LYNCH'S FIVE SPATIAL ELEMENTS (AS DISNEYLAND ELEMENTS – SARAH PERRY)**
>
> - *Paths* are "channels along which the observer potentially, occasionally, or customarily moves" [Lynch]. In Disneyland, these include footpaths, the railroads, and even the paths that rides take through their environments.
> - *Landmarks* are distinctive features of the landscape used for navigation, but used externally for navigation rather than entered into. Signs and towers are **landmarks**. In the case of Disneyland, the Matterhorn could be a **[hub]** or **landmark**, depending on how it is used.

- *[Hubs] are junctions (of paths) or concentrations of activity that people travel to and from, and enter into. In Disneyland, railroad stations, ride entrances and exits, and attractions like Sleeping Beauty's Castle form [hubs].*
- *Edges are linear elements not considered as paths, but rather as boundaries (with different levels of permeability). The Rivers of America at Disneyland form an edge; they may be crossed by boat or canoe, and form a natural boundary to foot traffic.*
- *Districts are medium-to-large two-dimensional areas that the observer mentally enters "inside of". Within Disneyland, the districts are the different lands: Fantasyland, Frontierland, etc.[9]*

These five **spatial elements** make up players' mental map of the storyscape, provide navigation guidance, and represent physical geographical features to which digital elements can be anchored. Crucially, they are all generally detectable or inferable from GPS data (either by reading topology or accessing spatial datasets via platforms like Niantic's Lightship). This means that as well as designing for these **spatial elements** in **location-specific** design, storytellers could potentially detect and procedurally refer to or incorporate these elements into **location-agnostic** and semi-**agnostic** narratives.

We'll use these five **spatial elements** as our components of spationarrative **layout** (Figure 3.1.1).

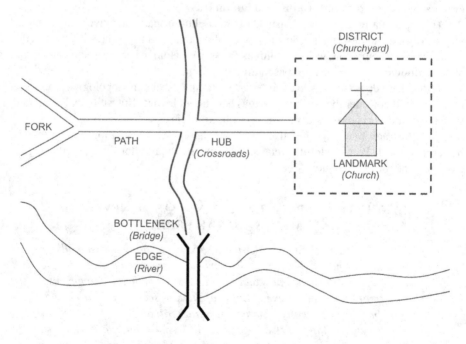

FIGURE 3.1.1   Example map of **spatial elements**

Paths

Any designated or demarcated "channel" for travelling along. Pre-existing paths provide players with clear navigation guidance: *follow the path/road/trail* is straightforward to communicate with in-fiction dialogue or narration. **Paths** can also be helpful in clearly demarcating **forks** where the player can make decisions through **spatial agency** (More on this in 3.2: BEING THERE.)

It's also very possible to augment new digital **paths** onto landscape, allowing you to provide navigation in **path**-less places (though this has safety and accessibility implications – more on this in Appendix A).

In **location-specific** design, **paths** can help storytellers closely curate players' spatial experience by defining **journey times** and moving the player through areas with a specific mood or feel, to support a particular story moment. (More on **journey times** shortly when we look at **spatial pacing**.)

In **location-agnostic** design, **paths** could be drawn algorithmically between content **nodes** with the same kind of wayfinding used in GPS map. Algorithmic wayfinding has limited context-awareness, so it's difficult to predict the **journey time** or the landscape your player will move through. **Locagnostic** storytellers have to embrace that serendipity.

Paths often interlink content **nodes**, but they are also, themselves, spationarrative content. If the player spends time journeying between different content **nodes**, their IMAGINATION should still be engaged during these **journey times** so their experience is in-character and **diegetic**. Delivering content as the player is moving along a **path** allows you to unfold content in a specific linear order during journeys, with some control over **pacing** (even if the wider storyscape is nonlinear). Your storytelling could also exploit the texture and mood of the **path**, refer to physical features the player passes, or augment new visual features to look at.

Bear in mind that players don't necessarily follow **paths**! There's almost always more than one route between locations. Players will generally take the **path**-of-least-resistance, but some players rebel, others explore, others simply get lost. If you *need* players to follow a specific **path**, in **location-specific** design you may be able to use a physical **bottleneck** (see 3.1.2). But generally, if you *want* players to follow a certain **path**, consider ways to make that **path** expressive of the player's **spatial agency**. Choosing a **path** should help players express their IDENTITY in the story (More on **spatial agency** in 3.2).

The shape formed by **paths** will in many ways define the shape of the player's experience and the "mental map" they form of the storyscape. **Path layout** is key to helping players navigate and express agency. According to Short, "a streetmap design allows the player to think of the structure of the world in terms of streets with a number of subordinate locations". In other words, link major content **nodes** to major **paths** (or *arterials*) with a network of interlinking subordinate **paths** (or *capillaries*). With this sort of **layout** "the player automatically creates a hierarchy between two types of location: *arterials*, which can be remembered with respect to each other, and *cul-de-sacs*, whose location only needs to be remembered with respect to the arterial".[10] In this way content **nodes** can be conceptualised and easily navigated.

A streetmap structure is useful when you want players to progress a linear story through spatial progress: it provides a strong spine to STAGE a story on, and can be relatively easily read from or algorithmically imposed on the player's local geography. If on the other hand you want players to freely explore a nonlinear "sandbox" space, you'll need to focus more on **landmarks** for navigability.

Landmarks

Landmarks are valuable as aides to navigation, and are particularly helpful in anchoring digital landscape to physical for **merged reality moments**. *Ingress* functions by designating physical **landmarks** like public art, monuments and statues – many tagged by players themselves – as in-game content **nodes**, and *Pokémon GO*'s digital geography built on that same dataset. This means that the abstract map icons of Gyms and Pokéstops have solid physical anchors, which aids their memorability and navigability. The types of **landmarks** used in Niantic LBGs are often semantically identified in GPS datasets so could be algorithmically identified for use in **locagnostic layouts**. But access to these datasets may require substantial license fees. A version of Niantic's own global dataset including its **landmarks** is available for developers through its Lightship platform.

Landmarks don't have to be right in front of the player to be meaningful. Augmenting distant **landmarks** can be helpful to create a sense of a wider fictional world beyond the player's immediate surroundings. A distant-but-visible physical **landmark** like a skyscraper can act as an anchor, even if you're re-skinning it as a wizard's tower or a giant beanstalk. Short suggests portraying distant **landmarks** which can be seen from multiple different locations to provide orientation.

Layouts can be built around **landmarks** to help players draw their "mental maps". You could select (or algorithmically determine) a prominent **landmark** the player can see from multiple **vantage points** – a large tree, a hill or a skyscraper – and distribute your content **nodes** in relation to it. That way "different areas of the map can be understood not merely as north and south of each other, but – more simply – as north or south of a central point. The player builds a hub-like conception of the game world".[11] This provides a much clearer **layout** to STAGE a story around than a scatter of unrelated content **nodes**.

Hubs

Whether or not they're arranged around a **landmark**, **hubs** are where **paths** intersect or where players might congregate. **Hubs** are common in videogame level design: they allow access to a range of content, and encourage or require players to return to the same area several times during progression. If players return to the same place with predictable regularity it allows for story-driven changes to be shown in that place over time, whether that's magical plants slowly overtaking a train station, or a budding romance with a shopkeeper character. Change is what drives narrative, and this over-time experience of narrative progression in an augmented place is powerful for STAGING emotional effects.

In **location-agnostic** design **hub** areas could be imposed algorithmically onto maps by reading identifiable generic features like public squares, parks or even the player's own home. Remember that rural players will almost always need to travel further to a public gathering-place. But any crossroads can be a **hub**, and all crossroads have an inherent spatial drama – there's a reason you go to crossroads to make a deal with the devil.

Edges

An **edge** is the opposite of a **path**: a physical feature which can't be easily crossed, which divides up the accessible areas of a space and shapes player movement within the storyscape. An **edge** is not just an area of impassible terrain: it runs through space in a line, which is powerful for building players' mental maps. Emily Short uses the analogy of "rivers": "any geographical feature that runs through or beside several locations reinforces a sense of continuous space... coastline, a wall that runs past several locations, a cliff[12]..." Examples could also include railway lines and fences. These could be reimagined or reskinned as lava rivers, force fields or leylines depending on your narrative.

Co-opting physical **edges** into a spationarrative **layout** allows you to fence-in player movement, and potentially direct them down specific **paths** or even **bottlenecks**: you could give players the objective of crossing a river, guaranteeing they will move across one of the available bridges. Bear in mind that in spatial design terms, **edges** present barriers and friction to the player, so they're an important part of gameplay. You could require players to follow the **path** of a dragon flying as-the-crow-flies across a landscape, so players are forced to navigate around local **edges** – transforming the player's local geography into an obstacle course.

Districts

A **district** is a "medium-to-large" area with a distinct identity, like a neighbourhood. (It might also be a **hub**, e.g. a very large town square.) **Districts** are containers of spatial meaning, so they can be helpful for navigation – communicating to the player that the story all takes place within a named **district** is useful for defining outer **boundaries**, for example. **Districts** can also provide clear changes in geography to add texture to spationarratives – moving from ordinary streets to a busy shopping precinct will likely come with a change of mood which could help your STAGING.

However, many **districts** are relatively ill-defined; even if they have specific **boundaries** demarcated in GPS datasets these may not correspond to physical **edges** or players' perception of where a **district** begins. You could simply define a fictional **district** onto real space using augmented graphics or drawing on a map: depending on your story you could designate an area of space as the "infected zone" or the "magic kingdom".

Let's explore how these five **spatial elements** could be used to build up a spationarrative **layout** in **location-portable** design.

CHALLENGE #16: LOCATION-PORTABLE LAYOUTS

Goal: Explore the challenges and opportunities of augmenting **layouts** on multiple locations.

SUMMARY

Select two **places** in different parts of the world which share a similar **spatial element**, and obtain maps for each place. For example, you could identify areas of two parks which have a similar **edge** like a river, or two neighbourhoods both clustered around a **landmark** like a hill or skyscraper.

Conceptualise a spationarrative which reimagines the **spatial element**.

Develop three **characters** or other **content nodes** with narrative relationships to your chosen **spatial element**. You could reimagine a hill **landmark** as a smoking volcano, and **develop** three worried townsfolk characters in three different locations nearby. Or reskin a river **edge** as a magical leyline and **develop** three scattered ritual stones the player must visit to purify it.

Abstractly **diagram** the location of each **content node** in relation to your chosen **spatial element**. E.g. arrange your three **content nodes** in a **hub layout** around a **landmark** (say, three worried villagers at different **vantage points** around the volcano). Or arrange them in a "streetmap" structure which provides a clear **path** over or through an **edge** (say, arranging three ritual stones either side of the river, incorporating a bridge which players must cross and where you can STAGE content).

This **diagram** is your spationarrative **layout.** Now **overlay** the **layout diagram** onto BOTH maps, and identify where each content node should be placed in both physical geographies.

Finally, **write** dialogue/narration for each of the character/content elements. Refer specifically to the **spatial feature** to anchor the digital layer in local geography, but ensure the content is **portable** and works in BOTH locations.

TASKS

- **Select** two **places** which share a **spatial element**. Obtain **maps**.
- **Conceptualise** a **locagnostic** narrative which reimagines the element.
- **Develop** three **characters** or **content nodes**.
- **Diagram** a spationarrative **layout** with **content nodes** arranged in relation to the **spatial element**.
- **Overlay** the **layout** onto both **maps**.
- **Write** narrative for your spationarrative and a typical player's journey through it.

BONUS CHALLENGE

How well did your **layout** fit each chosen location? Did you find yourself prioritising one location in your design? Consider a **location-agnostic** version: how would your **layout** need to algorithmically adjust to fit different geographies?

GENERAL AUGMENTED STAGING: SPATIAL PACING

Short's second principle of interactive fictional geography is "control access to parts of the geography in a way that sets the desired **pace** for the game, through puzzles and other design techniques". **Pacing** refers both to a story's sequence of events, and the timing of when those events occur. To **pace** a spationarrative we don't just need to know the sequence of events; we also need to consider the **journey time** required to move between spatial content **nodes**, and find ways to choreograph players' movements.

Agency and Pacing

Layout has a big impact on **pacing**. As Ritchie says, "while the physical environment can potentially constrain narrative pacing, in that travel across space requires a passage of time perhaps inconsistent with narrative purposes, movement through space can also be used to frame enacted narratives".[13] The duration spent journeying between different content **nodes** affects how an experience feels and the narrative the player maintains in their head as they play.

Most **location-agnostic** LBGs treat locations as "templated spaces".[14] LBGs algorithmically distribute content **nodes** (e.g. Pokéstops) across generic geographical elements, most often **landmarks**. Content **nodes** have only a general relationship to their geography (e.g. water-type Pokémon might spawn near bodies of water), but the distance between **nodes** is determined partially by game design (for example, PokéStops tend to be a minimum distance apart). But the general **pacing** of the player's experience is still unpredictable and serendipitous.

Whereas, in **location-specific** design, we can impose more **pacing** by defining **paths** and other **layout** elements. But **pacing** will still be subject to the player's **spatial agency**. **Journey times** will vary from player to player. **Pacing** is part of the player's agency as an embodied protagonist. We can't meticulously **pace location-specific** spationarratives; instead, as Ritchie says, "by influencing the perception and the movement of the audience through the physical world, embedded narrative elements can be emphasised and consequently chronologically arranged to convey a narrative".[15]

Furthermore, duration is one of the easiest variables to detect and respond to in digital storytelling. Say you want to create a sense of urgency: a character might urge the player to hurry to a content **node**. If the player chooses to take, say, longer than ten minutes to arrive, the character they meet could **conditionally** respond to the duration, perhaps asking them why they dawdled. Players could even arrive *too late*. Thanks to the principle of **panopticon**, once this level of consequentiality is established, the player will understand that the time they spend in-between **nodes** is in-character, **diegetic** and consequential.

DWELL TIMES AND JOURNEY TIMES

Think carefully about the overall duration of a spationarrative, and the different ways you want your players to experience this time. If you want your player to remain static at a **node** while you narrate, this is **dwell time**. Remember players are not a passive audience; they are actively present in the spationarrative. This means that keeping players static always risks their attention actively wandering.

A **node**'s maximum **dwell time** is the longest duration you can reasonably ask players to dwell without critical loss of their attention. This varies from player to player and with other factors, especially weather. So it's always better to keep your storytelling brisk. In audio, players' attention usually begins to wander after as little as 90 seconds' **dwell time**. Graphical augmentation of the environment via headsets may increase maximum **dwell time**, but any time a player is made passive in the narrative, they will quickly be distracted by the real world. Only ask players to dwell if there is something for them to actively sense, interpret or form a relationship with.

Journey time is the duration while the player moves between **nodes**. People move at very different speeds so your available duration is uncertain. **Test journey times** with different people with a range of mobility needs. If your **conditional pacing** feels punitive or some players miss out on content due to **journey times**, consider adding an accessibility mode with longer durations suitable for those with different mobilities. More on designing for different mobilities in Appendix A.

Consider implementing modular journey content; slower-moving players could trigger additional content to fill longer **journey times**. Ensure that modular content is non-essential, since faster-moving players may miss it entirely. Consider whether modular content should be interrupted or continue to play if the player arrives at the destination **node**. Your goal is to provide the right amount of content to cover different **journey times**. But **journey time** content doesn't need to seamlessly fill time; there's nothing wrong with augmented players experiencing silence.

Diegetic and Nondiegetic Durations

As Ritchie says, "the experience and changing perspective of moving through a space is an enacted narrative".[16] The story doesn't unfold through the storyteller positioning content **nodes** on a map; the story is in the player's experience of moving through these **nodes**, in hybrid with their IDENTITY and physical features of the geography. The story is unfolding any time the player exists in an augmented place embodying an augmented IDENTITY. Spatial narratives are not "on pause" even when players are not in direct contact with the content, say if they're currently journeying between content **nodes** in an LBG.

Motive.io's mobile game *CodeRunner* (2011) was a **location-agnostic** AR game designed to be played in any North American city. It dramatised the player's interactions with standard urban features like gas stations, buses and convenience stores. The player was cast as a spy, and might be asked to perform a mission by going to a convenience store and staying nearby to "hack" it. The game's content management system read online datasets such as live weather and even bus timetables to generate contextual events: the narrative might respond to whether it was raining; in order to evade pursuit players might be prompted to get on a bus which was just arriving.

CodeRunner's narrative was a loose structure of vignette **nodes**, in-between which player-characters journeyed or waited to be contacted about missions. But even when players weren't in direct contact with content, the game had still augmented a dimension of play onto their experience of the city.[17]

Pacing in spatial narratives doesn't mean filling every square inch of space-time with narration. Most stories have a lot of implied silence, and there's nothing wrong with an embodied player-character experiencing silence as part of their **diegetic** protagonist journey. It's more important to establish compelling player IDENTITY and **objectives** which alter how they relate to places around them in an ongoing way. This creates a spatial story the player continues telling themselves during the natural silences of embodied experience.

Traditional concepts of immersion are not just about immersing (or submerging) us in a different place; there's often also a suspension of time. Brooks says "when we are drawn into narrative time so completely that we lose track of presentation time, we are immersed... For a few moments, we as audience can leave the cares of our time and put on the simpler cares and tailored joys of characters we have just met".[18]

Brooks identifies two types of time in the experience of narrative: "Presentation Time", the time that passes at its regular rate while a story is being told, and "Narrative Time", the internal time of the story in which we're immersed. Presentation Time is the real-time duration of the story's telling: "a real-time experience encompassing the narrative experience... the time during which one is in the movie theatre theatre".[19] Whereas in almost all stories the Narrative Time moves at a different rate to the real world (with the exception of movies shot in realtime, like *High Noon* (1952) and *Run Lola Run* (1998)). Narrative Time could jump over minutes, days or years, run in slow-motion or even backwards.

But an augmented reality is STAGED in the real world, where time is manifestly passing. The player's perceptual apparatus constantly senses time move forward. So there's a risk of juxtaposition if we try to manipulate Narrative Time: players are looking *through* augmented media *at* the world, in which time is going on at its usual unforgiving rate. Hence, in AR/spatial storytelling it's hard to skip around in Narrative Time the way a film does with editing or a novel does with ellipses and elision. We certainly can't put reality into slow-mo or fast-forward.

But this doesn't mean an augmented/spatial story's **diegetic** Narrative Time needs to match the unwavering march of realtime. Our experience of time is fundamentally relative. So in AR/spatial we can still create slippages in time. They're best positioned when the narrative is focused on the player's internal experience (like **journey times**), not when the player's attention is focused on physical places where time's passing is most manifest.

Key to this is the idea that the Narrative Time of augmented/spatial experiences is continuously passing *within the player* even if there isn't any durational content currently happening like narration or dialogue. A *Pokémon GO* player is still *hunting Pokémon* even if they're not actively flicking Pokéballs; their augmented IDENTITY and augmented relationship to place is not "on pause" when journeying between the content

nodes. In these **diegetic** interstitial periods, the player's experience of time is highly relative, and so these are durations where manipulation of Narrative Time can take place.

This implies is a third type of time in AR/spatial narratives: not quite "Presentation Time" i.e. realtime duration, and not quite "Narrative Time" i.e. the depicted duration. It's a hybrid of real-time and the subjective experience of the player's internal narrative: the "**Relative Time**" of embodied experience.

With **Relative Time** augmented **pacing** can be as relative as players' own inner experience; slowing to a crawl during a boring lecture or passing in a blink during a delightful conversation.

The artist David Hockney explored depicting **Relative Time** in the visual medium of photo collage. Hockney was accustomed to creating the illusion of space and time in paintings, but a photograph has no illusion of time:

> The photograph didn't really have life the way a drawing or a painting did... It's a fraction of a second, frozen. So the moment you've looked at it for even four seconds, you're looking at it for far more than the camera did... If [an image] is the same time at the top left-hand corner as it is in the bottom right-hand corner, there's something wrong with time. It's stopped.[20]

Hockney responded to this lack of temporality in photographs by creating "joiners", photo collages depicting objects or people from multiple perspectives and multiple temporal moments, such as *The Scrabble Game, Jan 1st 1983*. The collages composit multiple photographs of the same scene taken over time; multiple "frozen fractions of a second" combine into a coherent image with a sense of duration.

Locagnostic pacing for augmented narratives is best handled with a similar "temporal collage" approach. We can't stop time from passing all around the player whilst we tell them the story. And we risk juxtaposition if we try to cut and edit time too much. In a sense we need to do what Hockney did by collaging photos: create interlinked moments of Narrative Time, but empower and exploit the player's relative experience of time and let their subjective perspective take the lead when moving between those moments.

This means storyboarding moments of content where Presentation Time and Narrative Time both run effectively in realtime, but separating these moments with **Relative Time**. The **Relative Time** "gaps" become the journeys, pauses, ellipses and other idle moments which make up ordinary experience – and provided that we have successfully augmented the player, their "enacted narrative" will continue throughout.

This is partly why AUGMENTING IDENTITY is so key: when the player is in-character, any **Relative Time** they spend can be **diegetic**, even if they're not in direct contact with authored content. Remember, *the most important reality you're augmenting is the player themselves*.

Conditional Pacing

How do we ensure story moments are deployed (or better still, triggered by players) at the most effective, emotive time? And how do we prevent players from seeing key story events in the wrong order?

Short describes an example of **spatial pacing** in interactive fiction. Say the storyteller wants the player to meet a "king" character, but only AFTER they have met a "vizier" character:

> The author guards the king's audience chamber with a servant who must be bribed; [the author also] places a bag of gold in the guest bedroom, so that the player is guaranteed to explore that area before proceeding. In order to reach the guest bedroom, the player must pass through the hallway, where the palace vizier is wandering around.

In this way, the storyteller can guarantee the player will meet the vizier before they meet the king:

> Carefully applied, this method can even disguise the linearity of a fairly strict narrative design, by making a string of events (which always happens in the same order) appear to be a natural outcome of the geography of the setting and the goal the player is pursuing.[21]

The player can't initially meet the king because they can't physically access the guarded audience chamber. In Interactive Fiction this is mediated by code, not physical space. If the storyteller doesn't want the player to access the audience chamber, they can exclude the possibility in the game's logic. If the author wants the player to only be able to access the audience chamber under certain circumstances, they can lock off (or "**gate**") the audience chamber in the game's logic by making access to it **conditional**. **Conditionality** means using IF->THEN statements to determine logic.

In Interactive Fiction this is usually handled by creating and editing **variables** in an event script. The event script is usually a text document or spreadsheet and is separate to the actual code base of an interactive project. The event script manages the content by giving all content assets a specific name by which they will be triggered. It also lists **variables** which track all the consequential things the player can do.

In industry-standard Interactive Fiction scripting language Twine, **conditionality** is controlled by **variables** usually denoted by $, e.g. "$BagOfGold". **Variables** can be assigned different values, and the computer uses IF > THEN logic to trigger certain events IF a **variable** has a certain value. Let's look at an abstract example of **conditional** scripting.

The storyteller wants to prevent the player from meeting the king until they have first met the vizier. So they want the door to be locked except IF the player has satisfied the **condition** of having the Bag of Gold in their inventory (which in turn guarantees they have met the vizier).

The author sets up a **variable**, "$BagOfGold" to track the bag of gold, and sets its value to "no". The author sets up another **variable**, "$KingsChamberDoor", and sets it to "locked".

IF the player approaches the King's chamber door, the game's logic checks the **variable** "$BagOfGold". IF "$BagOfGold=no", THEN "$KingsChamberDoor" remains "locked".

IF "$KingsChamberDoor=locked", THEN players are prevented from entering. It acts as a logic **gate**. (This could be represented in-narrative by the guard refusing to unlock the door unless bribed.)

IF the player enters the guest bedroom, meets the vizier, and acquires the bag of gold, THEN "$BagOfGold" is set to "yes".

IF the player now approaches the audience chamber door, the game's logic checks the **variable** "$BagOfGold".

IF "$BagOfGold=yes", THEN "$KingsChamberDoor" is set to "unlocked".

IF "$KingsChamberDoor=unlocked", the player can enter. (In-narrative this could be represented as bribing the guard.)

From these basic building blocks of **conditionality** it's possible to construct highly sophisticated interactive fictions with strong player agency. You can try your hand at one yourself shortly.

But Short's example didn't take place inside a physical royal palace; it took place in a virtual environment defined wholly by code. In augmented places, especially **locagnostic**, we may not be able to physically **gate** access to a space.

LBGs and other locative narrative experiences often have **variable**-driven **conditionality** systems similar to IFs and flatscreen games. Players input commands via touchscreen or by choosing where to physically go. These choices are tracked by **variables**. Content in the digital layer can be **gated** and locked off in the same way as in the example above. For example, player actions like using a "lure" in a location might alter **variables** controlling the likelihood of a Pokémon spawning in that location.

But it's more difficult to physically lock off physical places using **conditionality** that only exists in the digital layer.

In controlled **location-specific** settings it's possible to create **digital-physical gates** where digital **variables** indirectly determine player access to physical areas. For example, players could be given a passcode in the digital layer, which they must speak to a physical "bouncer" or type into a physical door lock. (We'll look at this type of **digital-physical gate** more in 3.1.2.)

But in **locagnostic** settings you generally can't **gate** off players' physical access to spaces using only digital **variables**.

Let's recreate the example above as a **locagnostic** augmented spationarrative, taking into account physical and digital access.

The storyteller wants the player to be prevented from meeting the king except IF the player has satisfied the **condition** of meeting the vizier.

The **location-agnostic** content system algorithmically designates an area of a nearby park as "Location:KingsChamber" defined by a set of <gps coordinates>. The vizier is at a set of different coordinates.

Without a physical **gate**, the player could simply walk into the KingsChamber coordinates without meeting the vizier. But we still need to prevent them meeting the king.

If the player arrives at "Location:KingsChamber" WITHOUT meeting the vizier, the storyteller could simply say the king isn't there:

The storyteller creates a **variable**, "$KingInKingsChamber", and sets it to "no". "$KingInKingsChamber" is only set to "yes" IF the player has met the vizier.

IF the player's <gps coordinates> match "Location:KingsChamber" the system's logic checks the **variable** "$KingInKingsChamber". IF "$KingInKingsChamber=no" THEN nothing happens. The player is physically at the KingsChamber coordinates, but digitally speaking the king's not there.

However, this approach arbitrarily makes the King's presence **conditional** on the player's actions. If the King were a real person his decisionmaking probably wouldn't be directly **conditional** on the player's actions. So instead, if the player does accidentally stumble upon the Location:KingsChamber without having met the vizier, the king could be there but refuses to see them without the vizier's blessing:

The storyteller creates a **variable**, "$PlayerMetVizier", and sets it to "no".

IF the player's <gps coordinates> match "Location:KingsChamber" the system's logic checks the **variable** "$PlayerMetVizier". IF "$PlayerMetVizier = no" THEN the king is present, but refuses to speak to the player until they have met the vizier.

IF the player's "<gps coordinates>" match the vizier's location, the player meets the vizier. The vizier greets you and gives their blessing for you to meet the king. "$PlayerMetVizier" is set to "yes".

The player returns to "Location=KingsChamber". IF "$PlayerMetVizier=yes" THEN the king greets the player properly.

If some time elapses and the player hasn't found the vizier, the player might have lost interest, or be pursuing other **objectives**, or be unable to locate the vizier. Regardless, since the player is **diegetically** enacting a character, we need to treat this delay as **diegetic**. It might be a deliberate choice by the player or an accident, but it must be incorporated into the ongoing narrative.

This is a good opportunity to demonstrate that real time has a **diegetic** presence in the story, and that the player's decisions have consequences (including decisions they may not have expected to be **diegetic** or consequential, creating a sense of **panopticon**). Maybe IF the player hasn't found the vizier, AND thirty minutes have elapsed, THEN the player receives an angry message from the vizier demanding that they visit him.

These are basic, abstract examples of **conditional** scripting. Even if (like me) you're not a coder, as a digital storyteller you should still familiarise yourself with the principles of **conditionality**. The best way to start learning is to use Twine (https://twinery.org/), an accessible and interactive scripting format with many quality tutorials.

CHALLENGE #17: CONDITIONALITY IN TWINE

Goal: Explore **conditionality** using an industry-standard format.

TASKS
- Use the **tutorials** at https://twinery.org/ to familiarise yourself with the Twine format.
- **Play** some classic Twine games exploring **conditionality**, such as Porpentine's *Crystal Warrior Ke$ha* (2013[22]).
- Use Twine to **develop an Interactive Fiction** with multiple endings.

Remember, good stories aren't just about "events" – they're about *change*. You don't necessarily have to unfold new story events by asking the player to continually progress through new environments. It can be powerful to have players remain-in or return-to places – e.g. **hubs** – and to use **conditionality** show how a place changes as a result of player actions, story events or the passage of time.

Roomscale/At-home Pacing

In **roomscale/at-home** experiences you're even less likely to be able to prevent the player from physically accessing certain areas. If your story hinges on a murder that has taken place in the player's kitchen, but you don't want them to discover the body until Act 2, you either need to provide in-story disincentives against them going into the kitchen until Act 2 (still no guarantee). Or you need to make sure the body isn't visible if the player enters the kitchen too early – and then you need a story reason why the body subsequently appears in the kitchen.

Some **roomscale** experiences centre on the player and have the story – and **pacing** – follow them wherever they are. *Hauntify* (Virtual Go, 2021) is a mixed reality horror game which populates a scanned multi-room space (usually a home) with ghouls which hunt the player. The game's goal is not to "kill" the player quickly but to deliver a satisfying horror experience, so **pacing** is all-important. The player-centred structure allows the designer to **pace** events for maximum impact: the ghouls always know where you are and slowly pursue you. But the **pacing** of being chased by an AR ghoul is an unpredictable combination of digital **variables** (like where and when the ghoul spawns), physical **variables** (the particular physical **layout** of the user's home) and hybrid digital-physical **variables** (how well the ghoul's AI wayfinding navigates the **layout**).

Digital Pacing for Real Objects

One prototype[23] feature of *Hauntify* allows the player to move into a room in their home and close the door to hide. The game detects the closed door and "masks" it, superimposing a digitally cloned image of the door over the top of the physical door. The game can fully control this digital door so it can be used to **pace** an event: a ghoul "breaks through" the door to attack the player. The real physical door has not been broken of course – all the events take place inside the headset. But it's an ideal **merged reality moment**: the player physically closed the door themselves just moments ago, anchoring their sense of its physicality. From the moment the door is digitally cloned, the storyteller has full control of **pacing** when the door will be broken through. But this digital event is still strongly anchored to the physical through the **merged reality moment**.

"Masking" and digitally "cloning" the door is an example of what researchers Kari, Schütte and Sodhi call "Object Rephysicalisation".[24] Using their 2023 "RealityToggle" tool, an object can be detected and a "co-aligned digital twin" – a digital clone of the object – superimposed on top to "virtualise" the object. At that point the digital object and the physical object are co-aligned – they exist in the same space. But in the virtual layer the "virtualised" object can then be moved by a virtual character, or damaged or destroyed like the *Hauntify* door.

But moving or destroying the "virtualised" object means masking the fact that the physical object is still there under the virtual layer. A "virtualised" empty space is augmented into the space where the physical object still is, masking the object and creating the appearance that it's been moved or destroyed: this is called "object elusiveness".

Ultimately it's this kind of visuotactile illusion which will allow for true **merged reality moments**, where the player can feel the tactile physicality of a solid object, but then also see it be changed, moved or reskinned in the digital layer. When augmented storytellers can appear to move, remove and choreograph physical objects, this will greatly enhance augmented storytellers' **pacing** powers. Timing is particularly important for horror, comedy and satire, so Object Rephysicalisation/Elision techniques will be essential for augmented storytellers to achieve sophisticated storytelling.

But, the real objects will still be there, beneath the "object elusiveness" mask. In the same way, though we can use our subjective experience of time to stretch and shrink the Narrative Time of even an augmented/spatial narrative, real time will still be there, ticking away underneath. We can't stop it, and unlike in stories, we can't control how time unfolds, what happens when or in what order.

Which is why it's also important to talk about another powerful approach to **pacing** where Presentation Time and Narrative Time can be almost entirely aligned: **emergent narrative**.

Emergence and Serendipity

As Short says, "if one has a specific story to tell, an expansive layout can make it hard to show the game to the player in the right order". Showing story events to players in a specific order will remain a major challenge in locative narrative design, particularly **location-agnostic**. But if your story's **pacing** is driven by serendipity, rather than sequencing, this is not an issue.

In a sense there's always an inherent serendipity to locative augmented reality, even **location-specific**. As the locative AR audio researcher Løvlie says in their essay on "Poetic Augmented Reality", "instead of being printed on paper, thus being turned into a physical mass product to be distributed around the world, [geolocated] text finds itself left hanging in the air, as an aural sculpture to be listened to by random passers-by".[25]

In **location-agnostic** LBGs the algorithmic **layout** influences the terrain through which players move, but in a fairly context-blind way. So players' experience **emerges** serendipitously as a hybrid of loosely-related digital and physical factors. Of course, this emphasis on serendipity suits the LBG format: they're often based on franchises with strong hunter-scavenger narratives like Pokémon or Monster Hunter. Many different locations could present supportive **layouts** for broad, serendipitous scavenger-hunt gameplay and narrative; the **pacing** of hunter-scavenging is also defined by serendipity.

Generally the context-blind **layout** and unpredictable **pacing** of algorithmically-located content makes it hard to impose heavily scripted narrative – but this is fine, because narrative will be that which **emerges** in the player's mind through hybridising digital, physical and imaginative factors.

Players are fully capable of composing coherent narratives from serendipitous and even random encounters with content. Provided the player's IDENTITY is augmented, so their actions are **diegetic**, they will tend to embrace or even rationalise randomness. After all, serendipity and randomness is part of any real-world adventure.

Researchers Saker and Evans coined the term *playeur* to describe how LBGs create an intentionally playful, serendipitous relationship between player and place.[26] *Playeur* is a play on *flâneur* or "stroller", used by the French poet Beaudelaire (1863) to describe a serendipitous wanderer and observer of urban life. Ideally, the augmented *playeur* is "an engaged actor who develops relationships with space and place through intentional playful activities",[27] who "moves through his or her environment using altered routes, frequenting new and unplanned-for spaces",[28] with the **pacing** of their experience **emerging** through serendipity. In this "strolling" style of play, your story might be an ongoing narrative dimension of the player's everyday life. And serendipity is a fun element to augment into the everyday.

In **emergent** narratives, story events are compelling because their **pacing** is determined by player agency and environmental **conditions**, not a storyteller's planned beats. Open-World Survival videogames in particular rely on **emergent** narrative. These games often take place in realtime (i.e. Narrative Time matches Presentation Time) so they can't use flashbacks or cuts to aid **pacing**. Instead the constant passage of time creates a sense of ongoing consequentiality. As one YouTuber describes, "when one stands stock still in a World War 2 shooter or something, the setting just freezes around you, until the next enemy spawn point is hit; the Nazi war machine coming to a humiliating halt with your inaction. But do the same in a survival game and the world will just keep existing. It doesn't care what you do. You have to be the one to take actions within it, and that rule is replicated across everybody playing in that world. Everybody is having their own, sometimes fiercely unique play experience".[29]

In other words, the Narrative Time and the Presentation Time are the same. This indifferent march of time is in some ways authentic to physical reality. Following this **emergent** model, persistent multiplayer LBGs like *Ingress* STAGE a living map of contested digital territories over the physical world. This sense of being part of an ever-changing world augments a compelling extra dimension of serendipity and competition to everyday life. (Some experiences use a hybrid of **emergent** and pre-scripted approaches; we'll look at some examples in Appendix B.)

Creating the **conditions** for **emergent** narrative is a complex combination of engineering and artistry. As the game writer Leigh Alexander says, "working in a generative mode is not actually labour-saving. In fact it might be more difficult". For an example of procedurally-generated narrative with a strong spatial component, watch Alexander's talk about hers and Brian Bucklew's prototype "generative celebrity murder roguelike" *McMansion* (2023[30]).

This type of managed, progression-oriented serendipity is kind of like gardening – the designer allows things to take their course organically, embracing unpredictability, while intervening in specific ways (e.g. **conditionally** triggering events). This means populating an environment with enough content to make it continually playful – relationships, oppositions, and the possibility of unexpected combinations.

Generative narrative design is challenging at the best of times – with too little stimuli a generative story might be tedious, and with too much it might become chaotic. And remember, you're STAGING this in the physical world, which is itself a highly unpredictable and **emergent** system. If you're creating digital serendipity in **location-specific** design, you might be able to control your environment like a garden: a walled-off, managed space. But in **location-agnostic** design your environment is more like a park, a mixed-use public space you don't control.

In short, creating the conditions for satisfying **emergent** spationarrative **pacing** means designing storyscapes which are as organised and regulated as a city but which *feel* as organic and spontaneous as a natural environment. In other words, *parks*. As the great architectural commentator Laugier said, "whoever knows how to design a park well will have no difficulty in tracing the plan for the building of a city [...] There must be regularity and fantasy, relationships and oppositions, and casual, unexpected elements that vary the scene: great order in the details; confusion, uproar and tumult in the whole" (1765[31]).

Provided you have "great order in the details", there's nothing wrong with a bit of "confusion, uproar and tumult" in a narrative. And remember, tumult is part of the authentic experience of the real world. In a sense, replicating and reflecting the real world's **emergent pacing** within a digital layer is just another kind of **merged reality** that anchors your digital experience to the real.

GENERAL AUGMENTED STAGING: BOUNDARIES

Short's third principle of interactive narrative geography is "disguise the edges of the map from the player so that [the player] doesn't feel claustrophobic".[32] We've talked about **edges** as geographical features within storyscapes, but here Short is referring to the *outer edges* of a storyscape, beyond which there is no content. We'll refer to these as **boundaries.**

In a videogame or interactive fiction the story world is only as big as the creator can depict with text or graphics. Storytellers need to expend resources to depict every room, location or zone the player can visit (and to imply any further territory beyond). So these purely digital storyscapes can feel claustrophobic – they're manifestly smaller than the real world. As a result videogame level designers develop what Short calls "techniques for making your game feel as though it is set in a larger contiguous world"[33] without having to implement content beyond its **boundaries**.

In contrast to videogame level design, as augmented/spatial storytellers we're usually building upon the existing world. (In fact Dustin Freeman, who helped develop Playlines's first AR installations, used to call our site-responsive **layout** process "**reverse level design**" – we'll look at this in more detail in 3.1.2.) Nonetheless some of the techniques and terminology of videogame level design are really useful to us, particularly in drawing **boundaries**. For more on the fundamentals of level design I recommend *Video Game Level Design* (2021) by Michael Salmond.

Videogame Boundaries

In videogames, level designers can create walls which the player cannot pass through. Many game levels are effectively series of corridors in a specific **layout** designed to guide the player sequentially through different situations or set-pieces and **pace** the emotional journey. But walls also disguise the game world's limited **boundaries**. Level designers often use the language of architecture to imply that the player is only seeing a small part of a larger building or neighbourhood or spaceship (or whatever). They might seek to imply the existence of rooms or wider architecture which doesn't actually exist, so level designers funnel players along a specific path, through a limited architecture, while creating the illusion that the player is intuitively navigating a much larger geography.

(Immersive theatre experiences deploy similar effects in physical experiential design: in London's *SAW: Escape Experience* (2022) audiences move into a room set-dressed as an elevator; the elevator appears to move, implying that players are going deeper into a multi-level complex when in fact the experience is all on one level.)

One common level design trick is to place doors along corridors, implying the existence of rooms beyond, but make the doors inoperable. But as Short says this carries risks:

> Used very carefully, the false door makes it seem as though the game environment is larger than the area the player is actually allowed to walk through. Make the door too interesting, however, and the player may waste a lot of time trying to open it, to her frustration. It's worst of all if she feels cheated... instead of impressing the player with the expanse of your game world, you've drawn attention to its limitations and wasted her time.

There are similar risks in locative AR/spatial media: in **location-agnostic** design we can't predict or control what doors might be nearby. In **location-specific** design we might be able to respond to physical doors in the location. But if you encourage players to open one door and reward them with content, this teaches the player that "opening doors" is one of the affordances of the experience. Without clear signalling there's a good chance that they will then try every door they see, whether or not those doors are part of your plan.

In outdoor videogame levels where the designer can't **boundary** the playspace with architecture, they often use geographical **edges** like cliffs or rivers which imply geography beyond but which are impassable. But not every level design can be confined in a canyon or circumscribed by rivers! Many outdoor levels are ultimately **boundaried** by "**glass walls**", barriers which the player's avatar can't pass through but which players can see through to an implied contiguous landscape beyond.

A lot of level design goes into disguising **glass walls** or disincentivizing players from approaching them, because the the effect of bumping into one can disrupt immersion (this is even more jarring in VR). With well-designed **glass walls** the level designer can be highly resource-efficient, guiding the player's spationarrative journey and implying it's part of a wider world while still giving the player a feeling of agency in navigation. But if a game fails to disguise its **boundaries** and players frequently and jarringly bump into **glass walls** the game might become notorious as a "glass tunnel", where the player can discern the claustrophobic dimensions of the actual playable space despite a wider world visible beyond.

Augmenting Boundaries

In contrast, augmented/spatial storytelling is STAGED in a portion of the real world, and the real world really does continue off in every direction beyond. As we've seen, although we can use **layout** techniques to spatially guide the player, and **pacing** techniques to control *when* content is released, we can't control *where* the player goes. As Short says, in the constructed environment of an Interactive Fiction or game "even a well-designed map can confuse a player who has access to too much of it at a time".[34] Out in the real world, the player's nearby geography is not necessarily "well designed" until we help them develop a "mental map". And that often requires **boundaries**, because otherwise the world extends in every direction.

Basically, in augmented/spatial reality we cannot impose **glass walls**. **Variables** in the digital layer can't directly lock off physical areas. If your player can see an area of the landscape, there's a good chance that they can move there. Unlike videogames, where the parameters of the player's agency are ultimately always coded in by the creator,[35] augmented players are squarely in the real world, where (in theory at least) they have full agency.

It is possible to digitally draw a **boundary** on a map or visually augment a barrier into space. But augmenting a "do not cross" line across a street in front of the player represents a juxtaposition which challenges players' suspension of disbelief. The player actually lives in the real world; they know its rules. By drawing a digital barrier you're asking them to believe they can't cross a barrier which they probably know they CAN – and the more visually convincing your augmented barrier, the more likely they are to try to assess its level of reality by testing the **boundary**.

Players have to agree to treat digital **boundaries** as real through "active creation of belief". So within augmented/spatial narratives, we not only need to draw clear **boundaries** but also to make them **diegetic**, providing in-story justifications for the **boundary**'s existence and placement. This works slightly differently across **location-specific, location-agnostic, roomscale** and **portable/generic-place** design.

Boundaries are particularly important in **location-specific** experiences, but **location-specific** design offers lots of tools. For example, creators can piggyback digital **boundaries** onto physical **edge** features. We'll examine various techniques in 3.1.2: Location-Specific Augmented STAGING.

Algorithmically-driven **location-agnostic** experiences like Niantic LBGs are often unboundaried: the player could travel in any direction and always find new content **nodes** waiting for them. This approach is suitable for those large hunter-gatherer LBGs whose content is procedurally spawned into any new geography around them. The content can be as unlimited as the physical geography (but not as varied; ultimately procedural content generation requires repeating loops of gameplay).

Roomscale experiences by definition take place in a physically bounded space and co-opt its existing physical **boundaries**. As we've seen many **roomscale/at-home** experiences augment "breaking through" graphics onto walls to create the illusion of a larger environment outside. This also exploits the emotive nature of the **boundaries** of the home, often with scenarios of transposing the home to a new environment or defending the home against incursion from attackers outside.

Location-portable experiences and experiences designed for **generic places** generally need to define **boundaried** playable areas in which some or all of the story unfolds.

Let's examine three general approaches to **boundarying** augmented storyscapes: **diegeticizing boundaries, foveating space** and creating **social boundaries**.

Foveating Space

The simplest technique to keep players within the bounds of a storyscape is to simply make it the most interesting place to be. Back in 1.1 we looked at **foveated rendering**, the trick where a VR headset dynamically blurs everything in the player's peripheral vision. We can invert this effect for augmented/spatial storytelling: creating areas of player focus by placing high levels of content and rewards within, and reducing focus on other areas by positioning no content outside.

A high-content-density area could be a crime scene, a job site or search area; it might be **boundaried** by hazard tape, picket fences or just a chalk line. Provided that the player's IDENTITY and **objectives** incentivise them to remain focused, in most cases they won't stray outside of the area during play. But we can't use **glass walls** so it's important to establish that player **objectives** can only be completed within the focused area, making everything outside peripheral.

Even if players stray, you don't necessarily need to alert them. If the player unwittingly leaves the **boundaries** of the content area, this doesn't mean they've left their augmented IDENTITY. They might have mistakenly crossed the **boundary** due to in-character curiosity. They might be unaware they've crossed the **boundary** and be continuing their ongoing self-narration. So you don't necessarily need to disrupt the story by alerting them that they're out-of-bounds, especially if you can gently guide them back in-bounds. If the player is still embodying their IDENTITY they'll likely find their way back naturally while hunting **objectives**. You could also prompt players in-story in ways which don't emphasise geographic **boundaries** but instead refocuses them on the content area: have a character contact the player and testily redirect them back to their objective, for example.

In addition to creating areas of focus, you can also imply a wider contiguous world beyond your **boundaries**, but make it clear that there's no content out there. Short describes these as "Trompe l'Oeil Vistas", i.e. viewpoints over illusory space with no real dimension, which depict contiguous space "but in such a way that it's clear to the player there's nothing interesting over there".[36]

Location-agnostic LBGs have pockets of emptiness: Niantic has a policy of not placing content **nodes** inside cemeteries. They can't physically prevent players from entering these spaces, but creating an absence of content prevents cemeteries being areas of focused play. However, it's in the nature of AR/spatial media that the played experience extends beyond any one **node** or area. Gameplay might cause players to shortcut through a cemetery on their way to a Pokéstop; there are no content **nodes** inside the cemetery but arguably the player is still hunting Pokémon, still STAGING the game within their own IMAGINED instance of the place.

In VR, creating absences to direct players' gaze means missing out on a chance to "greet the rebel". But in spatial narratives, creating spatial gaps in the content is the only way to fully disincentive "rebellious" players from trying to move into certain areas. This is particularly important if you're trying to prevent players moving into inappropriate or dangerous areas.

Bear in mind that while you can create absences in the digital layer, you can't ever augment emptiness onto the world. After all, augmenting means adding to, not subtracting from, the world – and the world always has substance. Creating an absence of digital content beyond a **boundary** always risks juxtaposition, because the player can see the world continuing beyond as normal. So when creating **foveated** space, consider what **diegetic** explanation you provide for *why* content only exists inside the **bound-aried** area. Why do your content **nodes** cluster around a **landmark** or only occur in a **district**? This will help anchor the spatial dimensions, build the player's **mental map**, and justify the **boundary** in-story.

(Remember also that creating areas of high content density doesn't necessarily mean filling places wall-to-wall with narrative. As we said back in 2.1 when looking at **plausibility,** spationarratives can contain lots of relatively unfocused, un-augmented peripheral space where you trust the player's IMAGINATION to play.)

Diegeticizing Boundaries

We can appropriate real-life **edges** like rivers, railway lines, coastlines or fences to use as in-story **boundaries**. This anchors the digital **boundary** to a physical feature. It's your job as a storyteller to then come up with a way to incorporate the **edge** into your story – **diegeticizing** it – in a compelling way. That might mean telling the player that a river is haunted by a million lost souls, or visually reskinning it as a river of lava.

Physical **edges** can often be read from GPS datasets, so in a **location-agnostic** experience it might be possible to algorithmically detect **edges** near the player and co-opt them as **boundaries** (or detect suitably-bounded areas nearby and direct the player to them).

But spationarrative **boundaries** don't necessarily have to be physical barriers. More conceptual **boundaries**, like the outer limits of a park or **district** might be readable from GPS datasets. If you inform the player that their digital spy-hunt or magical forag-ing quest will take place entirely within the bounds of a **district** like a park, they can rely on the language of geography to understand the **boundaries** without you having to augment them in. This is a form of **merged reality** and makes the players unlikely to bump into a **boundary** accidentally – though bear in mind that conceptual **boundaries** like the borders of a park can be ambiguous and open to interpretation.

Social Boundaries

Creating **boundaries** which carry in-story social risks can be highly effective. **Social boundaries** can clearly show the existence of more world beyond, while keeping play-ers within the content area for emotive, **diegetic** reasons. If the story tells the player that they will embarrass themselves or disappoint someone if they stray beyond a **boundary**, this provides a clear **diegetic** justification for the **boundary** with clear emotional stakes.

Some players will always rebel, but a **social boundary** implies consequences which can be enforced by giving the player responsive content instead of trying to "glass tun-nel" them. In other words, a **social boundary** is an opportunity to deliver content to "reward" the rebellious player, showing them they are in an environment of real consequence. Of course, the story has to make good on its threats. Players need to actually experience consequence content after they've crossed a boundary. So there should be a buffer zone outside a **social boundary**, in which the social consequence content is triggered if the player strays. Providing consequences for crossing **boundaries** can be part of their hybrid spationarrative experience, since it shows the player they are BEING SEEN and the story is paying attention.

These social consequences need to be articulated clearly enough to motivate players to turn back, rather than to continue testing the **boundary**; the best way to do this is to make clear that beyond a certain threshold the player will encounter only the absence of content, perhaps because their violation of the **social boundary** puts them simply "beyond the pale".

Some players will always rebel and test **boundaries**, especially **social** ones; in the absence of **glass walls** our job as storytellers is to clearly indicate **boundaries** where necessary, and provide motivation for players to stay where the story is. But in augmented/spatial media, we also have to respect their freedom to simply wander off, since that's part of their embodied experience of BEING THERE in real world.

CHALLENGE #18: BOUNDARY A LOCATION-AGNOSTIC STORYSCAPE

Goal: Explore different techniques to create spationarrative **boundaries**.

Select two similar **places** in different parts of the world. You could choose two famous parks of similar sizes (e.g. Sefton Park in Liverpool and Lalbagh in Bengaluru) or two museums or airport lounges you're familiar with.

Find **maps** of the two **places** and **identify** common **spatial elements** between the two. Examine the physical and conceptual **boundaries** of the **places** and **identify** any similarities and differences.

Conceptualise a single storyscape to augment into both **places**. The storyscape should focus content inside the **boundaries** of each **place**. Anchor the storyscape by referring to local **spatial elements**.

Make sure your concept justifies the **boundaries**. You might **diegeticize** them by anchoring them to physical **edges**, or threaten narrative **social** consequences for crossing them. Consider also how to justify the absence of content outside the **boundary**.

Write example narration/dialogue for the beginning of the experience, depicting the area of **focus** and identifying the **boundaries**.

Write example narration/dialogue alerting the player when they're approaching a **boundary**. How will you highlight the **boundary** to the player and motivate them to explore in a different direction? What will happen if the player tests the **boundaries**? **Write** narration/dialogue for the consequences.

TASKS
- **Select** two similar **boundaried** places with **maps**.
- **Identify** common **spatial elements** and the nature of their **boundaries**.

- **Conceptualise** ONE storyscape to augment on BOTH places.
- **Justify** the storyscape being confined within the places' **boundaries**.
- **Write** intro narration/dialogue.
- **Write** narration/dialogue for players approaching a **boundary**.
- **Write** narration/dialogue for players violating a **boundary**.

Let's summarise the key points of General Augmented STAGING before moving on to Location-Specific STAGING in 3.1.2.

GENERAL AUGMENTED STAGING: SUMMARY

How do we GENERALLY activate player IMAGINATIONS to help STAGE digital narratives in real places?

- *Remember to augment the place, not overwrite it.*
- *Players are copresent in augmented/physical places. Spationarratives should be interwoven and "intervolved" with location.*

How do we design/co-opt layouts for augmented spationarratives?

- *Help the player build their "mental map" with clear spatio-narrative **layout**.*
- *Use or incorporate the five **spatial elements**: **paths**, **landmarks**, **hubs**, **edges** and **districts**.*

How do we pace augmented spationarratives?

- *Spationarrative **pacing** can't be tightly controlled or predicted, even in **location-specific**.*
- *Understand the experiential difference between Presentation Time and Narrative Time, and the subjective **Relative Time** the player spends in-between. Use IDENTITY to help keep **Relative Time diegetic**.*
- *Consider **emergent** narrative for authentic and serendipitous **pacing**.*

How do we create and communicate the boundaries of augmented spationarratives?

- *Communicate, justify and/or enforce **boundaries** without trying to create **glass walls**.*
- ***Foveate space**: create and justify areas of high content density and emptiness.*
- *Create, appropriate or **diegeticize** existing **boundaries**.*
- *Build **social boundaries** to enforce **boundaries** with narrative consequence.*

NOTES

1. Jay Springett, *World Running dot Guide* (ongoing) https://docs.google.com/document/d/1XRm39aH8APXVqjzKYptz7-NQ-3AAXNVrgcjm9oBMOec/edit retrieved 22 Jun 2023.
2. Springett (ongoing).
3. John Horton, "'Got My Shoes, Got My Pokémon': Everyday Geographies of Children's Popular Culture", *Geoforum* 43:1, 2012.
4. Pokémon GO: Mobile media play, place-making, and the digital wayfarer, Larissa Hjorth, Ingrid Richardson, *Mobile Media & Communication* 5:1, 2017, https://doi.org/10.1177/2050157916680015, citing Horton "'Got My Shoes, Got My Pokémon', 2012, 4–13.
5. Emily Short, "Challenges of a Broad Geography", *IF Theory Reader*, Kevin Jackson-Mead, J. Robinson Wheeler (eds.) 2011, https://emshort.blog/how-to-play/writing-if/my-articles/geography/ retrieved 9 Nov 2023.
6. Ritchie, 2014.
7. Short, 2011.
8. Kevin Lynch, *The Image of a City,* MIT Press, Cambridge, MA, 1960.
9. Sarah Perry, "Cartographic Compression", 3 Sep 2015, Ribbonfarm, https://www.ribbonfarm.com/2015/09/03/cartographic-compression/. For clarity these examples are presented in a different order to the original.
10. Short, 2011.
11. *Ibid.*
12. *Ibid.*
13. Ritchie in Farman, 2014.
14. Arpita Bhattacharya, Travis W. Windleharth, Cassandra Lee, Amulya Paramasivam, Julie A Kientz, Jason C. Yip, and Jin Ha Lee. "The Pandemic as a Catalyst for Reimagining the Foundations of Location-Based Games", *ACM on Human-Computer Interaction* 5, 2021.
15. Ritchie, 2014.
16. *Ibid.*
17. Motive.io, About Us https://www.motive.io/about-us/.
18. Brooks, 2003, p. 5.
19. *Ibid*, p. 4.
20. David Hockney, *Bigger & Closer (not smaller & further away)*, Lightroom, 2023.
21. Short, 2011.
22. Porpentine, *Crystal Warrior Ke$ha,* 2013, https://xrafstar.monster/games/twine/kesha/ retrieved 13 Dec 2023.
23. As of Jan 2024.
24. Mohamed Kari, Reinhard Schütte, Raj Sodhi, "Scene Responsiveness for Visuotactile Illusions in Mixed Reality", *ACM Symposium on User Interface Software and Technology* 2023, https://mkari.de/scene-responsiveness/.
25. Anders Sundnes Løvlie, "Poetic Augmented Reality: Place-bound Literature in Locative Media", *MindTrek* 2009.
26. Leighton Evans and Michael Saker, "Everyday Life and Locative Play", *Media, Culture & Society* 38:8, 2016.
27. *Ibid.*, p. 13.
28. Leighton Evans and Michael Saker, "The Playeur and Pokémon GO: Examining the Effects of Locative Play on Spatiality and Sociability", *Mobile Media & Communication* 7:2, 2018.
29. SovietWomble, "What's So Strange About the Forest [2014]", 9 May 2023, https://www.youtube.com/watch?v=PUWg905fGTA, retrieved 14 Nov 2023.

30. Leigh Alexander, "McMansions of Hell: Roguelikes and Reality TV", Roguelike Celebration 2023, https://www.youtube.com/watch?v=NjYS8XmeaiY&ab_channel=RoguelikeCelebration.
31. Marc-Antoine Laugier, *Observations sur l'Architecture*, Paris 1765, Wolfgang Hermann, Anni Hermann (trans.), p312.
32. Short 2011.
33. *Ibid.*
34. *Ibid.*
35. See Jack Halberstam, quoted in Brice, 2013.
36. *Ibid.*

Location-Specific Augmented STAGING

3.1.2

Location-specific design gives us particular tools to respond to place, create strong **merged reality moments** and recontextualise the player's relationship to the world around them.

In his paper "Poetic Augmented Reality", Anders Sudnes Løvlie describes what's possible when poetry or literature are "place-bound" via locative media:

> The work, the text or the experience is in permanent dialogue with the world, so that rather than [being] submerged in some alternate reality [the player is] engaged with the world with a heightened sense of engagement and mobilization.[1]

The augmented player is not transported into a virtual other-place or dragon's cave. They are engaged with the manifest world around them, with all its physical sensations and real emotional stakes, while also being co-present in a digital instance of that place. When you know precisely where the player will be, you can refer to the specifics of that location in ways which merge the place into the story's setting. This can create especially heightened "engagement and mobilisation".

Location-specific augmented narratives have another advantage: they can be significantly easier to prototype. Creating **location-agnostic** experiences like Niantic-style LBGs may require algorithmic content generation and huge, complex datasets; third-party platforms like Niantic's Lightship can help, but they require some technical expertise and often license fees. Whereas, as we've seen, we can prototype a **location-specific** spationarrative by simply recording a site-responsive audio track and playing it as the player moves through a place.

In the previous chapters we've done CHALLENGES focused on exploring individual design techniques. In this and the following chapters we'll start bringing it all together with a series of **Storyscape Design CHALLENGES**. These CHALLENGES all focus on a single place chosen by you. You'll develop several different narrative audio layers for that place to test out various ideas, and ultimately bring them all together into a coherent spationarrative.

DOI: 10.1201/9781003379294-18

To explore basic **location-specific** STAGING techniques we'll first examine how to hear and bring to the surface the existing history of a place through AR/spatial media.

Then we'll return to Short's three principles of digital narrative geography: **layout, pacing** and **boundaries**, and see how these work differently in **location-specific** design. In particular we'll see what we can learn from the techniques of videogame spatial design through "**reverse level design**".

LOCATION-SPECIFIC STAGING: SURFACING LAYERS OF HISTORY

The relationship between places and stories is a bit of a paradox: most places are real, and most stories aren't. Yet it's the ongoing "stories-so-far" in spaces that create "real" and meaningful *places*.

As we've seen, in a sense all augmented stories start *in medias res*. When a player enters an augmented place (or a place is augmented around them) they are joining a narrative of that place which is *in medias res* and *in situ*: already in-place as well as in-progress.

Building hybrid storyscapes means responding to the physical landscape. As the landscape architect Sierra Bainbridge says, this means "uncover[ing] the sometimes revelatory and sometimes terrible secrets that the landscape holds… See[ing] the hands that shaped it and the bodies held within it".[2]

Highlighting the *in-situ* history of a place always recontextualises our relationship to that place, because *context is everything*. As Ritchie says, "the perception of a playground would be altered were we to know that a horrible crime had been committed at that place".[3]

Spatial researcher Mark Sample puts it more simply: "location is not compelling (until it is *haunted*)".[4] Fortunately, most places are.

It Happened Here

Because *context is everything,* the place and local context in which a spationarrative takes place will always influence players' experience. As the historian G.M. Trevelyan said,

> The dead were and are not. Their place knows them no more and is ours today… The poetry of history lies in the quasi-miraculous fact that once, on this earth, once, on this familiar spot of ground, walked other men and women, as actual as we are today.[5]

One of the main use cases of location-sensitive technology has been to provide contextual cultural and historical information. Locative social network FourSquare partnered with History Channel back in 2010 to provide historical digital tidbits near historic sites[6]; Niantic's first app, *Field Trip* (2012) provided local information including history; the largest non-generative locative AR cultural installation to date, Storyfutures' Story Trails project (2023), embedded local histories and voices in towns around the UK.

Technological developments in AR (often combined with AI) are expanding our ability to digitally visualise a place's past while present at the place. But keep in mind that effective augmented/spatial storytelling never fully overwrites a place's past OR its present. Using augmentation to dramatise a historical event *in-situ* doesn't transport the player back into a virtual past; it brings some of that history into co-presence with the player's contemporary experience of that place. The two become commersive. As ambient literature researcher Amy Spencer says,

> there must be space for the language of the place to enter the story, such as through the presence of strangers, sounds, buildings, and other physical elements. The effect is to connect both the physical world and the narrative in a hybrid experience where the boundaries of each are porous.[7]

When AUGMENTING PLAYERS we had to leave room for the player – and in the same way, when AUGMENTING specific PLACES we have to leave room for the place.

Let's try this out with the first in a sequence of **Storyscape Design CHALLENGES**, in which you'll develop a detailed **location-specific** spationarrative. You're going to create a linear audio tour which guides the player along a **path** through a **place** and describes or dramatises an event in the **place**'s history.

CHALLENGE #19: STORYSCAPE DESIGN PART 1: LINEAR NONFICTION

Goal: Augment a place with a linear **location-specific** audio spationarrative, based on the location's history.

SUMMARY

Select a public **place:** historic buildings, marketplaces and parks all work well. Obtain a **map**.

The player will move around the **place** visiting individual locations within it (we'll call these individual locations **nodes**).

Research the **place**'s history. Keep digging until you **identify** an historical event or context that's highly specific to the **place**. This could be a single event like a protest or pageant, or a context over time like ritual or industry.

Outline a narrative of the historical event/context. This could be a factual depiction or fictionalised dramatisation.

Think about how you would tell a friend the story. What would be the beginning, middle and end? What context would they need to understand beforehand? What knowledge and emotion would you want them to be left with afterwards? **Aim for a 10–15min narrative.**

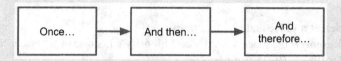

FIGURE 3.1.2a   Diagram of linear story beats

Structure the story in chunks or "**beats**". A **15 min** narrative should have **a minimum of 5x beats**. One simple beat structure is[8]:

Once Upon A Time (starting context)

Then Something Happened (initial catalyst)

Then Because of That...

And Therefore (conclusion)

Draw a **diagram** of the **beats** as a linear sequence (Figure 3.1.2a):

Now, the fun part. **Visit the place**. Think about the historical narrative as you move through the place. How would you change your telling of the story if you were telling it to a friend while moving through the **place**?

Where within the **place** would you start to best correspond to the story's beginning? Are there specific **nodes** you could move through which would represent different beats or be suitably emotive?

Plot the story to the **place**. Superimpose your story diagram onto the map. Place each **beat** at appropriate **nodes** within the **place**. Draw **paths** connecting the **beats/locations** in the linear sequence.

Write the dialogue/narration for each **beat/node** in sequence. This text will be played as audio when the player is on-site. Think about narration style: is the player hearing a neutral narrating voice, dramatised voices from the past, or a historian character who is co-present with the player?

Your player has to navigate between **beats/nodes**. **Write navigation** dialogue/narration to guide players along the **paths** between each **beat/node**. Keep this **navigation** in the same style as the other content.

Each **beat** should be anchored to its **node** and the wider context of the **place**. Find opportunities for **merged reality moments** by referring to or **diegeticizing** things the player might see, hear, smell or touch.

Return to the location for initial **testing**. Read your script aloud as you follow your story **path**, and **time** the **dwell times** and **journey times**. If possible, **test** with a friend.

Refine your script to provide clear **navigation** and minimise unnecessary **dwell time,** while providing enough **journey time** for all potential players to participate.

Finally, **record dialogue/narration audio**. You may want to consider recording on-site to capture the atmosphere of the location, but remember your player will be on-site too; don't let your recording overwrite their ambient experience of the place.

Continue to **test and refine** your experience with different players, particularly the anchoring to place, the **navigation** text and the timings.

TASKS

- **Select a place** and obtain a **map**.
- **Research** the place's history and **identify** a historic event or context.
- **Outline** a **10–15min** narrative.
- **Diagram** the narrative as a linear series of **beats.**
- **Visit the place.**
- **Plot** the narrative to the **place**. Superimpose the story diagram onto the map, placing **beats** at **nodes** and drawing **paths** between.
- **Write** dialogue/narration for each **beat/node.**
- **Write navigation** dialogue/narration for each **path.**
- **Test** and **refine**.
- **Record audio**
- Continue to **test** and **refine.**

BONUS CHALLENGE

Use a geotagging platform like caught.nu to geolocate your recorded audio within the location, triggered when players are in player proximity to the location. Utilise the platform's **conditionality** tools to implement and test **conditionality** as a locative layer.

BONUS CHALLENGE

Consider ways to add physical elements create more **merged reality moments**: could you place physical signage, hide messages or artefacts, or even station costumed performers in the place?

TIPS FOR AUDIO NAVIGATION

Audio spationarratives give us a great way to prototype, but without visuals they can be challenging for players to navigate.

Imagine you are on a phone call with a friend trying to guide them through a place. You know what the place looks like, but you don't know exactly where they are or which way they're looking. Think about what **landmarks** they might be able to see, and remember that instructions which seem logical when looking at a map may not be helpful on the ground. Contextual instructions like "go uphill" or "towards the big tree" are often more helpful than abstract directions like "go left" or "head North".

Most people can only remember a couple of navigational instructions in a row. If one of your **paths** would require multiple complex instructions to navigate, break the **path** down into multiple **paths** with **nodes** in-between.

Consider also the tone of your instructions. How can you tell the player what to do in a way that's **diegetic** and sympathetic to the tone and mood of your narrative? How can you invite players to reflect on their surroundings, and motivate them to move with purpose through the narrative? Consider challenging them, asking questions or using cliffhangers.

LOCATION-SPECIFIC STAGING: LAYOUT

Location-agnostic designs tend to be **sandboxes** full of redundant content **nodes** which players navigate freely based on self-defined **objectives**. They don't create the expectation of a carefully-curated spationarrative experience. But **layouts** for **location-specific** spationarratives must respond to the real space your player moves through.

Let's look again at Emily Short's three principles of interactive fictional geography, and apply them to **location-specific** design. First: **layout**. When developing a **location-specific** spationarrative, it's crucial to visit the place and allow its layout to shape your ideas, in order to create "space for the language of the place to enter the story".

The Language of Space

What we do is figure out which is the best route on site and then I generally stand around a lot and see what patterns evolve... When I'm walking the site, it gives me ideas and situations—this could be cool here, this kind of sound would work well here. The site gives me ideas... What's weird about it is that it's like writing three-dimensionally.[9]

Janet Cardiff

In her site-specific work, immersive artist Janet Cardiff first develops the story concept as "a response to the location, almost as if the site becomes a Rorschach test that I am interpreting".[10] She then creates a spationarrative **layout** in a hybrid process where the textures and tone of the place influence the story structure, and the story's structure influences the story path through the place:

We plan [paths] that can go through places that can affect the person's body in different ways. Like a narrow alley will make you feel a bit weirder, then an open space. It's like if you're making a drawing you want texture, you want a certain kind of line, and then you want darkness, you want light.[11]

Videogame level designers are able to carefully architect and choreograph the player's emotional journey through virtual spaces, so the place helps tell the story. Whereas when STAGING digital narratives in specific locations, especially public places, we have relatively little control over the **layout**, let alone other factors like the presence of others, the weather etc. So instead of building a new place to tell a story, like a level designer, we need to respond to and build a story around a real place. The brilliant developer and designer Dustin Freeman, who created probably the first iBeacon-driven audio AR theatre narrative,[12] coined a term for this site-responsive **layout** process: **reverse level design**. Where a videogame level designer constructs a virtual setting to help tell the story, **reverse level design** is about shaping a narrative to a real physical place.

In many videogames there is a singular or primary path of linear progression – this is called the **critical path** – and the level designer's job is to guide the player along that path, often while "glass tunneling" them to a greater or lesser extent. Some level designs feature multiple optional, intersecting or parallel **critical paths** so players progress along a linear or semi-linear story, but with more genuine freedom to explore the geography. These designs with multiple **critical paths** are sometimes called "Immersive Sim"-style level designs, and they are closer to real architecture than the "glass tunnels" of games built around singular, linear **critical paths**.

The "Immersive Sim" level design approach is relevant to us in applying **reverse level design** to physical places, because "Immersive Sim" levels are likely to have a lot of redundant rooms and extra spaces – just like physical places do. As Short says, "even a small building in real life is likely to have more rooms than would be interesting to simulate in a game. […] Service rooms, like bathrooms and closets, are often left out of [game] locations, just as novels rarely mention every time the protagonist uses the toilet".[13]

But these everyday spaces like toilets, stairwells, closets or dead ends can be some of the most emotive places for STAGING spationarratives. In Playlines' early AR theatre we sought out "service rooms" like bathrooms or closets and used them to STAGE intimate moments or opportunities for emotive or transgressive player behaviour, because these places often had heightened dynamics of BEING (UN)SEEN. These kinds of places feature heavily in "Immersive Sim" level design.

Uncritical Paths: *Goldeneye*

Goldeneye 007 (1997), the most influential console shooter of all time, stood out from its competitors partly because its levels – which included military facilities, yachts and archival buildings – felt like real places with authentic **layouts** and realistic "service rooms" (showcased in the iconic and unprecedented entrance into a bathroom via an air vent in the "Facility" level). This was achieved partly because *Goldeneye*'s development team, included lead environmental artist and trained architect Karl Hilton and "wildly talented architecture school dropout" Duncan Botwood who, as game researcher Alyse Knorr says, "took a lot away from architecture school about the flow of spaces and how people engage in them".[14]

Goldeneye's memorable but sometimes frustrating **layouts** came about because these architecturally-minded designers applied a type of **reverse level design** – closely basing levels on film sets from the *Goldeneye* movie, which were in turn based on real locations in Russia and Cuba. At a time when movie tie-in games were a byword for terrible game design, the *Goldeneye* developers exploited their access to the actual movie sets and architectural plans, even shooting reference video walkthroughs on one of the first digital cameras. This "made for a stunningly realistic gaming experience at a time when most first-person shooters took place in sci-fi labyrinths or cartoonish dungeons".[15]

The movie sets were a starting point, but even they omitted real details of usable buildings, so Hilton would "add in extra bits he imagined the Russian bad guys would need in their base[s]". *Goldeneye* had originally been developed as a "rail shooter", where the player could aim but couldn't move freely, instead moving automatically along the **critical path**. Environment Lead Hilton said "some of those early builds had bits missing because you'd never be able to see them". After the game came off the rails, Hilton "remember[s] going back and filling in the holes".[16]

Goldeneye's realistic **layouts** could be confusing: players needed to apply real-world logic to navigate realistically-laid-out archives, barracks and supply rooms. But it's not a coincidence that these authentic **layouts** made for some of the first truly great first-person multiplayer levels. Filled with nooks and crannies, but with an intuitive architectural logic, *Goldeneye* **layouts** allowed a generation of console kids (including myself) to stage ambushes and grudge matches with their friends that felt visceral and real because they felt like they took place in real places. The influence of those practical **layouts** on today's blockbuster "Immersive Sims" like *Cyberpunk 2077* (2020) cannot be overstated; like me, many of their level designers grew up on *Goldeneye*.

The realistic, even redundant level layouts of "Immersive Sims" reward players' flexibility, logic and intuition, but it can also be frustrating without a designer smoothing the player's flow along a **critical path**. As the game critic Patrick Gill says,

> Game devs have mastered the art of guiding us through our adventures with funnels, lights, landmarks, and clever suggestions. And even in those games that have hidden paths, shortcuts and diversions, there's a certain sense you get when you're approaching what I call a "desirable dead end": you're creeping through a dungeon and the tunnel splits. You know that one path will take you forward, and the other will be a quick diversion that ends in a little treat. A chest with a nice little potion or a special sword, and then it's just a quick jaunt back to the critical path.
>
> But in an Immersive Sim, that second path keeps going; it winds around and around and somehow you come out at the beginning of the level. Or maybe right above your objective... It's such a fundamental shift in level design that it can be kind of anxiety-inducing. You might worry that you're going the wrong way, or missing some delectable bit of content.[17]

"Desirable dead ends" are a feature of **critical path**-driven design, while the redundant **paths** of "Immersive Sims" are authentic to real physical **layouts**. With AR/spatial media, especially with headset-based visuals, we have new opportunities to augment digital "funnels, lights, landmarks, and clever suggestions" to guide players along **critical paths** through real places. We can even begin to superimpose "desirable dead ends", secret areas and Easter eggs into real places.

Reverse level design is the art of situating and/or superimposing compelling and navigable spationarrative **layouts** in real places. How can we **diegeticize** aspects of physical places and stimulate the player to imaginatively STAGE the digital story there? Like in **location-agnostic** design, we need to build on the five **spatial elements** to STAGE the story and help players create their spationarrative "mental maps".

Augmenting Spatial Elements: The Location-Specific Approach

Let's look again at our version of Short/Lynch's five **spatial elements**: **paths**, **landmarks**, **hubs**, **edges** and **districts**.

Now, instead of algorithmically detecting and augmenting these elements via GPS datasets, we need to find these elements in our chosen specific place, then use them as the underlying structure on which we STAGE the story and choreograph the player's spationarrative journey through it.

Paths

If your spationarrative has a **critical path** (i.e. if there are specific content **nodes** the player must see), it's best to piggyback on actual physical **paths** where possible. This makes navigation easy to communicate since you can refer to the world's manifest features. But you can also superimpose new **paths** onto space. Whether you're selecting **paths** or drawing new ones, as Cardiff says you should look for the for texture, line, darkness or light of different places along the path and think about how they will make your player feel.

Short described how a "streetmap" **layout** can aid the navigability of content **nodes** in relation to **paths**. But in the real world, like "Immersive Sims", there will often be multiple possible **paths** between **nodes**. If the player has a choice of **path**, their choice should reflect their **diegetic** agency. Visit the site and identify likely **paths** between **nodes** – usually but not always the shortest routes or **paths**-of-least-resistance. Also identify alternate **paths** the player might choose, and consider the different texture, mood and duration of those routes, as well as players' possible **diegetic** motives for choosing that **path** (as well as meta-diegetic motives, like if one path is longer but sheltered from rain).

Landmarks

With **location-specific** design we're able to select specific **landmarks** rather than reading them from datasets, so they can be the basis for highly contextual **merged reality moments**.

Remember that physical **landmarks** must be seen on a site visit to understand their potential relationships to the player and the wider world. Take a coffee shop: depending on your story, you may be able to guide the player to that exact coffee shop by name, or to visually reskin elements of the building as a steampunk coffee-house. But there are other ways the coffee shop could provide spationarrative anchors; you could direct players could follow the smell of coffee, or refer to groups of people queueing at certain times of day.

Hubs

Players often return to **hubs** multiple times, which is useful if your story shows locations or characters changing over time. It's also useful if you're giving players persistent **objectives**, like in "farming" or "gardening" gameplay (which could be anything from farming digital crops to maintaining an alien zoo).

Hubs also create a social context since they're where players and non-players both are most likely to congregate and influence one another' experience. The social dynamic of a place is an intangible quality which can't be read from datasets, so being able to anticipate, respond to and incorporate social dynamics in **hub** spaces is a particular strength of **location-specific** design. (More on this in 3.3: OCCUPYING SPACE.)

Edges

It's often useful make the **boundaries** of your storyscape correspond to physical **edges**, since they're manifest and easily adopted into your player's augmented mental map. Looking for **edges** on a site visit is also a good opportunity to think about the accessibility of your experience. Features which may not seem like an **edge** to some can be completely impassible to others: to a wheelchair user an uncut kerb between road and sidewalk is an impassible **edge**. (More on accessibility in Appendix A.)

When **paths** intersect with **edges** they sometimes create **bottlenecks** which funnel players through a single **path**, like bridges, tunnels or gaps in fences. You might use **bottlenecks** to keep players on a singular **critical path**, so you can STAGE mustsee content **nodes** there. Physical **bottlenecks** might also have a claustrophobic texture which can support your storytelling. If your experience is multiplayer, **bottlenecks** may also share some qualities of **hubs** as congregation places for fellow-players, creating clusters of players with social dynamics you can exploit.

Districts

Not all **districts** are visible from a map, because this isn't just about named neighbourhoods; any area with a distinct mood or texture can be part of your spationarrative canvas. Remember that **districts** in particular may change seasonally or with time of day, or manifest different social dynamics. Ultimately this is one of the most important elements of visiting locations as part of **reverse level design**: to feel your way through the space, ideally at different times and under different conditions.

LOCATION-SPECIFIC LAYOUT CASE STUDY: *PANOPTICON GO*[18]

In 2021 my team at Playlines prototyped a "surveillance assault course" mobile AR app which augmented a layer of site-specific stealth gameplay onto The Strand, a busy area of central London. We identified the locations and fields-of-view of all the real-world CCTV cameras in the area, and superimposed the cameras and their fields-of-view as hazards on a GPS map. Players were required to get from a start point to the goal without moving into any camera's field-of-view as augmented on the map. If the player moved into a field-of-view they would be "spotted" and penalised. This hybrid digital/physical gameplay was *heads-up* and required players to spot and orient themselves to the physical cameras to

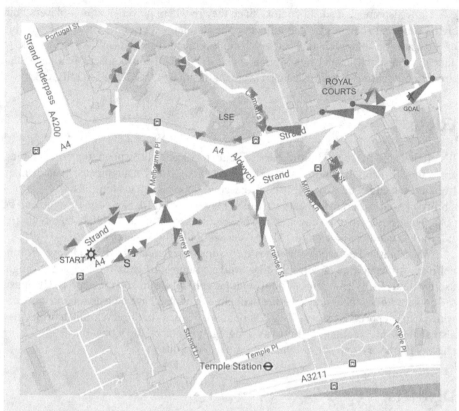

FIGURE 3.1.2b   An early prototype map of the *Panopticon Go* game area. Each dot is a camera. Grey cones denote fields-of-view. Google (2021), Strand, London. Available at: http://maps.google.co.uk (Accessed: 6 Mar 2021)

find blindspots. So players were required to navigate via the mobile map but also simultaneously needed to be alert to the physical environment (Figure 3.1.2b).

The prototype superimposed a **layout** of digital/physical hazards on the actual streets. It didn't define any **paths**; players were encouraged to determine their own routes. The game showed street and building names on the map, providing **landmarks** for orientation, and also treated the cameras as both physical **landmarks** and digital content **nodes**. The prototype was single-player with a designated start point and singular goal, so did not use a **hub** (though we have plans for a multiplayer version which would take advantage of players congregating in certain areas). The prototype occupied only a relatively small area of space but later versions were designed to use the River Thames as a natural **edge**. **Edges** in the built environment, such as the fences around the Royal Courts, provided inaccessible areas which added to the challenge. We also had to be aware of **districts** such as the London School of Economics campus, which had a definable mood (and a greater concentration of cameras).

Reaching the goal without being spotted on CCTV was, by design, nearly impossible. The goal was positioned in a literal **bottleneck** with high levels of surveillance, part of the "ring of steel" high-security surveillance system around the financial district of London. All players funnelled down a single street to the goal and were spotted on CCTV. Our intention with the design was to raise awareness of the dangers of facial-recognition CCTV – using AR to appropriate the street furniture of urban life, and critiquing state surveillance through gameplay by alerting players to the physical presence of cameras as "gameplay hazards" all around them.

In a later CHALLENGE we'll try out ideas for placing your players into spatial **sandboxes** to explore and set their own **objectives**. But for now let's try a CHALLENGE where you need to drive players towards a specific spationarrative goal while giving them freedom to choose a **path**.

CHALLENGE #20: STORYSCAPE DESIGN PART 2: MULTI-PATH LAYOUTS

Goal: Explore how players encounter the **layout** of locations with multiple optional **paths**.

Select a **place** and obtain a **map**. (Use the same **place** as **Storyscape Design Part 1** if possible.)

Conceptualise a simple spationarrative to augment into the location. **Outline** the player's IDENTITY and objective. The player might be a pilgrim finally approaching home, or trying to reach a planetary escape shuttle in time.

Identify a start point and goal.

Don't define a **path** for the player. Instead, identify at least **three potential paths**: some obvious, some not-so-obvious.

Conduct a **site visit** and feel out the texture and tone of the different potential routes. **Shoot a video walkthrough** of each of the **potential paths**.

Test your route choices by asking a friend to find a **path** from start to goal. Did they follow one of your predicted routes? What was their emotional dynamic like? **Refine** your **path** choice and narrative accordingly.

You're now going to add story elements to the **video walkthroughs** to show how your narrative would respond to the player's choice of **path**.

Watch the video walkthroughs and **write** dialogue/narration for each of the three **paths**. Refer specifically to the surroundings and/or highlight the player's agency in choosing a route. How does moving through this route feel, and how does that support the storytelling? Why might the player have chosen this route? How does this reflect on their protagonist IDENTITY? How might diegetic characters or non-players SEEING them interpret their actions?

Record dialogue/narration and choreograph it to the **video walkthroughs**. **Test** again with friends.

TASKS

- **Select** a **place** with a start and goal
- **Conceptualise** a spationarrative with a player-character IDENTITY and objective.
- **Outline** the narrative.
- **Visit** the site and identify three potential **paths**.
- **Test** and **refine paths**.
- **Shoot video walkthroughs** of the **paths**.
- **Write** dialogue/narration reflecting each **path** choice.
- **Record** audio choreographed to video **walkthroughs.**
- **Test.**

LOCATION-SPECIFIC STAGING: SPATIAL PACING

Short's second principle of interactive fictional geography is *"control access to parts of the geography in a way that sets the desired pace"*. As we've already seen, **location-specific** design gives us a decent amount of control over spationarrative structure and how a player moves through **nodes**/beats via **layout**. However in an embodied narrative, **pacing** must also be defined by players' actions. We don't necessarily know the **paths** they'll choose between **nodes**, which might determine the order in which events unfold, and we can't the control their **journey** and **dwell times** which define their experience of duration. These variances reflect the player's agency, and we need to treat their choices as **diegetic**.

Pacing augmented/spatial reality narratives usually involves finding ways to detect players' physical position or actions, and triggering digital events accordingly. In a headset-based **table-scale** experience, hand-tracking might be used to respond to players' physical gestures; in LBGs geolocation is used to respond to players' **spatial agency** (as in the **conditionality** examples back in 3.1.1).

Location-specific design allows us to trigger and STAGE digital events much more contextually. But increasing contextuality also raises the expectation of congruence between player actions in the physical layer and events in the digital layer. In **location-specific**, to create effectively paced **merged reality moments,** we need to create a cause-and-effect relationship between digital and physical events. This requires us to use **spatial logic gates** to precisely trigger digital content in response to player actions. We might also need to maintain a record of the **game state** in order to remember and respond to the player's previous choices, not just the choice they're making in-the-moment.

Conditional Pacing: Spatial Gates

In 3.1.1 we saw how flatscreen Interactive Narratives can create **logic gates** to prevent player-characters from accessing certain areas unless they satisfy certain **conditions**.

We also saw how in **location-agnostic** AR/spatial narratives we usually can't physically **gate** off places, though we can respond to player's general GPS location and vary content accordingly. To create more contextual and **location-specific pacing** we'll need to trigger events more precisely, using **spatial gates.**

In Playlines' location-based AR hip-hop opera *CONSEQUENCES* we combined bluetooth iBeacons with smartphones to detect players' position, and triggered new content **nodes** – contextual audio – as the player physically entered new rooms or areas. This also allowed players to branch the story by choosing where to go next: for example, players could choose to follow different NPC characters in the audio layer by choosing between different **paths** at a physical **fork**. Their choice of **path** would lead them to different rooms which would trigger different content, and also create a **variable** so that the consequences of their choice persisted throughout their experience. (More on **forks** in 3.2: BEING THERE.)

In *CONSEQUENCES* each room in the venue had its own content **node** and backing track, so our goal was to make the entrance to each room into a **spatial gate** so we could detect when players entered. The background music had to change and the appropriate story audio be triggered as soon as players crossed the threshold of the room.

We positioned beacons at each rooms' entrance to create a **spatial gate**. When the player's device detected that beacon, it triggered that room's content. But bluetooth iBeacons are relatively imprecise. During prototyping players sometimes experienced false positives: their device would detect a beacon early, and a room's content would be triggered well before they'd passed through the **gate** into the room. In order to create reliable binary **spatial gates** we got good at using tinfoil to shape the signal broadcast by the beacons, so that the beacon was detected only upon entering the relevant room.

This type of **spatial gate** creates a basic **merged reality moment**: a physical cause with a digital effect. Enter the room and the backing music changes, and NPC characters in the audio layer respond to you entering, establishing your commersive presence both in the physical room and the room's digital narrative layer.

With the addition of some physical infrastructure it's possible to physically block players from entering a physical room until they've satisfied **conditions**, creating a **conditional gate**. Escape Rooms often showcase digital → physical **gating**: players might interact with digital puzzles to trigger physical events like unlocking a door.

In **location-specific** controlled spaces we can construct simple, solid digital → physical **gates** by e.g. giving a passcode to a player via the digital layer; that passcode then opens a physical door lock in the location. We've already seen how in the Playlines installation *Coming Out*, a "VIP area" was guarded by a costumed "bouncer" actor with a velvet rope at the entrance. The bouncer would prevent entry, **gating** off the VIP space, unless the player spoke a password; the password could only be obtained via the digital layer.

Originally the password-bouncer **gate** was designed to prevent players from accidentally entering the end location early. But *Coming Out* gave players a choice over which of three storylines to pursue, and we soon realised that the three different storylines could give different **conditional** passwords. That way, when the player spoke their password it physically manifested which storyline they'd chosen in the digital layer.

This created a solid digital-physical **spatial gate** as well as a more sophisticated **merged reality moment**, where players' earlier choices about where to go in the physical layer caused later consequences in the digital story layer. The bouncer actor could respond to each password in a manner appropriate to the earlier choices made by the player. Players who chose a "friendly" storyline would be given a certain password in the audio layer; speaking this password to the bouncer, the player would be greeted warmly. Players on different storylines would be given different passwords, which would result in them being turned away or even threatened by the bouncer, reflecting that player's earlier choices in the story.

Game State

The **game state** is a digital record of the player's choices and status, similar to a save file created when a player saves their game. A **game state** contains all the relevant **variables** so the game can maintain or reproduce the player's story-so-far, including the consequences of any prior player choices. When *Coming Out* players spoke their **conditional** password to the bouncer, they were manifesting their digital **game state** in the physical world. Players didn't realise it, but the password they gave sent a signal across the barrier between digital and physical, indicating to the bouncer-performer which storyline the player had chosen.

With Internet of Things technology, networked physical devices could respond to players' digital **game state**: if the player chooses to go rogue, advertising billboards could display in-story "wanted posters" of them; door locks could open for players if they have the right keycard in their digital inventory. In controlled spaces like immersive theatre and theme parks, digital-physical instance management software like Clockwork Dog's COGS can trigger networked doors, lighting and even smoke machines based on players' actions or **game state**.

There's a lot we can learn about **location-specific spatial pacing** from theme parks. They're the ultimate in controlled narrative spaces: as scholar Margaret King says, theme parks are a "four-dimensional symbolic landscape".[19] Theme parks increasingly use digital instance management software, mediated by player-worn wearables or apps on player's phones, to track players' **game state.** This in turn can be used to reflect players' choices back at them, and to **pace** players' experience.

Super Nintendo World at Universal Studios Hollywood (2023) allows players to progress and unlock content with a "story mode". Visitor wristbands are linked via QR codes to a mobile app which narrates a simple story and directs the player through a sequence of physical minigames in the park. On completing a minigame the player's unique wristband code is scanned and their **game state** updated, with story progress displayed via the app – which also displays live leaderboards.[20] Bringing this type of persistent digital gameplay out into the park enables a physical → digital → physical gameplay loop with a strong BEING SEEN element: the "Final Boss" of Super Nintendo World is unlocked via progressing the storyline, and fought in a group with other players, allowing for a degree of public social cachet for completing the "story mode".

However, this physical → digital → physical loop in gamified physical attractions can also create **zero-sum pacing** issues. Capacity is limited by physical space so physical minigames often have queues. Physical gameplay components are generally **zero-sum**, i.e. they're the same for all players, so some players might find a minigame too challenging while others find it unsatisfyingly easy.[21] And though players can BE SEEN succeeding, it's also difficult for players to avoid realising that they're just one protagonist among many in the park. The story can tell you you've saved the day, but it risks *ludocorporeal dissonance* if you can see other heroes queueing up to save the same day just moments after you.

By contrast, the legendary hidden game *Sorcerers of the Magic Kingdom* at Walt Disney World Florida (2012–2021) used game kiosks disguised as ordinary themed set-dressing; the kiosks would detect special trading cards then activate hidden screens on which visitors could battle Disney villains. Players progressed a persistent storyline by scanning a unique visitor Key Card[22] at kiosks, allowing their **game state** to persist even between park visits. (Today, *Uncharted Adventure* (2022) enables similar app-driven scavenger hunt gameplay aboard Disney cruises.[23])

Gameplay progress in *Sorcerers of the Magic Kingdom* could trigger some physical "Easter Eggs", such as activating nearby animatronics. But the **pacing** was controlled at the digital level, enabling **non-zero-sum** storytelling, so different players could experience different challenge levels and storylines at the same game kiosk. Content could also be added over time to extend or improve the **pacing** of the experience. The hidden nature of the game also created a BEING SEEN dynamic; players were able to "magically" activate screens and hidden props, creating a sense of secret knowledge and cachet.

However, most augmented/spatial experiences, even **location-specific** ones, don't take place in fully-controlled spaces like theme parks. In public, using door locks and other networked devices requires permissions for every device. And even in fully-controlled spaces, it can be risky to make the **pacing** of potentially plot-critical moments hinge on technology you can't directly control: networked door locks still break; doors are propped open by cleaning staff; advertising billboards can malfunction or be bought out.

Digital Pacing with Physical Performers

One powerful way to provide visible, accessible AND highly responsive digital → physical **pacing** is to mediate some story moments through real actors, like the "bouncer" example above.

Passing information about a player's **game state** to a trained actor can allow the actor to respond to the player in-story with appropriate pre-rehearsed dialogue. They might be able to respond to or trigger story **conditions** by giving **objectives** or dropping clues. This creates **merged reality moments** with a human face.

Let's say that early in the digital layer of a story a player has to make a choice: slay or befriend a dragon. Later in the story, the player enters a physical location designated as an inn, and you want to reflect the consequences of their earlier decision via interaction with the real human innkeeper (an actor). Depending on the player's **game state**, you want the innkeeper to respond with appropriate dialogue and give the players one of two **objectives** reflecting their earlier choice. Giving the wrong **objective** to the wrong player will create juxtaposition (e.g. if a player chose to slay the dragon, the innkeeper should not give them the objective of inviting their new dragon friend to tea.) The player's slay/befriend choice is stored as a **variable** in the **game state**, but you need to get that information across the digital-physical boundary to the actor.

You could give the player a specific password manifesting their choice, as in the bouncer example above. Or you could embed a password within an otherwise innocuous phrase; players who chose to slay the dragon could be told to go to the inn and ask for ale, while players who befriended the dragon could be instructed to ask for wine. Each player unwittingly sends a **game state** signal to the innkeeper who can then respond to them appropriately. But players are always the most unreliable link in a digital-physical transmission; they might misinterpret, rebel against or simply forget their **conditional** instruction, especially if it seems innocuous.

Depending on how much control you have over the space and the player's navigation, you may be able to force the player to unwittingly signal their choice via **layout**. Players who slew the dragon could be directed via **layout** to enter the inn through the East door, while players who befriended the dragon are guided to the West door. But again, players are unpredictable, easily confused and downright disobedient.

Ideally you could update the innkeeper actor live about the **game state** of each player as they approach. This can be as simple as using a radio headset. Central operations staff could track player **game state**, and update the innkeeper actor via radio as each player approaches. But this is manpower-intensive and difficult to scale; sustainable large-scale experiences usually require automated event triggering, e.g. with signals automatically sent to a device the actor can access.

GAME STATE AND LIVE PERFORMERS CASE STUDY: *THE HEADLANDS GAMBLE*

If your story has a contemporary setting you have plenty of options to incorporate everyday communications technology into the story as a way of passing information across the digital → physical boundary. First Person Travel's acclaimed *The Headlands Gamble*[24] (2015) was a weekend-long live mystery where players interacted with real-world actors and props, including staying in a period hotel and driving a classic car to story locations.[25] Multiple players played the game separately but simultaneously, interacting with the same *in situ* actors in carefully timed slots, without encountering one another. So the **pacing** of each player's storyline had to be managed as well as the realtime resourcing of story components like live actor scenes.

First Person Travel's instance management platform Charter maintained a **game state** for each player and triggered both digital and physical events. The player's car was equipped with a dashboard tablet, which communicated key information to players but also tracked their progress and detected their decisions through interface input and GPS. A "Travel Agent" staff member tracked and managed storylines live, but many **game state** signals were automated and sent **conditionally**. For instance, players entering a given GPS area in the car might receive a message on the car tablet triggered by their location. The content of this message might be **conditional** based on **game state** tracking of previous player decisions.

Director Gabe Smedresman's goal was to minimise players' use of technology in favour of a physical props and actors. But behind the scenes the instance management platform was vital to manage the threads of **spatial agency** and **merged reality moments**: as Smedresman says "if we relied on all these people to talk to one another it'd be kind of a mess, and some piece of ad hoc information might go amiss".[26]

Actors stationed in story locations had access to a mobile app which displayed live information including the arrival times of player groups, players' names and statuses, and their relevant **game state**. This determined what content the actors delivered to which players. Actors manually updated players' **game state** by accessing the platform after each player interaction, recording what information player had already accessed, which clues they'd received, and which clues other actors might need to deliver.

The experience also incorporated "vendors" – real-world businesspeople such as the hotel's real-world staff – who weren't trained actors but who could deliver small elements of story. Vendors didn't have time to learn the interface and parse all the data, so the platform would simply SMS message vendors with simple prompts so they could play their part in the story's **pacing** and create **merged reality moments** – like "tell the guests in Room 32 *'there is a red envelope under your hotel bed'*". As Smedresman says, "that's the magic – those are the kind of moments that make it feel real – when it incorporates someone you don't expect to be part of the experience".

Complex interactive narratives with intersecting plotlines require **pacing** that keeps all the parts moving at a predictable rate – including the players. *Headlands* game days were carefully scheduled with different player groups arriving at locations in sequence. This meant players needed to progress consistently. Smedresman says *Headlands* didn't implement **gates** to block progress – "you don't want to end the story in the middle!" Smedresman's challenge was: "how do we create a rewarding arc, with as much feeling of participant agency as possible, but in a cost efficient manner – we don't want to have actors or other story resources waiting around not being seen". This risk of story resources *not being seen* is one of the inherent risks of branching narrative. This is sometimes called a *hard branch*, a player choice which causes players to see some content but cuts off other content as a consequence. This is the price of player agency. But as Smedresman says "there's an extreme logistical cost to hard branches in the real world, with real actors". If you plan, resource and rehearse a scene, and players' choices mean they never see it, you're leaving that content unused on the cutting-room floor.

For Smedresman, when players have made choices, they should be made aware of other possible outcomes on other branches: "if people don't know that a branch was a consequence of something they did, they won't appreciate it in the same way. You need to surface those mechanisms… people who got the secret ending thought *everyone* got the secret ending, while people who didn't, didn't even know it was there".[27]

Branching storylines and **game states** tend to be built around binary yes/no choices. They might create the illusion of nuance through storytelling and the cumulative effect of multiple decisions. But this also adds complexity, and ultimately the nuance exists only in the players' IMAGINATION. Trained immersive actors are able to combine pre-rehearsed dialogue with improvisation, subtly dropping gameplay-critical clues into conversation while responding in an individuated way to each player, reflecting both their digital **game state** and their real-world demeanour. This is a great strength of augmenting immersive theatre with digital elements. (But bear in mind that a live actor is usually better utilised in improvising around a few key prompts, rather than releasing heavily-scripted **conditional** information or dictating precise **pacing**. That's what computers are for.)

As AR technology develops, some of these early hybrid digital-physical **gate** designs and other **pacing** solutions will no longer be necessary, while others will continue to be refined. In experiences like *Headlands Gamble,* actors might soon wear headsets which visualise colour-coded **game states** as icons above each player, or even be fed clues and dialogue lines via heads-up display. Just remember that in hybrid spationarratives, however much you're able to digitally manage **pacing**, as much as possible it should create authentic, organic-feeling encounters with the real world.

CHALLENGE #21: STORYSCAPE DESIGN PART 3: SANDBOX WITH CONDITIONALITY

Goal: Explore the process of populating a location with augmented content and introducing **conditionality**.

Select a public **place** and obtain a **map**. If possible continue using the location from **Storyscape Design Parts 1&2.**

Visit the **place** and explore. You're NOT going to be specifying a **path** or linear spationarrative for the player, instead creating multiple **content nodes**. **Identify** at least 5x **nodes** where the player could encounter characters or other story elements in the audio layer.

Conceptualise a **fictional storyscape** which could be overlaid on the **physical place**. You could reimagine the place as a classic RPG village with an inn, item shop and various townsfolk. Or dramatise the **place's** far future with robots going about everyday business.

For each of the **nodes** you identified, **outline** a character or story asset the player encounters there. Remember that the player is free to roam the **place**, so they may encounter **nodes** in any order. All the content/characters should be part of a coherent world. Consider ways to cohere different elements of the world together: characters could suggest the player go visit other characters or all refer to a larger plot.

Add conditionality to at least two of the **nodes**. Visiting these **nodes** should trigger different content based on whether the player HAS or HAS NOT already visited another **node**. So a character at the church might tell you to visit the cafe; if the player has already visited the cafe the character at the church might ask them what they think of the café's disreputable owner.

For each **conditional node**, articulate the **conditionality** based on **game state** stored as **variables**, like in this example:

NODE: Church
IF $VisitedCafe=no THEN trigger content "Church Character Suggests Cafe Visit"

IF $VisitedCafe=YES THEN trigger content "Church Character Asks What Player Thinks Of The Cafe"
NODE: Cafe
IF $VisitedChurch=NO THEN trigger content "Cafe Character Suggests Church Visit"
IF $VisitedChurch=YES THEN trigger content "Cafe Character Asks Player To Help Them Rob The Church"

Write the content for each **location**, including each **conditional** story element. **Record** the content as audio.
Test the content, including the **conditionality**, by playing the audio to friends on-site. Does the **conditional** content make sense in all possible situations the player can create, (including returning to locations multiple times)?

TASKS

- **Select** a **place** and obtain a **map**.
- **Visit** and identify **5x nodes** within the **place.**
- **Conceptualise** a **fictional storyscape** to overlay.
- **Outline** a story element for each **location**.
- **Add conditionality** to 2x **nodes** based on player actions.
- **Record** audio.
- **Test**.

BONUS CHALLENGE

Use caught.nu's **conditionality** tools to implement and test **conditionality** as a geotagged locative layer.

LOCATION-SPECIFIC STAGING: BOUNDARIES

In 3.1.1 we looked in general at the importance of augmented/spatial **boundaries** to keep player's emotional experience focused in the storyscape and to "disguise the **edges** of the map from the player so that [the player] doesn't feel claustrophobic". For Short,

The author's mission is to help the player pretend that the world continues forever in all directions—and perhaps envision what lies in those directions—while making it clear which areas are worth focusing on for the purpose of advancing the game.[28]

In **location-specific** spationarratives, the storyscape is a designated story-rich area of the world. But the real world continues off in every direction beyond, so we need to draw **boundaries** to make the player's experience coherent and navigable and keep them within the bounds of our content. With augmented reality we can draw new **boundaries** directly onto space or align them with real-world **edges,** either physical – like rivers – or conceptual – like the **boundaries** of a park.

In 3.1.1. we examined three techniques: **foveating space, diegeticizing boundaries** and creating **social boundaries**. Now let's see how these apply in **location-specific**.

Foveating Space

By creating focused areas of content you can show players which areas will reward their **diegetic** actions, and make everywhere else peripheral. In **location-specific** design we might augment the conceptual **boundaries** of a fictional **district** onto space to keep players within the area of focus, or co-opt physical or conceptual **edges** to help players build a clear "mental map" of where content can be found. It's best to situate players' **objectives** within the designated space. Remember you don't necessarily need to abruptly halt the story if the player strays out of bounds. Players' **diegetic** self-narration will continue out beyond the **boundary** unless contradicted, so it's best to gently guide them back in-bounds, or create buffer zones of content in which they can discover in-story consequences for crossing **boundaries**.

Even when augmenting a space without strong conceptual or physical **edges,** there are ways to convey in-story that no content can be found beyond a given threshold.

FOVEATING SPACE CASE STUDY: COMING OUT

In *Coming Out* (Playlines' 2016 audio layer installed at London's Tobacco Dock), players freely roamed the venue navigating a locative audio layer, hearing voices from characters speaking from thirty years into a fictionalised future.

(Many AR/spatial experiences, particularly history-based ones, augment asynchronous content into places, i.e. content which is in the same location as the player but set in a different time. As locative audio media researcher Løvlie says, "on the one hand the text has been embodied, in that it has been given an audible voice and a physical location to live in; on the other hand the body which created that voice is no longer present".[29] With *Coming Out* we wanted to try creating co-presence with characters from the future, i.e. characters who *weren't there yet.*)

The venue staff had asked us to discourage players from going into the basement – the area was empty and unsupervised. The narrative layer added content to other relatively empty areas of the venue, and there was a risk that free-roaming players might misinterpret navigation or otherwise explore downstairs in search of content. Access to the basement was via wide staircases which couldn't be blocked. So there was no physical **boundary** and an ambiguous conceptual **boundary** – and remember, this was an audio-only layer so we couldn't augment in a graphical **boundary**.

So we augmented emptiness into the basement using narrative. The audio layer depicted a version of the Tobacco Dock venue thirty years in the future: a vibrant community space in a London ravaged by climate collapse. So, early on in the experience, while the player was leaning over a balcony looking down into the basement space below, we established in-story that Tobacco Dock's basement was flooded by the Thames' rise due to climate change. This enabled us to build out the story world, and to make it clear that there was no content to be found downstairs.

Diegeticizing Boundaries

In **location-specific** design we're much more likely to be able to situate an augmented storyscape in an already-**boundaried** space like a building (or an island, or cave). AR/spatial technology may allow you to reskin or recontextualise a building or **district** as something else entirely, say, by augmenting a building's inner walls as the inside of a spaceship. But creating a solid "mental map" of **boundaries** is key for players to understand the parameters of their in-story **spatial agency**.

Often informing the player that an augmented/spatial narrative takes place wholly within a building or defined **district** like a park is enough to give the player a clear "mental map" and reduce the chance they'll accidentally or deliberately test **boundaries**. If your location is a museum, but your story depicts a dystopian future, inform players their adventure takes place within the Abandoned Museum (or the offices of the Evil Corporation which took over the Abandoned Museum). This helps merge story into setting, and **diegeticizes** the existing physical and conceptual **boundaries** of the space. Player's won't bother going into areas which are obviously outside the conceptual bounds of the museum.

However, bear in mind that augmented **boundaries** are consensual and require the player's willing "creation of belief": you can't "glass tunnel" the player or physically prevent them going anywhere (without implementing the kind of digital-physical **spatial gates** we covered under **location-specific pacing**). This means that narrative justification for **boundaries** shouldn't inadvertently motivate players to test those **boundaries**. Say you STAGE an experience inside a museum and tell the player they're trapped there by a curse or a horde of zombies outside. A certain type of player will immediately begin trying doors, wanting to venture outside to investigate. Remember also that even controlled spaces like immersive theatre venues are required to have multiple fire exits, so their **boundaries** can be surprisingly porous. If you tell a player they're trapped within a haunted castle and must find a way to escape, there's a real risk they will start opening fire doors.

In **roomscale/at-home** design, reskinning a room's physical walls as digital **boundary** walls is the most effective way to prevent players bumping into them. Many experiences like these depict a wider world outside the digital/physical **boundary** of the home. *Drop Dead: The Cabin*'s AR *Home Invasion* mode (2023) draws broken windows onto a room's physical walls: these are spawn points for zombies invading your home, but also situate your home in a wider horror-themed environment by showing virtual landscape outside. The objective is to *defend* the house so players are unlikely to test these **boundaries** by trying to escape through the false windows. And anyway, the player has a hybrid understanding of the storyscape and knows that their windows aren't really broken. (Even if the player accidentally bumps into a reskinned physical/digital wall, this lends physical substance to the digital wall so it's also a kind of **merged reality moment** – though not necessarily a positive one.)

Social Boundaries

Enforcing a **boundary** with social factors can be a tidy way to keep players in-bounds using their own ambient sensitivity to BEING SEEN. Short uses the example of eavesdropping, citing Andrew Plotkin's interactive fiction *So Far* (1996). The player approaches a locked door and can overhear characters in a room on the other side discussing plot-significant goings-on. As Short says, the depiction of the room beyond "adds a sense of breadth and habitation to the world"[30] without requiring the room to be accessible – so the **boundary** is clear but the world feels bigger than the playable space (like in the "Trompe L'Oeil vistas" Short described earlier).

In **location-based** design we can deploy an equivalent effect: allow the player to eavesdrop or peep beyond a **boundary**, but make it clear that if the player crosses the **boundary** they will be noticed. The in-story consequences of being noticed can vary: in the case of eavesdropping, if the player breaks through the **boundary** they will at the very least disturb the people they're overhearing, cutting off access to content.

Eavesdropping is a common literary trope, particularly in Shakespeare, and it can be a highly emotive situation in which to place embodied players. Eavesdropping activates players' sense of BEING (UN)SEEN and helps build both their social and spatial sense of the storyscape (we'll look at this in more detail in 3.3: OCCUPYING SPACE.)

Plays like *Much Ado About Nothing* and *A Midsummer Night's Dream* often show characters eavesdropping on one another. In AR/spatial adaptation of these plays, the storyteller could create **boundaries** and control player flow by demarcating eavesdropping areas. Violating the **boundaries** of eavesdropping areas would disturb the overheard characters, cutting off the player's access to eavesdrop content. (Even in a **location-agnostic** or **generic-place** design, e.g. a version designed to work in any garden or forest, a **layout** of eavesdropping areas could help contain and guide players without requiring on-site barriers.)

LOCATION-SPECIFIC AUGMENTED STAGING: SUMMARY

How do we activate players' IMAGINATIONS to help STAGE digital narratives in specific locations?

- *Create contextual **merged reality moments**, but be conscious of players' higher expectation of congruence between digital and physical layers in **location-specific** experiences.*

How do we design/co-opt layouts for augmented spationarratives in specific places?

- *Understand the role of **critical path** in spationarrative – are you creating linear progression or a sandbox?*
- *Take inspiration from game-level design, particularly realistic "Immersive Sim" **layouts***
- *Use **reverse-level design** to select emotive routes through real places.*
- *Utilise the specifics of **paths, landmarks, hubs, edges,** and **districts.***

How do we pace augmented spationarratives in specific places?

- *Implement **spatial gates** to track and respond to player movements.*
- *Implement digital-physical **spatial gates** to make player access to places **conditional**.*
- *Explore ways to manifest or transmit players' **game state** from digital to physical, using e.g. passwords*
- *Physical performers can add drama and help manage some digital-physical **conditionality**, often supported by instance management software.*

How do we create and communicate the boundaries of augmented spationarratives in specific places?

- *Situate the **boundaried** playspace in a wider story world.*
- *Use **objectives** to **foveate space** and/or justify it in-story.*
- *Co-opt and **diegeticize edges** but avoid motivating players to test them.*
- *Enforce **social boundaries** with consequences, using **diegetic** social factors like **eavesdropping**.*

NOTES

1. Tom Abba, Jonathan Dovey, Kate Pullinger (eds.) *Ambient Literature: Towards a New Poetics of Situated Writing and Reading Practices*, Palgrave Macmillan, London, 2021, p. 19.
2. Sierra Bainbridge in B. Cannon Ivers (ed.), *250 Things a Landscape Architect Should Know*, Birkhäuser, Basel, 2021, p. 9.
3. Ritchie, 2014.
4. Mark Sample, "Location Is Not Compelling (Until It Is Haunted)", in Farman (ed.), 2014, p. 68.
5. G. M. Trevelyan, *Autobiography of an Historian,* Longmans, Green, London, 1949.
6. Jolie O'Dell, "History Channel Launches Foursquare Campaign and a New Badge" Mash-able, 13 Apr 2010, https://web.archive.org/web/20110101062810/http://mashable.com/2010/04/13/history-channel-foursquare/.
7. Amy Spencer, "Reading Ambient Literature: Immersion, Distraction, and the Situated Reading Experience", *Poetics Today* 42:2, 2021.

8. Thanks to Chris Hogg for this story structure.
9. Janet Cardiff, from Walsh and Enright 2001.
10. Janet Cardiff, "The Missing Voice: Case Study B" 1999 https://cardiffmiller.com/walks/the-missing-voice-case-study-b/.
11. Bradley (ed.) 2019.
12. Dustin Freeman, Joshua Marx, *The Painting*, Speakeasy, San Francisco, 2015.
13. Short, 2011.
14. Alyse Knorr, *Goldeneye 007*, Boss Fight Books, Los Angeles, 2022, p. 21-29.
15. *Ibid.* p. 36.
16. *Ibid.* P. 41.
17. Patrick Gill, "Tears of the Kingdom's New Thing Is Actually Pretty Old", *Polygon*, 8 Jun 2023 https://www.youtube.com/watch?v=kKS4s-2sKVw.
18. *Street of Eyes*, Playlines with support from King's College Culture. Rob Morgan, Anya Tye, Jerry Carpenter, Muki Kulhan, 2021.
19. Margaret King, "The Disney Effect: Fifty Years after Theme Park Design" in Kathy Merlock Jackson and Mark West (eds.), *Disneyland and Culture*, McFarland, London, 2011, p. 223.
20. Tom Bricker, "Strategy Guide for Super Nintendo World", Disney Tourist Blog, Jan 2023 https://www.disneytouristblog.com/guide-super-nintendo-world-universal-studios-hollywood-tips-tricks/.
21. Tom Bricker, "Ride Review: Mario Kart in Super Nintendo World", Disney Tourist Blog, Jan 2023 https://www.disneytouristblog.com/ride-review-mario-kart-bowsers-challenge-super-nintendo-world/.
22. Michael Andersen, 'Sorcerers of the Magic Kingdom Brings Dueling to Disney', *Wired*, 22 Mar 2012 https://www.wired.com/2012/03/sorcerers-of-the-magic-kingdom-brings-dueling-to-disney/.
23. Scott Sanders, '"Disney Uncharted Adventure", Disney Cruise Line Blog, 19 Sep 2022 https://disneycruiselineblog.com/2022/09/disney-uncharted-adventure-interactive-experience-debuts-aboard-the-disney-wish/.
24. *The Headlands Gamble*, First Person Travel, 2015 https://www.firstperson.travel/theheadlandsgamble.
25. Hilary Moss, "A Romantic Weekend for Two: Solving a Crime", *New York Times*, 19 Jan 2016 https://www.nytimes.com/2016/01/19/t-magazine/travel/headlands-gamble-first-person-travel.html.
26. Gabe Smedresman, personal correspondence, 30 Nov 2023.
27. *Ibid.*
28. Short, 2011.
29. Løvlie, 2009.
30. Short, 2011.

BEING THERE

3.2

How do we give players a sense of presence in a hybrid physical-digital storyscape?
What makes a good moment of spationarrative agency?

FOUND YOU

In 1.2 the second pillar of VR immersion, BEING, focused on showing VR players that their presence is **diegetic** and consequential in the virtual world. When AUGMENTING PLAYERS back in Section 2, BEING evolved into IDENTITY-BUILDING, because co-constructing an augmented IDENTITY is essential for the player's actions and emotions to feel **diegetic**.

Now we're AUGMENTING PLACES, our job as storytellers is to give augmented players a strong sense of BEING THERE in fictionalised, digitised versions of the world. The player needs to feel fully co-present with any story elements augmented into their immediate reality.

This is complex because players are always already *somewhere* before augmentation begins, and we cannot overwrite all their physical sensations of BEING THERE. In fact those physical sensations of the real world lend augmented/spatial storytelling solidity and emotional weight. We need to create a continuity with the player's ongoing experience of BEING physically present in the real world, while instancing an augmented version of the world around them.

Much of this section will focus on extending our work on **layout** to allow players to express **spatial agency** in augmented places – for example by designing **forks** in the road where they can feel their presence in the hybrid spationarrative through agency and making spationarrative choices.

But keep in mind that as Løvlie says, even non-interactive geolocated text can "directly invoke[] the co-presence of the reader with the voice of the text"[1] – if it builds a strong sense of BEING THERE.

> It's snowing. It's cloudy. The sun is shining and it's hot. There's a hail storm. My voice holds four seasons and any weather, it will always stay here and never know who you are. And yet something may be staring at you just now, from a window you cannot locate, unreal, like Lee Harvey Oswald in the dark.[2]

This poem by Endre Ruset was written for a specific street in Oslo and geotagged there as part of the "place-bound literature"[3] project *textopia* (2009). *textopia* geo-texts

DOI: 10.1201/9781003379294-19

were accessible with early locative mobile technology, and as Løvlie says the project "requir[ed] the user to physically traverse the landscape of the story in order to traverse the text of the story".[4]

textopia texts were tagged to a location, but the technology couldn't detect any local conditions or the player's **game state**. It was context-blind, yet Ruset's read-only poem is still highly contextual. The poems voice acknowledges that it cannot know who the player is or what the weather is doing, hence it "holds four seasons and any weather". Yet by deploying BEING SEEN the poem emphasises the player's co-presence with the voice of the poem, grounding the player in the place through the gaze of an imagined "Lee Harvey Oswald". The poem is universal, encompassing any weather, yet also individuates and situates the player with the unforgiving focus of a sniper's scope. *You – yes you – you're being watched.*

The question is, how do we build on literary techniques like this with more context-aware AR/spatial technology? How do we show players they are BEING THERE in an augmented storyscape?

BEING THERE THROUGH NAVIGATION

Unlike other media, AR/spatial storytelling is almost always first-person. Even if the player observes other characters through a smartphone like in Niantic's *Peridot* (2023), the player's vantage point defines their relationship to the action and implies their presence – behind the "camera", but present in the scene. Like VR, in headset-based AR/spatial, the player's perspective and vantage point is fully subjective and fully controlled by them, not framed by a director or cinematographer. Hence for Duncan Speakman, "immersion might mean there is no vantage point" defined by the creator – only the individual and subjective first-person **vantage points** of each individual player.

Similarly, whatever the meanings of a place, the experience of BEING THERE is always first-person too. It's *egocentric*, i.e. subjective to individual experience and perspective. In fact, technology seems to be making the experience of BEING in places ever-more **egocentric**.

Until very recently all maps were **allocentric**: a paper map was a fixed image you had to read and decipher to find your location. This meant comparing symbolic features on the map to physical features in the world – locating yourself in the map image and orienting the map in relation to the world. But smartphone GPS maps don't have a fixed image or reference point: they usually begin centred on your location. Our experience of GPS maps is **egocentric**.

As the locative media researcher Stuart Dunn says "the glowing blue dot in the middle of Google Maps identifies where you are in relation to the features around you [**egocentric**], whereas an **allocentric** map printed on paper is static and you have to determine where you are in relation to the features".[5]

EGOCENTRIC AND ALLOCENTRIC MAPPING

Neuroscientists often describe our brains' spatial orientation and spatial reasoning using two frameworks:

The **egocentric** framework depends on our own organism's cues, in other words, our own position and point of view.

The **allocentric** framework relies on remembering, recalling, and recognizing environmental stimuli called **landmarks** that progressively compose a mental image about a place.[6]

- **Allocentric mapping**: arbitrary & fixed, top-down perspective, requires orientation.
- **Egocentric mapping**: relative & dynamic, centred on the player, subject to their perspective.

As we've seen, many LBGs are map-centric experiences, which suits the hunter-gatherer aesthetic of games like *Pokémon GO* and *Monster Hunter Now* (2023). But **egocentric** mapping via a mobile device can significantly reduce users' sense of BEING THERE in a physical place. Have you ever navigated through a location using a smartphone map, then relised you barely looked up from your device to see the actual place around you? Using an **allocentric** paper map requires orientation to physical **landmarks**, so players have to "find themselves" by looking up from the map and paying attention to their surroundings. Whereas an **egocentric** GPS map can provide waypoints or draw **paths** which players can follow without ever looking up from their device – reducing the opportunity for a hybrid physical-digital experience.

Research shows that people navigating places using **egocentric** smartphone maps remember less about the places compared to those using **allocentric** paper maps. This "suggest[s] that the spatial representations or 'optical knowledge' of mobile media impair[s] the formation of cognitive maps".[7] You're less likely to form memories of place using an **egocentric** map because your main knowledge of the place is temporary "optical knowledge"[8] (i.e. what's on the screen in front of you), compared to the "mental map" you build up using spatial awareness and orientation by physical features.

Most mobile LBGs are pretty "heads-down": players' experience consists of looking down at their screen more than interacting with real surroundings. So you're less likely to gain memories of place, and a sense of BEING THERE.

This "heads-down" effect is similar to "minimap blindness" in flatscreen videogames. Most open-world game interfaces used to feature small **egocentric** contextual "minimaps". But designers noticed that players tended to focus on the small 2D maps rather than the lovingly-rendered virtual world. As game journalist Andrea Castellano says, "the top-down map view provides more instant information [or "optical knowledge"] than the in-game world itself. No matter the genre, you subconsciously start to play the minimap".[9] "Minimaps" began to disappear in the late 2010's as designers started to replace them with heads-up navigation aides like compasses or contextual instructions referring to **landmarks**. These resulted in players paying attention to their surroundings instead of the minimap and feeling more presence.

Out in the real world, in order to create a hybrid spatianarrative experience it's essential to get players' attention up off device maps and onto the real world. Otherwise you risk creating what Huck *et al.* call "dichotomy of immersion": "the peculiar situation in LBGs whereby a player's attention is constantly divided between the physical world... and the screen of their mobile device". This split is "usually dominated by interaction with the screen at the expense of interaction with the landscape".[10]

Headsets may resolve some of these issues, since they can superimpose graphics onto our "heads-up" field of view.. We're already seeing car manufacturers like Volkswagen augmenting navigation data directly onto windshields with heads-up displays,[11] and headsets are able to translate map data into videogame-style wayfinding graphics in users' fields-of-view, like following augmented arrows. This will allow for more hybrid encounters with physical/digital places.

But augmenting arrows into the player's field of view isn't strictly **allocentric**, as it bypasses orientation and navigation by **landmarks**. There's a risk that players can context-blindly follow heads-up digital wayfinding, still without much engagement with their physical location. As Dunn says "we are increasingly thinking of routes through our environment as a given route defined by a computer, which we follow, rather than something that we have to triangulate ourselves using observation of our environment. And this undoubtedly affects the way we look at things".[12] This type of superficially contextual wayfinding via heads-up display can lead to context-blindness in players. It's just another form of temporary "optical knowledge" which doesn't become memory or narrated experience of place.

To build players' "mental map" of a storyscape, and properly situate them within it, we need to combine **egocentric** and **allocentric** techniques. Navigation should build players' top-down **allocentric** sense of features' physical relations to one another, as well as activating their first-person, street-level **egocentric** perspective. This might mean providing some heads-up wayfinding, but also physical navigation clues requiring players to examine and orient to the environment.

In **roomscale/at-home** experiences, the player will often already have a strong "mental map" with both an **egocentric** and **allocentric** sense of the layout of their home. In controlled spaces like immersive theatre or theme parks, you may be able to design layouts to be highly memorable or provide physical navigation signs which are fully **diegetic**.

If you're superimposing a storyscape onto a public place, it can be useful to encourage players to examine their surroundings to navigate – as long as what they're seeing can be **diegeticized**. To create a compelling spatianarrative, we need to show players they aren't just following arrows. Augmented/spatial navigation should alert players to the fact that they are within a living and breathing storyscape which exists **allocentrically** beyond their own **egocentric** perspective. You might allow players to ask augmented characters for directions along their way, or place digital signposts at junctions and **hubs**, indicating players' **objectives** but also pointing to other nearby **landmarks** to help build their larger "mental map" of the storyscape. Even **egocentric** wayfinding graphics can be **diegeticizied** and situated in place, rather than presented as an abstract

HUD interface – for example, players could follow footprints augmented on the floor rather than arrows floating in space.

This combined **egocentric/allocentric** approach becomes even more important when asking players to express **spatial agency**. If you present players with a "**fork** in the road" where they can make a choice, their spationarrative experience will be much more powerful if they understand the choice within a larger, living spationarrative context.

SPATIAL AGENCY: FORKS

In flatscreen and VR games players might express their agency through button inputs, via touchscreen or through gestures. Some VR games allow players to move in the virtual world by physically walking (walking-in-place technologies like Disney's HoloTile[13] even allow VR players to walk indefinitely without reaching the physical bounds of their space). But in location-based augmented/spatial media players are already BEING THERE in the real world. This means they can physically "vote with their feet" and choose a **path** or destination in physical space, and in doing so, express their **spatial agency**. **Spatial agency** has a continuity with their everyday experience, so it's crucial we acknowledge and **diegeticize** it.

The most basic **spatial agency** mechanic is a "**fork**-in-the-road".

A **fork** is a physical and metaphorical manifestation of choice. Different **paths** take players to different destinations, excluding other possible roads-not-travelled. Whether the player is choosing an "infiltration route" through their own home in a mixed reality combat game like *Espire 2*, or choosing between paths in a hybrid physical-digital theme park, augmenting forks with narrative weight can make the player's choices feel emotive and consequential. Different **paths** may move through different physical terrain with different feel and texture, which can support spationarrative storytelling. And with **conditionality** using **gates**, different **paths** can trigger different content. This content could trigger immediately AND/OR alter **conditional variables**, so that the consequences of a choice at an earlier **fork** can follow the player and occur later in the narrative.

Broadly speaking, there are two approaches to designing spationarrative **forks**: **location-agnostic** and **location-specific**. A **location-agnostic fork** happens wherever the player happens to be; a **location-specific fork** is STAGED in a specific location and players have to go there.

Location-agnostic forks commonly, but not exclusively, occur in **location-agnostic** experiences like LBGs and **roomscale**. Since they're context-blind, designing narrative for location-agnostic forks tends to focus on the destinations, not the physical properties of the **fork**.

Two destinations might be algorithmically placed on a top-down map of a neighbourhood. The **fork** is wherever the player happens to be when they choose between the two destinations. To the player's first-person perspective, the physical properties of the **fork**, and the experience of choosing a **path**, is subject to wherever they happen to be. (In other words, players' experience of the **fork** is **egocentric** because it is defined by their position and perspective.)

For example, a post-apocalyptic LBG might superimpose a layer of survival gameplay over an ordinary neighbourhood. A quest might ask players to choose between going to a physical gas station to collect fuel or a physical supermarket to collect food. The algorithm finds suitable physical gas stations and supermarkets near the player and augments them as destinations. The **fork** is **location-agnostic**: it's defined both by the algorithm and their starting location. Another player who lives in the same neighbourhood might be choosing between the same two destinations, but their **fork** location might be different based on their different starting location. Another player playing in a different neighbourhood would have a wholly different experience.

In **roomscale** the player's spationarrative experience of a fork will be largely **location-agnostic** and determined by the features of their own home: in *Hauntify* the gameplay might present the player with a **fork** choice of turning left into their kitchen or right into their bedroom when chased by a ghost. The spationarrative qualities of this **fork** will vary hugely between players' homes.

Location-specific forks occur in **location-specific** experiences where the designer can STAGE a choice at a specific physical **fork**. The **fork** can be selected by the storyteller for specific spationarrative effect. In other words, players' experience of choosing a **path** at the **fork** is **allocentric**, because the fork was selected "top-down" by the storyteller, and the spationarrative experience of BEING THERE is defined by the specific features and **landmarks** around the **fork**.

For example, in a theme park, the player might be asked to choose between supporting the rebellion or the authorities; this choice is then spationarratively manifested as a choice between going to a hot dog stand or a drinks stand. The storyteller can STAGE this choice so it happens at a specific **fork**: for example, if the moment of choice is triggered when the player exits a specific ride, the storyteller can determine the specific location of the **fork** and knows the specific feel of the **paths**.

LOCATION-AGNOSTIC FORKS

- Common in **location-agnostic** LBGs and **roomscale**.
- **Fork** location is wherever the player is choosing between two destinations.
- Players navigate **egocentrically**; local features and **landmarks** define the spationarrative experience.

LOCATION-SPECIFIC FORKS

- Only in **location-specific** and controlled spaces.
- **Fork** location is selected by the storyteller, and likely to be chosen for the texture and feel of a physical **fork** or **hub**.
- Players navigate **allocentrically**; the storyteller's choice of fork defines the spationarrative experience.

In **location-specific** design, a key part of any site visit is identifying *in-situ* **fork** features. These might be literal **forks**-in-the-road or stairs going up or down (or simply places where the player can choose to stay or go).

The advantage of **location-specific forks** is that the storyteller can determine a lot of the texture and feel of the moment of choice and subsequent **paths**. The downside, as with all **location-specific**, is the challenge of getting players to come to an exact location.

Location-specific fork qualities:

There are four key qualities to look for when selecting **location-specific forks**: they should be *(i) distinct, (ii) navigable, (iii) asymmetrical* and *(iv) expressive.*

Distinct

A **fork**'s two or more available **paths** need to be clearly distinguishable, both in terms of what the player sees and in terms of tracking the player.

A momentous story choice might feel underwhelming if the physical **fork** is a choice between two identical corridors or two arbitrary directions in a forest.

If you're using GPS or indoor tracking with iBeacons, the two **paths** need to be far enough apart that the system can distinguish location. To avoid false positives you often won't be able to trigger content until the player moves a few meters down one of the **paths**. Write triggered dialogue with this delay in mind.

If you're using a headset, you're likely to be combining mapping data with camera tracking of the environment. This allows much more precision but isn't foolproof; headset cameras could easily confuse two unmarked corridors or two bits of forest. In a controlled space you can help headset sensors visually distinguish **paths** with marker images (these can be disguised as everyday objects like posters).

A particularly distinct **fork** is created if you ask players to choose whether to *go* or *stay*. But remember your tracking system needs to give time to distinguish *going* from *staying*; the player who decides to *go* may take time to make up their mind and clear the area, but the *stay* content shouldn't trigger until they've actually made that choice.

Navigable

It's not enough for **paths** in a **fork** to merely be distinct; you also need to be able to unambiguously communicate to the player which **path** represents which choice. As Chris Hardman says in "Walkmanology", "actors rehearse, audience don't. Whatever [audiences] are asked to do must be instantly understandable to a significant cross-section of the populace".[14] Any uncertainty the player feels should be **diegetic** uncertainty about *which* path to choose, not extra-diegetic uncertainty about *which **path** is which.*

Depending on how much you're graphically reskinning a location, you might be able to co-opt existing physical signage to distinguish paths. If you're in a controlled space you may be able to place physical signage to provide unambiguous navigation; this is an opportunity for a **merged reality moment**, so find ways to make this signage **diegetic**.

Even if you're significantly decontextualising the location in the narrative you might be able to co-opt contemporary physical signage. In *Virtual Ambrose,* the story significantly recontextualised some parts of Kingston's Grand Theatre. The Orchestra Pit under the stage became a symbolic Hell. We couldn't hang any signs contradicting the existing modern fire safety signage. So, when directing players to the Orchestra Pit/Hell, we simply told players to follow the signs to "The Pit", appropriating existing signage.

Asymmetrical

In videogame choice design, narrative designers tend to treat each branch of a choice as a legitimate progression of the story, so each branch tends to trigger roughly equal amounts of content.

The real world, by contrast, is pretty uneven. If you're choosing one of two pubs to walk to, even if the pubs are of equal quality, the distance between the two is unlikely to be exactly equal. **Journey time** will be just one of many factors you weigh up, alongside beer quality and weather. These are the kind of factors your player considers when choosing **paths** in the real world. This means we need to embrace asymmetry in **fork** selection.

The natural **asymmetry** of physical storyscapes means that spationarrative **fork** choices don't have to be equilateral; a **fork** doesn't have to be a choice between apples and apples, any more than it has to be a choice between identical corridors. It's much more important that the sensory experience of making the choice is **expressive**.

Expressive

The goal of creating a **fork** is to get players expressing their agency and augmented IDENTITY in the spationarrative. So choosing between **paths** at a **fork** should express the narrative choice they're making in terms of mood and texture.

There is always a poetry to space: going downstairs feels very different to going up; moving through a large, airy space will contrast with a confined corridor; old or ill-maintained places have a very different feel to new ones. Some places have a feel of intimacy, furtiveness or transgression; in Playlines' AR theatre shows we often placed intimate or confrontational story branches in venue toilets, or encouraged players to go to the smoking area for disruptive or antisocial choices.

This doesn't necessarily mean that the initial appearance of a **path** has to match the desired emotion; there's nothing wrong with surprising a player with where a path goes.

Think about some **forks** in the geography near you. What kinds of spationarrative choices could they represent? One **path** might be the safe, long way round, while another is a hazardous shortcut. One might be a well-trodden route, another a plunge through the undergrowth to follow something glimpsed or overheard. One **path** might be a frontal assault while another a sneaky pincer move.

CHALLENGE #22: IDENTIFYING LOCATION-SPECIFIC FORKS

Take your current location as a starting point. **Identify** a physical **fork** in the geography nearby – a choice of corridors, a forking path, a stairway.

Assess the **fork**. Does it fulfil the qualities of being *distinct*, *asymmetrical*, *navigable* and *expressive*?

Now **conceptualise** story with a choice that takes place at this fork: a spationarrative moment where this **fork** would present a compelling and *expressive* choice to the player. Think about what the player can see, hear, smell and touch at the **fork**. What will it feel like to make the choice? Where will each **path** end up? Will the feel of the **path** and its destination be what the player expected?

Write dialogue/narration for the moment of choice, and dialogue/narration for each **path**.

Record it as audio and **test** by playing the audio to a friend at the **fork** and then playing the relevant **path** audio. Ask them what spationarrative factors motivated their choice, and **refine** your design.

TASKS

- **Identify** a suitable nearby **fork**. Apply the criteria of *distinct, navigable, asymmetrical* and *expressive*.
- **Conceptualise** a spationarrative choice for the **fork**.
- **Write** choice dialogue/narration for the choice moment and each **path**.
- **Record** audio.
- **Test** and **refine.**

BONUS CHALLENGE

Now **identify** a **location-agnostic fork**. Can you apply the same narrative concept and choice moment?

Use a map of your local area (ideally a paper map, not GPS). Rework your spationarrative choice moment as a choice between two nearby destinations. For example "Go to the nearest gas station or go to the nearest church" or "go to the canteen or the library".

Using your current location as the start point, make the choice. Then select a different start point, and choose again. What are the different spationarrative qualities of each of the resulting **forks**? How could you amend your narrative concept to fit these conditions? If you need to conceptualise a new narrative, why is it different?

SPATIAL AGENCY: HUBS

The above criteria for **forks** assume that you're creating binary branches where player choices progress the story along one or more distinct **paths** leading to different destinations.

An alternative structure is to create a **hub,** from which the player can select multiple **paths,** and to which they'll return. As we saw in 3.1 **hubs** create the opportunity to express narrative not just by progression through places but by showing changes to a place over time. The texture and mood of the **hub** location will have a spationarrative impact, and the same criteria of *distinctiveness, navigability, asymmetry* and *expressiveness* all apply to the **paths** radiating off a **hub**.

With **hubs** the *navigability* and *expressiveness* of the RETURN routes also becomes a factor. Do you ask players to exactly retrace their steps back to the **hub** or can they find a different route? Or can you connect or loop **paths** so players find their way back to the **hub** without retracing their steps?

CHALLENGE #23: STORYSCAPE DESIGN PART 4: BRANCHING PATHS

Goal: Augment a place with a branching **location-specific** spationarrative.

SUMMARY

Select a public **place** with multiple **node** locations within it. Obtain a **map**. Identify a natural **fork** or **hub** with **paths** that are *distinct, navigable, asymmetrical* and *expressive*.

Visit the place and **conceptualise** a spationarrative where the player will make a defining choice at the **fork** or **hub**.

Consider how much you want to define the **path** the player will take, what **locations** they may visit, and how the **fork** or **hub** may appear and feel under different conditions. The spationarrative should have at least two possible endings in which players end up at different **nodes**.

Outline your narrative as a series of **beats** and **diagram** it as a branching narrative, like this:

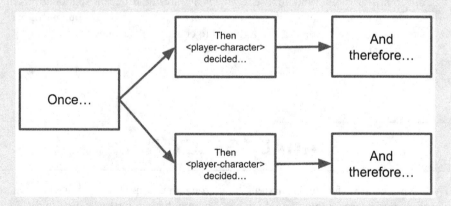

FIGURE 3.2   Diagram of basic branching story beats

Plot the story onto the **place** by superimposing the story diagram onto the map. Determine the location of each **beat/node** and the **fork** or **hub**.

Write the content for each **beat/node**, **navigation content** to be played on **paths,** and any content to be played at **destinations**. **Write** the decision content for the **fork/hub**, motivating the player to choose their **path** and responding to the spationarrative qualities of the **fork/hub**.

Revisit the place and **test** for **dwell times** and **journey times**, then **refine** your spationarrative.

Record the content as audio and then **test** onsite, assessing the effectiveness of the **fork/hub**. **Refine**.

TASKS

- **Select** a public **place** with a **fork/hub**.
- **Visit.**
- **Conceptualise** a spationarrative with at least two end **nodes**.
- **Outline** and **diagram** the narrative.
- **Plot** the story to the **place**.
- **Write** the content.
- **Revisit, test** and **refine**.
- **Record audio**.
- **Test** and **refine**.

BONUS CHALLENGE (A)

Refresh yourself on "greeting the rebel" (1.1). Identify three rebellions players might perform at the starting location (e.g. going indoors, going downstairs, remaining still). Treat these as valid choices and write dialogue/narration to acknowledge and **diegetically** incorporate this player agency. Assuming the player still reaches one of the ending **nodes**, how is their earlier rebellion reflected in the narrative?

BONUS CHALLENGE (B)

Make your experience design **location-portable**. Select a new place. Overlay your existing branching narrative diagram onto a new place and adapt the spationarrative to a new location. How easy is it to find a new place which fits the overall structure? Does the narrative need to change to fit the new place? Can you efficiently reuse or repurpose the same assets?

BONUS CHALLENGE (C)

Use a geolocation platform such as caught.nu to implement your design as a locative digital layer. Use caught.nu's **conditional** triggering to implement **conditionality**. Test your **fork/hub** with real players.

Remember, BEING THERE only becomes meaningful when it has an observable impact on the people and places around us. The techniques of **spatial agency** are important to build players' sense of BEING THERE in an augmented place. But it's vital we show players that their BEING THERE has an impact on that place.

We also need to show that when a player manifests their agency by physically BEING in a place, they also lose control over how they may BE SEEN by others in that place. This is what we'll examine next, when we look at the very last of our pillars of emotional immersion: OCCUPYING SPACE.

BEING THERE: SUMMARY

How do we give players a sense of presence in a hybrid physical-digital storyscape?

- *Use narrative to create **co-presence** with digital elements: acknowledge, incorporate or dramatise local features and the player's presence.*
- *Understand that players' experience of place is always first-person and **egocentric**.*
- *Combine **egocentric** and **allocentric** approaches to navigation so players' experience is individual but context-aware.*

What makes a good moment of spationarrative agency?

- *Design **forks** and **hubs** as physical and metaphorical manifestations of augmented IDENTITY and **spatial agency**.*
- *Construct **location-agnostic forks** for local relevance to the player.*
- *Select **location-specific forks** to be distinctive, navigable, asymmetrical and expressive.*

NOTES

1. Løvlie, 2009.
2. Ruset, E. *textopia*, 2009, in Løvlie 2009.
3. Løvlie, 2009.
4. *Ibid.*
5. Stuart Dunn, personal correspondence, June 2022.
6. Cristina Fernandez-Baizan, Paula Nuñez, Jorge Arias, Marta Mendez. "Egocentric and Allocentric Spatial Memory in Typically Developed Children", *Brain Behaviour* 10:5, 2020.
7. Jason Kalin, Jordan Frith, "Wearing the City: Memory P(a)laces", *Rhetoric Society Quarterly* 46:3, 2016, p.4.
8. *Ibid.*
9. Andrea Castellano, "The Slow, Necessary Removal of Game Mini-Maps", *DualAnalog*, 15 May 2018 https://www.dualanalog.com/the-slow-necessary-removal-of-game-mini-maps/.

10. Jonny Huck, Paul Coulton, Adrian Gradinar and Duncan Whyatt, "Abstract Feature Representation as a Cartographic Device for Mixed-Reality Location-Based Games", *Conference: 23rd GIS Research UK Conference,* 2015.

11. "The augmented reality heads-up display", Volkswagen, https://www.volkswagen.co.uk/en/electric-and-hybrid/software-and-technology/driving-technology/augmented-reality-head-up-display.html.

12. Stuart Dunn, personal correspondence, 2022.

13. Disney Imagineer Makes History, Disney, 18 Jan 2024 https://www.youtube.com/watch?v=68YMEmaF0rs&t=230s&ab_channel=DisneyParks.

14. Hardman, 1983, p. 45.

OCCUPYING SPACE

3.3

Why is it important to give players a sense of OCCUPYING SPACE in the story-scape?

What spationarrative techniques make players feel that their presence is consequential and has an impact on an augmented place?

FINDING YOURSELF

In 3.2 we looked at ways to make players' narrative choices correspond unambiguously to physical **layout** elements like **hubs** and **forks**. By combining **allocentric** and **egocentric** navigation and carefully designing **forks** and other choice points, we can allow players to express their augmented IDENTITY and agency through BEING THERE in a space. But reality doesn't always present us with unambiguous, binary forks-in-the-road. And the destinations we end up in are rarely exactly what we expected when we began a journey.

In the real world simply BEING THERE isn't quite enough. Even if the player is present in an augmented place and can choose where to go, they might still only have the kind of mute, voyeuristic presence which activates the **Swayze Effect**. In the same way that augmented objects need to cast augmented shadows to appear real, augmented IDENTITIES need weight and consequentiality. They need to OCCUPY SPACE.

Augmented players have one foot in the digital realm, in which their choices, however emotionally subjective, will ultimately be expressed as a set of binary yes/no, true/false **variables**. But they also have one foot in a physical place, where things are much more analogue. In the real world, however we express our agency, we don't necessarily have control over the outcomes, nor how our choices are SEEN by others. We also never have the full picture: unlike digital realities, physical reality is **zero-sum**, so we can't be in two places at once or SEE all sides of an event. It's these factors which give meaning and consequence to our choices in physical reality.

In order to anchor players securely in authentic-feeling augmented places, we need to replicate these **zero-sum** qualities of the physical world in our hybrid digital-physical spationarratives, giving players the feeling of meaningfully taking up space.

In Section 2 when we were AUGMENTING PLAYERS the pillar BEING SEEN evolved into BEING SELF-CONSCIOUS, because an augmented IDENTITY is only fully-formed when we can see the impact it has on other people.

Now, for the final pillar of AUGMENTING PLACES, BEING SEEN will evolve into OCCUPYING SPACE. We'll examine techniques to show players that the way they

DOI: 10.1201/9781003379294-20

OCCUPY SPACE embodies and expresses their augmented IDENTITY, and has an impact on the augmented place around them. That means highlighting not just players' **spatial agency** but their **spatial subjectivity**: how their position in space defines their perspective and cuts off their access to other possible perspectives and **vantage points**. It might also mean showing that players lose control of how they're perceived by NPCs and other players and non-players, perhaps even unwittingly becoming a performer in others' stories.

An AR narrative is embodied in its players and their relationship to the world. This means that more than any other medium, AR/spatial storytelling takes place not on a screen, in a virtual world or on a game board but instead OCCUPIES SPACE in the environment.

The word "OCCUPY" definitely comes with some weighty baggage. It's often associated with political protest. But places are ALWAYS political: according to Jennifer Eileen Cross, a *place* is a "space that has been imbued with meaning through personal, group, and cultural processes".[1] Many places have multiple contested meanings, like disputed territories or places of historical or religious significance to different groups. OCCUPYING SPACE always means negotiating our way through a place's different meanings, as well as adding our own narrative to the "stories-so-far" already at play there.

We all OCCUPY SPACE – that's how we know we're real. We all have the right to take up space. But our societies often make more space for some people than others. Some people have to assert their right to take up any space at all. This spatial marginalisation is part of many people's authentic experience, which is the fundamental substrate on which all augmented storytelling is built. So we need to create space for players' complex, contested experiences of OCCUPYING SPACE in our hybrid spationarratives. Otherwise, we risk overwriting or excluding many of the "pieces of self" which augmented players bring with them into spationarratives.

Digital layers can be **non-zero-sum**. As AR/spatial technology proliferates and places begin to digitise, different people might perceive the same place as a playable game board, an art gallery or a site of political protest. All those different instances of a place could coexist simultaneously, layered onto space. Some digital instances of a place might even be encrypted or invisible to those without the right hardware or access – but they might still manifest by prompting different people to act and OCCUPY SPACE differently.

This is the fundamental dichotomy at the heart of augmented/spatial storytelling. We're now able to create **non-zero-sum** layers of information, story and adventure, and overlay them on the world to make it more usable and magical. These layers don't need to compete with one another: as John Hanke says, many of us might soon be able to "theme the world" as we choose, without one user's "theming" interrupting or even being visible to another. But humans have to occupy space; so the emotional and political consequences of different "world-themes" will take place in **zero-sum** reality, the physical environment we all share. A liveable environment is a **zero-sum** commodity, and in the face of conflict and climate catastrophe our ability to digitise and dramatise our environment brings with it certain responsibilities.

This chapter represents the final pillar of emotional storytelling in AR/spatial. But it's not the final piece of the puzzle; that's down to you. In the final CHALLENGE, Storyscape Design Part 5, you'll bring together all the techniques we've examined so far to create a coherent location-based spationarrative. As you apply this chapter's techniques to your own storytelling, consider questions like *How can we create spationarratives which ask players to contest the meanings of places, or examine the meanings they themselves assign? Can AR/spatial storytelling give players the experience of asserting*

*their right to OCCUPY SPACE? Can we use digital spationarratives to stimulate play-
ers to take meaningful action in the real world?*

Questions like these reflect the power, and potential harm, inherent in our new tools
for reimagining and recontextualising the world. When we're OCCUPYING SPACE,
augmented or otherwise, the stakes are high. For starters, space is always politicised and
territorialised because the **zero-sum** nature of space means people occupy drastically
different perspectives or **vantage points**.

SPATIAL SUBJECTIVITY: VANTAGE POINTS

In real life it's impossible to adopt a completely neutral **vantage point**. And in aug-
mented/spatial media the storyteller can't define one. Due to the **blended** nature of
augmented IDENTITY, even if multiple augmented players play the same character
their IDENTITIES and perspectives will all be different. But **vantage points** have a big
impact on how players perceive story elements. As Ritchie says, in locative narratives
"a change in physical location or in point of view can physically reveal information or
reinforce a feeling that influences the reception of the story".[2]

Vantage point can also impact how players feel SEEN by the story. A player
OCCUPYING a **vantage point** might be physically "taking a stance" in relation to the
other characters and narrative elements, which is in turn subject to others' gaze.

Eavesdropping is one type of **vantage point** which emotively invokes BEING SEEN.
We've already mentioned eavesdropping as a means of drawing a **social boundary**
while also showing that the story world extends beyond the **boundary**. Eavesdropping
is also a strongly embodied experience. Players might need to move or maintain a **vantage point** to avoid being spotted and losing access to overheard content. This means
the players' relationship to story elements is anchored in to their physical embodiment
and BEING SEEN.

Eavesdropping isn't confined to spy stories. Shakespeare is full of eavesdroppers,
though this can sometimes stretch suspension of disbelief since on stage the eaves-
dropper needs to be visible to the audience (and they'll often speak aloud at theatrical
volume). This stage-whispering was one of the conventions of Elizabethan theatre, like
the soliloquy and all the cross-dressing. But Act 2 Scene 3 of *Much Ado About Nothing*
(1599) plays with this convention. The overheard characters are well aware they're being
eavesdropped on; in fact, they set up the situation to plant an idea in the eavesdropping
Benedick's ear. Benedick is forced to hide in ever more ridiculous places in order to
keep listening, and the audience is privy to the spectacle of him BEING (UN)SEEN.[3]
In an immersive STAGING of an eavesdropping scene, this might turn into fun spatial
gameplay: players would feel strongly embodied, alert to how they physically OCCUPY
SPACE because of the risk of in-fiction consequences if they're spotted.

Players might perceive different interpretations of the same events from different
vantage points. This shows players that their OCCUPATION of space is all-important.
They might experience this subjectivity of perspective during the story, or only later
realise how subjective their perspective was when they compare interpretations with
other players. In storytelling this is called the *Rashōmon* Effect, named after Kurosawa's

1950 movie, in which the same events are interpreted in wildly different ways by different characters based on their **vantage points** and preconceptions.

Let's take another classic Shakespearean scene where **vantage point** is all-important: Act 4 Scene 1 in *A Midsummer Night's Dream* (1595). The audience witnesses the fairy queen Titania with her fairy attendants and her lover Bottom (whose head has been magically transformed into a donkey). There are many different dynamics in this scene: it's bringing together all the plotlines which have taken place in different parts of a forest. Comedy comes from the beauteous Titania being enchanted to love an ass – but also from the fact that Bottom is a pretty decent guy, at least compared to Titania's husband Oberon, who is spying on them nearby and who set the whole thing up with his fairy servant Puck. Also in the scene, but UNSEEN, are four young runaway lovers in a magical sleep – they've had their own plotline of confusion, heartbreak and love potions, and soon the grown-ups will arrive to wake them up and demand an explanation.

Many separate but entwined plotlines, with characters spying on, overhearing or just-missing each other as they move through an enchanted forest. In Shakespeare's day these characters would all share the same stage. But in an augmented/spatial STAGING these events could all be positioned in different locations in a real forest, allowing players to potentially become as lost and as subject to serendipity as the characters. Like in the "scarcity model" of Punchdrunk Theatre, the player's choice of where to go and which storylines to see would manifest **zero-sum** choice of **vantage point**. Different players would emerge with very different interpretations of events glimpsed through the trees.

But you don't need a whole forest to create this effect: scene 4:1 could be staged in-the-round with Titania and Bottom as its centrepiece and all the other eavesdropping, spying or sleeping characters arranged at different **vantage points** around it. Like any in-the-round theatre performance, the audience would gain a different perspective on the action depending on their position – only in this case, choosing different **vantage points** could also place the player among different groups of characters also eavesdropping or caught up in their own business. Giving players agency to choose which characters' **vantage points** to share would create space for players' subjective interpretations, expanding on the play's ambiguities. If the player positioned themselves near Oberon and Puck they might hear them bickering and mocking Titania as they spy on her. Players positioned among Titania's fairies might find out whether they also mock her or are supportive of their queen's new lover, which is ambiguous in the play as written. If the player finds themselves among the sleeping lovers, they might even find out what actually happened during the time the four spent sleeping together half-naked in an enchanted forest.

Shakespeare purists might object, of course; the point is that by forcing the player to choose to OCCUPY a specific space we show them that perspective on the story is just one among many entwined "stories-so-far" – just like in real life.

CHALLENGE #24: THAT'S NOT HOW I REMEMBER IT: SPATIAL SUBJECTIVITY

Goal: Explore the impact of **vantage point** on spationarrative.

This is a development of **CHALLENGE #15: Unreliable protagonists** back in 2:3. That challenge focused on subjective perspective as a component of augmented IDENTITY: now use the same concept (or develop a new one) to explore the same ideas in a spatial context.

Identify a **place** and **conceptualise** a spationarrative. Your goal is to create a short scenario which could be perceived very differently by players witnessing it from different **vantage points.**

Identify at least TWO different **vantage points** in the **place** from which players could witness the scenario.

Outline the scenario and any characters, and ensure that players at different **vantage points** will perceive it differently.

Obtain a **map** and **plot** the spationarrative onto the **place.**

Write summaries of the scenario for EACH of the **vantage points**, articulating each version or perception of the scenario.

Test, ideally with two or more friends independently experiencing each **vantage point.**

TASKS

- **Identify** a **place.**
- **Conceptualise** a scenario with multiple subjective interpretations.
- **Identify** at least TWO **vantage points**.
- **Outline** the scenario.
- **Plot** the scenario onto the place.
- **Write** perspective summaries for each **vantage point**.
- **Test.**

BONUS CHALLENGE

After the central incident is seen from different **vantage points**, guide all players to a single location and encourage them in-story to compare perspectives on what they saw. How does the encounter with different perspectives affect each player's sense of IDENTITY and agency?

SPATIAL SUBJECTIVITY: PLAYER-AS-PERFORMER

The way a player OCCUPIES SPACE in a spationarrative is an external manifestation of the player's augmented IDENTITY. As the great Looney Tunes animator Chuck Jones said, "we are not what we look like. We are not even what we sound like. We are how we *move*".[4] But most of us move in ways that are unconscious as much as deliberate. We don't have complete control over what we *are*, and certainly can't control how we're SEEN. In the same way that a place can have multiple meanings inscribed upon it by different people, the way a player OCCUPIES SPACE in a place may also be interpreted differently by different people. To create an authentic sense of BEING THERE we sometimes have to show players that their external manifestation of IDENTITY and agency might be misinterpreted or altered from others' **vantage points**.

In the *textopia* project, one geolocated text by R. Lothe was situated in an underpass and created a strong sense of play:

> *Oaaooo! Hoi, hoi! Such fun it is to shout here!*
> *What acoustics! Even the footsteps bang from wall*
> *to wall.*[5]

Perhaps the player might join in the shouting, or maybe they just enjoy the playfulness vicariously. After all, this sort of behaviour might invoke embarrassing feelings of BEING SEEN in public, just like in the *autoteatro* experience of Silvia Mercuriali's *wondermart* where player-performers are asked to draw a heart in the condensation of a supermarket freezer. Similarly, ZU-UK's **location-portable** immersive audio experience *Radio Ghost* (2023) plays with dynamics of BEING (UN)SEEN in a public shopping mall setting. Players are asked to "infiltrate" certain shops and identify consumer products while listening to critiques of commercialism; players are eventually "spotted" as infiltrators and must escape.

Radio Ghost players begin the experience in a group of three at the threshold of a shopping mall. The three players are arranged facing each other, each listen to individual audio layers via headphones which instruct them to enact certain behaviour. At first, players are prompted to enact the same behaviour simultaneously, reinforcing the three players' physical co-presence in the hybrid narrative. It seems like they're all listening to the same audio layer. But then the audio layers, and instructions, begin to diverge. Though the players are co-present in the location, they're fed asymmetrical content in the digital layer. The three players are given simple, emotive augmented IDENTITIES: "eldest", "baby" and "middle child". The "baby" player's audio layer might instruct them to perform a certain behaviour – like "look confident". But the other players will see the "baby's" behaviour from the outside – and in their audio layer, they're hearing audio which reinterprets the "baby's" enacted confidence as spoiled smugness. This sibling-like dynamic highlights that players are SEEING and BEING SEEN. Players thus become both performers to one another, with their perspectives defined by their physical and IDENTITY-driven **vantage point**.

As the theatre-maker and researcher Nathan Sibthorpe says, in experiences like this participants "must navigate the porous boundaries between the real world and their self-generated arts experience... participants become audience to themselves as actors".[6] The theatre scholars Chapple & Kattenbelt (2006[7]) describe this as *intermediality*, where the audience becomes one of the media which makes up the performance – as does the place.

In Playlines' AR audio theatre, multiple players were co-present in the location, so each player might also be a performer in other players' experiences. In the prototype *Virtual Ambrose*, set in Kingston, Ontario's Grand Theatre, players who acted out a "ritual" onstage became unwitting performers to other players. Similarly, in *CONSEQUENCES* all players were protagonists in their own experience and background characters in others' experiences. Even if two players in a given room might have made the same choices leading to the same **game state**, each one was on a unique protagonist journey as far as they were aware. Inspired by multichannel silent discos, in *CONSEQUENCES* every storyline climaxed with a final dance in the same room, with most players congregating at roughly the same time. So the finale had the communal feel of the end of a club night, but each player experienced a unique-seeming protagonist journey defined by the private **vantage point** of the audio layer.

CHALLENGE #25: STORYSCAPE DESIGN PART 5: BRINGING IT ALL TOGETHER

Goal: Augment a place with a branching spationarrative, implementing all the techniques of augmenting place. Ensure you exploit the presence of other players and non-players.

Design a spationarrative to be played by multiple players simultaneously. All players will end up in the same location, where **conditional** content will express the consequences of their earlier choices, and the presence of **other players** and **non-players** will be **diegeticized** into each player's individual subjective narrative.

Identify a public **place** with multiple **nodes** and at least one suitable **fork**, as well as an **end zone** – an open public area where players will gather.

Visit the **place** and **conceptualise** a spationarrative journey through this location for multiple players, where players will make one or more choices at **forks**, and all players will end up in the **end zone**.

Your spationarrative should incorporate the presence of **other players** and **non-players**. You could heighten the player's sense of BEING SEEN by giving them a secret or asking them to **roleplay**, or appropriate other players as characters in the story, e.g. as fellow-contestants in a deadly gameshow. You could also incorporate **player-as-performer** techniques by instructing some players to perform actions, then **diegeticizing** those performances into others' storylines.

Consider ways to differentiate different players' experiences: players could begin at different phased times, or from different starting locations. Consider how you can choreograph events so that players converge: you could start all players at the same time, or use external triggers (e.g. a clock striking) to choreograph players' actions like a flashmob.

Outline your narrative as a series of **beats** and **diagram it** as a branching sequence which **bottlenecks** back together in the **end zone** (Figure 3.3):

Plot the story onto the **place** by superimposing the story diagram onto the **map**. Define the **fork(s)** and **end zone**.

Add **conditionality** to each branching **path** AND the **end zone** location. All players will end up in this location, but there they should experience different content based on the consequences of their earlier **fork** decisions.

Write narration/dialogue for each **beat, path, fork** and the **conditional** content for the **end zone**.

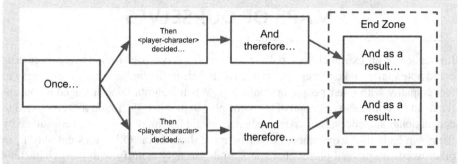

FIGURE 3.3   Diagram of branching story beats converging in End Zone

Revisit the **place** and **test** for **dwell times** and **journey times**, then **refine**.
Record the content as audio and then **test** onsite with multiple players simultaneously. **Assess** and **refine** the clarity of **navigation**, **durations** and the effectiveness of the **forks**. As much as possible, test under different physical conditions. How well does your narrative incorporate the presence of other people? Ask your players about their experiences, or find ways to stimulate them to compare notes. In what ways were their perspectives different?

TASKS

- **Select** a public **place** and obtain a **map**.
- **Visit.**
- **Conceptualise** a spationarrative with at least two endings.
- **Outline** and **diagram** the narrative.
- **Plot** the story to the **place**.
- Add **conditionality** to the **end zone** content based on player **path**.
- **Write** the content, exploiting the presence of **other players** and **non-players,** especially in the **end zone.**
- Revisit, **test** and refine.
- **Record audio.**
- **Test** onsite with multiple simultaneous players and non-players.

BONUS CHALLENGE

Consider ways to enhance the experience with physical additions to the place. Would set-dressing, signage or real performers improve the experience? **Conceptualise** two versions of the experience: a) a "live" version run at specific show times, with physical set-dressing, live performers and a critical mass of audience; b) an "on-demand" version which remains *in situ* and can be played in the location anytime, minus the live elements. Can your spationarrative work in both versions? Can you add modular elements to maximise the impact of the "live" experience while keeping the "on-demand" version coherent?

MAPS OF OURSELVES

Immersion is an extremely compelling storytelling force. But immersive experiences could potentially make players feel *too close* to their individual experience of a story to feel empathy with other people or characters. When Nandita Dinesh staged a conventional and an immersive version of the same play in parallel, she found that compared to conventional audiences, immersive audiences might be "more likely to be consumed by their own embodied experience (i.e. solely in the shoes of the Other they embody[8])". In other words, immersed player-characters might strongly identify with their character's perspective, but this might limit the empathy with other characters; empathy which they'd feel if they witnessed the drama from the outside.

We can balance this "Main Character Syndrome" using BEING SEEN and OCCUPYING SPACE techniques like the ones above. These techniques allow players and player-characters to SEE themselves from the outside as well as from within, and to encounter the presence of others in ways which build empathy.

One of the very first AR/spatial artworks I saw "in the wild" was *Un/Seen Evergreen* (2014), a digital sculpture of a tree placed in Valletta, Malta which was visible only through a smartphone. At the beginning of the project, the tree was a small sapling. But every time a new player downloaded the app and viewed the tree, it grew.[9] When I saw the tree it was almost two storeys high, a testament to the other players who had gone before me and who, in a strange way, were still co-present with me, manifested through the tree's growth.

Generally, the most powerful way to show players that they've OCCUPIED SPACE in a real consequential storyscape is to show them they've left a mark. A story is a map of change, so showing players that they have changed a place is often the best way to end an augmented/spatial narrative. This might mean seeing the liberation of a kingdom, or leaving behind a flourishing magical flowerbed. It could mean allowing players to digitally "graffiti" or tag a trace of their presence onto space, or supplant another player at the top of a local leaderboard. It might mean showing players the uniqueness of their own **vantage point** and perspective, or encouraging players to compare notes with others to discover the **spatial subjectivity** at play in the storyscape.

Situating a narrative firmly in an environment has always been a way for storytellers to stimulate empathy, through audiences' encounter with the traces left by other people. As the econarratology researcher Erin James says, "[n]arratives, via their power to immerse readers in environments and environmental experiences different from their own, can reveal perceptual points of difference, clarify the interests of those who imagine and inhabit an environment in a specific way, and expose readers to different or opposing points of view".[10]

As we explore the world, we're always self-narrating and building "mental maps". Ultimately, those stories and maps reflect ourselves as much as they depict the world. The writer Jorge Luis Borges once told a parable:

> A man sets out on a quest to discover the world. Through the years he populates a space with images of provinces, kingdoms, mountains, bays, ships, fish, rooms, instruments,

heavenly bodies, horses and people. A little before his death, he discovers that this patient labyrinth of lines traces the image of his face.[11]

But that's just one map; one story. If you're an AR/spatial storyteller (and if you've made it this far through the book, then yes you are) then ultimately the narratives which you augment into the world will reflect *you*. Your artistic priorities. Your conceptions of people and places. Your prejudices. But if you leave room for your players to OCCUPY SPACE, encounter other perspectives, and leave their mark, their experiences within those narratives can become much deeper and richer than just a single layer overlaid on the world. As augmented storytellers, we have an opportunity to show players that the world is bigger than themselves, no matter how rose-tinted their individual instance of reality.

This means that in hybrid digital-physical realities, the **zero-sum** limitations of physical reality are a feature, not a bug we need to correct. In the real world, choosing which road to take always means cutting off access to the roads-not-taken. This is what makes risk, sacrifice, love – the stuff of great stories – meaningful.

This is what allows stories to contribute positively to the real world, even though they're not real – by inspiring us to do the best we can with the limited time and space that is given to us.

We tend to think of stories, especially fantastical ones, as a means of escaping awhile from realit(ies) and even from ourselves. But the techniques of OCCUPYING digital narrative spaces should remind us that however many world-versions we're able to instance, nonetheless the real world is something we have to share, not something any one person or group gets to define – or escape.

OCCUPYING SPACE: SUMMARY

Why is it important to give players a sense of OCCUPYING space in the story-scape?

- *OCCUPYING SPACE in an AUGMENTED PLACE is what makes presence feel meaningful and authentic.*
- *Players can be co-present across multiple realities but cannot OCCUPY two places at once; this is what gives choices meaning.*

What spationarrative techniques make players feel that their presence is consequential and has an impact on the place and other players/people?

- *Create **spatial subjectivity** to show players their choices matter.*
- *Use **vantage points** to emphasise **spatial subjectivity**. Don't be afraid to make choices cost players content or opportunities.*
- *Exploit players' OCCUPYING SPACE to make them **performers** in others' experiences.*
- *Allow players to see how they have changed the spaces they OCCUPY as a result of the story.*

COMMON GROUND

Now we have our feet firmly on the ground, OCCUPYING SPACE across hybrid physical-digital places. But whether or not we realise it, the ground is shifting beneath us.

As AR/spatial storytellers, we're rapidly gaining access to unprecedented tools for fictionalising reality. Players could soon transcend the **zero-sum**, single-channel nature of the real world. But we all still need to OCCUPY physical space.

New technologies are allowing radical re-STAGINGS of reality. Even ordinary public spaces could become contested territories, visibly and invisibly, in different layers, for different players. People might soon be able to choose to live in game layers which wholly recontextualise the world, or in bubbles of **customised reality**. Increasingly players may feel an emotive stake in BEING THERE and OCCUPYING SPACE not in a shared consensus reality but in their individualised **divergent realities** – especially as these get entwined with real economies. Augmented/spatial technology might even empower ideologically **radicalised realities**. But the perspectives and behaviours and prejudices fostered in these divergent digital realities will impact the real world.

On the flipside, in shared consensus reality, powerful people can exercise an outsized level of reality-control, for example, by defining the recorded history or dominant narrative of a place. In **zero-sum** reality WHO tells a place's story (or adds their own story to a place) is a question of money and power. As Farman says, "a site's dominant narrative is often told through durable media such as stone inscriptions, while the narratives on the margins are relegated to ephemeral media such as graffiti or the spoken word".

Ultimately, the promise of augmented/spatial technology is the ability to leave each other notes in the margins of reality. But as storytellers, it's vital that we don't allow these technologies to give powerful people yet more control over reality, or allow those already marginalised to be pushed further into the margins of reality.

Spatial storytelling can show that the dominant narratives of a place are really just subjective perspectives, just one layer of meaning among many. Yet we still might not be able to "escape" dominant narratives: as the writer Alan Moore says,

> History, unendingly revised and reinterpreted, is seen upon examination as merely a different class of fiction; it becomes hazardous if viewed as having any innate truth beyond this. Still, it is a fiction we must inhabit.[12]

As we've seen, augmented/spatial storytelling doesn't really provide an "escape" from physical reality, or from history, or from ourselves.

But the techniques of OCCUPYING augmented SPACE show us that humans already all exist in slightly different versions of reality. AR/spatial media have a unique capacity to help people explore and compare notes on their diverse perspectives and **vantage points**. AR/spatial narratives can show players there's always more than one story at play in reality. Moore goes on:

> Lacking any territory that is not subjective, we can only live upon the map. All that remains in question is whose map we choose, whether we live within the world's own insistent texts or else replace them with a stronger language of our own.[13]

Augmented/spatial technology gives players and storytellers the opportunity to find our own "stronger languages" that can exist alongside the world's "insistent texts". These new hybrid digital-physical texts could potentially OCCUPY enough digitised space to challenge society's "dominant narratives" – or redraw the maps entirely. But there's also a danger that augmented texts, maps and languages could become so siloed and so divergent that they end up isolating people further and further from one another.

The ground is shifting beneath our feet: lacking any territory that is not subjective, us storytellers have a greater responsibility than ever. The dystopian possibilities of augmented/spatial technology are the flipside of all the storytelling techniques we've discussed so far. We'll examine these all-too-real risks in the next and final section: DIVERGENT REALITIES.

NOTES

1. Jennifer Eileen Cross, "Processes of Place Attachment: An Interactional Framework", *Symbolic Interaction* 38:4, 2015.
2. Ritchie, 2014.
3. For an example of this staging, see *Much Ado About Nothing* (film) (1993).
4. Chuck Jones, *Chuck Amuck: The Life and Times of an Animated Cartoonist*, Farrar, Strauss and Giroux, New York, 1999.
5. Lothe, R., *textopia* 2009, Løvlie, 2009.
6. Nathan Sibthorpe, "Leaving Space at the Table", 2 Dec 2019, https://thewritingplatform. com/2019/12/leaving-space-at-the-table/.
7. Freda Chapple and Chiel Kattenbelt (eds.), *Intermediality in Theatre and Performance*, Rodopi, Amsterdam and New York, 2006.
8. Dinesh, 2017, p. 65.
9. *Un/Seen Evergreen*, Shadeena / Martin Bonnicci 2016 http://unseen.shadeena.com/.
10. Erin James, *The Storyworld Accord: Econarratology and Postcolonial Narratives*, University of Nebraska Press, 2015, p. 208.
11. Jorge Luis Borges, 1983, attested by Nicholas Shakespeare, from the introduction to Bruce Chatwin, *The Songlines,* https://www.nicholasshakespeare.com/writing/bruce-chatwin-the-songlines/.
12. Alan Moore, *Voice of the Fire,* Top Shelf Productions, 1996, p. 306.
13. *Ibid.*

SECTION 4

Divergent Realities

JOURNEY THROUGH SPACE

Back in 1999 in the *headmap manifesto* Ben Russell foresaw a world where

> real space can be marked and demarcated invisibly […] what was once the sole pre-
> serve of builders, architects and engineers falls into the hands of everyone: the ability
> to shape and organise the real world.

Russell saw this as "a recolonisation of the real world" by users instead of institutions and governments: these users would be

> capable of augmenting, reorganising, and colonising real spaces without altering what
> is already there or notifying those being colonised.[1]

Today we might use words like "reclaiming" or "reappropriating" as well as "colonising" to describe how augmented/spatial technologies allow individuals to leave their
mark on real space. But as Figure 4.0 implies, there are very real risks that the digital
dimension of public space could end up being colonised and manipulated by powerful
interests – AND/OR could become chaotic, divisive and harmful.

The bulk of this book has focused on techniques to use augmented/spatial technology to reshape and recontextualise experience and space. This technology is still at a
very early stage, and we're still at the very beginning of a long journey of developing its
storytelling tools. But, in the words of augmented reality designer Galit Ariel,

> like any space voyage, or new technology, we must navigate it with a balanced sense of
> awe and caution. We want to be space explorers, not space invaders. After all, we are
> dealing with an already-inhabited planet.[2]

There is a real danger that without responsible storytelling, the very techniques
we've been developing may be used to supercharge divisive, false or manipulative narratives that already disrupt our lives, colonise and oppress people, and hasten the destruc-
tion of our environment. Stories can cause real, physical harm to us and our world. The
language of the fantasy epic and the noir mystery alike can be used to power narratives
of hatred and complacency.

Augmented/spatial technologies might allow players (those who can afford access)
to "shape and organise the real world" – or to shape personalised versions of the world

DOI: 10.1201/9781003379294-21

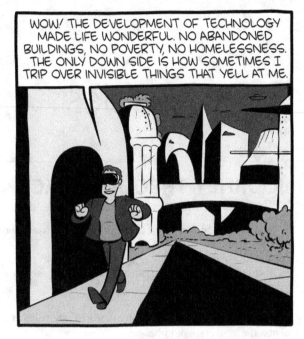

Using augmented reality to disguise social blight
turned out to be much cheaper than fixing it.

FIGURE 4.0 Zach Weinersmith, "Augmented", *Saturday Morning Breakfast Cereal*, 2 February 2024; reproduced by permission of Zach Weinersmith

to suit them. With emotive storytelling, players might feel a strong sense of BEING and belonging in their personal world-version, and this might shape their IDENTITY and their behaviour. Ultimately it's our sense of social consequence, BEING SEEN and being SELF-CONSCIOUS, which regulates our behaviour towards others and makes us act for the greater good. But without responsible storytelling, AR/spatial technology might make it easier to UN-SEE the situations and perspectives of others – or to reskin and **diegeticize** other people as NPCs, obstacles or enemies.

Augmented/spatial technologies might allow players (much more literally than ever before) to SEE the world as a space of gameplay – maybe as a network of contested territories, where gameplay conflicts bleed over and are STAGED in both the digital and physical worlds.

These technologies might enable unprecedented and even liberating new ways to BE and to project your chosen IDENTITY in the digital dimension – but they might also allow others to fully overwrite or even erase your IDENTITY in the privacy of their own perceptual model.

And none of this will change the **zero-sum** nature of the world, which we all ultimately need to share and conserve.

Augmented/spatial technology, and by extension augmented/spatial narratives, could empower some players to live in worlds of fantastically unambiguous, colour-coded morality.

Or worlds seemingly devoid of responsibility or consequence. Or worlds which reflect a monolithic worldview, excluding other perspectives. These narratives will be illusions. But they can still be dangerous. Responsible augmented storytelling, much more than other forms of narrative, requires **responsibility to reality**. Because, as Forbes says, "the meaning of reality is undergoing a paradigm shift". Soon the idea that there is a single consensus reality, some solid ground underlying all the subjectivity, might seem increasingly quaint.

In the light of AR/spatial technology's world-shaping potential in the near future, let's conclude the main section of this book by examining again our three hard-and-fast rules for augmenting reality: **context is everything**, **augment the player themselves**, and **you have a responsibility to reality**.

BETTER THAN LIFE: CUSTOMISED REALITIES AND AI

Augmented/spatial technology represents an unprecedented, existential shift in the way digital information pervades and influences our everyday lives. The technology is already proliferating and beginning to create divergent ways of re-IMAGINING and STAGING the world.

As I said at the start of this book, I've never been a big believer in "better than life" VR dystopias, where VR is so convincing that users forget what's real. The idea that audiences cannot tell the virtual from the real, and cannot tell fiction from fact, gets media coverage and even scaremongering every time a new technological medium emerges. Even the famous "panic" by Orson Welles' radio broadcast of H.G. Wells' *War of the Worlds* was likely sensationalised by contemporary media.[3] In a later interview H.G. Wells described the "panic" as "Halloween fun". Orson Welles agreed, describing it as

> the same kind of excitement that we extract from a practical joke in which somebody puts a sheet over his head and says "Boo!" I don't think anybody believes that that individual is a ghost, but we do scream and yell and rush down the hall.[4]

Throughout this book, we've seen that immersed players have to *play along*. What makes an experience or narrative immersive is not whether it's *convincing*; it just has to be *compelling*. But often, there's nothing more *compelling* than having our perceptions and prejudices affirmed. (The Red Dwarf sci-fi novel *Better Than Life* depicted a very plausible VR "paradise" which did trap users in the illusion – because the simulation gave users not what they *wanted*, but what they secretly thought they *deserved*.)

This is why I believe that even subtly **customised realities** in AR represent a far greater danger than VR simulations. Generally speaking, people "getting lost in a fantasy" doesn't represent a threat to our rights and our survival. The threat comes when people view the world through unbreakable ideological filters, or try to overwrite the plurality of the world with monolithic, totalitarian perspectives.

Humans are already prone to construct and dwell within ideological **echo chambers** which validate their perspectives and limit their empathy for those with other perspectives. In principle, when we venture out into the physical world, these selective realities run up against the real world and are juxtaposed with the plurality of different peoples' experiences. But as augmented/spatial technologies become more sophisticated and more entwined with ever-richer datasets, players might be able to choose to view the world not just through rose-tinted spectacles, but personalised x-tinted filters.

Context is everything, especially the socioeconomic context we live in. Augmented reality can re-imagine the world, but it can't remake it. As we'll see in Appendix A, justice cannot be augmented-in. That work has to happen in the real world. Spatial computing cannot correct the very-real inequities and dangers experienced by many people.

But **customised realities** could potentially allow users to overwrite or edit-out the injustice and suffering experienced by others. Perhaps not edit it out completely; just enough. We don't have to *believe* that other people are ghosts in order to *act* as though we can't see them.

With context-editing **customised realities**, augmented/spatial players might not simply SEE through x-tinted spectacles, but might dwell entirely within tinted-glass houses. And after long enough inside, anything breaking through from the outside and allowing in the colours of the real world might seem hostile.

In totalitarian systems, control over reality-curation might be monopolised by governments or state actors to enforce approved perceptual models.

In *laissez-faire* capitalist systems, players might end up ceding control over the curation and commoditisation of everyday experience to whichever platform provides the most convenient or most customisable realities. John Hanke has described a consumer right to "theme the world" however we choose – which might also imply the right of a corporation to sell us whichever world-theme they can monetise.

In either case, it's likely to be AI that enables reality-customisation at scale. AI represents a gigantic step-change in two areas key to augmenting reality: 3D modelling the world and creating contextual graphics and content. NeRFs (neural radiance fields) and stable diffusion already underpin many of the most sophisticated techniques for scanning and reskinning the world. Meanwhile, AI has led to a huge increase in companies' ability to create personalised services. This could help create living, evolving digital story worlds which can generate new assets fast enough for all players to receive a personalised experience. Or advertising which appeals to every user on a deeply personal level.

As Scott Belsky, Chief Strategy Officer at Adobe said in 2023, without AI, consumer personalisation is currently "segment-by-segment; even the best marketers in the world effectively segment all their customers and then they make various versions for those segments". But with AI, "why shouldn't I be able to make literally a custom asset for every single person in my database based on what I know about them, their profile or their gender and where they're based?"[5]

When Geoffrey Hinton, "the godfather of AI", quit Google in protest in 2023, "his immediate concern [was] that the internet will be flooded with false photos, videos and text, and the average person will "not be able to know what is true anymore."[6] With AR/spatial, that might start happening beyond the browser and out on the street.

"True" and "real" are very different things. Personalised augmented worlds might have a magical or cutesy aesthetic which distinguishes them from physical reality, but this doesn't stop them being compelling – or from changing our behaviour. Advertising doesn't have to be "real" to sell us things: it uses storytelling to feel authentic. We know that influencers and ideologues generally present idealised versions of reality, but we choose to engage with them all the same. We all tend to "create belief" in the fiction that we have a fair, rational grasp of how the world should work. As the philosopher Slavoj Žižek says, "ideology is the original augmented reality".[7]

Context is everything, but it's very personal and subjective. It influences our perceptions, our behaviour and ultimately our IDENTITY. Today our personal contexts can increasingly be read and inferred by machines. Those same machines might soon be able to generate messages, assets, products or even worlds which are designed to suit our contexts – or to adjust or hack our contexts.

Ultimately AIs will likely still be controlled and directed by people. But those people may well be in it for power or commercial gain. If people are being context-hacked in separate, impenetrable, non-interoperable, **divergent realities**, it may be difficult to tell for sure that it's even happening, or to know just how different your reality looks compared to someone else standing at the same bus stop. Again, philosophically, this is nothing new – but this will likely soon be happening at vast scale, as part of the commercial and cultural agendas of the world's largest corporations and institutions.

Spationarrative storytelling techniques allow players to feel like they're firmly anchored and genuinely BEING THERE in a digital-physical experience – but those storytelling techniques could be used to entwine players' sense of IDENTITY with a particular context, and to make them territorial and hostile to other IDENTITIES, contexts or ways of BEING. Without responsible storytelling, players might become ever-more contextually divergent even from people sharing the same bus stop.

BUT IS IT ARt?: AR GRAFFITI AND NON-ZERO-SUM CULTURES

The meanings of places have always overlapped and shifted. Remember, a space only becomes a *place* after it is "imbued with meaning through personal, group, and cultural processes".[8] But people often want to define a dominant context or narrative of a place, and push any other meanings to the margins – whether that's conquering or colonising a territory, or controlling the political meaning of a public monument. Meanings that are physically inscribed on a place, or are promoted by governments or establishments, or enforced by money or power – in **zero-sum** space those dominant meanings tend to last.

A public monument gives public prominence to its subject by OCCUPYING **zero-sum** SPACE. A label on a museum wall gives prominence to certain interpretations of an artefact, as decided by the curator. A graffiti tag on a wall OCCUPIES a surface which might belong to someone, or which might be exploited commercially. This is why graffiti is considered property damage, and also why it's so compelling: graffiti OCCUPIES SPACE in the reality of everyone passing by (at least until it's painted over by the authorities). Graffiti is inherently **zero-sum**: overwriting another artist's tag has been considered disrespectful since graffiti's first golden era in late 70s New York.[9] (As well as appropriating surfaces, those pioneering teenage graffiti writers always shop-lifted their paint for respect – this was called *inventing* the paint.[10])

In our world, the physical surfaces around us are overwhelmingly OCCUPIED by **zero-sum** commercialised meanings – advertisements, brands. Overwriting commercialised surfaces with graffiti creates "street art", art with an additional context of protest, anticapitalism or reclamation of public space. As Banksy said, "any advert in a public space that gives you no choice whether you see it or not is yours. It's yours to take, re-arrange and re-use... Asking for permission is like asking to keep a rock someone just threw at your head".[11]

As we've seen, to give our players a sense of truly OCCUPYING SPACE, we need to empower them to leave their own mark on augmented places. Numerous AR applications already exist for creating and viewing visual art tagged to public surfaces. As technology opens up read/write access to the digital dimension of reality, there's likely to be an explosion of comments, posts, memes and artworks tagged to popular landmarks, monuments and artefacts. A public square might be overlaid with multiple simultaneous instances of place: for different people the same space might be a graffiti gallery, a game terrain with a rich lore, or an unambiguous celebration of imperialist history.

This has even resulted in "guerrilla AR curations" of established gallery spaces: back in 2010 the artists Sander Veenhof and Mark Skwarek created the WeARinMoMA exhibition of early Augmented Reality art as a "guerrilla infiltration", placing a layer of AR artworks within New York's Museum of Modern Art without the museum's knowledge or permission. This digital layer was co-present with the physical gallery, but didn't OCCUPY SPACE, instead raising questions about who gets to OCCUPY and define a museum. As the artists said, "the criterion of whether something [is] placed within museum walls is no longer valid. Virtual artworks by "non artists" could mix with officially curated art within an official museum".[12]

In **zero-sum** physical reality, cultural institutions like museums and galleries tend to be the curators and arbiters of the meaning of physical artefacts. Museums and galleries' public role has traditionally been to digest culture into representative exhibits, and to digest the "stories-so-far" surrounding an artefact into a short label text. Traditionally, these label texts present a singular, theoretically non-controversial, nominally objective interpretation for the wider public – even if debate or nuance exists behind the scenes. After all, brick-and-mortar museums have a **zero-sum** amount of wallspace, and have to present culture in a digestible, single-channel form. But with **non-zero-sum** augmented/spatial interfaces, the limiting factor on curation is no longer space but interface.

With AR interfaces it's possible to imagine a "hyper-label" approach to curating culture. A physical artefact or monument could be the centre of a constellation of ongoing commentary, interpretation and appropriation, navigable in the digital layer via augmented interface. Or, a plurality of different artefacts could occupy the same space, like the "People's Platform" augmented reality app, which allowed users to visualise a range of replacement artworks for a toppled statue of a slaveholder, all augmented onto the same empty plinth.[13]

Augmented interfaces could turn physical monoliths into **non-zero-sum** "poly-liths". Expanding read/write access to reality might ultimately allow a greater variety of people to leave their mark on public space and assert their right to meaningfully OCCUPY SPACE – in the digital layer at least. As Farman notes, "technologies [which] layer stories, allowing many voices to be heard [...] can lead to an enabling of marginalised voices that have been silenced by those in power".[14] As Mark Sample says, this represents an opportunity for users to "turn locative media from gimmicky entertainment coupon books and glorified historical guidebooks into platforms for renegotiating space and telling stories about spaces".[15]

Except of course, there is another limiting factor on information design other than physical label-space: human attention. One of the dangers of unlimited **non-zero-sum** read/write access to the digital layer is cacophony. If we perceived an unfiltered feed of all the different augmented instances of a place we might be overwhelmed with an unmanageable stew of information and recontextualisations, like that shown in Keichii Matsuda's *HYPER-REALITY*.

Context is everything, but that also means *everything is context*. Trying to capture or understand all the possible contexts of a single place – or monument, or artefact – quickly becomes overwhelming.

The way we deal with cacophony is through filtering and curation, either by curating our own media or allowing a curator or algorithm to do it for us.

There are already companies engaged in licensing and selling the still-hypothetical advertising rights to the digital dimension of public spaces. They're gambling that large-scale reality-augmentation will soon be normalised, but also gambling that most brands, institutions and consumers will choose to participate in curated, institutional, public layers of augmented reality – main channels – which will be moderated and monetised and made accountable by commercial forces.

But in the **non-zero-sum** digital dimension there's nothing to stop some users superimposing alternative "guerrilla" augmentations onto a given surface, even if it has already been augmented by a commercial entity. Back in 2018 Farman was already articulating concern about locative stories geolocated at sites related to the Holocaust, arguing "alternative stories are not an advantage at some places".[16] If some people perceive a place through a layer of false or hateful messages, it may not even be possible to confront these pervasive alternate realities since they may only exist within invisible or encrypted "dark layers".

Augmenting reality starts by *augmenting the player*. Soon, augmented players might choose to view the world via a commercialised and curated context layer, or choose to view private, encrypted layers of unregulated content and guerilla context overlaid on real space. But either way these reality-curations may change how players behave out in physical, **zero-sum** reality. And in reality, the stakes are high.

AR BODIES, AR SELVES: RIGHTS IN AN AUGMENTED ERA

If an AR graffiti writer paints their tag across a McDonald's storefront, but it can only be seen by only those who opt-in to the AR graffiti layer, has that McDonald's private property been infringed?

Does the McDonald's have ownership rights over the digital dimension of their storefront, all the possible digital versions of that *place,* just because they own the physical *space*? Do they have the right to be notified of any digital message that's tagged in proximity to their building? What if the tag isn't geolocated at the McDonalds, but is viewable in relation to the McDonald's from certain **vantage points**?

This kind of **non-zero-sum** graffiti sounds kind of fun, when it's on a McDonald's. But what if someone digitally writes a slur across the front of your house, in a layer that you don't even know exists? What if they're doing so within an encrypted layer, perhaps marking your house out to a crypto-political group? Do you have the right to be notified? Should you have the right to access or edit that layer, when all the relevant data exists on someone else's server and inside someone else's headset?

Never mind buildings, what if someone could tag or even texture your body in real-time, as you pass them on the street, simply by viewing your body through AR glasses?

Augmented/spatial technology might soon open up digital read/write access to any physical surface. This raises complex questions about our right to OCCUPY space, and even our right to control how our bodies are SEEN. We might soon gain radical individual control over how we present our IDENTITY in the digital layer(s) – while others gain the power to SEE and re-IMAGINE our bodies however they choose.

It's already possible for stable diffusion-driven AI to graphically reskin human bodies in 3D, like how Virtual Production adds superhero suits onto motion-captured actors – but in realtime.

Meanwhile stable diffusion-driven "nudify" applications are already capable of inferring body shape and generating 2D deepfake porn of real people, including minors, sometimes based on just a single image[17].

What if someone viewing the world through AR glasses chose to scan and reskin you, retexturing your body with an AI-inferred 3D nude, mapped onto your physical body? What if they were able to do this in realtime, simply as they passed you on the street? This is no longer science fiction.

If this happens to you, have your rights been infringed? Does it make a difference if that person never shares or disseminates that imagery? Is there a difference, legally, morally, between doing this with technology and simply IMAGINING someone nude in the privacy of one's own head?

What rights do we have over the way our bodies, or our property, appear to others in the privacy of their headsets or digital layers or perceptual models? On the flipside, what right does an individual have to maintain a private perceptual model? What are the responsibilities and liabilities of the companies who provide the software, and the developers who create the augmentations? How much responsibility does an individual bear for actions they take while under the influence of an altered reality?

When you're augmenting reality, *the most important reality you're augmenting is the player themselves*. Any change to reality, even only in a digital perceptual layer, also changes *us*. We may well end up being augmented by this technology as much as it allows us to augment the world.

New uses and abuses of AR/spatial technology are likely to accelerate, particularly among young people. It's likely that very real harms will take place within encrypted augmented/spatial communities and "dark layers", which will be even more impenetrable and baffling to parents, lawmakers and governments than the internet communities of today. Yet they will be all around us.

One thing that's clear is that our capacity to augment people and places is going to rapidly outstrip legislation, policy and even public consciousness.

Even if laws were written asserting individuals' or companies' rights in the digital dimension, could these laws actually be enforced? The fundamental technology to detect physical surfaces and augment them with graphics can now be home-brewed by individuals in their bedrooms at little cost. Kids will always *invent* the paint they need to leave their mark on the world. Even if tech companies could be held to account for moderation or oversight of their reality-editing platforms, in practice the actual process of detecting and augmenting physical surfaces can't monopolised by a single company or platform.

Or can it? Because a Wild West of unregulated, "crypto-realities" and "dark layers" might not be the worst-case scenario.

Google actually hold a patent for the broad concept of "AR graffiti", US8350871B2, "Method and apparatus for creating virtual graffiti in a mobile virtual and augmented reality system",[18] originally filed by Motorola in 2009 and only due to expire in 2030. There's also US8968099B1, "Systems and methods of transporting virtual objects through a virtual world associated with a parallel reality game",[19] originally filed by Hanke *et al* at Google in 2012, subsequently transferred to Niantic and now returned to Google.

Microsoft holds the even more broadly-worded US10643394B, "Augmented reality", addressing devices which, "based on a plurality of local 3D models", generate

a global 3D model representing a portion of a real-world environment; determining a location of a 3D virtual object in the global 3D model; and generating augmentation data for rendering the 3D virtual object to be seen at a location of the real-world environment.[20]

Meanwhile, early in 2024 Apple sued the US patent office to keep its rights to the terms "Reality Composer" and "Reality Converter".[21] Apple's recent patents focus on environment tracking and notifications for nearby immersive content (perhaps compensating for their lack of access to Google and Meta's global-scale meshes), as well as **location-specific** device tracking, implying that Apple foresee implementations for on-site retail or sporting experiences.[22]

Baidu, Disney, Intel, Snap and Tencent all also hold, or have applied for, significant augmented/spatial technology patents. It's not yet clear how powerful these patents could be in allowing corporations to commercialise or even monopolise large-scale reality-augmentation. But it's clear the AR sector, and by extension the digital dimension of public space, is being carved up behind the scenes. Based on the last two decades of technological history, it seems likely that augmented/spatial platform economies will be worth billions, and be fully entangled in millions' of peoples' lives, long before corporations begin trying to enforce monopolies (and long before regulation can catch up with them). But sooner or later, patents like these could conceivably persuade governments to help enforce a corporation's commercial rights over millions of peoples' chosen realities.

Unlike the internet, a "spatial internet" won't necessarily be open. The internet was built upon an intentionally open and interoperable protocol, TCP/IP, which allows any terminal or node access to any other node. By contrast, developments for large-scale augmentation of reality are currently built on multi-billion-dollar global datasets and "visual maps", assembled at vast expense from a combination of satellites and drones and, increasingly, from data knowingly or unknowingly contributed by users. Unlike the baked-in interoperability of the internet, large-scale reality-augmentation and a "spatial internet" is likely to run on patented methods, proprietary hardware and licensed datasets. Platform holders who own the patents, the hardware AND the datasets will be the ones most invested in extending their existing multi-billion-dollar service/content/data business models out beyond the browser and onto physical streets.

In the 70's, those early graffiti writers stole or *invented* their paint for respect. But what if a company invented and patented digital paint, then got paid every time anyone viewed any digital painting? What if that company had the right to define what people could and couldn't paint, and who could and couldn't view a painting? What if they also owned all the digital canvas? It's possible that unlicensed "dark layers" or guerrilla curations of reality, run on home-brew software or ad-hoc hardware, will end up being vital dimensions for free speech. And, even more importantly, free *perception*.

HOW DO WE KNOW WHEN IT ENDS?

Cacophony or curation? Chaos or control? Do we resign ourselves to an unlimited proliferation of overlapping, impenetrable private sub-realities, pervasive and potentially radicalising ways of SEEING and BEING-in the world, which are invisible to outsiders?

Or do we cede *de facto* editorial control over much of our reality to monolithic companies who are ultimately in it for the money? Or to governments who might seek to control us?

And more importantly, what happens to the vast majority of people who can't afford access to these new, more usable, more information-rich realities? Will technology have-nots be left even further behind, and be stuck effectively living in a second-class world, even moreso than they do already?

Soon, a property-owner might lose control over the meanings and messages tagged to their space – regardless of whether or not the law says they have that control.

You, the owner-operator of a human body, may be able to project a digital IDENTITY of your choice, yet have no control over how others choose to digitally clothe your body, or replicate it or rub it out, or place it in a different context.

In retrospect, the virtualisation of reality began long ago. Many different cultural shifts, as well as technological developments, got us to this point. We can now conceive of humans living in instances of reality that are isolated and non-interoperable and invisible to one another. When we view the world from within these instances, how will we know where the augmentation ends and the real world begins? As Duncan Speakman asks, "If there are no end credits, how do we know it's over?"

This is where narrative comes in. Our ability to story-tell, to "run off-line cognitive simulations", was a crucial factor in human evolution. As Lisa Cron says in *Wired for Story*, "opposable thumbs let us hang on; story told us what to hang on to".[23] Part of our evolved capacity for narrative-making is that broadly speaking, people *can* tell fiction from reality. For starters, stories are generally more satisfying than reality. Stories end. Reality continues off in every direction.

Still, it's closeness-to-reality that gives stories their power. Not through being *convincing*, but by echoing how reality makes us feel, and helping us explore how we feel about reality. Storytelling is imaginative play, and as the makers of the RPG *Stonetop* say, "play is practice, and practice is how you change yourself, how you change your world".[24]

Storytelling helps us make sense of the real world's uncertainties and ambiguities. It's an imperfect but evocative language for comparing notes on our subjective experiences. This doesn't mean "escape" from the world: our job as storytellers is to provide fantasy and "escapism" only as a means of relating to the real world. As Borriaud said, "art does not transcend our day-to-day preoccupations; it brings us face to face with reality through the singularity of a relationship with the world, through a fiction".[25]

In the 2008 sci-fi story "To Hie From Far Cilenia", the augmented Atlantis of *Rivet Couture* is viewable only through AR glasses. (In perhaps the story's only implausible detail, the glasses are manufactured by "a Swiss augmented reality firm that had recently bought out Google".) And yet it's not really the technology that creates the hybrid place: it's the community, and their shared emotional immersion. Their willingness to not just suspend disbelief but to actively create belief:

> That city – world-spanning, built of light and ideals, was tricked into existing moment-by-moment by the millions who believed in it and simply acted as though it was there.

Sci-fi authors have been exploring the implications of augmented/spatial technologies for decades. We are now on the cusp of realising these reality-changing technologies, and we still have far more questions than answers about how they will impact our societies. In the words of the late, great Vernor Vinge, whose 2006 novel *Rainbows End* inspired countless AR developers (including myself), "What if we succeed? Do you think that will be the end of it?"

What will it be like when we can incarnate new digital versions of ourselves, and instance new versions of the world built of light? Will this help speed up how we *create belief* in a better world, and how we work to prototype that better world? Or will we just imaginatively STAGE versions of the world which already suit us – or pay others to do it for us? And what will we do if we perceive our personal world-version being threatened?

One thing is certain, all those world-versions will need storytellers to help make them. How will that new generation of storytellers use their new capabilities, their radical new levels of influence over their audience? Will they collaborate with players' IMAGINATIONs? Or with their worst impulses? Or both?

The answers to these questions will be down to you.

As Mario Vargas Llosa wrote, "to pass off fiction as reality, or to inject fiction into reality, is one of the most demanding and imperishable of human enterprises – and the dearest ambition of any storyteller".[26]

Our capacity to "inject fiction into reality", and vice versa, is about to vastly increase – but this leaves us storytellers with a grave *responsibility to reality*. The dream of an augmented world – and potentially the dystopian realit(ies) – are both nearly here. As a storyteller, you will have access to incredible new tools to iterate on reality. And it's never been more important that you do so with empathy and care. Technology is accelerating, the world is getting more weird, our species is faced with very tangible existential threats – and yet the notion of what is "real", and whether that even matters, is becoming ever more complex and contested.

Luckily, we are also constantly inventing new narratives and narrative formats to help make sense of things. Those narratives don't have to be "real"; they just have to show us how much we share with other humans, and show us how to share the world, including its harsh realities.

Even though we're all engaged in "active creation of belief" throughout our everyday lives, nonetheless our experiences are all grounded in **zero-sum** physical reality. As Phillip K. Dick said, "reality is that which, when you stop believing in it, doesn't go away". Reality isn't going away anytime soon – certainly not its unfairness and harshness. But nonetheless it's belief – and our capacity to suspend our cynicism and disbelief – which allows humans to change our reality in ways large and small. The same capacity which makes us "narratable selves", and lets us imagine "possible selves", also allows us to believe in the possibility of a better world.

I started this book by telling you to go out and "**PROVE ME WRONG**". But I hope I'm proven right about one thing. Technology by itself will not make the world better – but I believe that YOU can.

So get out there, imagine extraordinary new realities, and make them real – whatever that means to you.

NOTES

1. Ben Russell, *Headmap Manifesto*, 1999, p. 1, http://www.technoccult.net/wp-content/uploads/library/headmap-manifesto.pdf.
2. Ariel, 2018.
3. Jefferson Pooley, Michael Socolow, "The Myth of the War of the Worlds Panic", Slate 2013 https://slate.com/culture/2013/10/orson-welles-war-of-the-worlds-panic-myth-the-infamous-radio-broadcast-did-not-cause-a-nationwide-hysteria.html.
4. Interview with H.G. Welles and Orson Welles, KTSA, 30 Oct 1940 https://youtu.be/OYeUCqSjY2w?si=_g_WADiacL3UXVVg.
5. Scott Belsky, interview by Ben Thompson, Stratechery, 13 Apr 2023 https://stratechery.com/2023/an-interview-with-adobe-chief-strategy-officer-scott-belsky/.
6. "The Godfather of A.I". Leaves Google and Warns of Danger Ahead, *New York Times*, https://www.nytimes.com/2023/05/01/technology/ai-google-chatbot-engineer-quits-hinton.html.
7. Slavoj Žižek, "Ideology Is the Original Augmented Reality", 26 Oct 2017, https://nautil.us/ideology-is-the-original-augmented-reality-236862/.
8. Cross, 2015.

9. Joyce Wadler, "Graffiti: Learning to Appreciate 'Art' on Someone Else's Walls", Washington Post 16 Nov 1981, https://www.washingtonpost.com/archive/politics/1981/11/16/graffiti-learning-to-appreciate-art-on-someone-elses-walls/97c112cf-455c-4f83-a24e-e99a7e04719c/.
10. Norman Mailer, *The Faith of Graffiti*, 1974, Reprinted 2009, Lebowski, Amsterdam, p. 11.
11. Banksy, *Wall and Piece*, 2005, Century, London.
12. Sander Veenhof and Mark Skwarek, DIY Day MoMA: "WcARinMoMA", 9 Oct 2010, https://www.sndrv.nl/moma/.
13. "Edward Colston: Virtual Statues Appear on Slave Trader's Plinth", *BBC*, 8 Jun 2021 https://www.bbc.co.uk/news/uk-england-bristol-57387363.
14. Farman, 2014, p. 193.
15. Mark Sample in Farman, 2014.
16. Farman, 2014, p. 193.
17. Skylar Harris, "High Schooler Calls for AI Regulations After Manipulated Pornographic Images of Her and Others Shared Online", *CNN*, 4 Nov 2023 https://www.cnn.com/2023/11/04/us/new-jersey-high-school-deepfake-porn/index.html.
18. https://patents.google.com/patent/US20100194782A1/en.
19. https://patents.google.com/patent/US8968099B1/en.
20. https://patents.google.com/patent/US10643394B2/en.
21. William Gallagher, "Apple Sues US Patent Office Over Augmented Reality Trademarks", 27 Feb 2024, https://appleinsider.com/articles/24/02/27/apple-sues-us-patent-office-over-augmented-reality-trademarks/amp/.
22. David Schloss, "Apple Has a Wide Array of Research to Command the Future AR and VR Market", *Apple Insider*, 22 Mar 2024. https://appleinsider.com/articles/24/03/22/apple-has-a-wide-array-of-research-to-command-the-future-ar-and-vr-market.
23. Lisa Cron, *Wired for Story*, Clarkson Potter, UK, 2012.
24. Jeremy Strandberg, *Stonetop*, p. 13.
25. Bourriaud, 2002, p167–168.
26. Mario Vargas Llosa, quoted by Nicholas Shakespeare, https://www.nicholasshakespeare.com/writing/bruce-chatwin-the-songlines/.

Appendix A: Inclusion, Accessibility and Safety

INCLUSIVE APPROACHES

All artists have to work within the operational realities of their chosen medium. Augmented/spatial technology can allow us to re-imagine the world, but not to remake it. As an augmented/spatial storyteller it is part of your job to make your story compatible with your audiences' different realities as far as possible. The world presents different obstacles and restrictions to different people. If you choose to make art in physical reality, the hardest and most unpredictable medium of all, then it's part of your professional responsibility to make sure your experience works as much as possible for all potential players.

Augmented/spatial media has sometimes been used to highlight the lack of accessibility in public places, as in AR artist's Joseph Wilk's *Wheeltrails* project,[1] where wheelchair users left AR trails through urban spaces to explore the ways these spaces create disability. But AR/spatial media could also be used to hide or erase the experience of others. As the AR artist and activist Mark Skwarek observes "a recurring point of contention" among activists who use AR is the concern that "technology masks the evils of the world and that it detaches society from reality".[2]

This book, like all storytelling manuals, is about building empathy. That empathetic approach starts with you. Good storytelling in AR means augmenting the player's world, not trying to overwrite their world with yours. The different physical and social obstacles that a space presents to different people can't be simply augmented away, and justice cannot be augmented in. That work has to happen in the real world.

Figuring out how to ethically augment narratives into reality is likely to be the ongoing work of many years – and if you want to be a storyteller in this space, some of that work is on you. As with the rest of this book, the advice given below is not exhaustive or definitive. These are huge and consequential topics which can't be fully covered here; your work must be informed by your own empathy and willingness to learn and improve.

One key starting point is to seek out insight from fellow-practitioners and players with different perspectives and different ways of moving through the world. Do this early in any project and regularly throughout, and remember to treat those people as colleagues and customers, NOT fonts of free advice!

ACCESSIBILITY

Remember that an AR/spatial experience is only as accessible as the physical place in which it happens. This is particularly important in **location-specific** experiences. The disability advocacy charity SCOPE has a useful guide on assessing the accessibility of venues at https://www.scope.org.uk/advice-and-support/checking-event-venue-accessibility/.

A study by Clark, Singh and Barbareschi found a desire among disabled players "to let game developers know [they] are disabled and receiv[e] a more accessible experience".[3] For locative experiences in general, consider the **journey times** you implement and how they will be differently experienced by players with different mobilities. LBGs often require users with different mobilities to "navigate physically challenging environments to receive in-game rewards".[4] Some people already have to navigate the urban environment on "hard mode" because of a lack of accessibility in urban design, and long **journey times** can exclude many players from fully participating.

In the 2020–2022 pandemic when many more peoples' mobility was reduced due to lockdowns and social distancing, Clark, Singh and Barbareschi found that

> disabled LBG players voice[d] their delight as long-awaited changes were made due to lockdown restrictions. For instance, the walking distance necessary for eggs used to hatch rare Pokémon was halved. However, as lockdown restrictions have globally eased and people are now allowed to interact with one another in co-located spaces, games such as *Pokémon GO* have decided to revert to game rules that existed before the pandemic. Unsurprisingly, disabled users of LBGs have shared their frustrations with these changes… Following the backlash, Niantic decided to reinstate some of the changes in question.[5]

Consider the usability of your chosen technology platform, and how you can make it usable for more players. Most mobile AR experiences assume that players can simultaneously move and hold a device; but wheelchair users need their hands to move. Shape Arts' *Unfolding Shrines*[6] is a good example of an AR experience which provides accessible controls to allow wheelchair-users to screen tap to move around an augmented artefact. This project highlights an affordance that non-wheelchair-users often take for granted.

Headsets of all kinds have significantly different affordances for different people, particularly neurodivergent people. Consider whom you might be excluding by choosing to use a headset-based experience, and how you can mitigate this. You can find a summary of current efforts to increase the accessibility of headset-based experiences in Dudley, Yin, Garaj & Kristensson's study "Inclusive Immersion"[7] and more resources at XRAccess: https://live-xraccess.pantheonsite.io/resources/.

Live experiences in public may present barriers to those with different mobilities or who are neurodivergent. Consider these starting points for accessibility (inspired by accessibility principles developed by live game designers Coney for smartphone adventures/digital experiences in public places):

- **Seek input from a wide range of perspectives and treat this as professional advice.**
- In advance: share as much information as possible about the experience (potentially as an "opt-in", if you'd like to preserve the mystery for other players).
- Key information to share in advance includes duration, location, likely crowds, ground conditions, availability of toilets (including accessible toilets), parking, public transport access, step-free access, noise and lighting themes and content.
- Consider the lighting and soundscapes of locations, and provide refuge spaces where possible.
- Wherever possible, allow players to be able to pause experiences and to go back if they've missed something.
- Provide captions/transcripts for all audio.
- Where possible provide a visual story or storyboard to accompany any text.
- Offer a choice of font, font size and colour contrast for all text.
- Position **dwell time nodes** in locations where players can sit down.
- **Test, test, test!**

INEQUALITY

As well as physical/sensory accessibility, consider the **socioeconomic inequalities** which impact different players' realities. Think about the ways in which certain locations might be differently welcoming, accessible or dangerous to different people for sociocultural reasons. Particularly if some people might be subject to discrimination or violence.

If a player is playing *Pokémon GO*, and they come across a Pokémon which they can't reach because it's on the other side of a chain-link fence, the game is still functioning as-designed. However, if a player is unable to access a Pokémon because they don't feel safe moving around in certain areas or at certain times, the game has inadvertently ported-in some of the injustices of the real world. de Souza e Silva *et al* argue that LBGs

> have the potential to add playfulness to ordinary life spaces. However, in order to be playful, a space needs to be safe… people are "free" to play when they trust that strangers in the city will behave in a certain way.[8]

Not everyone gets to play freely in urban space. de Souza e Silva *et al* point out that in *Pokémon GO* communities in some areas, "instead of drifting around, players normally leave their houses with the specific goal of going to a safe place in order to play" due to "deeply ingrained social and economic inequalities [which] affect personal safety and mobilities".[9]

Some players are potentially subject to violence because of their racial, gender or sexual identity. Research shows that "*Pokémon Go* play follows a pattern of marginalization and harassment in public spaces that lead minority populations to have a more difficult gameplay experience".[10] Remember also that context-blind algorithms can still be influenced by inequalities in the datasets they use. Juhász and Hochmair (2017) found that Pokéstops and Gyms in South Florida and Boston were originally created by *Ingress* players, who are mostly "White, male, and tech-savvy",[11] "leading to a concentration of virtual landmarks in commercial and downtown areas and fewer in non-White or residential areas".[12]

For players who experience discrimination and violence in the real world, augmented/spatial reality doesn't offer an "escape". One pandemic-era study cites the voice of a Native American *Pokémon Go* player:

> As a Native trainer, I have been profiled by security, I have been targeted as suspicious while playing in well-lit areas while a White man ten feet away wearing all black is seen as "normal".

Another player in the same study related the experience of people of colour playing LBGs who "didn't feel safe playing [Ingress] because not being arrested/shot/killed was a higher priority than a game".[13]

Whatever your background, do not lose sight of the fact that safely and playfully exploring a given environment is a relatively rare privilege. Consider ways you could increase safety and mitigate dangers for your players – including exempting certain players from certain rules.

REPRESENTATION

Augmented/spatial media have a particular responsibility to represent the plurality and diversity of our reality. Consider the IDENTITIES of non-player-characters you include in your story, and examine your biases about how you're representing the real world's diversity of age, race, ethnicity, gender, sexuality, physical ability, neurodiversity, mental health and socioeconomic status.

Some AR/spatial experiences represent players as avatars, and future experiences may be able to reskin the body of the player (or even other people) as avatars. Clark, Singh and Barbareschi found that being able to represent your own identity via LBG avatars is a priority for players, particularly for people of colour and disabled people.[14] If your experience includes avatars, especially if they can be customised, then as far as possible ensure that the available avatar options represent the same diversity of IDENTITY as your potential audience. As the VR LARP creator Nadja Lipsyc says, "what body we wear, what space we create, those are not simply a creator's preference or some fan service; those are statements on the digital future we are vouching for, and we now have very concrete options to challenge our usual aesthetics".[15]

We're just starting to scratch the surface of the sociocultural implications of augmented avatars. Remember that your ***responsibility to reality*** means making sure your work does not contribute to the erasure of marginalised people and identities.

ROLEPLAYING SAFETY

As we saw in 2.2, **roleplaying** is a complex emotional process, especially if you're augmenting people's IDENTITIES. This should always be done with care. When IDENTITY is involved, different players may find different experiences difficult or even traumatic.

Augmented storytellers need to develop tools to give players control over their level of **diegetic-ness**, e.g. by allowing players to quickly switch to a fully un-augmented view in a headset. It may be necessary for digital artefacts augmented into places to carry a tag or visual signifier to ensure they can always be discerned from real objects, and that their provenance can be traced so that abusive content can be removed.

AR safety tools could also give players ways to adjust their closeness to the experience in the event they encounter content which makes them uncomfortable. Remember Mashiter's 5th C, **Comfort**, is a vital component of creating compelling **roleplay** characters. Where possible give players the agency to control their level of involvement in the fiction in cases of challenging content. One system commonly used in tabletop roleplaying and LARP allows all players to define **lines and veils**, coined by designer Ron Edwards and developed by numerous indie game communities. Per Lotte Reinbold,

> Put simply, a **line** is something which will never come up as part of a campaign or session, while a **veil** ensures that whilst an action or event might take place, this will happen 'off-screen': mentioned in passing, but not dwelled on in detail and not a significant part of any plot or encounter.[16]

Lines are hard limits established by players to preclude certain content or experiences. **Veils** are a "pan away" or "fade to black" moment, allowing content to be **diegetic** but limiting players' emotional proximity to it. For a starting point on lines and veils, read Reinhold's post at https://www.dicebreaker.com/categories/roleplaying-game/opinion/lines-and-veils-rpg-safety-tools.

PHYSICAL SAFETY

Immersion is an agreement, not a trick, and so ultimately players bear responsibility for their own behaviour even in an immersed state. After all, however good the magic show, it would not be acceptable to assault a stage magician in retaliation for them sawing your spouse in half. Immersion does not work by "distracting" players from reality – but emotionally immersed players can be highly distracted, and as creators we have to acknowledge our part in this and work to remind players to keep themselves safe in a dangerous world.

Making sure your audience is safe is part of your professional responsibility. This includes ensuring that your experience doesn't inadvertently contradict or undermine safety rules in a location.

In **location-specific** experiences, **test** under a wide range of conditions to make sure your experience doesn't obscure safety information or inadvertently imply that players should violate safety **boundaries**, go into unsafe areas, or behave inappropriately. However you are reskinning or reimagining a place, ensure that fire safety doors and signage are clearly visible at all times.

Be particularly aware of the risks inherent in gathering large groups of people at venues or in public places. Ultimately, audience sizes in specific locations will always be limited by the **zero-sum** nature of the real world. Crowds and public gatherings may represent fire or crush hazards, be subject to policing, or cause unsafe or intimidating situations for non-players. As a location-based storyteller, it's part of your job to consider the occupancy limits and fire regulations of your chosen places. Consider how your experience might create unpredictable conditions and behaviours.

In public **location-specific** design, be cautious about the potential risks when adding set-dressing. In particular, planting mysterious objects in public places has potential safety and legal ramifications.

In **location-agnostic** design, the context-blindness of geotagging algorithms may create hazardous situations for players. Back in 2004, ten years before *Pokémon Go*, the Slashdot community discussed *Mogi*, an early Tokyo-based LBG. In a remarkably prophetic post, a commenter named MikeFM correctly predicted many aspects of contemporary LBG design. In fact, the only really incorrect part of MikeFM's vision is that they presumed future LBGs would be inherently safe:

> I don't think you need to worry about people swerving thru traffic to dodge [digital] monsters or collect treasures because most likely all such items would be placed on the map by someone actually going there and either electronicly [sic] marking the location or leaving a real key item in a cache. It's unlikely that the game's masters would purposely put objects in places that might cause the player or others harm.[17]

Like pretty much everyone at the time, MikeFM assumed that the content in future LBGs would continue to be geotagged by hand, by a human, who had some contextual understanding of the hazards and affordances of real space.

But manually geotagging content is prohibitively labour-intensive and expensive, which is likely why *Mogi* was never accessible outside Tokyo. Niantic's big leap was using their access to Google's mapping datasets to algorithmically populate environments worldwide with content, enabling LBGs to scale and become profitable.

But because geotagging algorithms curate content into places in context-blind ways, research has identified "risks of accidents related to a lack of attention or getting into dangerous, improper, or even forbidden places for the sake of picking up some rare Pokémon character".[18] Evans and Saker cite stories "involving players unwittingly putting themselves in physical danger by focusing on the digitality of their smartphones at the expense of the materiality of their environment",[19] which could lead to injury or even death.[20]

The potential risks of this kind of context-blind augmentation only increase in headsets. If your experience overlays graphics onto the player's entire visual field, you bear responsibility to ensure that the graphics cannot mislead players into hazardous situations or obscure physical security or safety information and signage. Consider how your players will navigate everyday obstacles like steps or roads while engaged in a headset-based experience; if there is any significant risk of increased harm in ordinary use, your experience is not ready for public consumption. Examine your biases, and seek input from other people with other perspectives; your assessment of the risks of a headset-based may not match other peoples', especially if you're accustomed to using headsets.

From a legal perspective, it's not yet clear how much liability creators might bear if a player gets hurt while their reality is being augmented. Most likely there will be precedent-setting test cases in various jurisdictions over the next few years. In order to avoid liability, most LBGs and similar games provide legal messaging which alerts players to the fact that there may be hazards in the environment, and makes it clear that players bear responsibility for their safety while playing. Your experience may well need to provide similar messaging.

This advice on Inclusion, Accessibility & Safety for augmented/spatial media merely scratches the surface of a huge and consequential new field of research. Remember, as creators and storytellers, some of this work is on us. Make sure that you approach augmented/spatial design with responsibility, empathy and a willingness to incorporate the needs and insights of others. As technologist Galit Ariel says in her 2018 talk "How AR can make us feel more connected to the world",

> we must ensure that we develop augmented reality that leverages the physical richness of this world rather than trying to "overcome" it. To create disciplines and practices that are inclusive and positive. And if we do so, we will have the privilege and joy of exploring, together, a new space full of endless imaginative worlds. Amazing journeys await us right here on planet Earth.[21]

NOTES

1. Joseph Wilk, https://art.josephwilk.net/projects/wheeltrails_r&d.html.
2. Skwarek in Geroimenko 2014, p. 24.
3. *Ibid.*
4. Maximillian Clark, Aneesha Singh, Giulia Barabareschi, "Towards Greater Inclusion and Accessibiliy for Physically Disabled Players in Location Based Games". *ACM Human-Computer Interactions* 7, 2023.
5. *Ibid.*
6. https://www.shapearts.org.uk/unfolding-shrines.
7. J. Dudley, L. Yin, V. Garaj, et al., "Inclusive Immersion: A Review of Efforts to Improve Accessibility in Virtual Reality, Augmented Reality and the Metaverse", *Virtual Reality* 27, 2023 https://doi.org/10.1007/s10055-023-00850-8.
8. de Souza e Silva *et al.*, 2021.
9. *Ibid.*
10. *Ibid.*
11. *Ibid.*
12. Levente Juhász and Hartwig H. Hochmair, "Where to Catch 'em all? – A Geographic Analysis of Pokémon Go Locations", *Geo-spatial Information Science* 20:3, 2017.

13. Arpita Battacharya, Travis W. Windlehearth, Cassandra Lee, Amulya Paramasivam, Julie A. Kientz, Jason C. Yip, Jin Ha Lee, "The Pandemic as a Catalyst for Reimagining the Foundations of Location-Based Games", *Proceedings of the ACA on Human-Computer Interaction* 5, 2021.

14. *Ibid.*

15. Nadja Lipsyc, "Comments on VR, Larp, Technology, Creation" in *Liminal Encounters: Evolving Discourse in Nordic and Nordic-Inspired Larp*, Kaisa Kangas (ed.), Ropecon, Finland, 2024.

16. Lotte Reinbold, "Lines and Veils, and Other RPG Safety Tools, Open Up Tabletop Roleplaying for Everyone", Dicebreaker, 29 Apr 2021, https://www.dicebreaker.com/categories/roleplaying-game/opinion/lines-and-veils-rpg-safety-tools.

17. MikeFM (12491), 2 Apr 2004 https://games.slashdot.org/comments.pl?sid=102633&cid=8751549.

18. Licoppe, 2016.

19. Evans and Saker, 2018, citing A. Frank (2016), "Six Pokémon GO Tips for the Ultimate Beginner", Retrieved from https://www.polygon.com/2016/7/9/12136310/pokemon-go-tips-how-to-play-beginners and E. Rosenberg (2016, August 22), "In a Safeguard for Children, Some Civil Liberties Groups See Concerns," *The New York Times*, p. 14.

20. Evans and Saker 2018, citing J. Soble (2016), "Driver in Japan Playing Pokémon Go Kills Pedestrian", *The New York Times,* 26 Aug 2016 http://www.nytimes.com/2016/08/26/business/japan-driver-pokemon-go-kills-pedestrian.html.

21. Galit Ariel, TEDWomen 2018.

Appendix B: Sliders for Defining Augmented/ Spatial Experiences

As we've seen, augmented/spatial experiences can run the gamut from intensive public competitive clashes to chill dimensions of digital farming augmented onto everyday life. Different experiences could create wildly different relationships between the *author*, the *audience*, the *content*, and the *context*.

Augmented/spatial media are always subjective and difficult to define, especially since technology platforms and media markets are evolving and hybridising so rapidly. However, it's vital that we begin to develop a vocabulary to communicate the different design aspects of augmented/spatial experiences. This vocabulary is important in order to communicate to players what they can expect of an experience, and what it will expect of them. It's also important in order to communicate clearly to team members and funders.

We also need to begin to build a collective memory of immersive experience design practice. Many early videogames are now difficult to access without expensive and specialised hardware or illegal emulators. Without the development of a collective design vocabulary, the legacy and learnings of generations of game creators could easily be lost. Many augmented/spatial experiences will be similarly ephemeral, so developing a design vocabulary is critical to preserve and continue developing augmented/spatial media.

But since AR/spatial is so subjective and hybrid, rather than try to provide a comprehensive set of definitions, this Appendix proposes a prototypal set of **sliders**. These are axes between two extremes. Each **slider** represents an aspect of augmented/spatial narrative design, with two definite extremes and a space in between for subjectivity and hybridness. For example, almost all AR/spatial experiences fall somewhere on the **slider** between the two extremes of **location-specific** and **location-agnostic**.

Think of the **sliders** like the character-generation sliders in an RPG videogame, where a "nose size" slider might allow the player to choose a nose size on a spectrum between the extremes of "large" and "small".

You might assume your project is a clear binary at one extreme of a **slider**, e.g. if you know that you want your concept to be 100% **location-agnostic**. But there are very few hard, binary definitions in augmented/spatial reality, and there probably won't be any anytime soon. (Not even *Pokémon GO* is completely **location-agnostic**.) More importantly, placing your idea on a **slider** will encourage you to challenge your assumptions. When you define an aspect of your design somewhere along a **slider**, think about

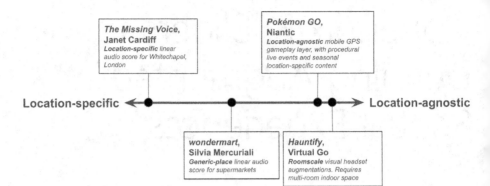

FIGURE B1 Example **slider**

the possibilities if you nudge the idea a little further along; what if your experience was largely **location-agnostic**, but had elements of **location-specific** live events like *Pokémon GO*'s Raids? What if it was subject to real seasons, or the phases of the moon? What if it asked players to perform good deeds in the physical world?

See Figure B1 for an example slider. A range of other sliders are listed below. Take a project idea you're working on, and try defining it by drawing out the **sliders. Use** a pencil and put a dot on each slider at one of the extremes, or somewhere in between. Wherever feels right. Then try out new ideas by nudging the dots one way or another. (You can always put more than one dot on the **slider** too – your experience design might work very differently under different circumstances.)

Alternatively, you could assign numerical values to each **slider**, for example assigning "1" to **location-agnostic** and "5" to **location-specific**, with "3" in the middle. This might allow you to chart out various different kinds of immersive experiences. But resist the idea that these sliders can be used to "grade" one experience as better or more interesting than another. Any possible configuration of these **sliders** could be a great and groundbreaking experience.

You could also use the **sliders** as a creative exercise: blindly assign random dots to each **slider**, then try to imagine what kind of an experience would satisfy that definition. What would a **protagonist-agnostic, location-specific** experience with a high degree of **performativity** and a high degree of **emergence** look like?

Feel free to add to, use, misuse or adapt these **sliders** to suit your own thinking.

(Note that these **sliders** are designed to help define new or unique affordances of augmented/spatial experiences. As such they don't cover design aspects already common in other interactive design disciplines, such as Replayability or Linear Vs. Branching narrative.)

The sliders are organised under loose headings, reflecting the aspects of the player's experience each **slider** might influence: **WHERE, WHEN, WHO, WHAT** and **WHY**.

WHERE:
Location-specific – Location-agnostic
Public place – Private place

WHEN:
Time-specific – Indefinite
Live – Asynchronous

WHO:
Roleplay – Protagonist-agnostic
Multiplayer – Solo
Anonymous – Performative

WHAT
Scripted – Emergent
Minor reality reskin – Major reality reskin
Private augmentation – Public augmentation

WHY
Creator-defined objectives – Player-defined objectives
Worldbuilding – Worldbuilt

WHERE

Location-specific – Location-agnostic

Is the experience designed for a specific place or could it work anywhere?

Chapter 3.1 deals with this **slider** in detail. Remember that this **slider** will have significant implications not just for your design but also for your distribution and business models: more on this in Appendix C.

As a general rule, **location-specific** experiences are restricted in space and therefore accessible only by a limited audience, but can lead to more contextual storytelling. It may also be easier to orchestrate the presence of other players for **live** or **multiplayer** experiences.

A **location-specific** layer could exist *in-situ* in a place **indefinitely**, for example enabling **asynchronous** gameplay, e.g. if multiple different players helped cultivate a digital flowerbed over time in a public square. Alternatively, **location-specific** experiences sometimes have **time-specific** showtimes like immersive theatre, allowing for e.g. choreographed **multiplay** or incorporation of highly contextual **merged reality moments** such as using real actors.

Remember, even with **location-specific design** you may well need to consider how to make an experience **portable** in order to make it sustainable.

As a general rule, **location-agnostic** experiences allow more potential players to access, allowing greater possibilities for **emergent** and **multiplayer** play. **Multiplayer** play could be **indefinite** and **asynchronous**, as in the territory capture of *Ingress*, or with a critical mass of players the experience could orchestrate **live time-specific** events such as *Pokémon GO*'s Raids.

Location-agnostic design is relatively context-blind, so it can result in more gen-eralised storytelling. There's a risk that your story could feel like it could be happening *anywhere*, and to *anyone*. However, clever **locagnostic** writing can feel responsive to a place despite context-blindness.

WHERE

Public Place – Private Place

*Is the experience intended to take place in a **public** environment or a **private** one such as a home?*

The **public – private** status of an experience may have a large impact on your player's psychology as they play. If an experience is likely to take place in **public**, this implies that players might BE SEEN by others they don't know in a way they can't control.

Use this **slider** to think about how the social dynamics of your chosen **locative category** might influence the player's emotional relationship to the content. If wearing a headset, might they be concerned about the "doofus factor"? Bear in mind that the same location could have different dynamics of **Public – Private** depending on times of day or year.

Public – Private may also have implications for accessibility. Players are likely to feel safe in the **private** space of their own home and have the appropriate **access** to it. Whereas a **public** space might be inaccessible, or might be an unsafe space for some players due to socioeconomic factors, inequality or discrimination (see Appendix A.)

This **slider** is distinct from the **Private augmentation – Public augmenta-tion slider** (see below). If an experience takes place in a **public** place but it uses **private augmentation**, e.g. being mediated entirely on the user's phone screen or via headphones, the user's experience might effectively feel private overall (see "Walkmanology" in 0.7).

An enclosed or controlled space such as an immersive theatre environment is less **public** than a public square. If there is a large audience population in a controlled space, players may still feel that they are BEING SEEN by others, like they would be in a **public place**. However this is also subject to the dynamics of **public-private augmentation**. A group of players could be all sharing the same **diegetic** layer of **public augmentation**, e.g. all wearing headsets and collaborating to fight an augmented monster, but this could be taking place in a **private place** like a home.

Your experience might ask players to do things that might look strange out-of-context to bystanders – this is handled under a different slider, **Anonymity – Performativity.**

WHEN

Time-specific – Indefinite

*Is the augmented instance temporary? Is it **conditionally** active at certain times? Or is it always-on and always in-progress?*

This **slider** asks WHEN players can access the experience and under what circumstances. Do players have to attend the experience at a specific moment or moments? Or can players access the experience anytime?

An **indefinite** experience can be dipped-into by players, perhaps becoming a playful dimension of the player's neighbourhood or daily commute.

If your experience is based around a one-off time-limited event, it is a 100% **time-specific**. If the experience could remain accessible and/or in-situ indefinitely with the content unchanged (so long as its technology platform remains online) it is 100% **indefinite**.

If an experience has specific showtimes (e.g. an hourly event or nightly showtime in a weeklong run) it's still **time-specific**. An **indefinite** experience could be potentially active anytime but only activated **conditionally** under certain circumstances, e.g. only being active when it's raining. A game which is playable anytime but whose **mechanics** change on a day/night cycle would be **indefinite** with elements of time-**conditionality**.

A **time-specific** experience can be highly contextual, responding to a specific moment in time to create **merged reality moments**. A **time-specific** and **location-specific** experience could refer specifically to a physical event e.g. a parade. A **time-specific** and **location-agnostic** experience could refer specifically to a temporal event happening worldwide, e.g. a World Cup final.

WHEN

Live – Asynchronous

*Must players interact with the experience (or other players) **live** in realtime? Or can different players interact at different times and return later to see what's changed?*

A **live** experience unfolds and must be interacted with in realtime, e.g. witnessing a one-off story event, or playing realtime PvE co-op with a friend in *Monster Hunter Now* (2022). An **asynchronous** experience can be interacted with by different players at different times – e.g. capturing a portal in *Ingress* and returning the next day to find it has been recaptured by another player, or contributing a leaf to a digital tree which grows over time as more players contribute, as in *Un/Seen Evergreen*.

Live multiplayer experiences can have great immediacy and contextuality, allowing players to play in realtime with current events or fellow-players, but this relies on a critical mass of players all coinciding and accessing the experience at the same time. Whereas **asynchronous multiplayer** allows players to interact with the game or with each other without having to coincide at the same point in time. For this reason, most LBGs have both **live** and **asynchronous mechanics**, to ensure that players have something to do both at busy times/locations and quieter times/locations.

Non-**multiplayer live** experiences could be one-off events in the digital layer which happen at **time-specific** moments and which must be interacted with in realtime, like a **solo** augmented experience timed to coincide with a solar eclipse.

Note that this **slider** has some overlap with **Time-specific – Indefinite**, but they define different things. An experience could be **indefinite** but have **live** elements, such as an always-open gladiatorial arena in which anyone can challenge another player in realtime.

An experience could be **time-specific** but have **asynchronous** elements, e.g. a month-long virtual community garden into which any player can contribute seeds at any time, which all flower at the full moon, and then disappear.

WHO

Roleplay – Protagonist-agnostic

*Is your player **roleplaying** an entirely composed character provided by the story, or playing as themselves?*

We examined the implications of this slider in detail in Chapter 2.2.

Similar to **Location-specific – Location-agnostic**, this **slider** determines how specific you can be about certain story elements. In a fully **roleplayed** experience you can tell the player WHO they are (though not WHAT they care about or WHAT they should do next). Remember this approach can easily end up leaving no room in your experience for the player. Help players co-create their **blended** augmented IDENTITY, e.g. with *anagnorisis* and *mise-en-**self*** techniques.

Remember player-characters are almost always somewhere in-between these extremes. Their IDENTITY within the story will be a composite of themselves and your storytelling.

WHO

Multiplayer – Solo

Is the player's experience impacted by the presence or actions of other players?

This slider has an enormous impact on the player's psychology. Even if there is no digital evidence of other players' participation at a given moment, if the player knows that **multiplay** is possible then this will have an impact on their play by activating their BEING SEEN instincts.

Even if the player can only leave their mark via **anonymous** and **asynchronous** interactions like adding their name to a leaderboard, that player is alerted to the fact that the augmented layer is a partially social environment.

Note that this slider defines whether a player's in-layer actions could impact *other players*. If players' actions could be observed or have an impact on non-players or ordinary bystanders, this is tracked by the **Anonymous – Performative slider.**

WHO

Anonymous – Performative

When the player is playing, are their in-layer actions manifest to non-players? Do they behave normally? Could a bystander tell that the player is playing an augmented experience?

This slider reflects the social dynamic of actions the player enacts as part of the experience. If the player could fully participate in an experience without their outward behaviour appearing unusual in their local context, the experience is fully **anonymous**. If the player is asked to perform in-story or in-character actions which are potentially visible to others, and which don't make sense absent the narrative or gameplay context, it is fully **performative**.

So an audio-only guided tour of a park experienced through headphones would be 100% **anonymous**. A game of *Monster Hunter Now* might be mostly **anonymous** because the player is just navigating normal space while interacting with a smartphone, but the **path** they take through a place might not make sense outside the context of the game layer, so their behaviour is slightly **performative**.

Autoteatro experiences like Mercuriali's *wondermart*, which asks players to draw a heart on the condensation of a supermarket freezer cabinet, have a significant **performative** element, though can still be very personal experiences. A **location-specific** competitive duelling game which displays the leaderboard on physical billboards would be highly **performative** because player actions are being broadcast publicly outside of the game layer. In flashmob-like live games such as *Gentrification: The Game*, a major part of the dynamic is player SELF-CONSCIOUSNESS and the **performative** impact of player behaviour on passers-by.

Remember that the player's actions can be fully in-character while still being **anonymous**: an experience which tells them to blend in or *just act normal* is designed to dramatise their everyday actions inside their own heads, without manifesting decontextualised actions to bystanders.

This **slider** is distinct from **Public place – Private place**, which is about the social dynamics of the space in which the player is playing. It's also distinct from **Public augmentation – Private augmentation**, which is about whether the digital elements of the experience can only be seen by one player, or can be seen by multiple players.

WHAT

Scripted – Emergent

Are the events of the experience pre-determined? Or are they an unpredictable product of interacting systems?

We examined **emergent** design under **spatial pacing** in 3.1.1. **Emergent** design creates serendipity and spontaneity, and often encourages replay. However it is more difficult to create structured **pacing** of **emergent** story **beats** compared to **scripted** narrative.

Scripted story events can still be injected into **emergent** narratives: open-world survival videogames like *Subnautica* (2016) often use a hybrid of **emergent** and **scripted** story. Players are free to explore and encounter serendipity, but the story also advances through **scripted beats** by driving players to specific story locations with **objectives**, or **conditionally** triggering **scripted beats** at **hub** locations after players have made a certain amount of general progress.

In a **location-agnostic** augmented narrative, hybrid **emergent/scripted pacing** could mean players freely explore and encounter serendipity, but the Narrative Time advances through phases or seasons, altering the texture and feel of the general experience and triggering story **beats**. LBGs releasing "seasonal" content is an example of a semi-**scripted** approach to otherwise **emergent** games.

Persistent multiplayer **emergent** narratives can be combined with **scripted** or semi-scripted events managed in realtime by human gamesmasters, such as the massive shared PvE instance of *Helldivers 2* (2024).

Emergent structures can sometimes create far larger and grander experiences than scripted ones. In PvP (Player versus Player) **multiplay**, **emergent** elements and lack of creator-defined objectives tend to result in game experiences defined by players' meta-objectives like curiosity, ambition, factionalism and mischief. That makes them very human spaces. In the words of Andrew Groen, historian of massively multiplayer emergent galaxy *EVE Online* (2003–), "it's a virtual space, but a virtual space where causation and human ambition matters, and that makes it a space that matters to history".[1]

WHAT

Minor Reality Reskin – Major Reality Reskin

How much is reality being altered by the augmentation? How different is the player's augmented experience from immediate physical reality?

This **slider** summarises the extent to which you're digitally altering the player's sensory experience of the world, e.g. through graphical reskinning. If you're only augmenting small graphical touches, it's **minor reality reskin**. If you're fully reskinning the world, it's **major reality reskin.**

This is specifically about how much you're overwriting the world; *imaginatively* augmenting the player isn't covered under this slider. If you use an open-ear audio layer to whisper to the player *"you are secretly a dragon"*, this might completely recontextualise their perceptions, but 99% of their sensory experience is still the real world. This is still a **minor reality reskin**. Whereas if you use a headset to re-texture every surface of a street to look like a nighttime Victorian metropolis, this is a **major reality reskin**.

This is a very broad and subjective **slider** and will mean different things with different implementations and different technologies.

WHAT

Private Augmentation – Public Augmentation

Is the player's instance of the experience perceivable only by them? Is the player in a private instance of reality or a shared one?

If the augmentations the player perceives are perceivable only by them, existing only to the player's perceptual **vantage point**, they are **private augmentations**. If the augmentations are publicly visible to anyone with the appropriate hardware and software, they are **public augmentations.**

A piece of digital graffiti which is viewable only by a small group via a private opt-in channel, undetectable to anyone else, is strongly **private**. Whereas the same piece of digital graffiti posted to a location's "public channels", like a location-tagged public social media post, is strongly **public**. If the digital graffiti is freely viewable to everyone with platform access, it's a **public augmentation.**

If the player leaves a digital note anchored to their fridge, reminding them to buy milk, and this note is not visible to anyone else, it's 100% **private augmentation**. Whereas a **public augmentation** could be a major boss spawn in *Monster Hunter Now* designed to attract players to fight in **live** co-op PvE. If the monster is viewable on multiple devices, and located and oriented the same way for everyone; it is a fully shared **public** instance.

Note that players could be playing the same game, but not necessarily sharing **public augmentations**. If a game allows players to build *Minecraft*-like digital buildings in public places, and these buildings are visible to other players, they are **public augmentations**. If the player can make their buildings invisible even to other players, they are **private augmentations**.

This slider defines aspects of your content's reach and **accessibility** and your player's social relationship to the content. Many of the most dystopian aspects of augmented/spatial technology have this slider at their heart. Are your players viewing a fully bespoke, private **customised reality**? Or a shared, public version of reality? How much right do we have to maintain a private perceptual model of the world? How much right do we have to privately impose augmentations onto the bodies or property of others? More on these key questions in Section 4.

WHY

Creator-defined Objectives – Player-defined Objectives

*Does the player pursue defined **objectives** within the experience? Do they set their own **objectives**?*

If the narrative or **objectives** are entirely defined by the creator, they are **creator-defined**. If the player is able to entirely set their own objectives, e.g. in a sandbox like *Minecraft*, they are **player-defined**.

Note that players may choose to engage with other players' **player-defined** meta-objectives, like "speedrun the game as fast as possible". See the **Audience** section of Appendix C for examples of different types of player engagement with internal and meta-objectives.

WHY

Worldbuilding – Worldbuilt

Is the story world already built? Can the player's actions have a material impact on the story world?

Does the player's participation engage them in the ongoing shaping of the narrative or world of the experience? Are they engaged in **world-building**?

Note that the player who follows the plot of a linear adventure game and "saves the world" according to the story ISN'T engaged in **worldbuilding** – any in-storyline changes to the game's world were defined by the creator before the player even began playing.

Whereas if it's possible for the player's actions to become part of a game world's ongoing player-defined *lore*, then the world is not pre-**built** and players CAN engage in **worldbuilding**.

Creating worlds where players can make a genuine difference through **worldbuilding** is difficult: it requires players to be able to effect permanent creative changes which are visible to others, which requires moderation and editorial at scale AND/OR requires the world itself and its storylines to be highly malleable, which requires asset creation at scale.

For example, say it is possible for a player to kill a boss NPC and then capture, redesign and rename the boss's castle, having permanent effect on the world for all players. This creates a powerful and thrilling context of BEING SEEN: the player has left a substantial mark on a living world. But to allow this, the game's creators might need to ensure that a) any ongoing storylines involving the boss are altered to include the boss's death, with the appropriate knock-on effects, b) the player has robust tools to redesign the castle and doing so doesn't negatively disrupt other players, and c) moderators review the castle's new name to make sure it isn't a slur. All of these processes require resourcing and oversight.

Online games with strong elements of **worldbuilding** exist, such as *EVE Online* in which most events are driven by player actions within an intricate functional economy. Games of this type are difficult and expensive to build and maintain, and are often chaotic and unforgiving. However, virtual worlds in which it's possible to make a true difference hold a strong appeal, especially for augmented/spatial experiences taking place in the real world.

Researchers like Jay Springett focus on "Worlding" or "Worldrunning" as emerging possibilities and design disciplines. If you like the idea of being a Worldrunner, read Springett"s *Worldrunning.guide*.[2] This is a particularly exciting area of potential development for augmented/spatial media: can we create living, persistent, coherent and consequential digital dimensions augmented onto the real world?

NOTES

1. Andrew Groen, *Empires of EVE*, 2016, p. iii.
2. Jay Springett, *Worldrunning.guide*, ongoing, https://docs.google.com/document/d/1XRm 39aH8APXVqjzKYptz7-NQ-3AAXNVrgcjm9oBMOec/edit#heading=h.z0500e4podv3.

Appendix C: Example Concept Development Framework

This section outlines an example **framework** for developing your augmented/spatial narrative ideas into full concepts. The goal is to provide a structure for planning and articulating your ideas in a way that's clear and systematic. Communicating your ideas to potential audiences is a crucial part of creative work. And before you even reach your audience you will most likely need to communicate your ideas to potential partners, team members and funders.

Note that this framework doesn't focus on the process of *pitching*. Pitching a marketable proposition is a storytelling skill which you will probably need to cultivate to one extent or another. If you're going out looking for support or investment, remember your story idea will be just one component of a wider proposition. The key skill of pitching is to present your idea as a bankable solution to a clearly-articulated need or opportunity. This includes understanding the existing or potential demand for a certain type of content. For an example of how to start thinking about pitching, try the CO-STAR Value Proposition Framework at https://www.dsc.org.uk/wp-content/uploads/2016/05/co-star.pdf.

Even if you're not aiming to create a marketable proposition, remember that players have a **zero-sum** amount of time and attention. If you can learn to present your ideas in terms of their value to the end-user, this will be helpful in refining your narrative into its most attractive form.

This **framework** covers the early concepting phase of a project, rather than the later production phase, and as such it doesn't provide exhaustive guidance on budgeting and project management. However, the **budget** phase below contains general advice on how to establish your concept's budgetary parameters, and includes links to resources and example budgets.

Much of this **framework** is based on lessons learned and mistakes made in my own career. As with the rest of this book, it's not intended to be exhaustive or definitive. Feel free to adapt, hack or ignore parts of this **framework** to suit your needs.

First we'll examine some **general skills** which will serve you well as an augmented/spatial storyteller.

This is followed by the full **concepting framework**, organised into a step-by-step list of key **concepting phases** to help you develop from initial idea, through platform and budget considerations, all the way to testing.

The **framework** closes with **three pieces of general advice** drawn from my own experience.

GETTING STARTED: WHAT SKILLS DO YOU NEED?

If your ambition is to be an augmented/spatial storyteller, the most important skills you'll need are **flexibility** and **audacity**. First, the flexibility to adapt to the myriad requirements, rejections, roadblocks and "operational realities" involved in producing entertainment in the real world. Second, the audacity to maintain your narrative vision and your working practice in ways that are coherent, compelling and empathy-building.

I've spent my career making immersive stories using whatever tools were available (often on "barefoot budgets") so in addition to narrative design I've also picked up skills like production, budgeting and collaboration. I had to develop this wide range of creative and production skills because I was working in early, unproven technologies. As augmented/spatial media mature and markets are established, it will increasingly be possible to build a career as a specialist storyteller in the field without needing those other skills.

But keep in mind, interactive media are inherently multidisciplinary; especially immersive media. As one analysis of the UK Immersive Industry put it in 2019,

> It may be that in fifty years' time, today's VR and AR headsets have become the fore-runners of some other form of immersive staging that makes them look like the zoetrope or praxinoscope – those Victorian optical devices that we now understand as the precursors of cinema.
>
> And just as the pioneers of cinema at the end of the 19th Century could not foresee Hollywood, we don't know where immersion will go. But when Cinema did get there in the 1920s, it sucked in every kind of creative talent, from the whole world, to create an industry. Writers, musicians, designers, technicians, performers, investors; it took them all to build what we now recognise as cinema.[1]

Whatever your creative skills, they're going to be needed if we're going to fully explore the potential of augmented/spatial storytelling.

Technical skills are not essential to working in augmented/spatial media, but a basic grounding in common technical tools is always useful. Some experience working with **conditionality** is very helpful in thinking about interactive story design. Refresh yourself on **spatial pacing** in 3.1.1 including **CHALLENGE #17: Conditionality in Twine**.

Some experience with game development environments is always helpful. Even basic skills in development platforms like Unity or Unreal will help you prototype your ideas quickly and inexpensively. If (like me) you find this intimidating, you can get started by simply watching beginners' guides on YouTube, or doing short online courses to find your feet.

Collaboration – and compromise - will almost certainly be vital skills. Sometimes, especially if you are a writer within a larger team, it might be part of your role to be an advocate for the story, to ensure that resources are allocated to make the story the best it can be. But you need to balance this with understanding the overall equation of the project. Often it will be on you to reach out and understand the considerations of budget, time and logistics which affect other collaborators or teams within a project, whether that's graphics, music, code or production. Even if you are a specialist storyteller, remember that every single department or discipline is engaged in telling the story. Often the best way to ensure a strong creative collaboration is to be the biggest fan of the story within the team. This means communicating the evolving story to the team, ensuring that all members are excited about the story you're telling together and understanding other team members' priorities as well as your own.

CONCEPTING PHASES

The goal of this **framework** is to provide you with an example structure and step-by-step process for each phase of developing an augmented/spatial concept. The **concepting phases** are presented in a specific order to encourage you to be systematic in your thinking. Approaching a project as a series of distinct phases can help prevent you getting too far ahead in developing one area (such as the **script**) without having considered limitations or practicalities in other areas (such as the **budget**).

But bear in mind, every new idea may cause you to rethink concept areas, or force you to weigh up your priorities. Concept development isn't a very efficient process; it requires a lot of iteration, backtracking, reassessment and compromise. The **concepting phases** are presented in a specific order, but many of the phases are not truly finished until the project is launched. The final phase is **iteration**, and if you reach that point you will likely have already gone through several iterations of earlier phases. Don't be surprised if some core ideas which were once at the very heart of your concept end up being dropped or completely changed by the end.

The **concepting phases** are organised into five general areas, reflecting the role they play in the holistic development of a concept:

HEAD
 Theme(s)
 Audience
HEART
 Player Agency
 Core Objective
 General Mechanics
 Player IDENTITY
 Story Overview
HANDS
 Locative Category
 Platform
 Budget & Scope
 Access
GUTS
 Story Beats
 Story Mapping
 Script

LEGS
  Prototyping
  Testing
  Iteration

HEAD

Theme

You might already have a rough concept idea. You might have a sense of how you want your experience to *feel*. But before you go any further it's worth thinking about what you want it to be *about* and summarising this in a handful of words. This is the **theme.**

Your **theme** should be your guiding star throughout development, keeping you on-track and keeping you honest about *why* you're telling this story.

Your **theme** should be SHORT, six or so words at maximum. A rule of thumb I use is the **mouthful rule**: your **theme** should be short and punchy enough that you can communicate it clearly with your mouth full – and I mean *full* – of food. Take a big bite of sandwich then say your draft **theme** to a friend – if your friend gets it, then you have a clear and communicable **theme**, as instantly recognisable as the silhouette of an iconic cartoon character. Example **themes** might be:

> *vengeance;*
> *persistence is rewarded;* or
> *we must care for one another.*

Every story decision you make should ultimately be in service of your **theme**, and eventually ANY element which doesn't express the **theme** can be cut. However, **theme** shouldn't constrain your initial thinking. After progressing in other phases, you may circle back and find the **theme** has changed. **Theme** iterates throughout development, so stay honest and remember to keep updating it. If you find a key story element is straying away from the **theme**, then either that element is extraneous, OR it's a sign your thinking may have evolved and the **theme** needs updating.

Audience

The **audience** is your ultimate endpoint, so why start thinking about **audiences** so early in the process? Remember, your player is a vital collaborator and co-storyteller. You need to leave space for them in your story from the very beginning.

Plus, your story simply doesn't exist if no-one plays it! So you should have some understanding of the type of person you are hoping to attract. For large projects, this might mean performing demographic research or market analysis. For smaller projects, identify one or more similar existing projects which attracted an **audience** size you could realistically emulate, then try to identify who that **audience** was and why that project appealed to them. Again, be realistic.

Identifying your **audience** will also help you verify early on that the relevant people can actually **access** your story and the **platform(s)** it uses. If you're also responsible for promoting or marketing the final product, this will be even more important.

Find ways to humanise your eventual **audience** and keep them foremost in your mind as you develop. You could find photos or illustrations of a diverse range of example players and stick them up around your writing area. Or write example "user journeys" telling the story of a player's experience of your project, and how it fitted into their day – including what they had for breakfast. Or give your players names in your script – Shreya and Dan, not Player 1 and Player 2.

Some experiences appeal to specific types of player, while others attempt to have something for everyone. To get you thinking, below are two examples of ways that creators have categorised different types of player.

The first list is based on a classic taxonomy of videogame players based on work by game researcher Richard Bartle, creator of the first MUD (Multi-User Dungeon, a precursor to multiplayer games).[2] The second is adapted from a recent taxonomy of immersive theatre audience types by Tom Maller, Creative Director of *Peaky Blinders: The Rise*.[3]

(Note that the vast majority of players don't fit squarely into a single category, and instead share aspects of different categories.)

FOUR TYPES OF VIDEOGAME PLAYER (BASED ON BARTLE'S TAXONOMY, 1996)

ACHIEVERS

Also called "Diamonds". Achievement Hunters, showboats, early-adopters. Players who emphasise gaining points, levels or other concrete measures of in-game success. Cosmetic accolades are their own reward. Multiplayer and social dynamics revolve around progression and status.

EXPLORERS

Also called "Spades". Glitch-hunters, horizoneers, completionists. Tend to dig around, seek discoveries and pursue meta-objectives. Engage strongly with the digital world but less with its defined constraints or **objectives**. Social dynamics might revolve around meta-objectives like finding glitches or secrets.

SOCIALISERS

Also called "Hearts". Guild leaders, lobby butterflies, chat-focused streamers. Tend to seek emotional engagement with NPCs and/or fellow-players. Social dynamics are an end in themselves. Might use games as social platforms and ignore the story or **mechanics** altogether.

KILLERS

Also called "Clubs". Speedrunners, min-maxers, esports athletes. Motivated by competition and powergaming. Tend to engage with skill-based mechanics and seek ways to maximise competitiveness. Social dynamics revolve around winning.

SEVEN TYPES OF IMMERSIVE THEATRE AUDIENCE (BASED ON TOM MALLER, 2023)

FAN PLAYER

A diehard fan of the original IP or work a show is based upon, and/or a subject matter buff. Will often fixate on a detail or pursue a key character or storyline.

NARRATIVE PLAYER

Has already engaged with the narrative either as existing IP or through research. Seeks to maximise exposure to story proceedings, e.g. witnessing the beginning, middle and end, or seeking new content in a well-known story world.

OBSERVER PLAYER

Highly present, and often costumed to fit in, but doesn't want to be forced into the spotlight. (Maller advises performers not to force these players into interactions, but also not to dis-include or turn their back on them.)

GROUP PLAYER

Arrived in a group and will stay in a group. Their goal is to compare notes on the experience and/or have a collective experience. Often attending as part of a social occasion which is a meta-textual part of their engagement, e.g. a birthday. (Maller advises recruiting these players for group tasks or granting them IDENTITY as a faction.)

SOCIAL PLAYER

Engages with the experience as an in-fiction social environment, not a narrative progression. Is likely to want to BE SEEN as much as to SEE. Likely to dwell in social environments like **hubs** or bars. Seeks characterful encounters not story **beats**.

THE FRESH FACE

Unfamiliar with immersive formats, a first-timer. They've come straight from work because someone had a spare ticket. Can metamorphose into any of the other player types, but needs clear rules of engagement and routes into interaction.

EXPLORER

Will challenge the experience, seeking its secrets, edges and under-explored possibilities. (Maller suggests giving these players an **objective** – but if you tell them to turn right, they might turn left, push boundaries, start reading a character's diary.)

HEART

Player Agency

Agency is at the heart of all interactive design – according to Calleja, players "do not merely consume a pre-established piece of media, but instead are active participants in the creation of their experience".[4] This is even more true in augmented/spatial media because the player is co-present in everyday reality, not an authored virtual world.

Emily Short defines **agency** as "the player's ability to affect the world and story". **Agency** depends on the amount of information you give the player and whether or not you've made them care about it: "if the player cannot guess or does not care where the action will lead, there is no **agency**".[5]

The key questions for now are HOW MUCH **agency** you want the player to have, and how much you want them to FEEL they have. These questions will greatly impact the **mechanics** and your choice of **platform**.

An augmented/spatial experience doesn't necessarily need a high level of **agency** – more **agency** doesn't inherently make digital experiences better. In augmented/spatial media, even if the player doesn't engage in gameplay or make decisions which branch the narrative, they are still co-tellers and co-creators of the story. If you have a strong story you want to tell, with a fixed beginning, middle and end, and you want your player to join you for the ride, go for it. Don't be tempted to add unnecessary decision points if really you just want them to follow a single specific **path**. If a player is required to interact merely to progress the action along a linear path, that's not **agency** – it's just a tax on the player's participation.

If you do want to give a high level of **agency**, remember that a rewarding experience of **agency** doesn't necessarily mean giving the player exactly what they want. Augmented/spatial media often tell better stories, AND feel more authentic to real experience, when they don't necessarily give us exactly what we expected. (See "Empowerment and Entitlement Simulators" in 2.1.)

For a general discussion of **agency**, read Short's 2009 blog post "Types of Action and Types of Agency".[6] For detailed technical analysis on how **agency** is designed and how it influences players try Gordon Calleja's *In-Game: From Immersion to Incorporation*[7] (2011), and for a more philosophical treatment try C. Thi Nguyen's *Games: Agency as Art*[8] (2020).

Core Objective

Wait a minute, we haven't even decided on **platforms** yet – why are we talking about the nitty-gritty of **objectives**? Well, this isn't about individual quest goals – this is about integrating your player's experience with the **theme**.

The player's fundamental **core objective** is what the story makes them want to *do*. Integrating this **objective** with the **theme** means that whatever your player wants to *do* also makes them feel like part of the story.

Core objectives should be expressible as basic verbs. An **objective** verb should clearly articulate an emotive desire. They must also exist in relation to the **theme**. Example **core objective verbs** include *survive, create, thrive,* or *discover the truth*.

At any point in the experience, it should be clear to the player what their objective is and why they should care about it. It's the interface's job to convey the **objective**, and the story's job to make the player care about fulfilling it. Again, in an experience with relatively low levels of **agency**, this **core objective** could be very simple: *explore*, or *find out what happens next*. Like any **objective**, this is the driver behind the player's participation.

Objectives make things personal. As we saw in 2.2, players dramatise their goals as "possible selves" in order to internalise them. In the same way, **objectives** are a crucial part of how players discover and relate to their augmented IDENTITY.

Objectives also make for resource-efficient storytelling: a player who has internalised an **objective** will self-narrate and maintain their active "creation of belief" within the story, even at times when they're not in direct contact with content.

General Mechanics

Every interactive experience has **mechanics** of one kind or another. These are the functions, interfaces or gameplay with which the player interacts. However simple or complex your concept, you need to understand the types of interactions you are asking of your players, and how different players may experience those **mechanics**.

In a linear, low-**agency** experience, it may be that the only **mechanic** is simply *follow a path*. If you're planning a complex gameplay system, don't try to fully design it during this early concepting process. Instead try to summarise your mechanics as basic verbs in relation to your **core objective**. If your **core objective** is *survive*, a **mechanic** verb might be *gather fuel* or *plant crops*.

A good interactive narrative does not simply provide an in-fiction explanation of the **mechanics**. Narrative and **mechanics** should be integrated so that interactions feel like a practical and emotional expression of the player's place in the story.

From a narrative perspective, **mechanics** define how play *feels* and how the player participates in the story's **theme** by attempting to fulfil the **objective**. So the mechanics, objectives and theme are all interrelated and should support not contradict each other. If your **mechanics** are simple, e.g. *follow a path*, then the player's emotional experience will be defined by *following*. This could create dissonance if your intended **theme** is *discovery*. But if your **theme** is, say *revenge*, then you could let the player know that by simply *following a path* they can fulfil their **objective** of *discovering the true culprit*.

If you play videogames then you probably already have pretty good instincts for what makes a good gameplay **mechanic**. But gameplay design is a complex topic far too large to cover here. Two good starting points are Jesse Schell's *The Art of Game Design*[9] (2008) and Anna Anthropy and Naomi Clark's *A Game Design Vocabulary*[10] (2014).

Player IDENTITY

You should now be able to outline what kind of character you're asking your player to BE in the augmented narrative.

If your experience is highly **protagonist-agnostic** this might be very loose – the player's in-game IDENTITY might simply be a version of themselves who has engaged with the **core objective**. Refer to 2.2 for techniques on how to help players assert a **blended** IDENTITY, e.g. through *anagnorisis* or *mise-en-*self.

If you have a strong element of **roleplay** you might be asking players to adopt established characteristics or backstory which give them a specific relationship to the story world. If so, think about how you will convey enough information to the player to help them successfully **roleplay** without overloading them. They need to be able to feel fluent in their **IDENTITY**, so **roleplaying** even a strongly characterised role shouldn't feel like a test the player might fail. Again, refer to 2.2: use the **5 C's** to create a compelling but empathetic role the player can step into:

Connections
Capabilities
Commitments
Conflict
Comfort

Interacting with the **mechanics** may be part of how players establish/discover their **IDENTITY**. But remember that in augmented/spatial media much of **IDENTITY-BUILDING** takes place inside the player's imagination, often in the **diegetic Relative Time** which takes place when the player is in-character but not in direct contact with narrative content (See **spatial pacing** in 3.1.1).

Resist the urge to ask the player to **mechanically** define their **IDENTITY** through making binary yes/no choices, like in a binary "morality system". This could unnecessarily corral a subjective IDENTITY within a restrictive definition.

Story Overview

Finally! Storytime, right? Well, this isn't about writing out the whole plot yet – it's about being able to summarise what your story is going to *do*.

You should now be able to write an **overview** of your concept's story in a single ~250 word paragraph. Write this **overview** the way you would verbally summarise the concept to a stranger if you only had a minute.

If you struggle to summarise the story in this way, you are probably including too much extraneous detail that the listener doesn't need. Refine your **overview**. You're not trying to compress the events of the story into this paragraph, you're trying to give an overall sense of the **theme**, what makes it compelling for players, and the beginning, middle and end of the emotional journey.

(You may not want to give away the story's ending in the **overview** – but make sure the **overview** suggests how the ending will resolve the **theme** and the player-character's journey, AND what the stakes are.)

This process will help you find the core of your story, and may well help clarify the **theme**, **objective** and player **IDENTITY**.

If you find it's just not possible to explain the core of the story and communicate the **theme** and **objective** in one minute, then your **overview** has too much complexity. Consider refining elements out of the **overview** – then seriously consider whether those elements are needed in the concept altogether.

Overviews are challenging to write. If you're struggling, think about *what you want the player to feel*.

The events of the narrative should all *express, complicate* or *resolve* aspects of the **theme**. Look at how your **mechanics** interact with the **objectives** and think about how the player might want to *express, complicate* or *resolve* the **theme** through their **agency**. Then think about what you want your player to come away from the story *feeling*. These are the elements to include in the **overview** – everything else is just detail to be fleshed out later.

HANDS

Locative Category

Now is the time to decide which **locative category** your experience broadly fits into. Section 3 of this book was devoted to selecting and utilising place(s). Refer to each sub-chapter of 3.0 if you need a refresher on the **locative categories**:

Location-Agnostic
Location-Specific
Generic Places
Location-Portable
Roomscale/At-home
Table-Scale

Remember that most experiences incorporate aspects of multiple categories – for example, **location-specific** experiences are often also **portable** for economic reasons. If your experience is a hybrid, use the **sliders** in Appendix B to explore and express its nuances.

Whatever locative category you use, remember the five **spatial elements** which will give the spationarrative experience texture: **paths, landmarks, hubs, edges** and **districts**.

Platform

Let's get real. It's time to select the technologies and/or software on which the digital components of your experience will be built and accessed by players. The **platform** might be a mobile browser, the App Store for the Apple Vision Pro, or a bespoke headset installed in a specific venue.

It may be that **platform** choice has been self-evident to you from the start, or you may have been keeping an open mind as you formulated **mechanics** and "game-feel".

Regardless, **platform** choice should be locked-in only after research, because **platform** defines much more than functionality. This decision will also probably define your distribution and marketing models.

What is the reach and **accessibility** of a given **platform**? This constrains your audience and demographics. What kinds of development tools are available, and will they fit your purposes efficiently? Have similar projects been released on the **platform**, and did they succeed? Will the **platform** still be **accessible** by the time your development is complete? What is the **platform's** licensing model and how will it affect your bottom line?

This book focuses on storytelling principles not specific **platforms**, in order to keep it relevant in the ever-shifting technology landscape. However familiar you are with that landscape, research your **platforms** and, if possible, seek out insights from fellow developers. Look for Developer Diaries, conference talks or postmortems by creators who've worked on similar projects to yours. Challenge your own assumptions – smaller **platforms** can blow up (or disappear) very quickly, while giant monoliths can change their rules or topple seemingly overnight.

Budget & Scope

You should now be able to summarise your entire project on a single page: what it is about, who it is for, how it will feel, how it will be distributed. This is enough to get a sense of what resources it will take to produce.

The **budget** will probably cover money, but should definitely cover TIME – particularly yours. Be ruthlessly realistic about how much money and time you and other potential team-members can supply to build the project. Then add AT LEAST 10% for things to go wrong. Make sure you treat team members the way you would want to be treated.

If you're seeking investment or planning to use crowdfunding, research similar projects which have been successful in their goals – and similar projects which *weren't*. If you're planning return-on-investment, research the profitability of comparable projects and realistically assess what you can achieve. Form a strategy for achieving your **budget** goals and remember to present your project as a bankable solution to a problem or opportunity.

Budgets can be very intimidating – they certainly were for me – but ultimately they are just spreadsheets. Watch some YouTube videos about basic spreadsheet skills, then open one up and start entering the numbers you know and highlighting those you don't. The *GameDev Business Handbook*[11] includes example budget templates[12] to get you started. Those examples are for medium-sized projects, but the principles are the same for small and large budgets.

Don't be afraid to seek help, but build your own understanding of **budgeting** too. It's easy to want to leave the calculations to someone else, but the **budget** is where creativity meets reality, so it's a vital tool for executing the story.

Once you have a sense of the **budget**, refine the size and **scope** of the project so you can actually make it within that **budget**.

Scope by enumerating the various assets, fees, licenses and contingencies you will need to build the project, and estimate their costs – scriptwriting, art assets, music, voiceover recording and licensing etc. – as well as the costs of implementing each of these in the platform. Research similar projects or talk to potential team-members to estimate the hour- or day-rates for developing different elements, and the number of hours or days required, or request quotes from potential contractors etc. Consider marketing and distribution costs.

Consider insurance, legal fees, software license fees, physical implementation costs, onsite costs, voiceover fees (including actor buyouts and editing). This will be an ongoing and iterative process, as some costs ALWAYS get forgotten, so continue updating the **budget**.

Consider outsourcing – throughout the digital industries, components such as art assets, music, and character design are outsourced to individual specialists. Even if you are just starting out, don't be afraid to search online for specialists. Examine online portfolios, find specialists you like and contact them about their rates. As long as you can give a clear brief for what you want, you will seem as professional as anyone else! If in doubt, ask specialists what kind of information they need in order to quote costs.

Don't forget that your experience will need to be **tested** – add AT LEAST another 10% budget for this.

When you have an initial **scope,** compare your estimated costs with the available **budget**. Then, most likely, it is time to start cutting things out.

Creativity is about compromise. Be realistic. It's much better to reduce your ambitions and make a smaller experience you can realistically finish. It's better than making half of a larger experience that no-one but you will ever see.

Access

You now know roughly WHAT you want to make, WHO you are making it for, and HOW it will reach them. Now is the time to find ways to maximise the number of people you can reach. How expensive is your chosen platform for the end user? Are there hidden costs or privacy issues which put some players off? What is the physical, social and economic **accessibility** of your chosen **location category** and **platform**? What are the affordances of your **mechanics**, and how will they be experienced by people with different abilities, identities or perspectives? Who might you be excluding without even realising it? See Appendix A for some guidance, but remember there's always more work to do.

GUTS

Story Beats

Defining the story as a series of key **beats** will help ensure you have a clear beginning, middle and end, and also help you break down the story into parts to determine what isn't working.

There are many different structures you can use to help guide you in writing **story beats**. The specific affordances of augmented/spatial narratives will influence the effectiveness of different **beat** structures, and probably lead to new AR/spatial-specific **beat** structures being developed. This will undoubtedly be a rich area of creative research and argument for artists and researchers for years to come.

The most basic beat structure is in three beats: "Beginning, Middle, End" or "Setup, Climax, Resolution".

In *Technique of the Drama* (1863) the German playwright Gustav Freytag developed a basic five-beat "pyramid" which was highly influential on later storytelling models:

FREYTAG'S PYRAMID (1863)

Act 1: Exposition. Introduction of characters and backstory, and indication of the central emotions or conflict through an inciting incident.

Act 2: Rising Action. Characters try to achieve their goals, conflicts begin to increase.

Act 3: Climax. A key turning point takes place and/or the tension reaches its peak.

Act 4: Falling Action. Events begin to lead to a resolution. Things may seem at their darkest. The audience experiences suspense or doubts their expectations about how the story will resolve.

Act 5: Resolution. The central emotions or conflicts are resolved, and any loose ends are tied up.

(Bear in mind that unlike modern story models, these Acts aren't necessarily meant to be roughly equal in length: in a modern film Acts 3, 4 and 5 might all happen in the last half hour.)

Joseph Campbell's "Hero's Journey" (1949) expanded Freytag's basic model into twelve steps based on his study of myths (we talked about some of the strengths and weaknesses of this model in 2.1). In *Save the Cat!* (2005) screenwriter Blake Snyder developed this further into 15 beats. For more detailed guidance consider writing manuals such as Brian McDonald's *Invisible Ink* (2010).

Owen Kingston's 10-beat Adaptive Narrative Plot Beats structure for immersive theatre experiences is particularly helpful: for more, watch the video of Kingston's characteristically gruff-but-inspiring talk at the Immersive Experience Network in 2023.[13]

ADAPTIVE NARRATIVE PLOT BEATS – OWEN KINGSTON, PARABOLIC THEATRE (2023)

1. Setup
   Often pre-show, an opportunity for the audience to explore the world of the show. Possible informal interaction with characters and other audience. Engagement with world-building materials. Opportunity to buy a drink or six.

2. Theme Stated

What your story is about; the message, the truth. Usually, it is expressed negatively on first hearing it. The rest of the show will prove the opposite to be true.

3. Catalyst

The moment where everything changes and the story begins. It is the telegram, the act of catching your loved-one cheating, allowing a monster aboard the ship, the Red Telephone ringing, etc. The "before" world is no more, change is underway. The adventure has begun.

4. Debate

Change is scary and for a moment, or a brief number of moments, the protagonists (the audience) doubt the journey they must take. Can I face this challenge? Do I have what it takes? Should I go at all? Space must be given to feel the weight of this if the protagonists are going to really "buy in". They must choose to lead rather than be asked to follow.

5. Fun and Games

The audience get to experience the idea you sold them. They get to have fun playing in the world they paid to experience. Where you deliver on the promise of the premise in your marketing. Everything that exploded into their minds when they first heard about your show should happen, and it should happen here.

6. Midpoint

Just when you thought you had it figured out, this is the moment when things twist. [...] The tone of this moment sets up the ending. The protagonists might get everything they think they want ("great!") or don't get what they think they want at all ("awful!"). But not everything we think we want is actually what we need in the end.

7. Bad Guys Close In

Doubt, jealousy, fear: foes both physical and emotional regroup to defeat the goals of the protagonists. The challenges get harder. The threat of failure is tangible. If it hasn't already, the clock starts ticking. Shit gets real.

8. All is Lost

The opposite moment from the Midpoint ("awful"/"great"). The moment that the protagonists realise they've lost everything they've gained, or everything they have now has no meaning. The initial goal now looks even more impossible than before. Something or someone dies. It can be physical or emotional, but the death of something old makes way for something new to be born.

9. The Long Dark Night of the Soul

The protagonists hit rock bottom, and feel like they may have failed. There is space to mourn the loss of what has "died" – the dream, the goal, a character, etc. You must fall completely before you can pick yourself back up and try again. Like the debate, this beat must be given space to land.

10. Finale

In some way, the Theme triumphs. Either it is realised through success, or through failure you learn its lesson and value, or something in between. A good finale will usually follow a recognisable pattern:

> *Gather the team*
> *Execute the plan*
> *"High tower" surprise*
> *Dig down deep*
> *Execute new plan[14]*

Story Mapping

Time to start **plotting** your story to your chosen place(s). Refresh yourself on the techniques of **layout**, **spatial pacing** and **boundaries** in 3.1: STAGING.

If you are creating a **location-specific** or **-portable** experience, **story mapping** is an in-depth, onsite process. Visit the place and explore it thoroughly for possibilities. Find a good **map** of the place, then start penciling your **beats** onto different locations to create **nodes** and **paths**. Remember to consider **access** and make sure the place will enable the **mechanics** for your target **audience**.

Think about **dwell times** and **journey times** – how long will a **node** ask the player to stay in a location, and how long will they spend journeying between locations? Can you fill that **Relative Time** (see 3.1.1) with story or engage their sense of **IDENTITY** or **objective** so that time becomes **diegetic**?

Consider how it will feel to BE THERE. Different conditions could affect the spationarrative qualities of the place. Utilise **reverse level design** and use the place's mood and texture to support each **beat**, particularly at **forks**. Consider whether to select **forks** location-specifically or to focus on destinations with a **location-agnostic fork** approach.

Above all, consider how you are using or augmenting the various possible meanings of the place (or inviting the player to challenge them). Give players the opportunity to feel they're OCCUPYING SPACE and have a chance to leave a mark.

If your experience is **location-agnostic**, story mapping is still important but more abstract. Think about how your **mechanics** and **beats** might interact with various different places worldwide. Do some **beats** or **mechanics** only suit certain location types or work under certain **conditions** e.g. weather or time of day? List out a range of environmental possibilities next to each of your **beats** and think about how each **beat** might feel different in different places or under different circumstances. Remember that both **dwell time** and **journey time** are made uncertain in **location-agnostic** – you have no idea how long players may want to (or be able to) spend in a location, or how long it will take to travel between locations. Ensure you have compelling **objectives** and IDENTITY so that this **Relative Time** is **diegetic** (i.e. the player continues telling themselves a story during Relative Time).

For **generic place** and **roomscale/at-home** narratives, consider ways to utilise the emotive experience of **home**. Consider algorithmically assigning story beats to location types within a contained space, e.g. "kitchen". Consider the probable texture and spationarrative dynamics of those location types, while leaving enough subjectivity for local variations. Think about how you can use augmentation to impose new meanings onto objects, or to impose **pacing** onto objects, e.g. with object rephysicalisation (see **spatial pacing** in 3.1.1).

For **table-scale** experiences the **place** matters less; consider creating a physical mockup of your stage area or building it in a developer environment like Unity, then "puppet" your story assets to work out the **layout** and **pacing**. Remember to consider the impact of **vantage point**.

Script

Finally! Time to tell your story. At this point, it's over to you.

Explore writing formats to find what suits you best – screenwriting software like Final Draft might be useful for linear narrative, wikis might help with broad world building, and project-writing software like Scrivener might help with complex multi-part narratives. After years in the games industry, I personally tend to write dialogue and narration directly into a spreadsheet as it helps me think of each line as a discrete editable component – especially helpful if dialogue will be recorded as voiceover.

Remember that *talk is cheap*. Even if your emotional relationship to the script is the driver for the whole project, it is usually cheaper and easier to change elements in the script compared to changing elements in any other **project phase** in this **framework**. This is why the story often ends up changing to absorb constraints and blockers encountered in other **project phases**. Remember to balance being both flexible and audacious. Maintain your vision, but be ready to compromise.

LEGS

Prototyping

You're now ready to begin **prototyping** your experience. You may have already **prototyped** basic **mechanics** in order to test their core appeal, but it's now time to create rough-and-ready examples of the experience. One approach is to prototype individual components like **mechanics** or individual **beats**, e.g. as simple paper prototypes. Another approach is to build a "vertical slice"; a small snapshot of the project finished to near-final quality, e.g. a chapter or short sequence. Make sure you don't spend too much time on polishing a **prototype**; any **prototype mechanic** or vertical slice may end up making it into the final experience, or it may be discarded altogether.

Refer to the Introduction for tips on minimum-viable prototyping using available tools. Consider prototyping on paper or using audio to explore your **mechanics** and **beats** in-principle.

Testing

Testing is vital to all good storytelling, particularly where technology is involved. **Test** your prototypes early, and continue **testing** throughout development as often as you can – really every single phase in this **framework** could be followed by an individual testing phase where you sense-check your thinking with friends or colleagues.

Be systematic and honest with yourself, and ask for the kind of feedback that will be helpful, not the kind of feedback you secretly want.

And always assume that outcomes from **testing** will require **iteration** – if you make time for **testing** but don't make time to implement unexpected changes, you're not really **testing** at all.

Iteration

Finally… no **phase** in this **framework** is truly "final" until the project is released. **Iteration** is the process of repeatedly reviewing, altering and evolving the various components of the project in response to changes in circumstance, new ideas, or the outcomes of **testing**. Changes can take place in every single **phase** at any time, and every change is an opportunity for you to review your assumptions and revisit **project phases** to find ways to fix, enliven or streamline your project.

GENERAL ADVICE

---

1. **Finished is better than perfect.**
   There's only one thing better than perfect, and that's *finished*. "Finished" in this context means delivered, implemented, executed, out in the world. "Finished" does not mean you are happy with the end product, or that it has stopped evolving. It means that it's *done,* enough for you to *move on.* As the Oscar-winning screenwriter Bill Condon puts it, "no piece of writing is ever finished. It's just due".

   Or, as the designer of *Thousand Year Old Vampire* Tim Hutchings says, "A year of revisions can make something 5% better, but even better than that 5% is making three totally new projects in that same amount of time".[15]

   If this isn't what you want to hear, then flip the advice around: **a "perfect" idea is probably un-finishable**. This is particularly the case for your first project. Don't spend years trying to perfect your first project, and miss out on the experience of finishing off a project and putting it out into the world.

If you have a dream of what your first project should be, a beautiful and perfect-able concept, you owe it to that concept to *not try to do it first.* Make something else, make it fast, make it badly, get it out into the world, and move on. Come back to your perfect-able dream project later, when you know you're willing to compromise to get it made.

2. **Play to your strengths.**

If possible, try not to imitate the kind of work that's already out there. Make the kind of work you want to see in the world. Make work which you can make well with the skills you already have, or the skills you're excited about acquiring. If you try to chase down what already exists, or make what the market seems to want, you're selling yourself short. If you have a skill or a perspective which you don't see out there, then you've got a chance to make something unique.

3. **Always list things in threes, so you have time to think of a third thing.**

I'm definitely not just making this third piece of advice up on the spot; absolutely not. The point of this third piece of advice is that as an immersive creator, you have to be able to *delegate to your future self.*

Any immersive project is a huge and complex iceberg, far too big to wrap your head around all at once. Managing it will mean using different parts of your brain which function well at different times. If you can't solve a particular creative problem RIGHT NOW, trust that you *will* be able to solve it later. In the meantime, drink some water, eat something, make progress on other fronts.

Trust your future self; after all, they will be a more experienced creative than you are. If you can't solve a story problem right now, you're probably better off going for a walk, discussing it with a friend or simply going to bed. You may well find you return with a solution or a new angle on the problem.

List things in threes, even if you haven't thought of the third thing yet: trust your future creativity to find something to fill that space and make the most of the creative opportunity you've given yourself.

NOTES

1. *Framing Immersion*, 2019.
2. Richard Bartle, "Hearts, Clubs, Diamonds, Spaces: Players Who Suit MUD", 1996 http://www.mud.co.uk/richard/hcds.htm.
3. Transcribed by the author at IEN Immersive Design Symposium, 9 Oct 2023
4. Calleja, 2011, p. 56.
5. Emily Short, "Types of Action and Types of Agency", 3 Mar 2009 https://emshort.blog/2009/03/03/types-of-action-and-types-of-agency/, retrieved 31 Oct 2023.
6. *Ibid.*
7. *In-Game: From Immersion to Incorporation* (2011), Gordon Calleja, MIT Press.
8. *Games: Agency as Art* (2020), C. Thi Nguyen, OUP USA.
9. Jesse Schell, *The Art of Game Design: A Book of Lenses*, Elsevier, Burlington, USA 2008.

10. Anna Anthropy, Naomi Clark, *A Game Design Vocabulary: Exploring the Foundational Principles Behind Good Game Design*, Addison-Wesley Professional, 2014.
11. *The GameDev Business Handbook* (2017), Michael Futter, Bithell Games http://www.gamedevbizbook.com/.
12. Example Template Indie Game Budgets, via The GameDev Business Handbook https://docs.google.com/spreadsheets/d/1L9aadgdwSd4Gb4vshBJjYFKtK-zHG1I_eQygcA0UOjk/edit#gid=769526996, retrieved 19 Oct 2023.
13. Owen Kingston, 10 Beat structure for Adaptive Narrative in 'Writing for Immersive Experiences', Immersive Experience Network - Huddle 1, 20 Feb 2023, https://youtu.be/d0ptCizUpiM?si=L5_Oh7pK7DJN6ZPE&t=854 14:14.
14. *Ibid.*
15. Tim Hutchings, *Thousand Year Old Vampire* (2021) Appendix IV, Interview with Sean Hillman for EN World.

Glossary

allocentric: In mapping, a fixed-image approach e.g. a paper map which users must interpret and orient to relate to physical features

anagnorisis: Discovery of a character's own IDENTITY as a dramatic revelation

bottleneck: A place where paths must converge due to geographical constraints

conditional/conditionality: Subject to logical cause-and-effect. Certain condition(s) must be satisfied (or not satisfied) before a conditional event occurs.

critical path: In game design, the primary path of progress

diegetic: Existing or taking place within the world of the story

diegeticize: Bringing or hybridizing physical elements into the world of the story

diegeticizing boundaries: In spationarratives, a technique of incorporating or appropriating physical boundaries like **edges** into the narrative

district: A spatial element: a distinct area, neighbourhood or region

dwell time: Realtime duration a player spends stationary, e.g. at a content node

echo chamber: A perceptual model in which all incoming news or commentary is filtered for ideological content, potentially resulting in skewed or radicalised perspective

edge: A spatial element: a physical linear barrier, e.g. river

egocentric: In mapping, a user-centric approach, e.g. a mobile GPS map which centres on the user by default

emergent: Unscripted storytelling which emerges through a combination of systemic possibilities

fait accompli: A done deal; an event already in-motion; an offer you can't refuse

foveate/foveating: Mimicking the selective gaze of human vision

foveated rendering: A technique in VR which imitates normal vision; the centre of the gaze is rendered in high-resolution while the peripheral is blurry

game state: In an interactive experience, the variables making up the current status and progression of an individual player or instance

gate: In **conditionality**, a function which prevents progress along a given axis until one or more conditions are met

generic place: Design or functionality for a specific globalised type of place e.g. a supermarket

glass wall: In game design, an invisible wall preventing progress

hub: A spatial element: a meeting place or place where paths cross

in medias res: In narratives, a story which begins partway through; already underway

In situ: Already on-site or in-position

journey time: Realtime duration a player spends travelling between content nodes; varies between users

landmark: A spatial element: a distinct visible feature

locagnostic: Short for **location-agnostic**; design or functionality which could work anywhere. Contrast **location-specific**

location-agnostic: Design or functionality which could work anywhere. Contrast **location-specific**

location-portable: Design or functionality which is initially location-specific but modular in design so it can be remounted in new places

ludocorporeal dissonance: Brendan Sinclair's term for a disconnect between the experience of a spatial game and the experience of space

merged reality moment: A hybrid digital-physical narrative moment; anchors digital elements in physical reality

mise-en-**self:** An establishing or characterising moment for a player-chacracter IDENTITY: the IDENTITY equivalent of *mise-en-scene* or an establishing shot in cinema

node: In spationarratives, a location where one or more content elements are located

panopticon: Where the possibility of BEING SEEN anytime leads to individuals behaving as though BEING SEEN all the time

passthrough: Augmented reality in which a device films live footage of the outside world then "passes" it to a screen with added augmentations. Contrast **See-through**

path: A spatial element; a channel players can move along

protagnostic: Short for **protagonist-agnostic**; narrative design in which the player and protagonist are the same person, hence the protagonist could be anyone. Contrast **roleplay**

protagonist-agnostic: Narrative design in which the player and protagonist are the same person, hence the protagonist could be anyone. Contrast **roleplay**

roleplay: Narrative design in which the player-character's IDENTITY is characterised within the world of the story. Contrast **protagonist-agnostic**

roomscale/at-home: Design or functionality which scans and augments the user's own home or similar enclosed indoor environment

see-through: Also called "hard" or "true" AR, where augmentations are added on a transparent display and overlaid on normal vision of the real world

spatial subjectivity: Spationarrative design which empahises the player/player-character's subjective viewpoint, e.g. through vantage point

spatial agency: Expression of the player's agency through movement or action in space

spatial gate: Spatial equivalent of a logic **gate**; a specific location where player progress can be prevented until certain conditions can be fulfilled; can also be used to detect player progress through a specific location

spatial pacing: Geographic elements of a spationarrative's structure, duration and timing

Swayze Effect: Matt Burdette's term for the disoncerting effect of being UNSEEN in VR

table-scale: Design or functionality which augments a flat surface without reference to wider context

unreliable narrator: A narrator who is biased, subjective or otherwise not all-knowing

unreliable protagonist: A player-character who is alert to the subjectivity of their perspective

variable: In **conditionality,** used to track changes in game state

visuotactile congruence: Correspondence between what the player sees and feels; crucial in VR immersion

zero-sum: Any situation in which two elements cannot co-exist without loss. E.g. two physical objects cannot share the same space. Digital layers are generally non-zero-sum; they can coexist in the same space

Index

A

Abovitz, Rony, 15
Abrash, Michael, 14, 15
Accessibility, 246–247, 261, 274, 275
Active creation of belief, 75–76, 113, 153, 173, 242
Agency, 44–47, 270; *see also* Spatial agency
    diegetic agency, 188
    and pacing, 161–162
AI, *see* Artificial intelligence
Alexander, Leigh, 170
Allocentric framework, 207–209
Anagnorisis, 100, 101, 103, 106, 272
    augmented, 100
    and character development, 102–104
Anonymous – Performative slider, 259
Anthropy, Anna, 271
Apple, 13, 15, 21, 239
Apple Vision Pro, 12, 14, 15, 116, 273
AR bodies, 237–240
Arcane: Enter the Undercity (2021), 119
AR graffiti, 235–237, 239
Ariel, Galit, 5, 231, 251
Aristotle, 100
Arrival of the Train (1895), 3
AR selves, 237–240
Artery (1982), 111
Artificial intelligence (AI), 12, 27, 143, 148, 151, 168
    customised realities and, 233–235
    diffusion-driven, 238
The Art of Game Design (Jesse Schell), 271
The Assembly (2016), 53, 111
Asynchronous multiplayer, 258
Audience, 16–17, 93, 100, 104, 119, 120, 144, 220, 221, 267–269, 278
Audio, 31–33
Audio prototyping, 30–31
Augmented anagnorisis, 100
Augmented IDENTITIES, 94, 99–104, 108, 109, 113, 130, 133, 154, 218, 223
Augmented players, 2, 12, 23, 29, 49, 56, 69, 70, 73, 76, 77, 88, 93–94, 98, 109, 116, 117, 127, 153, 173, 180, 205, 218, 219, 220, 237
Augmented reality, 5, 12, 13, 14, 27, 32, 74, 103, 109, 125, 146, 149, 163, 169, 200, 231, 234
    "establishing shot" of, 77
    virtual reality vs., 9–10
Augmented SELF-CONSCIOUSNESS, 121–124
Augmented shadows, 81, 218

"Augmented Shadow" (Joon Moon), 81, 116
Augmented/spatial advertising, 22
Augmented/spatial experience, 5, 21, 56, 76, 142, 143, 163, 195, 253, 263, 270
Augmented/spatial media, 3, 4, 5, 9, 10, 14, 16, 18, 20, 67, 70, 76, 77, 93, 120, 130, 153, 176, 209, 220, 245, 248, 251, 253, 263, 265, 270, 272
Augmented/spatial realities, 5, 7, 12, 14, 21, 26, 29, 44, 62, 64, 81, 100, 110, 173, 192, 248, 253
    moving from virtual realities to, 66
        dragon's cave, 68–69
        hybrid realities, 69–70
        parallel realities, 66–67
        unified sensory models, 67–68
Augmented/spatial technology, 2, 3, 6. 20, 27, 29, 67, 69, 74, 77, 139, 147, 228, 229, 231, 232, 233, 238, 239, 245, 261
    BEING in VR to IDENTITY-BUILDING and BEING-THERE in, 56–57
    BEING SEEN in VR to BEING SELF-CONSCIOUS and OCCUPYING SPACE in, 63–64
    SEEING in VR to IMAGINING and STAGING in, 48–50
Augmenting/appropriating others, 126–127
Augmenting boundaries, 172–173
Augmenting IDENTITY, 98, 106, 113, 164
AUGMENTING PLACES, 7, 64, 133, 137, 140, 218
    BEING THERE, 205
        egocentric and allocentric, 207–209
        spatial agency: forks, 209–213
        spatial agency: hubs, 213–216
        through navigation, 206
    general augmented staging, 153
        boundaries, 171–177
        hybrid spationarratives, general principles of, 153–154
        layout, 155–160
        spatial pacing, 161–171
    location-specific augmented staging, 180
        boundaries, 199–203
        layout, 185–192
        spatial pacing, 192–199
        surfacing layers of history, 181–184
    locative categories, 139
        generic places, 145–146
        location-agnostic experiences, 141–143
        location-portable design, 146–147

287

location-specific experiences, 143–145
roomscale/at-home, 147–148
table-scale, 149
OCCUPYING SPACE, 218
common ground, 228–229
finding yourself, 218–220
maps of ourselves, 226–227
spatial subjectivity: player-as-performer,
222–225
spatial subjectivity: vantage points,
220–222
place vs. space, 138–139
AUGMENTING PLAYERS, 73, 74, 133
from augmenting players to augmenting
places, 133
IDENTITY-BUILDING, 93
augmented identity, techniques for building,
99–104
compelling roleplay characterisation, 98–99
immersive theatre, identity-discovery in,
104–112
not quite yourself, 93–94
ongoing identities, 113–114
protagonist-agnostic identities, 95–97
roleplay identities, 97–98
IMAGINING, 75
active creation of belief, 75–76
beginning augmentation, 76–91
desireability, 81–86
faits accompli, 86–91
plausibility, 79–81
SELF-CONSCIOUSNESS, 116
augmented, 121–124
augmenting/appropriating others, 126–127
diegetic, 118–121
discovering others, 129–131
player-as-performer, 124–126
unreliable protagonists, 127–129
Augmenting spatial elements, 155–156
location-specific approach, 187–188
Augé, Marc, 145

B

Bainbridge, Sierra, 181
Banksy, 236
Barabareschi, Giulia, 246, 248
Barefoot budget, 85, 265
Barrett, Felix, 105, 118, 119
Bartle, Richard, 268
Beat Saber, 23, 44, 52
Beginning augmentation, 76
desireability, 81
exclusivity, 85–86
purpose, 83
secrecy, 84–85
stakes, 84

faits accompli, 86–91
plausibility, 79–81
BEING in VR, 51
characterised VR identities, 53–54
to IDENTITY-BUILDING and BEING-
THERE in augmented/spatial, 56–57
identity-discovery, 54–56
out-of-body experience, 51–52
protagonist-agnostic VR identities, 52–53
BEING SEEN in VR, 59
to BEING SELF-CONSCIOUS and
OCCUPYING SPACE in augmented/
spatial, 63–64
being (un)seen, 62–63
feeling seen, 59–61
Swayze Effect, 61
BEING SELF-CONSCIOUS and OCCUPYING
SPACE, from BEING SEEN in VR to,
63–64
BEING THERE, 5, 7, 56, 59, 154, 176, 205, 235
egocentric and allocentric, 207–209
spatial agency
forks, 209–213
hubs, 213–216
through navigation, 206
Belsky, Scott, 234
Björk, Staffan, 142
Blending, 110, 111
conceptual blending, 100, 110
Blending identities and building complicity,
109–112
Bodily data, 23
Borges, Jorge Luis, 226
Boundaries, 151, 155, 159, 176, 181, 189, 199–202,
250, 278
augmenting, 172–173
diegeticizing, 175
social, 175–177
videogame, 171–172
Brice, Mattie, 83
Brillhart, Jessica, 44, 45, 46, 47
Brooks, Kevin, 43, 59, 60, 62, 75, 163
Brownlee, Marques, 45
Budget, 264, 274–275
Burdette, Matt, 61
Burroughs, Edgar Rice, 5
ByteDance, 148

C

Calleja, Gordon, 19, 76, 270
Cardiff, Janet, 30, 31, 120, 144, 185, 188
Carter, Erica, 138
Castellano, Andrea, 207
Cavarero, Adriana, 113
Chapple, Freda, 223
Character development, anagnorisis and, 102–104

Characterisation, Five C's of, 98–99
Characterised VR identities, 53–54
Chess, 18
Clark, Maximillian, 246, 248
Clark, Naomi, 271
CodeRunner (2011), 162–163
Coleridge, 43
Community Memory, 21
Compelling roleplay characterisation, 98–99
Conceptual blending, 100, 110
Conditionality, 122, 165, 166, 167, 168, 192,
        198–199, 209, 224, 265
Conditional pacing, 164–168
    spatial gates, 192–194
Conrad, Joseph, 130
Context, 10, 29, 77, 234, 235, 237
Context-blindness, 143, 208, 250
Conway, Steven, 83
Core objective, 270–272
Covid-19 pandemic, 60
Cox, Courtland, 55
Creane, Jessica, 77, 110
Critical path, 185–186, 187, 188, 189
Cron, Lisa, 241
Cross, Jennifer Eileen, 219
Cross, Tristan, 60, 61
Customised realities, 26, 27, 234
    and AI, 233–235
    in AR, 233

D

Davies, Hugh, 18
De la Peña, Nonny, 62
Desireability, 81, 87
    exclusivity, 85–86
    purpose, 83
    secrecy, 84–85
    stakes, 84
De Souza e Silva, 247
Deus Ex: Human Revolution (2011), 54
Dick, Phillip K., 242
Diegesis, 109, 110
Diegetic, 18–19, 46, 47, 59, 64, 88, 93, 96, 108, 109,
        110, 116, 127, 157, 167, 169, 173, 188,
        200, 205, 208, 211, 249, 278
Diegetic agency, 188
Diegetic and foveated seeing, 45–46
Diegetic and nondiegetic durations, 162–164
Diegetic IDENTITY, 96, 127
Diegeticizing boundaries, 173, 175, 201
Diegetic mood, 118
Diegetic motivations, 96
Diegetic-ness, 249
Diegetic SELF-CONSCIOUSNESS, 118–121
Diez, Daniel, 14
Diffusion-driven technology, 63

Digital pacing
    with physical performers, 195–199
    for real objects, 168–169
Dinesh, Nandita, 117, 129, 226
Discovering IDENTITY, 100
Discovering others, 129–131
Districts, 156
    general augmented staging, 159–160
    location-specific augmented staging, 189–192
Divergent realities, 26, 27, 235
    AR bodies, AR selves, 237–240
    AR graffiti, 235–237
    customised realities and AI, 233–235
    how do we know when it ends?, 240–242
    journey through space, 231–233
    non-zero-sum cultures, 235–237
Dixon, Dan, 123
Domhan, Tobias, 144
Donald, James, 138
Don Quixote, 25, 81, 82–83, 85
Doofus factor, 117, 256
Doom (1993), 54
Dragon's cave, 68–69
Drop Dead: The Cabin's Home Invasion mode
        (2023), 148
Dudley, J., 246
Dunn, Stuart, 206, 208
Dwell time, 146, 162, 192, 215, 225, 278

E

Echo chambers, 26, 234
Edges, 156
    general augmented staging, 159
    location-specific augmented staging, 189
Egocentric framework, 207–209
Emergence and serendipity, 169–171
Emergent design, 260
Emotional immersion in VR, 41–42
Entertainment colonisation, 126
Environment-tracking technologies and SLAM,
        10–11
"Establishing shot" of augmented reality, 77
Evans, Leighton, 21–22, 170, 250
Example concept development framework, 264
    concepting phases, 266–267
    general advice, 280–281
    getting started: what skills do you need?, 265–266
    guts
        script, 279
        story beats, 275–278
        story mapping, 278–279
    hands
        access, 275
        budget and scope, 274–275
        locative category, 273
        platform, 273–274

head
    audience, 267–269
    theme, 267
heart
    core objective, 270–271
    general mechanics, 271
    player agency, 270
    Player IDENTITY, 271–272
    story overview, 272–273
legs
    iteration, 280
    prototyping, 279–280
    testing, 280
Exclusivity, 85, 103
Experience, 18
EXtended Reality (XR), 12, 13

F

Fait accompli, 86, 87, 89, 90, 95, 103, 148
False IDENTITY, 102
Farman, 236, 237
Fauconnier, Gilles, 110
Field Trip (2012), 182
Filter bubbles, 26
First Encounters (2023), 148
Five Nights at Freddy's: Special Delivery (2019),
    95
Flanagan, Mary, 126
FourSquare, 181
Foveal vision, 45
Foveated rendering, 45, 174
Foveating space, 174–175, 200–203
Fowles, John, 83
Freeman, Dustin, 185
Friedlander, Larry, 56, 59
From Dreamer to Dreamfinder (Schneider), 106

G

A Game Design Vocabulary (Anna Anthropy and
    Naomi Clark), 271
Game state, 192, 194–195, 196, 197
Garaj, V., 246
General augmented staging, 153
    boundaries, 171
        augmenting boundaries, 172–173
        diegeticizing boundaries, 175
        foveating space, 174–175
        social boundaries, 175–177
        videogame boundaries, 171–172
    hybrid spationarratives, general principles of,
        153–154
    layout, 155
        augmenting spatial elements, 155–156
        districts, 159–160
        edges, 159

hubs, 158–159
landmarks, 158
paths, 157–158
spatial pacing, 161
    agency and pacing, 161–162
    conditional pacing, 164–168
    diegetic and nondiegetic durations,
        162–164
    digital pacing for real objects, 168–169
    emergence and serendipity, 169–171
    roomscale/at-home pacing, 168
General mechanics, 271
Generic places, 145–146
Gill, Patrick, 187
Glass walls, 172, 173, 176
Goffman, Erving, 97–99
Goldeneye 007 (1997), 186
Goldeneye's realistic layouts, 187
Google, 21, 239
    global mapping data, 142
Google Glass (2013), 116
Gorilla Tag (2021), 44
GPS apps, 10, 21
Graphics augmentation into space, 11–12
Groen, Andrew, 260

H

Half-Life (1998), 47
Hamlet on the Holodeck (Janet Murray), 19
Hanke, John, 9, 14, 21, 22, 27, 94
Harding, Chris, 111
Hardman, Chris, 31, 211
Harper, John, 98, 99
Hauntify, 148, 168, 210
Hayler, Matt, 139
The Headlands Gamble (2015), 196–197, 198
Headmap manifesto (Ben Russel), 1
Headsets, 10, 12, 13, 14, 208, 246
Heads-up display (HUD), 11, 209
"Hero's Journey" (Joseph Campbell), 276
"Hero's journey" structure, 86
The Hero With a Thousand Faces (1949), 86
High Noon (1952), 163
Hill, Leslie, 117
Hilton, Karl, 186
Hinton, Geoffrey, 234
Hitchcock, Alfred, 87
Hjorth, Larissa, 25
Hochmair, Hartwig H., 248
Hockney, David, 164
Horizon Worlds (2019), 53
Hosokawa, Shuhei, 31
Hubs, 156
    general augmented staging, 158–159
    location-specific augmented staging, 188–189
Huck, Jonny, 208

HUD, *see* Heads-up display
Hutchings, Tim, 280
Hybrid realities, 69–70
Hybrid spationarratives, general principles of, 153–154
HYPER-REALITY (Keichii Matsuda), 22, 237

I

IDENTITY, 93–96, 99, 103, 107, 108, 113, 272
    asserting, 106–108
    blending IDENTITIES and building
        complicity, 109–112
    discovering, 100
    ongoing IDENTITIES, 113–114
IDENTITY-BUILDING, 93, 117
    augmented identity, techniques for building,
        99–104
    compelling roleplay characterisation, 98–99
    immersive theatre, identity-discovery in, 104
        asserting identity, 106–108
        blending identities and building complicity,
        109–112
    ongoing identities, 113–114
    protagonist-agnostic identities, 95–97
    roleplay identities, 97–98
IDENTITY-BUILDING and BEING-THERE,
        BEING in VR to, 56–57
IDENTITY-discovery, 54–56, 100
    in immersive theatre, 104
        asserting IDENTITY, 106–108
        blending IDENTITIES and building
        complicity, 109–112
I-know-something-you-don't feeling, 103
IMAGINING, 75
    active creation of belief, 75–76
    beginning augmentation, 76
        desireability, 81–86
        faits accompli, 86–91
        plausibility, 79–81
    and STAGING, SEEING in VR to, 48–50
Immersion, 19–20, 76, 249
Immersive Experience Network researchers, 109
Immersive journalism for VR, 62
Immersive theatre, identity-discovery in, 104
    asserting identity, 106–108
    blending identities and building complicity,
        109–112
Immersive theatre shows, 119
Inception attacks, 24
Inclusion, Accessibility and Safety, 245
    accessibility, 246–247
    inclusive approaches, 245
    inequality, 247–248
    physical safety, 249–251
    representation, 248
    roleplaying safety, 249
Ingress (2014), 22

Instinctual experience, 118
Instruction-based theatre, 145
Iteration, 280

J

James, Erin, 226
Jenkins, Henry, 113
Jensen, Adam, 54
Jicol, Crescent, 44
John Carter of Mars (Edgar Rice Burrough), 5
Jones, Chuck, 222
Journey through space, 231–233
Journey time, 157, 161, 162, 183, 212, 246, 278
Juhász, Levente, 248
Juxtapositions, 66
    dragon's cave, 68–69
    hybrid realities, 69–70
    parallel realities, 66–67
    unified sensory models, 67–68

K

Kaplan, George, 88
Kari, Mohamed, 168
Kattenbelt, Chiel, 130, 223
King, Margaret, 194
Kingston, Owen, 276
Knorr, Alyse, 186
Kristensson, 246

L

Landmarks, 155
    general augmented staging, 158
    location-specific augmented staging, 188
Language of space, 185–186
La Poutre, Johannes, 144
Larp, 98, 109
Laugier. Marc-Antoine, 171
Layer, 17
LBGs, *see* Location-Based Games
Lenticular design, 109
Leung, Ghislaine, 147
Li, Meng, 76
Licoppe, Christian, 66–67
Lingan, Cesar Lucho, 76
Lipsyc, Nadja, 248
Live multiplayer, 257–258
Llosa, Mario Vargas, 241
Locagnostic design, 143
Locagnostic layouts, 158
Locagnostic players, 143
Location-agnostic design, 140–141, 250
    advantages of, 142
    disadvantages of, 142–143
Location-agnostic experiences, 141–143, 154, 173,
        180, 209, 255

Location-agnostic forks, 209, 210, 213, 278
Location-agnostic LBGs, 161, 169, 174, 210
Location-agnostic narratives, 143
Location-aware devices, 1
Location-Based Games (LBGs), 10
Location-based technology, 10
Location-portability, 146, 147
Location-portable design, 146–147
Location-portable experiences, 146, 147, 173
Location-portable layouts, 160
Location-specific audio narratives, 30
Location-specific augmented staging, 180
    boundaries, 199
        foveating space, 200–203
    layout, 185
        augmenting spatial elements, 187–188
        districts, 189–192
        edges, 189
        hubs, 188–189
        landmarks, 188
        language of space, 185–186
        paths, 188
        uncritical paths, 186–187
    spatial pacing, 192
        conditional pacing: spatial gates, 192–194
        digital pacing with physical performers,
            195–199
        game state, 194–195
    surfacing layers of history, 181–184
Location-specific competitive duelling game, 259
Location-specific design, 138, 140, 141, 144, 146, 147,
        156, 157, 161, 172, 173, 180, 181, 185, 188,
        189, 192, 200, 201, 210, 250, 255
Location-specific experiences, 141, 143–145, 173,
        210, 246, 250, 254, 255, 257, 273
Location-specific narratives, 146
    advantages of, 144
    disadvantages of, 144–145
Location-specific spatial pacing, 194
Locative categories, 139, 273
    generic places, 145–146
    roomscale/at-home, 147–148
    table-scale, 149
Loiperdinger, Martin, 3
Lopez, Francisco, 78
Lothe, R., 223
Lucas, George, 86
Ludocorporeal dissonance, 67, 69, 70, 195
Ludonarrative dissonance, 67, 69
Lynch, Kevin, 155
Lyons, Katie, 109
Løvlie, Anders Sudnes, 169, 180, 200, 205, 206

M

Machon, 118
"Magic circle" of game, 77

Magic Leap, 15–16
Main Character Syndrome, 84, 226
Major reality reskin, 261
Malinowski, Caitlin, 9
Maller, Tom, 126
Marketplace of realities, 27
Markus, Hazel, 95
Mashiter, Chloe, 98, 99, 109
Masked ghost-audiences, 105
Masque of the Red Death (2007), 118
Massey, Doreen, 138–139
Matsuda, Keichii, 22
McConachie, Bruce, 110
McWhirter, Joshua, 20
Medea (c.431 BCE), 100
Melcher, Charles, 96
Mercuriali, Silvia, 145, 223
Merged reality moments, 79–81, 84, 107, 125, 141,
        143, 145, 146, 148, 158, 169, 188, 192,
        195, 197, 202, 211, 255, 257
Meta's Horizon Worlds (2019), 53
A Midsummer Night's Dream (1595), 221
MikeFM, 250
Miller, George Bures, 30, 120, 144
Minimaps, 207–208
Minor reality reskin, 261
Mise-en-self techniques, 106–108
Misplaced IDENTITY, 101–102
Mitsubishi Electric Research Laboratories, 59
Mixed reality, 12, 13
Monster Hunter Now (2023), 207
Montgomery Bus Boycott, 56
Moon, Joon, 81, 116
Moore, Alan, 228
Murray, Janet, 19, 75, 76

N

Nair, Vivek, 23
Nelson, Noah J., 119
NeRFs, see Neural radiance fields
Neural radiance fields (NeRFs), 234
Niantic, 9, 22, 94, 116, 142, 158, 174, 182, 250
Night Walk for Edinburgh (2019), 120
Non-diegetic, 18, 99, 119, 120, 123
Non-multiplayer live experiences, 258
Non-zero-sum, 18, 195, 219, 236, 237, 238
North by Northwest (1959), 87, 88, 103, 120
Nurius, Paula, 95

O

Object Rephysicalisation, 168, 169, 279
OCCUPYING SPACE, 218
        common ground, 228–229
        maps of ourselves, 226–227
        spatial subjectivity

player-as-performer, 222–225
vantage points, 220–222
OCCUPYING zerosum SPACE, 235
Oedipus Rex (c.429 BCE), 100
Overmappings, 2, 103

P

Pacing, 161, 163; *see also* Conditional pacing;
          Digital pacing; Roomscale/at-home
          pacing; Spatial pacing; Zero-sum pacing
Panopticon effect, 85, 125
The Paradise Institute (2001), 120
Parallel realities, 66–67
Paris, Helen, 117
Passthrough technologies, 14–15
Passthrough vs. see-through, 14–16
Patel. Nilay, 15
Path layout, 157
Paths, 155
     general augmented staging, 157–158
     location-specific augmented staging, 188
Peaky Blinders: The Rise (2022), 119
Peitz, Johan, 142
Performance of self, 97–98
Perry, Sarah, 155
"Phantom Ride" films, 3
Physical reality, 2, 3, 9, 11, 41, 76, 79, 85, 218, 227
Place vs. space, 138–139
Platform, 273–274
Plausibility, 79–81, 87, 111
Player, 16–17, 29; *see also* AUGMENTING PLAYERS
     asynchronous multiplayer, 258
     augmented, 2, 12, 23, 29, 49, 56, 69, 70, 73, 76,
          77, 88, 93, 98, 109, 116, 117, 127, 153,
          173, 180, 205, 218, 219, 220, 237
     live multiplayer, 257–258
     locagnostic, 143
     rebellious, 46–48
Player agency, 166, 170, 270
Player-as-performer, 124–126, 222–225
Player-characters, 17, 84, 163, 192
Player IDENTITY, 163, 271–272
Players' IMAGINATIONS, 76, 154, 241
PlayStationVR, 44, 52
Poetic Augmented Reality, 169
Pokémon GO, 10, 11, 24, 25, 66, 94, 116, 139, 142,
          143, 163, 207, 247
Portal (2007), 54
Possible selves, 95–97
Prepare to Dive (2024), 147
Privacy, 23–25
Private augmentation, 256, 261
Protagnostic character, 103
Protagonist-agnostic identities, 52–53, 94–97, 105, 108
Prototyping, 279–280
     audio prototyping, 30–31

Public augmentation, 256, 261
Public-private augmentation, 256, 259
Punchdrunk, 105, 119

Q

Quixote, Don, 82, 83, 85

R

Radio Ghost (2023), 145, 223
Rashōmon Effect, 220
Realities, 29–30; *see also* Augmented/spatial
          realities; Customised realities;
          Divergent realities; Hybrid realities;
          Parallel realities
Reality customisation, 20, 25–28, 234
Rebellious players, 46–48
Refusal, 87
Reinbold, Lotte, 249
Relative Time, 164, 278
Reskinning, 12
     eXtended Reality (XR), 13
     mixed reality, 13
     spatial computing, 13–14
     XR, mixed reality, and spatial computing, 12
Resonance (2015), 47
Reverse level design, 181, 185, 186, 187, 278
Richardson, Ingrid, 25
Ritchie, Jeff, 69, 155, 161, 162, 181, 220
Rivet Couture, 103, 241
Rogers, Buck, 5
Roleplay, 95, 100
Roleplay IDENTITY, 97–98, 102–103
Roleplaying, 56, 86, 90, 93, 94, 97, 98, 99, 103,
          127, 272
Room-scale, 77
Roomscale/at-home design, 147–148, 201
Roomscale/at-home pacing, 168
Rosenberg, Louis, 13, 68
Rosenblat, Mariana Olaizola, 23
Run Lola Run (1998), 163
Ruset, Endre, 205–206
Russel, Ben, 1, 231

S

Saarenpää, Hannamari, 142
Saker, Michael, 170, 250
Sample, Mark, 181
Sanchez, Maria Vives, 62
SAW: Escape Experience (2022), 172
Scenography, 9
Schell, Jesse, 271
Schneider, Ron, 106
Schroeder, Karl, 22, 103
Schuster, Joe, 5

Schütte, Reinhard, 168
Scope, 274–275
Script, 279
Scripted story events, 260
Secrecy, 103
SEEING in VR, 41, 43
    diegetic and foveated rendering, 45–46
    to IMAGINING and STAGING in augmented/
        spatial, 48–50
    rebellious players, 46–48
    SEEING ≠ BELIEVING, 43–44
    SEEING with agency, 44–45
See-through visors, passthrough technologies vs.,
    14–16
Self, performance of, 97–98
SELF-CONSCIOUSNESS, 74, 113, 116, 259
    augmented, 121–124
    augmenting/appropriating others, 126–127
    diegetic, 118–121
    discovering others, 129–131
    player-as-performer, 124–126
    unreliable protagonists, 127–129
SFZero (c.2006), 95
Shape Arts' Unfolding Shrines, 246
Shirky, Clay, 118
Short, Emily, 154, 155, 157, 158, 159, 161, 165, 166,
        169, 171, 172, 173, 174, 181, 185, 186,
        187, 188, 192, 199, 202, 270
Sibthorpe. Nathan, 105, 223
Siegel, Jerry, 5
Simultaneous Localisation and Mapping (SLAM)
        technology, 11, 21
Sinclair, Brendan, 67, 69, 140
Singh, Aneesha, 246, 248
Skwarek, Mark, 236, 245
SLAM technology, see Simultaneous Localisation
        and Mapping technology
Slater, Mel, 62
Sleep No More, 118
Sliders, 253–254
Sliders for defining augmented/spatial experiences
    anonymous – performative, 259
    creator-defined objectives – playerdefined
        objectives, 262
    live – asynchronous, 257–258
    location-specific – location-agnostic, 255–256
    minor reality reskin – major reality reskin,
        260–261
    multiplayer – solo, 258–259
    private augmentation – public augmentation,
        261–262
    public place – private place, 256
    roleplay – protagonist-agnostic, 258
    scripted – emergent, 260
    time-specific – indefinite, 257
    worldbuilding – worldbuilt, 262–263

Smedresman, Gabe, 196–197
Smith, Heather Dunaway, 2–3, 88, 111
Social boundaries, 175–177
Socioeconomic inequalities, 247
Sodhi, Raj, 168
Sony, 13, 124
Sony Walkman, 31, 124
Space
    journey through, 231–233
    place vs, 138–139
Space, occupying, 218
    common ground, 228–229
    finding yourself, 218–220
    maps of ourselves, 226–227
    spatial subjectivity
        player-as-performer, 222–225
        vantage points, 220–222
Spatial agency
    forks, 209
        asymmetrical, 212
        distinct, 211
        expressive, 212–213
        navigable, 211–212
    hubs, 213–216
Spatial computing, 12, 13–14
Spatial-contextual datasets, 21, 23
Spatial internet, 240
Spatial pacing, 148, 161
    agency and pacing, 161–162
    conditional pacing, 164–168
    diegetic and nondiegetic durations, 162–164
    digital pacing for real objects, 168–169
    emergence and serendipity, 169–171
    roomscale/at-home pacing, 168
Spationarrative dissonances, 140, 147
Speakman, Duncan, 73, 77–78, 93, 137, 240
Spencer, Amy, 182
Springett, Jay, 31, 70, 153, 263
Squires, Judith, 138
Staging, 151
    all the world's a stage, 151–152
    egocentric and allocentric, 207–209
    general augmented staging, 153
        general augmented staging: boundaries,
            171–177
        general augmented staging: spatial pacing,
            161–171
        hybrid spationarratives, general principles
            of, 153–154
        layout, 155–160
    location-specific augmented staging, 180
        boundaries, 199–203
        layout, 185–192
        spatial pacing, 192–199
        surfacing layers of history, 181–184
    navigation, 206

occupying space, 218
    common ground, 228–229
    finding yourself, 218–220
    maps of ourselves, 226–227
    spatial subjectivity: player-as-performer, 222–225
    spatial subjectivity: vantage points, 220–222
spatial agency: forks, 209
    asymmetrical, 212
    distinct, 211
    expressive, 212–213
    navigable, 211–212
spatial agency: hubs, 213–216
Starship Home (2024), 148
Star Wars, 18, 86, 87
Story beats, 260, 275–278
Story mapping, 278–279
Story overview, 272–273
Strohecker, Carol, 56, 59
Superman, 5
Swayze, Patrick, 62
Swayze Effect, 61, 62, 218

T

Table-scale, 77, 149, 192, 279
Testing, 280
Textopia, 205, 206
Theme, 267
Thornhill, Roger, 87–88, 103
TikTok, 148
Tired of Giving In, 59
Travelling While Black (2019), 54, 60
Trevelyan, G.M., 181
Turner, Mark, 110

U

Uncritical paths, 186–187
Unfolding Shrines (Shape Arts), 246
Unified sensory models, 67–68
Unified world-model, 70
Unreliable narrators, 127
Unreliable protagonists, 127–129
Use of Force (Nonny de la Peña), 62

V

Van Doorn, Victor, 96
Vantage points, 46, 127, 129–130, 220–222
Veenhof, Sander, 144, 236
Vermeeren, Arnold, 76
Videogame boundaries, 171–172
Videogames, 17, 47
Video passthrough, 11–15
Vinge, Vernor, 241
Virtual Ambrose, 125, 211

Virtual Reality (VR), 41, 153
    vs. augmented reality, 9–10
    BEING in VR, 51
        characterised VR identities, 53–54
        to IDENTITY-BUILDING and BEING-THERE in augmented/spatial, 56–57
        identity-discovery, 54–56
        out-of-body experience, 51–52
        protagonist-agnostic VR identities, 52–53
    BEING SEEN in VR, 59
        to BEING SELF-CONSCIOUS and OCCUPYING SPACE in augmented/spatial, 63–64
        being (un)seen, 62–63
        feeling seen, 59–61
        Swayze Effect, 61
    juxtapositions, 66
        dragon's cave, 68–69
        hybrid realities, 69–70
        parallel realities, 66–67
        unified sensory models, 67–68
    moving to augmented/spatial realities, 66
        dragon's cave, 68–69
        hybrid realities, 69–70
        parallel realities, 66–67
        unified sensory models, 67–68
    roomscale in, 147
    SEEING in VR, 41, 43
        diegetic and foveated seeing, 45–46
        to IMAGINING and STAGING in augmented/spatial, 48–50
        rebellious seeing, 46–48
        SEEING ≠ BELIEVING, 43–44
        SEEING with agency, 44–45
Visuotactile congruence, 51–54, 76
Visuotactile incongruities, 67
Von der Au, Simon, 79
VR, *see* Virtual Reality
VRChat (2014), 44, 53–54

W

Walkman, 31, 124
Walkmanology, 31, 111, 211
Warren, Jason, 104
Welles, Orson, 233
West, Timoni, 49
Wheeltrails project (Joseph Wilk), 245
Wilk, Joseph, 245
Williams, Roger Ross, 55
Willing suspension of disbelief, 43
Wizards Unite (2019), 142
Wolfenstein 3D (1992), 54
Wonderbook: Book of Spells (2012), 107
Wondermart (2009), 145
World-mapping, 21–23

X

XR, *see* EXtended Reality

Y

Yin, L., 246

Z

Zero-sum, 17–18, 64, 218, 219, 227, 228, 235–236, 242, 250, 264
Zero-sum pacing, 194
Žižek, Slavoj, 235

Printed in the United States
by Baker & Taylor Publisher Services